Community Music Today

Edited by
Kari K. Veblen, Stephen J. Messenger,
Marissa Silverman, and David J. Elliott

Published in partnership with
NAfME: National Association for Music Education

ROWMAN & LITTLEFIELD EDUCATION

A division of
ROWMAN & LITTLEFIELD PUBLISHERS, INC.
Lanham • New York • Toronto • Plymouth, UK

Published in partnership with NAfME: National Association for Music Education

Published by Rowman & Littlefield Education
A division of Rowman & Littlefield Publishers, Inc.
A wholly owned subsidary of The Rowman & Littlefield Publishing Group, Inc.
4501 Forbes Boulevard, Suite 200, Lanham, Maryland 20706
www.rowman.com

10 Thornbury Road, Plymouth PL6 7PP, United Kingdom

British Library Cataloguing in Publication Information Available

Library of Congress Cataloging-in-Publication Data

Community music today / edited by Kari K. Veblen, Stephen J. Messenger, Marissa Silverman, David J. Elliott.
   p. cm.
   "Published in partnership with NAfME: National Association for Music Education."
   ISBN 978-1-60709-319-0 (cloth : alk. paper) — ISBN 978-1-60709-320-6 (pbk. : alk. paper) — ISBN 978-1-60709-321-3 (ebook)
   1. Community music. 2. Music—Social aspects. I. Veblen, Kari K. II. Messenger, Stephen J. III. Silverman, Marissa. IV. Elliott, David J.
   ML3916.C645 2013
   780—dc23
                                                                                    2012032635

∞™ The paper used in this publication meets the minimum requirements of American National Standard for Information Sciences—Permanence of Paper for Printed Library Materials, ANSI/NISO Z39.48-1992.

Printed in the United States of America

Contents

List of Figures and Tables   v

Foreword   vii
  Lee Higgins

Acknowledgments   ix

1 The Tapestry: Introducing Community Music   1
  Kari K. Veblen

PART I: COMMUNITY MUSIC IN GLOBAL CONTEXT

2 Community Music in North America: Historical Foundations   13
  Jeffrey E. Bush and Andrew Krikun

3 Community Music in the United Kingdom   25
  Kathryn Deane and Phil Mullen

4 Community Music in the Nordic Countries: Politics, Research,
Programs, and Educational Significance   41
  Sidsel Karlsen, Heidi Westerlund, Heidi Partti, and Einar Solbu

5 Community Music in Africa: Perspectives from South Africa,
Kenya, and Eritrea   61
  Elizabeth Oehrle, David Akombo, and Elias Weldegebriel

6 Community Music in Australia and New Zealand Aotearoa   79
  Brydie-Leigh Bartleet, Shelley Brunt, Anja Tait, and Catherine Threlfall

7 Community Music in East Asia   99
  Chi Cheung Leung, Mari Shiobara, and Christine Yau

PART II: INTERCONNECTIONS

8   Intergenerational Music Learning in Community and Schools   121
Carol Beynon and Chris Alfano

9   Music Learning as a Lifespan Endeavor   133
David Myers, Chelcy Bowles, and Will Dabback

10   Community Music through Authentic Engagement:
Bridging Community, School, University, and Arts Groups   151
*Sylvia Chong, Debbie Rohwer, Donna Emmanuel, Nathan Kruse,
and Rineke Smilde*

11   Digital Communities: Sharing, Teaching, Exploring   169
Stephen J. Messenger

PART III: MARGINALIZED MUSICS AND COMMUNITIES

12   Marginalized Communities: Reaching Those Falling Outside
Socially Accepted Norms   185
Sheila Woodward and Catherine Pestano

13   Personal Growth through Music: Oakdale Prison's Community Choir
and Community Music for Homeless Populations in New York City   199
Mary L. Cohen and Marissa Silverman

14   Reaching out to Participants Who Are Challenged   217
Don DeVito and Arthur Gill

15   Diverse Communities, Inclusive Practice   231
Magali Kleber, Dochy Lichtensztajn, and Claudia Gluschankof

PART IV: PERFORMING ENSEMBLES:
ARTISTRY, ADVOCACY, AND SOCIAL JUSTICE

16   Community Choirs: Expressions of Identity through Vocal Performance   249
Susan Avery, Casey Hayes, and Cindy Bell

17   Instrumental Ensembles: Community Case Studies from Brazil
and the United States   261
Don Coffman and Joel Barbosa

18   Expressing Faith through Vocal Performance   273
Hussein Janmohamed, Cindy Bell, and Mehnaz Thawer

19   Community Music and Sustainability Worldwide: Ecosystems of
Engaged Music Making   287
Huib Schippers and Richard Letts

20   Resources in Community Music   299
Janice L. Waldron, Steven Moser, and Kari K. Veblen

About the Contributors   305

List of Figure and Tables

FIGURES

5.1 *Mwana Wa Mberi*. Transcribed by David Akombo   76

7.1 Ways of Transformation and Representation of Red Songs
in the Historical Context   111

7.2a Harmonization—Transformation and Representation of the
Red Songs in the Modern Political Context   114

7.2b Consumerization—Transformation of Red Songs in the
Modern Commercial Context   114

15.1 Linking Concepts and Theories in Model of Music Pedagogical
Process as Total Social Fact (Kleber, 2006)   233

TABLES

4.1 The Ideal-Typical Characteristics of the Three Metaphors
of Learning (after Paavola and Hakkarainen, 2005, 541)   54

19.1 Nine Domains of Community Music in Australia
(Bartleet, Dunbar-Hall, Letts & Schippers, 2009)   291

Foreword

In 2000, I presented a spoken paper on collaborations and a workshop on carnival street drumming at a community music seminar organized by both Kari Veblen and David Elliott. Hosted at the University of Toronto, the seventh International Society of Music Education's commission for Community Music Activity symposium included a wide variety of presentations that reflected the commission's broad considerations of what constitutes community music. During the initial plenary session and introductory papers, I can remember that I had felt frustrated that the discussions were rather unwieldy and unfocused. In order to be productive, and to make the most of the opportunity, I took a self-reflective look at my own history in order to reveal why I was feeling this way. As a community musician from the UK, it wasn't long before my reflections revealed the socio-political baggage inherited from the growth and development of community music from within my country of origin. This was an important moment for me because it was during this particular event that my community music self was challenged. In short, I was forced to consider both the contexts that I had been working in and the language that I used to describe my practice.

At this time there were very limited materials to help orientate those of us for whom coming to terms with community music from an international context was a struggle. There was little in the way of written materials, no journal to call our own, scholarly writings were few and far between, project reports and practical how-to's seemed scarce, community music programs and courses were, on the whole, just getting off the ground, and there were certainly no books with "Community Music" emblazoned down the spine! With the visibility of applied ethnomusicology, community music therapy, and cultural diversity in music education gaining more traction, the landscape of musical discourse was changing and as a result community music was becoming more prominent. Today, the printed version of the *International Journal of Community Music* is in its fifth year, project reports and music workshop guides are now more readily available, there has been a tremendous growth in community music education and training throughout the higher education sector, regional world networks are on the increase, and of course we now have this book, *Community Music Today.*

A testament to the development of what we now might frame as a field of practice, *Community Music Today* presents a remarkable collection of twenty essays. In resonance of Kari's introductory metaphor, this book "threads" the many ways of community music into a tapestry of voices—each singing a celebratory song of people, participants, places, equality of opportunity, and diversity. The four editors have assembled an impressive array of over fifty contributors who are intent on sharing their stories and their contextual perspectives. As a collection of community music moments from the across the globe, what strikes me is a general resistance toward any sense of homogeneity, a refusal to ground community music in any one definitive statement. This is how it should be, a tacit acknowledgment of differences woven into a network that releases the sheer joy of experiencing the diversity of work that can be named community music.

Although this collective writing project refuses to be assimilated into any singularity, my personal proposition is that "hospitality" runs deeply through the practice of community music and, as such, is implicit throughout all of these narratives. Whether the content area is historical, intergenerational and lifelong, from within schools or with technology, with marginalized peoples, or as community cultural development, there is always a certain "welcome" at play—what I would call an "act of hospitality." From within many community music events there strives to be a cultivation of trust, respect, and responsibility brought forth through collaborative human endeavor. Musicking of this nature is cultivated through a reciprocal "call" and "welcome" that can foster deep and lasting relationships. Often a response to an unjust situation, community music practice has at its heart a commitment to cultural democracy, a call for both action and appropriate intervention, a system of support and respect for the many cultures and communities across the world. With no claim of superiority or special status, cultural democracy advocates that people need to create culture rather than having culture made for them. Following this, I would say that community musicians and those that advocate for their work are dreamers. Not in the sense of processing an unfocused mind but rather those who imagine an emergence of something different, something that might disturb and transform a situation that appears fixed and static. As optimists then, I would add that the authors featured in this book are constantly asking themselves "Why not?" They are defiant; always challenging those that suggest something cannot be done. Always seeking possible solutions to create music-making opportunities.

It is an honor to be asked to write this foreword, particularly in "front" of, or maybe better put, standing on the shoulders of, so many community music pioneers. From my first international community music interactions in 1998 (a quite remarkable event in Durban, South Africa, organized by one of the book's authors Elizabeth Oehrle) and on through subsequent encounters with many of the book's contributors, I can honestly say I am delighted to see this collection of essays published. I have no doubt that it will enrich the field and add its own particular accent to a growing number of texts and practices that seek to explore and release community music making.

Lee Higgins
Visiting Associate Professor, Music Education
Boston University

Acknowledgments

First, I must thank my father Thomas Clayton Veblen, who loves music of all kinds and who is endlessly fascinated with the ways that people interact communally. As well, thank you to my co-editors Stephen James Messenger, Marissa Silverman, and David J. Elliott for their mighty efforts and enthusiasm! Thank you to all who contributed their words with so much generosity, and to Kathryn Fenton for some judicious word cutting. And, as a former High Hog, I must give a nod to friends at the Wild Hog in the Woods Cooperative Coffeehouse in Madison, Wisconsin, celebrating its thirty-fifth birthday in 2013. Still running on a shoestring, still going strong. I learned so much about community music there.—Kari K. Veblen

To Dory and Regan Messenger, the best people I know.—Stephen J. Messenger

To David Elliott and Kari Veblen, without whom I would never have found my "official" way to community music. To my mother, Miriam Gaffney, who shepherded me from one community music school to another because she knew I needed to make music. And, most significantly, to two educators: Carol Lounsberry, my elementary school music teacher, who recognized my burgeoning musicianship when I was seven years old, and pianist Gregory Haimovsky, who convinced me to pursue music at a professional level and who continues to inspire everything musical in my life.—Marissa Silverman

At the age of six, I began going to Mrs. Fenwick's Community Music School. Situated in the countryside, this farmhouse is where I took my first jazz piano and trombone lessons. To those teachers, Valentino Cinanni, my piano teacher, and Steve Richards, my trombone teacher, my deepest gratitude for passing on their musicianship in such supportive and caring ways. Also, to Dave Price, Phil Mullen, Lee Higgins, and Kari Veblen, all of whom taught me so much about community music. To them, I am grateful.—David J. Elliott

Chapter One

The Tapestry:
Introducing Community Music

Kari K. Veblen

In your hands you hold a labor of love, the creation of many hands, and, even in its embryonic stages, a source of much debate. More than fifty musician, educators have shared their projects, perspectives, and passions . . . and all of us believe that this endeavor is important, both to ourselves and to everyone who loves music, plays music, and facilitates music making.

For me, this book illuminates the work of community music workers who improvise and reinvent themselves and their vision in order to lead through music and other expressive media and attempt to answer the perennial question "What is Community Music (CM)?" by defining it through a broader international tapestry of contextual shades, hues, tones, and colors.

Why does CM so vigorously and so robustly resist categorization? Helen Phelan of the Irish World Academy of Music and Dance suggests that definitions "must by their nature, deal with abstractions and generalizations . . . the danger of definition is that it diminishes the particularity of event-based activities, and strips them of the specificity of cultural, political or social context (2007, 145)."

In definitional approaches, Phelan finds "a tendency to move from one extreme of the discourse to another; to propose an understanding which emphasizes the complete uniqueness of a phenomenon, on the one hand, or to see it as ubiquitous, on the other. In other words, some approaches to defining Community Music may emphasize its uniqueness, and those characteristics which set it apart from other forms of music-making, while others may view all music-making as Community Music (2007, 145)."

While the wide-angle panoramic view that Phelan refers to—"others may view all music-making as Community Music"—might convey the sweep of CM activities, its essence would be lost (2007, 145). Such a panorama dissipates the tensions that CM promotes as a site of inquiry. CM consists of, but is not limited to, informal music making, which includes teaching and learning dimensions. These activities weave their way through amateur and professional, formal and informal, institutional and non-institutional contexts. Projects may be occasional, one-time, or ongoing. Thus, the CM tapestry is local, personal, political, multifaceted, and, above all, fluid.

With this in mind, this book takes as its point of departure the many ways in which CM is understood. Community music is examined through global contexts, interconnections, marginalized musics and communities, and performing ensembles.

COMMUNITY MUSIC IN GLOBAL CONTEXT

One way to explore community music is through the ways in which it is interpreted in different places. While music has long been part of community, documentation and recognition of CM, as such, is comparatively recent. Some countries have a history of sustained programs, while others are just beginning to pay attention to the organizations and networks that further these projects. The prevailing cultural perspectives of each locality naturally color individual visions of what CM is and can be.

Jeff Bush and Andrew Krikun explore networks, organizations, and individual enterprises in North America. They note that one of the earliest advocates of CM in the United States was music educator Peter Dykema, who defined CM in 1916 as "not so much the designation of a new thing as a new point of view . . . Stated positively and concretely, community music is socialized music" (p. 218). Dykema goes on to talk about the efforts in his day to give all people opportunities to hear and make music. He describes some programs as being motivated by profit and some as initiatives of public-spirited citizens. Dykema feels that all of these new programs are important because they give "the opportunity to every man and woman for free and frequent participation in music" (p. 223).

Almost 100 years later, Dykema's comments remain central to an understanding of CM in North American society. Music making and music teaching/learning are certainly a major part of the dynamic. However, social factors, which include aspects of identity, heritage, group solidarity, healing, bonding, celebration, and other factors— "socialized music," as Dykema puts it—are also essential (p. 218). In their chapter, Bush and Krikun explore other advocates such as Janet Schenck and Max Kaplan as well as the role of organizations such as the National Association for Music Education (NAfME), the North American Coalition for Community Music (NACCM), and the National Guild of Community Schools of the Arts in the United States.

The United Kingdom has long been a site for social reforms, particularly since the Victorian era when Charles Dickens and others began to write of the plight of the poor. Kathryn Deane and Phil Mullen take up the more recent thread of continuing initiatives in social work and arts advocacy. Their chapter traces the influence of Sound Sense, the organization for CM workers organized in the 1980s. Sound Sense has the overarching raison d'etre for further access to music for all and defines CM in three ways: first, CM involves musicians from any musical discipline working with groups of people to enable them to develop active and creative participation in music; second, CM is concerned with putting equal opportunities into practice; and third, CM happens in all types of communities, whether based on place, institution, interest, age, or gender group, where it reflects the context in which it takes place (Macdonald, 1995). One case study that epitomizes the current work in England is provided through Phil Mullen's compositional and improvisational work with children through the Sing Up program (pp. 25–40).

Scandinavia continues to sustain a history of support for CM initiatives. "A Nordic definition of the term," write Sidsel Karlsen, Heidi Westerlund, Heidi Partti, and Einar Solbu, "emphasizes that community music activities encompass a wide range of musics and music-related activities and imply a focus on lifelong learning and an open-access attitude" (pp. 41–60). Although the term is used sparingly in Scandinavian countries, the field is full-bodied. In their chapter, the authors explore interactive historical and political forces and the interplay of formal and informal music education in the grand fabric of music making. Three in-depth case studies are offered in the contexts of choirs, wind bands, churches, music therapy, and other situations. The Ole Bull Academy located in Voss, Norway, was established in 1972 to nurture Norwegian folk music, reaching over six thousand students in the past forty years. In the case of *Festspel i Pite Älvdal,* an annual festival held in northern Sweden, festival-goers participate in genres ranging from classical to folk, pop, and rock. In Finland, the online music portal Mikseri (www.mikseri.net) offers access to copyright-free pieces and opportunities to upload one's own music to members, and membership is free.

Elizabeth Oehrle, David Akombo, and Elias Weldegebriel offer three different interpretations of CM from Africa. Oehrle details the case study of her South African Ukusa program. *Ukusa* means "sunrise" in Zulu, and the thriving Ukusa music project, based in Durban, South Africa, has provided access to a wide variety of cultural opportunities over the past twenty years. Weldegebriel defines community music in Eritrea, a country populated by nine different ethnic groups each with unique language and musics, in terms of its cultural diversity. The Amsara Music School, founded by the Eritrean Peoples' Liberation Front in 1985, is the seminal institution currently teaching music for social transformation with contemporary music serving the function of resisting colonialization and promoting nationhood. The role of women *Isikuti* musicians among the Isukha people of Kenya is the subject of the final case study in this chapter. Akombo explains that much of African history is written from a male perspective, yet it is most often the women who are keepers of informal education in Africa.

CM activities from Australia and New Zealand Aotearoa are chronicled by Brydie-Leigh Bartleet, Shelley Brunt, Anja Tait, and Catherine Threlfall. They identify the place of CM in these neighboring Pacific nations as a "group activity where people join together to actively participate in the music-making process. Musical interactions include playing, listening, watching, moving, creating, and recording." Furthermore, community music activities in Australia and New Zealand "are reflective of a geographical community, a community of interest, or an imagined community and involve complex webs, networks, or pathways through which music making happens in-person or on-line" (pp. 151–168).

Case studies explored in the Australian/New Zealand context include an Australian nationwide community music research initiative (Sound Links), narratives from the remote Northern Territory (ArtStories) and the Cuba Street Carnival from Wellington, New Zealand. Although each case study (Sound Links, an Australian nationwide community music research initiative; ArtStories in the remote Northern Territory; and the Cuba Street Carnival in Wellington, New Zealand) presents a unique perspective, there are common themes: place-making or the connections between people and geography, commitment to social inclusion, and the ways in which inspired and inspiring individuals take action as CM workers.

A final chapter in this section surveys selected CM projects in East Asia. Chi Cheung Leung, Mari Shiobara, and Christine Yau present projects and research from Hong Kong, Japan, and mainland China. Leung shares his personal experience of the operation of his modern Chinese orchestra in Hong Kong. The Chinese modern orchestra consists of traditional Chinese instruments, such as the *dizi, pipa*, and *yangqin*, reinterpreted in this modern ensemble with newly arranged and composed music. Shiobara offers a case study with Kinseikai, or "The Voices of Golden Brocade Society," a Japanese singing group. This group in a suburb of Tokyo meets to pass on and enjoy *min'yō,* traditional Japanese songs. In this weekly gathering of professional and amateur singers, this art continues an unbroken oral tradition and offers outreach through school to younger singers. Yau explores the use of Red Songs and their transformation in China over the course of sixty years. Red Songs, revolutionary songs originally composed to promote communism in the People's Republic of China over sixty years ago, are being revived by the government to create community in modern urban China. However, as Yau notes, song competitions in an affluent shopping mall illustrate the dichotomy that exists between the vision of community and the new ways they are used to promote consumerism and individualization.

INTERCONNECTIONS

CM programs characteristically emphasize lifelong learning and access for all. Shaped by the participants they serve, programs may accommodate populations from the prenatal to the elderly, including intergenerational mixed groups and the hard-to-serve and privileged. Participants include people from diverse cultures, ability levels, socioeconomic circumstances, and political and religious traditions.

While some programs are geared toward marginalized and disadvantaged populations, taking place in sites such as hospitals and prisons, others are intended to celebrate and entertain, with parks, community centers, and campgrounds as their settings. A variety of alternative structures, formal and informal, planned and unplanned, exist to teach, experience, and perform music.

Intergenerational music—music that is made when people of different ages and generations come together—is the theme of the chapter by Carol Beynon and Chris Alfano. They note that research suggests that the benefits of intergenerational activities for seniors occur by being appreciated for their contribution, while children gain from increasing individualized learning activities. In many intergenerational situations, it is assumed that the older person knows more than the younger one, which is consonant with traditional interactive roles of teacher and student tied to age and experience. However, as Beynon and Alfano point out, there are some community settings where the young learn alongside adults, with a significant and synergistic impact upon each other, challenging the traditional notion of adult as teacher, role model, or expert and child or adolescent as novice learner.

Conventional wisdom sees music learning as the domain of the young. However, David Myers, Chelcy Bowles, and Will Dabback present a compelling case for music learning as a lifespan endeavor. Their chapter notes that access means both availability and gaining understandings and skills to further meaningful engagement. They believe, therefore, that it is important to identify the ways individuals change throughout their lives in order to design suitable delivery systems for diverse learners. The authors explore the history of music education, changing demographics, characteristics of adult learners, and motivation. Citing current research in this area, Myers, Bowles, and Dabback suggest that musicians working with adult learners may find the greatest success when they shift from a teacher to a facilitator role and provide practical strategies for implementing music programs for seniors.

The importance of intersections between community, school, university, and arts groups is the subject of the chapter by Sylvia Chong, Debbie Rohwer, Donna Emmanuel, Nathan Kruse, and Rineke Smilde. Chong documents and describes the funding of three current partnerships between schools and tradition bearers in Singapore. Culturally and demographically a mix of British, Malaysia, Indonesian, Chinese, and Indian peoples, Singapore is favored with vibrant musics and arts. As part of national cultural policy, the Singapore National Arts Council promotes the work of tradition bearers in the classroom. Debbie Rohwer, Donna Emmanuel, and Nathan Kruse explore university outreach ensembles in one Texas community through a seniors' band, a dulcimer ensemble, and a mariachi group. Located within the university setting, the Mariachi Águilas initiative aims for authentic engagement with the community. Finally, Rineke Smilde reports on the Netherlands experience "Opera in the Bus." This case study investigates the role and attributes needed for a community worker or animateur.

One of the most revolutionary advances in CM is through online media and modes. The advent in social networking allows entry into a kaleidoscope of musical genres and enables people to connect and learn musically in radically new ways. In his chapter on online jamband communities, Stephen J. Messenger considers the earliest jambands, beginning with the Grateful Dead. He analyzes the phenomenon of tapers and the taping of concerts and live festivals then shared via the Internet. Here too, according to Messenger's analysis, the touchstone of *communitas* in CM holds firm as members act out the social compact of their group by contributing and sharing information. Messenger notes how themes of creative musicking, social capital, and resistance to hegemonic commercial systems are played out through the deliberate community building in online jamband groups.

As shown in these case studies, the concept of community may be a contested notion because community is both an observable reality and an ideal. Some communities base their identity in culture or heritage while others are artistically connected. In some instances, community may be re-created or re-imagined. In other cases, community is found in virtual spaces, geographic locations, or both, an interplay between formal and informal contexts. Currently music scholars are documenting the interfaces and interconnections between social cultures and musical cultures, as they mirror, shape, and reflect each other.

MARGINALIZED MUSICS AND COMMUNITIES

Some CM initiatives are based on the premise that the personal and social well-being of participants is as important or more important than overt musical instruction. For many disadvantaged or marginalized people, CM activities nurture individual and collective identities. Creativity, improvisation, and personal exploration may be accommodated through music and arts interventions or opportunities. People who fall into this category may include immigrants entering a new culture; at-risk youth; those in prisons, shelters, and institutions; those who have suffered abuse; and the dispossessed.

Sheila Woodward and Catherine Pestano write of their music projects for youth who have fallen outside regular educational systems. These include at-risk students, juvenile offenders, and those encountering oppression as members of a minority. Woodward describes Diversion into Music Education (DIME), her program based in South Africa and the United States. Established in 2001, DIME initially focused on incarcerated American children and South African children within the court systems who were facing possible imprisonment. Later, this program reached larger numbers of children and expanded to include American juveniles assigned to diversion programs and other teenagers who were considered at-risk. This program offers participants marimba and djembe ensemble experience and cross-continental communication between the groups. Pestano contrasts two programs, one UK-based and the other located in the province of Vojvodina, Serbia. The UK-based project serves at-risk students who have been diverted from mainstream schools. The Serbian program is a creative participatory outreach for ethnically oppressed (such as members of the Roma community) as well as marginalized, disabled Serbian youth.

In their chapter "Personal Growth through Music," Mary L. Cohen and Marissa Silverman share musical interventions that address social alienation. Both projects are grounded in notions of restorative justice, an emerging area of study surrounding practices that restore and build community. A collaboration between the University of Iowa and the Oakdale Prison, Cohen's project engages inmates and volunteers in singing with social, ritual, and performance aspects. One innovative feature is the introduction of sharing through reading, writing, biography, and CD projects. Silverman considers two CM interventions involving homeless persons in New York City. The first project, the Music Kitchen, founded by Kelly Hall-Tompkins, brings concerts to homeless people eating at soup kitchens. The second project is the music therapy program in the 30th Street Men's Shelter at New York City's Bellevue Hospital, begun by Noah Shapiro in 1987. The Bellevue project engages homeless men with psychiatric challenges with music, related arts, and current events in order to help re-socialize participants, eventually moving them to more stable and permanent housing.

Other marginalized populations that may be reached through music participation include those with disabilities. Don DeVito and Arthur Gill examine programs from the United States, Pakistan, and West Africa, including current international initiatives and partnership links and programs in the Asian Pacific, Middle East, United Kingdom, and North America, for individuals who are challenged. DeVito's program at the Sidney Lanier Community Music Program (CMP) in Gainesville, Florida, combines music education and community-based instruction in school and outreach contexts. The program engages adults and students with moderate to profound disabilities and their families. In some cases, the participants live in assisted care facilities. Using a wide range of musics, from singing, drum circles, band ensembles, and movement, DeVito's program reaches students challenged with autism, Down syndrome, cerebral palsy, and other developmental disabilities. Community musicians guest in the classes teaching Australian didgeridoo and Brazilian *pifano* (a three-hole flute), Kenyan singing and dances from Peru, and other experiences. In addition to hosting local guests, this program links (via Skype) to programs in a half dozen other localities. One of these partners is Arthur Gill, who works with eighty children in Pakistan.

Themes of diversity and inclusive practice are illustrated through the work of Magali Oliveria Kleber, Dochy Lichtensztajn, and Claudia Gluschankof. Magali Oliveria Kleber from Brazil describes how social capital, social networks, and music education positively affect many lives. Her "Villa Lobinhos Project" in Rio de Janeiro, Brazil, promotes the music teaching and learning activities and inclusion of children and young people from underserved communities as well as outreach for faculty and pre-service teachers from Londrina State University. Kleber maintains that music education in other contexts can benefit from knowledge gleaned from these emergent environments.

Dochy Lichtensztajn examines the success of the Kadma Program-Live Music Encounters in the north of Israel, where Jewish and Palestinian elementary school students, although divided by cultural and national splits, unite by listening to symphonic concerts. As pedagogical director for the Levinsky School of Music Education Program "Live Music Encounters," Lichtensztajn has created a web of partnerships for the benefit of children and their communities. Claudia Gluschankof discusses her involvement teaching music on a voluntary basis, at the only school where Jewish children attend located in an Arab town. Gluschankof notes that her challenges were many, among them the need to find the right child-appropriate repertoire.

PERFORMING ENSEMBLES: ARTISTRY, ADVOCACY, AND SOCIAL JUSTICE

Many CM initiatives center on performing ensembles and active music making. In this section, authors address the underlying reasons for such ensembles through case studies that highlight artistry, advocacy, and social justice.

Susan Avery, Casey Hayes, and Cindy Bell explore community choirs from an American perspective. Avery writes of the prevalent traditional community choir, most often peopled with older singers, both working and retired. Citing 2009 research by Chorus America, she notes that over thirty-two million Americans sing weekly in community-based choirs. Membership profiles, organization, repertoire, and dynamics are probed for keys into the success of this popular form of musical expression. The importance of choral singing in affirming identity is highlighted through the flourishing GLBT (gay, lesbian, bisexual, transgender) choral movement. Hayes emphasizes the significant role that GLBT choirs play in creating a voice in catalyzing social change for social rights, including the freedom to love. He describes the beginnings of the San Francisco Gay Men's Chorus on the city hall steps in 1979 as a spontaneous crowd singing to protest the murders of gay rights advocates Harvey Milk and George Moscone. Hayes notes that GLBT choirs are beginning to come to grips with a changing dynamic: as civil liberties are attained, the choirs' role may be changing from education and advocacy to musical excellence.

Don Coffman and Joel Barbosa document the benefits and experiences of instrumental performing ensembles in North America and Brazil with two case studies. Coffman describes work with the Iowa City New Horizons Band (ICNHB), an affiliate of the New Horizons International Music Association (NHIMA), an organization with bands, choirs, and orchestras in North America, Ireland, and internationally, that share a newsletter, an Internet website (www.newhorizonsmusic.org), and national institutes or "camps." Begun in 1991 under the leadership of Roy Ernst, New Horizons groups offer opportunities to play music not simply to perform but to learn and improve music skills. Each NHIMA group is autonomous and usually works with a local music merchant who offers support such as rehearsal space, administrative oversight, or discounts on purchases. Similarly, Barbosa describes how civil wind bands are an essential part of Brazilian community and national identity. According to his research, the number of registered Brazilian bands has increased from 742 registered bands in 1975 to 2,086 by 2009.

Expressing faith through music is the focus of the chapter by Hussein Janmohamed, Cindy Bell, and Mehnaz Thawer. Through two case studies, the authors consider the role that singing plays in individual and shared worship. Janmohamed and Thawer chronicle the evolution of an Ismaili Muslim community youth choir in Vancouver. World events and resulting negative media compelled Janmohamed and others to increase dialogue in order to project positive views of Islam with the community beyond their mosque. Citing the thirteenth-century mystic poet Rumi (Barus & Moyne, 1995, p. 36), who wrote, "There are hundreds of ways to kneel and kiss the ground," Janmohamed describes his work helping young singers manifest what it is to be Ismaili Muslim and Canadian as they worship the divine (p. 279). Bell surveys the American phenomenon of Christian church choirs spilling out of Sunday morning into the community. She notes that much activity flies below the radar, groups are fluid and hard to document. While many choirs stand firmly in their pews, others take part in ecumenical choral festivals, seasonal performances (such as Handel's *Messiah*), camp meetings/crusades, and neighborhood gatherings.

Huib Schippers and Richard Letts explore the international ecosystems of engaged music making and issues of sustainability given modern globalization. Following a large-scale study undertaken for the International Music Council, the authors examine social dynamics and continuity of musical traditions through *Sustainable Futures*. This study focuses on nine traditions: Korean *samul'nori*, Mexican mariachi, Balinese *gamelan*, North Indian classical music, Western opera, Vietnamese *ca trù*, indigenous Australian musics, Ewe percussion from Ghana, and music from the Amami Islands in Japan. Schippers and Letts note that "systems of learning music are very often community-based, as are the contexts, values and attitudes that steer musical activity.

Even infrastructure, regulations, and the music industry are often driven, or at least strongly influenced, by communities" (p. 296)

Janice Waldron, Steven Moser, and Kari K. Veblen round out the book with a chapter of useful sources and websites for those hungry to know more about CM.

This book is both a response to and a testimony of the expanded awareness of what music is and what it can do, the place of music in people's lives, and the many ways in which it unites and marks communities. As documented in case studies throughout this book, CM workers may be musicians/teachers/researchers and activists, responding to the particular situations in which they find themselves, creating the CM tapestry's design. In places as separate as Sweden, Japan, and Kenya, pride of place and heritage is central to cultural identity and is nurtured by groups as dissimilar as the Ole Bull Academy, the "Voices of the Golden Brocade" singing traditional Japanese *min'yō,* and Kenyan women of the Isukha people who are the keepers of their cherished musical traditions. New ways of connecting act as the shuttle, happening intergenerationally, throughout the lifespan, through collaborative programs and through new technologies. While artistry and advocacy provide the warp and weft of this musical fabric, the needs of those at risk bind the CM cloth. All of these voices are the threads of the multifaceted tapestry of musical practices at play in formal, informal, non-formal, incidental, and accidental happenings of community music.

BIBLIOGRAPHY

Anderson, B. (1991). *Imagined communities: Reflections on the origin and spread of nationalism* (2nd ed.). London: Verso.

Borus, C., & Moyne, J. (1995). *The essential Rumi.* San Francisco: HarperCollins.

Boyd, D. M., & Ellison, N. B. (2007). Social network sites: Definition, history and scholarship. *Journal of Computer-Mediated Communication, 13* (1), 1–11. Retrieved from http://jcmc.indiana.edu/v0l13/issue1/boyd.ellison.html

Campbell, P., & Burnaby, B. (Eds.). (2001). *Participatory practices in adult education,* London: Erlbaum.

Dykema, P. W. (1916). The spread of the community music idea. *Annals of the American Academy of Political and Social Science, 67,* 218–228.

Mak, P. (n.d.) *Learning music in formal, non-formal and informal contexts.* Retrieved from www.emc-imc.org/fileadmin/EFMET/article_Mak.pdf

Phelan, H. (2008). Practice, ritual and community music: Doing as identity. *International Journal of Community Music,* 1(2), 143–158.

Schugurensky, D. (2000). *The forms of informal learning: Towards a conceptualization of the field* (Doctoral dissertation). University of Toronto. Retrieved from http://www.oise.utoronto.ca/depts/sese/csew/nall/res/19formsofinformal.pdf

Veblen, K. K. (2003). Community musicians, music educators and music workers: International dialogues. In E. Olsen Sampsel, *Proceedings of the 2002 ISME conference.* Bergen, Norway.

Veblen, K. K. (2012). Community music making: Challenging the stereotypes of traditional music education. In C. A. Beynon & K. K. Veblen (Eds.), *Critical perspectives in Canadian music education.* Waterloo, ON: Wilfrid Laurier University Press.

Veblen, K. K., & Olsson, B. (2002). Community music: Towards an international perspective. In R. Colwell & C. Richardson (Eds.), *The new handbook of research on music teaching and learning* (pp. 730–753). New York: Oxford University Press.

Part I

COMMUNITY MUSIC
IN GLOBAL CONTEXT

Chapter Two

Community Music in North America: Historical Foundations

Jeffrey E. Bush and Andrew Krikun

Although we can safely assume that music has played an integral role in North American communities from the time of the earliest human settlements, the promulgation of community music as an organized movement began to take root in the nineteenth century. Since that time, community music activities have included a panoply of musical styles and practices, encompassing community music schools, community bands, orchestras, choruses, church choirs and bands, labor choruses, industrial music groups, drum and bugle corps, and many other informal musical congregations, such as drum circles and jam sessions. Given the broad diversity of community music, a comprehensive history would be an impossible task. Instead, we highlight several educators, scholars, civic leaders, organizations, schools, and ensembles that have been instrumental in the history of community music in North America.

COMMUNITY MUSIC RESEARCH

The early historians of American music focused on the composers and compositions of the European art music tradition and largely ignored the contributions of musical performers from the diverse spectrum of North American musical styles (Crawford, 1993). Recent music historians have addressed these shortcomings and have attempted to present more culturally inclusive historical narratives, as well as document the history of previously marginalized groups, such as African-Americans (Chase, 1987; Crawford, 2001; Hamm, 1983; Hitchcock, 1988; Southern, 1997).

Despite the absence of these other musical styles from the music history books, folklorists began documenting traditional music following the Civil War. In the United States, interest in the traditional music of the African-Americans, Anglo-Americans, and Native Americans resulted in publications such as *Slave Songs of the United States* (Allen, Garrison, & Ware, 1867), *The English and Scottish Popular Ballads* (Child, 1882–1898), and *The Indians' Book* (Burlin, 1907). Ethnomusicologists incorporating sociological and historical models have conducted more recent studies of music in North American communities. Ruth Finnegan's study of music making in the English town of

Milton Keynes, *The Hidden Musicians* (1989), was the inspiration for the ethnographic study *Community of Music* (Livingston, Russell, Ward, & Nettl, 1993), which details the diverse musical activities taking place in the college town of Champaign-Urbana, Illinois. Other monographs use historical research methods to re-create community music traditions of an earlier time. These include Jennifer Post's *Music in Rural New England Family and Community Life* (2003) and Michael Saffle's *Music and Culture in America, 1861–1917* (1998). Mark and Gary (2007) describe the early community educational efforts of the singing-school movement in New England during the eighteenth century.

As has been the case in many parts of the world, the music of the native peoples of Canada was largely ignored until the latter half of the twentieth century. Early ethnomusicologists often made a haphazard attempt at collecting Indian and Inuit music, and early collections of songs were heavily Westernized. Over the past fifty years, an increase in the instruction and performance of these First Nations' music traditions has led to a more important role in the Canadian music landscape. A notable Canadian contribution is Gagnon's *Chansons Populaires du Canada* (1965), a series of transcriptions and information on the origins of French Canadian folk music (Kallmann, 1981). Edith Fowke has compiled over one thousand songs from Ontario, some published in *Traditional Singers and Songs from Ontario* and *Lumbering Songs from the Northern Woods* (Kallmann, 1981).

Groups of immigrants had a major impact on the musical life of Canadians. While the English and French were the two initial groups, succeeding immigrant groups have contributed to the Canadian music mosaic. In Newfoundland and the maritime provinces (Nova Scotia, New Brunswick, the Prince Edward Islands), the influx of Irish and Scottish settlers during the nineteenth century led to the establishment of Celtic music traditions. In Quebec, a center for French immigrants, the Catholic Church established itself as the center of early communities. Early French Catholic priests sought to convert the native peoples through music as well as church teachings. Southern Ontario (then called Upper Canada) was influenced by the English and, after American independence, Loyalists from the United States. Musical offerings were similar to those of the eastern United States, with opportunities such as singing schools being common. During the nineteenth century, primarily the urban centers of Vancouver and Victoria, British Columbia, enjoyed a cosmopolitan musical evolution as these centers were frequent jumping-off points for those heading for the gold fields of the Yukon and Alaska. As such, it was common to find a wide variety of amateur and semiprofessional European musical offerings in Vancouver and Victoria. The prairie provinces (Manitoba, Saskatchewan, Alberta) were settled later and were influenced by a variety of groups, including the Mennonites, Icelanders, and Ukrainians. Each brought a rich musical heritage that led to a variety of community music offerings.

COMMUNITY MUSIC ADVOCACY

Music educator Peter W. Dykema (1873–1951) was an early advocate of community music and a leader in the community singing movement in the early years of the twentieth century. After graduating with a master's degree from the University of

Michigan in 1896, Dykema began his career as a high school English and German teacher as well as a school principal. He went on to direct the music program at the Ethical Culture School in New York from 1901 to 1913 and spent the remaining years of his career as a professor of music at the University of Wisconsin (1913–1924) and professor and chair of the music education department at Teachers College, Columbia University (1924–1940). He served as president of the Music Education Research Council in 1916–1917 and also served as journal editor and chair of the Music Educators National Conference (MENC, now NAfME). As an avid amateur vocalist, he organized choirs at all of the schools at which he taught.

In his 1916 article, "The Spread of the Community Music Idea," Dykema offers a definition of "community music"—"a term that has obtained great vogue the past three years" (p. 218). He presents an inclusive and open definition of community music, stating, "It does not include any particular kind of music or any particular kind of performer. It is not so much the designation of a new thing as a new point of view" (p. 218). He sums up his definition with this democratic pronouncement: "Stated positively and concretely, community music is socialized music; music, to use Lincoln's phrase, for the people, of the people, and by the people" (p. 218). In 1919, he published *Twice 55 Community Songs*. The title refers to the first pamphlet of community songs published by the Music Supervisors National Conference (MSNC) in 1913, which consisted of a collection of fifty-five songs. Promoting a nationalistic and humanistic philosophy following the devastation of World War I, Dykema (1919) declares:

> This collection of songs represents a movement toward truer brotherhood and spiritual awakening through mass singing—an effort to liberate the spirit of the people through self-expression in song and add to growth in unity of thought and feeling which is the formulation of individual and national strength. (Preface)

The songbook contains a motley assortment of songs: patriotic songs, operatic arias, popular songs, Negro spirituals, Native American songs, college songs, and folk songs from Hawaii, Spain, France, and Scotland. The original songbook was followed by the expanded publication of *Twice 55 Plus Community Songs* (1929), which included some of the same songs from the earlier edition as well as new additions. Keeping to his multicultural credo, Dykema sought to include songs from many nationalities since America was a country of many nations.

From the start of the New Deal in 1933 to the end of World War II in 1945, civic leaders, musicians, and music educators studied the role of music in community life, hoping to create initiatives to promote amateur and professional music making as a positive social force. Summarizing a report of the Committee on Community Music of the Music Teachers' National Association, Dykema (1934) observed, "both as regards music and many other social activities, the year 1933 stressed the community idea to an extraordinary extent" (p. 13). Additionally, many community music projects were aided by the US government's Works Progress Administration (1935–1943), which provided federal funding to musicians, music educators, and researchers active in community music. Eric Clarke (1935) observes:

> The field is vast. Every detail in it is somebody's specialty, and many books on music particulars have been written by specialists; but musical activities in this country have

never been treated as a whole. Yet if people are ever to find an answer to these questions they must have a panorama—an airplane view, as it were—of the musical landscape to give those who may wish to come to earth a glimpse of interesting avenues to explore. And the eyes which see music must be those of the ordinary citizen rather than of teacher, player or institution. (v–vi)

Willem van de Wall was a seminal influence on the development of the field of music therapy, researching the role of music in institutional settings, including prisons, psychiatric hospitals, and general hospitals. He began his study and advocacy of therapeutic uses of music tending to the wounded soldiers in hospitals during World War I. During the 1920s and 1930s, van de Wall was employed by the Russell Sage Foundation as a writer and researcher. His impressive work culminated in the foundation's publication *Music in Institutions.* In *Music of the People* (1938), commissioned by the American Association for Adult Education, van de Wall describes community music in six localities—Westchester County, New York; Cincinnati, Ohio; Vermont; Kentucky; Delaware; and Wisconsin—and shares his views on a wide variety of community music practices.

Throughout his illustrious career, Max Kaplan was dedicated to community music and was lauded for his sociological research on music and music education, and most notably, his study of leisure. After receiving his education degree at Milwaukee State Teachers College in 1933, Kaplan worked for several years in Wisconsin as a social worker and research assistant before founding and directing the music department at Pueblo College, a small junior college in Pueblo, Colorado, in 1937. He remained at the college until 1944, striving to connect the curricular goals of the music program with the local community. In his final years at the college, he worked with his students to compile a survey of music in the city of Pueblo, which he self-published in 1944 as *Music in the City.*

Kaplan remained active in community music for the rest of his career. In the late 1950s, he chaired the MENC Music in American Life Commission VIII: Music in the Community, which contained the Committee on Music in Churches, the Committee on Music in Industry, the Committee on Music in Adult Education, and the Committee on Music in Community Agencies. The commission was primarily composed of professors from American colleges and universities but also included representatives from public schools, churches, music publishers, civic organizations, and companies. The commission published an informative report on the status of community music in 1958 (MENC).

PROFESSIONAL ORGANIZATIONS

Professional organizations of musicians and music educators and non-profit organizations dedicated to the promulgation of music in North American life have contributed greatly to the growth of community music. During the second half of the nineteenth century and into the early twentieth century, a number of professional organizations dedicated to music and music education were founded. These included the National Education Association (1870), the Music Teachers National Association (1876), the

Department of Music Education (1884), the Canadian Piano and Organ Manufacturers' Association (1899), the American Guild of Organists (1896), the National Federation of Music Clubs (1898), the Music Supervisors National Conference (1907), the National Bureau for the Advancement of Music (1916), and the Canadian Bureau for the Advancement of Music (1919).

The mission of MENC, The National Association for Music Education, one of the largest music organizations in the world with more than seventy-five thousand members, is to " . . . advance music education by encouraging the studying and making of music by all" (MENC). Throughout the organization's one hundred-plus years, the focus has largely been on public school (K–12) music education, even though many members participate in community music activities. In the 1980s, interest in community music activities increased, promoted by prominent music educators such as Charles Leonard and Mary Hoffman. In December 1995, David Myers and Chelcy Bowles submitted a proposal to the MENC Society for Research in Music Education (SRME) to establish a special research interest group (SRIG) for adult and community music. Included with this proposal were a petition and letters of support from prominent music education professors and researchers. At their annual meeting in April 1996, the SRME board voted to approve the creation of the Adult Continuing and Community Music Education SRIG (later changed to the Adult and Community Music Education SRIG).

The Adult and Community Music Education (ACME) SRIG held its first session on April 16, 1998, at the MENC Biennial Conference in Phoenix, Arizona. Formal events at all MENC Biennial Conferences from 1998 through 2006 have included panel discussions and invited speakers from adult education and international music organizations as well as several presentations on outstanding dissertations dealing with community music issues. Since 2005, the ACME SRIG has cosponsored three "Music and Lifelong Learning" symposiums: Madison, Wisconsin (2005), Ithaca, New York (2007), and Denton, Texas (2009). The group also publishes an annual newsletter and hosts a website that features an online database of pertinent publications created by Don Coffman and Laurie Bitters.

The National Federation of Music Clubs (NFMC) was conceived by Rose Fay Thomas. The wife of the renowned orchestra conductor of the Chicago Symphony, Theodore Thomas, Rose Fay Thomas was in charge of the musical segment of the World's Columbian Exposition held in Chicago in 1893. Her idea was to invite amateur women's musical clubs throughout the country to participate in the World's Fair Congress of Musicians. Initially, singing contests took place between the music club's choruses, which led to festivals and choral competitions. The federation was committed to the promotion of community music and was instrumental in providing opportunities to women to participate in music making. Ottaway (1935) describes the trailblazing role of the federation:

> Working with inadequate budgets or none at all, Federation apostles of music have pioneered in thousands of communities where there existed no interest in music and no music teaching in the schools. To arouse and maintain a permanent and active interest in music, to make music an integral part of life, to make the best music understood, to meet the need of the spirit in the reaction from the utilitarian and machine age are the ideals . . . (p. 225)

The NFMC remains active today with approximately two hundred thousand members in over 5,300 organizations and presents festivals and competitions across the United States, as well as sponsoring National Music Week (NFMC).

The National Bureau for the Advancement of Music was founded in 1916 by the National Piano Manufacturers Association, initially serving as a promotional vehicle to spur sales of pianos and other music merchandise (Koch, 1990). In his capacity as the director of the National Bureau for the Advancement of Music, C. M. Tremaine organized New York's first Music Week during the first week of February in 1920. With the participation of over 1700 local organizations, Tremaine (1920) hoped that his movement to spread music to "people of every class and of every variety of circumstances" (p. 9) would become a global phenomenon:

> The character and extent of the participation in this celebration make it certain that there will be hundreds, even thousands, of similar demonstrations, not only over our own country, but throughout the world. (p. 10)

In Canada, the Canadian Bureau for the Advancement of Music pursued similar interests to its American counterpart. The organization, chartered in 1919, began as an outgrowth of the Canadian Piano and Organ Manufacturers' Association's "Music in the Home" campaign—an early Canadian attempt at promoting community music. During the 1920s, it sponsored essay contests, community music weeks, and local music festivals. The bureau also functioned as the music committee for the Canadian National Exhibition beginning in 1921, focusing on entertainment, exhibition, and musical competitions (Kallmann, 1981).

A recent development in terms of national organizations is the North American Coalition for Community Music. Seventeen music educators met at the Hewitt School in January 2008 to discuss how to " . . . make music education more relevant and accessible to all." (NACCM) The deliberations noted there was a need for a continental organization that would develop and support all community music activities and would allow for interaction and learning between all interested community musicians and groups.

COMMUNITY MUSIC SCHOOLS

Community music schools have their roots in the music programs of the early settlement houses. The first and most influential settlement house was the Hull House in Chicago, co-founded by Jane Addams and Ellen Gates Starr in 1892 to improve the lives of recent immigrants. Although the Hull House offered music classes, the classes were limited to students demonstrating exceptional musical talent (Egan, 1989, p. 51). As other settlement houses sprang up in urban centers such as Boston, Philadelphia, New York, Milwaukee, Detroit, Toronto, and Baltimore, music departments were included in the educational offerings. Eventually, independent community music schools were established.

Janet Schenck was an early advocate and administrator for the community music movement. She was instrumental in convening the short-lived National Association of Music School Societies in 1910–1911 and chaired the Music Division of the National

Federation of Settlements and headed the Neighborhood Music School in New York. In 1923, Schenck published *Music Schools and Settlement Music Departments,* a report on the current state of community music schools commissioned by the National Federation of Settlements. She presents an overview of the organization and administration of community music schools with recommendations on curriculum development.

> We hear much these days of community music; and "music for all" has come to be a familiar slogan. But it is not enough merely to listen to music or to take part in the singing of a few community songs. If America is to become a truly musical nation, we must see to it that every child capable of creative artistic expression is guaranteed the opportunity of conscientious, exacting musical education under teachers of inspiration and ability. (p. 15)

The National Guild of Community Music Schools was established in 1937, initially composed of twelve schools based in Boston, New York, Cleveland, Buffalo, and Philadelphia. The purpose of the community music school was "to promote national culture through music based upon democratic principles. Such schools are unique in that they combine a high grade of music teaching with the fundamental principle that music is a vital part of living and is an essential element in the enrichment of the human spirit" (Egan, 1989, pp. 174–175). In 1974, the organization was renamed the National Guild of Community Schools of the Arts to include schools with an interdisciplinary arts curriculum. Today, the guild represents over four hundred member organizations, serves one million students, employs over sixteen thousand teaching artists, and reaches five million Americans through sponsored performances and exhibitions (National Guild of Community Schools of the Arts, 2009). Over the years, community music schools have produced a number of celebrated musicians, including Benny Goodman, Morton Feldman, Mario Lanza, Michael Tilson Thomas, and Dionne Warwick (Egan, 1989, pp. 374–377).

In addition, there are numerous other community music schools and organizations not affiliated with the National Guild of Community Schools of the Arts. Many of these schools focus primarily on musical styles historically outside the domain of formal music education, mainly folk and popular music. Two examples of non-traditional community music schools are the Ali Akbar College of Music in San Rafael, California (Ali Akbar College of Music, 2009), founded in 1967 in Berkeley, offering classes in the classical music tradition of North India, and the Paul Green School of Rock Music (The Paul Green School of Rock Music, 2009), founded in 1998 in Philadelphia, offering individual and group instruction in rock music in forty-nine schools across the United States. Extension divisions of colleges, universities, public schools, and religious organizations also offer classes and private instruction in music. In addition, private music instruction is offered in venues such as home studios and retail music stores.

COMMUNITY VOCAL ENSEMBLES

Community vocal ensembles take shape in a variety of forms: barbershop quartets, sacred and secular choral ensembles, opera and musical theater companies, and informal group singing.

One of the most enduring community vocal activities in North America is the barbershop quartet. The close harmony style of the barbershop quartet appears to be derived from African-American vocal quartets in the beginning of the twentieth century (Henry, 2001). The Barbershop Harmony Society, formerly known as the Society for the Preservation and Encouragement of Barbershop Quartet Singing in America (SPEBSQSA), presently has nearly thirty thousand members. The Sweet Adelines, an organization devoted to women barbershop quartet singers, was founded in 1945 in Tulsa, Oklahoma. Today, this international organization has nearly twenty-five thousand members as well as twelve hundred quartets and six hundred choruses. (Sweet Adelines, 2009). A splinter group broke off from Sweet Adelines in 1959 to form Harmony, Inc. Protesting the Sweet Adelines' racial discrimination policy, Harmony, Inc. dedicated themselves to a "focus on democratic principles" (Harmony, Inc., 2009).

The Toronto Mendelssohn Choir is one of Canada's most famous and longest performing amateur choirs. The organization was initially formed to perform unaccompanied mixed-voice literature. The ensemble has continued to change with the times, having performed with major North American orchestras and string and brass ensembles, as well as instrumental and vocal soloists. The organization continues to function with two primary groups: The Toronto Mendelssohn Choir (one-hundred-and-fifty-plus voices) and the smaller Toronto Mendelssohn Singers (seventy voices). As well as regular concerts in the Greater Toronto area (including annual performances with the Toronto Symphony Orchestra), the organization features a regular series of community singing workshops.

Most North American opera companies began their existence as community groups. Smaller communities still combine local amateurs with professionals, such as the Fargo-Moorhead Opera Company, North Bay Opera, Edmonton Opera, and Cedar Rapids Opera Theatre. Community music theater has been a popular form of musical entertainment since the early twentieth century and continues to flourish with companies in virtually every state and province. Many of these organizations have long histories of producing works with and for their communities, such as the Cincinnati Music Theatre (forty-six years) and the Worcester County Light Opera Company (seventy-two years). Many organizations alternate between theater and music theater, such as the 1937-established Mesa Encore Theatre. Smaller centers often rally behind their musical theater companies as an essential form of community entertainment. Examples include the Music Theatre of Wenatchee, the Music Theatre Idaho, and the Regina Lyric Musical Theatre. Another popular form of music theater includes organizations that focus on summer-only productions (e.g., Shenandoah Summer Music Theatre, Prizery Summer Theatre Celebration, Music Theatre of Wichita, and Summerstock Conservatory).

Although difficult to document, informal singing groups welcome community participants to gatherings regardless of their previous musical background. Recent examples of informal singing groups include the Walkabout Clearwater Chorus of the lower Hudson Valley in New York and the Ottawa Shape Note Chorus.

COMMUNITY INSTRUMENTAL ENSEMBLES

The growth of community bands in North America can be traced to the military bands of the eighteenth century. This was particularly true in Canada, where many settlements were started as garrisons for either the military or, in later years, the Royal Northwest Mounted Police (now the Royal Canadian Mounted Police). Community bands and primarily youth-based community bands continued their prominence due to the later arrival of instrumental programs in the public schools. This was particularly true in Western Canada, where urban centers were not as prevalent. Many fraternal orders and civic groups sponsored bands such as the Edmonton Schoolboys Band (established in 1935) and the Regina Lions Band (established in 1943).

A casual search of the Internet found listings for over eleven hundred community concert bands and orchestras in North America; undoubtedly, this only represents a portion of similar groups currently providing opportunities for community instrumental experience. The New Horizons International Music Association is a recent form of community music engagement. According to the New Horizons website, there are 8,500 ensemble members, and there are 200 "groups." Begun as the New Horizons Band Project in 1991 by Roy Ernst, the movement is built on the beliefs that anyone can play music and that seniors can benefit from the joys of music making even if they have never played music before. Originally designed as an opportunity for seniors, many of the ensembles accept adults of various ages. While most of the ensembles were initially bands, the inclusive approach and goals have fostered many New Horizons orchestras and other types of musical ensembles. When traveling, members are encouraged to "drop in" and play with other New Horizons groups. As well as regular rehearsals, the organization sanctions a number of music camps where members can get together with other like-minded musicians and experience a variety of music opportunities, such as chamber music and private lessons.

The Association of Concert Bands (ACB) is another example of an organization devoted to adult instrumental music making. The association, formed in 1997, seeks to promote all forms of concert bands, including community, municipal, and civic bands. ACB provides services to those interested in these forms of adult music making, such as providing blanket licensing agreements with music publishers, publishing a newsletter, acting as a clearinghouse for information important to community bands, and holding an annual conference.

Symphony orchestras and philharmonic societies became commonplace in nineteenth-century America. Included in the report of the MENC Music in American Life Commission VIII: Music in the Community (1958) is a definition of the community orchestra:

> The community orchestra is composed largely of non-professional musicians who play primarily because of an avocational interest in music. Usually the orchestra must depend upon the local community to supply the musicians and to provide financial support. Most

of these orchestras rehearse only one evening a week and give their concerts on Sundays or in the evenings. (p. 44)

According to this report, there were 694 adult community orchestras and 63 youth community orchestras existing in the United States in 1957. It was observed that these orchestras existed primarily in urban and suburban areas and the participants consisted of a great number of the local professional class, including doctors, lawyers, and teachers.

The League of American Orchestras was founded in 1942 and currently represents almost one thousand symphony, chamber, youth, and collegiate orchestras in North America, including numerous community orchestras. The goals of the organization are to provide resources for these orchestras in the areas of government advocacy, financial planning, education, and audience development (League of American Orchestras).

ETHNIC AND PRESERVATION GROUPS

The number and type of community ethnic and regional ensembles is essentially uncountable. Many of these began and continue to operate under the auspices of a community center or church and cater to the interests of select groups of enthusiasts. These ensembles may have been established to help immigrants remain connected with their culture and/or to teach the next generation about their heritage; however, they were often designed to give people a social outlet. Some types of instrumental ensembles have now become commonplace and popular enough to develop national or regional organizations. For instance, the Alliance of North American Pipe Band Associations is an umbrella group designed to bring together various regional piping and drumming organizations. The Alliance seeks to foster cooperation and communication between members as well as to provide a forum to discuss common issues. The International Bluegrass Music Association, founded in 1985, seeks to promote a greater appreciation of bluegrass music. There are associations for polka bands (Midwest Polka Association), Chinese music (Chinese Arts and Music Association), and harmonica playing (Society for the Preservation and Advancement of the Harmonica).

CONCLUSION

The documentation of community music history has grown steadily as North American musicians, music educators, folklorists, ethnomusicologists, and music historians have comprehended the social and musical significance of these practices. Records before the nineteenth century are scant due to the lack of formal music institutions and the informal nature of community music activities. However, the foundations of many of the movements and activities found in North American community music can at least partially be discovered. Perhaps more importantly, music making continues to be an energetic and thriving activity adopted by thousands of members throughout North

America. These endeavors include European traditional ensembles as well as ethnic, folk, and popular groups. As is the case with many forms of entertainment, organizations begin, flourish, and sometimes disperse based on their appeal to the population and the skills of dedicated community volunteers. Increased documentation and interest in community music making suggests that this story may still be at the introductory stage, with many more developments ahead.

BIBLIOGRAPHY

Ali Akbar College of Music. (2009). Retrieved from http://aacm.org

Allen, W. F., Garrison, L. M., & Ware, C. P. (1867). *Slave songs of the United States.* New York: Simpson & Co.

Alliance of North American Pipe Band Associations. Retrieved from www.anapba.org

Association of Concert Bands. Retrieved from www.acbands.org

Burlin, N. C. (1907). *The Indians' book: An offering by the American Indians of Indian lore, musical and narrative, to form a record of the songs and legends of their race.* New York: Harper.

Chase, G. (1987). *America's music: From the pilgrims to the present* (Rev. 3rd ed.). Urbana, IL: University of Illinois.

Child, F. J. (1882–1898). *The English and Scottish popular ballads.* Boston: Houghton Mifflin Co.

Chinese Arts and Music Association. Retrieved from www.uschinamusic.org/news

Clarke, E. T. (1935). *Music in everyday life.* New York: W. W. Norton & Co.

Crawford, R. (1993). *The American musical landscape.* Berkeley: University of California Press.

Crawford, R. (2001). *America's musical life: A history.* New York: W. W. Norton.

Dykema, P. W. (1916). The spread of the community music idea. *The Annals of the American Academy of Political and Social Science, 67,* 218–223.

Dykema, P. W. (1919). *Twice 55 community songs.* Boston: C. C. Birchard.

Dykema, P. W. (1929). *Twice 55 Plus community songs.* Boston: C. C. Birchard.

Dykema, P. W. (1934). Music in community life. *Music Educators Journal, 20* (4), 34–74.

Egan, R. F. (1989). *Music and the arts in the community: The community music school in America.* Metuchen, NJ: The Scarecrow Press.

Finnegan, R. (1989). *The hidden musicians: Music-making in an English town.* Cambridge: Cambridge University Press.

Green, J. P., & Vogal, N. (1991). *Music education in Canada: A historical account.* Toronto, ON: University of Toronto Press.

Hamm, C. (1983). *Music in the new world.* New York: W.W. Norton.

Henry, J. (2001, July/August). The historical roots of barbershop harmony. *The Harmonizer,* 13–17.

Hitchcock, H. W. (1988). *Music in the United States: A historical introduction* (3rd ed.). Englewood Cliffs, NJ: Prentice Hall.

International Bluegrass Association. Retrieved from www.ibma.org

Kallmann, H. (1981). *Encyclopedia of music in Canada.* Toronto, ON: University of Toronto Press.

Kaplan, M. (1944). *Music in the city: A sociological survey of musical facilities and activities in Pueblo, Colorado.*

Koch, F. W. (1990). Cooperative promotional efforts of the Music Supervisors National Conference and the National Bureau for the Advancement of Music. *Journal of Research in Music Education, 38* (4), 269–281.

League of American Orchestras. Retrieved from http://www.americanorchestras.org/utilities/about_the_league.html

Leglar, M. A., & Smith, D. S. (1996). Community music in the United States: An overview of origins and evolution. In M. A. Leglar (Ed.), *The role of community music in a changing world: Proceedings of the International Society for Music Education 1994 seminar of the commission on community music activity* (pp. 95–108). Athens, GA: University of Georgia.

Livingston, T. E., Russell, M., Ward, L. F., & Nettl, B. (Eds.). (1993). *Community of music: An ethnographic seminar in Champaign-Urbana.* Champaign, IL: Elephant & Cat.

Mark, M. L. (1992). *The music educator and community music.* Reston, VA: MENC.

Mark. M. L., & Gary, C. L. (2007). *A history of American music education* (3rd ed.). Lanham, MD: MENC/Rowman & Littlefield Education.

MENC. (1958). *Music education in a changing world. A report for the music in American life commission on music in the community.* Washington, DC: MENC.

MENC: The National Association for Music Education. Retrieved from www.menc.org/about/view/mission-statement

Midwest Polka Association. Retrieved from http://www.midwestpolkaassociation.com

NACCM. Retrieved from www.naccm.info

National Guild of Community Schools of the Arts. (2009). Retrieved from www.nationalguild.org

New Horizons International Music Association. Retrieved from www.newhorizonsmusic.org

NFMC. Retrieved from http://nfmc-music.org/cms

Ottaway, R. H. (1935). Historical highlights of the federation 1898–1935. In H. G. Weaver (Ed.), *Book of proceedings of the National Federation of Music Clubs, volume 1. Nineteenth biennial meeting, Philadelphia, April 23–30, 1935.* Ithaca, NY: National Federation of Music Clubs.

The Paul Green School of Rock Music. (2009). Retrieved from www.schoolofrock.com

Post, J. C. (2003). *Music in rural New England family and community life.* Durham, NH: University of New Hampshire Press.

Saffle, M. (1998). *Music and culture in America, 1861–1917.* New York: Garland Publishing.

Schenck, J. B. (1923). *Music schools and settlement music departments.* Boston: National Federation of Settlements.

Shansky, C. L. (2009). *A history of two community bands: The Franklin and Waldwick bands* (Unpublished doctoral dissertation). Boston University.

Society for the Preservation and Advancement of the Harmonica. Retrieved from www.spah.org

Southern, E. (1997). *The music of black Americans* (3rd ed.). New York: W. W. Norton.

Sweet Adelines (2009). Sweet Adelines. Retrieved from www.sweetadelinesintl.org

Tremaine, C. M. (1920). *New York's first music week.* New York: National Bureau for the Advancement of Music.

van de Wall, W. (1936). *Music in institutions.* New York: Russell Sage Foundation.

van de Wall, W. (1938). *The music of the people.* New York: American Association for Adult Education.

Veblen, K. K. (2003). Compelling connections: Community and music making in Canada. *Canadian Music Educator,* 45 (2), 25–28.

Veblen, K. K., & Olsson, B. (2002). Community music: Towards an international overview. In R. Colwell & C. Richardson (Eds.), *The new handbook on music teaching and learning* (pp. 730–753). New York: Oxford University Press.

Chapter Three

Community Music in the United Kingdom

Kathryn Deane and Phil Mullen

It is said that the winners write history. In community music in the United Kingdom, where everyone is a winner, there are many different histories. This may be because the histories look different, depending on how far back one looks, or because definitions of community music differ, depending upon who is doing the defining. This chapter will trace a path to a generally accepted description of community music in the United Kingdom today and then give an in-depth look at one project in England.

COMMUNITIES MAKING MUSIC TOGETHER

We begin in 1962, when Helen Crummy (1992) asked her son's primary school, located in an impoverished neighborhood of Edinburgh, if he could have music lessons. She was told that it took the school all its time to teach the children the three Rs, much less music. Crummy and other mothers responded by knocking on doors, finding local talent, and staging a People's Festival of music, drama, and the arts. Combining culture with satirical criticism, the people wrote and produced their own community musicals and historical productions, basing them on the area's myriad social concerns and issues. Immediately successful, it brought joy and a sense of self-fulfillment to the participants. The Craigmillar Festival exemplifies the idea of community arts as creative activities with deliberate social purposes, especially since its activities included "personal development and social cohesion; expressing or re-interpreting cultural, religious or ethnic affiliations; articulating feelings about social issues or local problems; and stimulating or contributing to local action, democracy and change" (Craigmillar Festival Society).

DEFINING COMMUNITY MUSIC IN THE UNITED KINGDOM

Although by the early 1970s an Association for Community Artists had formed, attempts to succinctly define community arts proved problematic, particularly for those who wanted it to be politically robust or theoretically distinct. A number of studies, inquiries, and commentators from the mid-1970s to the mid-1980s agreed that the idea of community arts encompassed an attitude toward the arts, implying a reflection on *why* the work is being carried out, rather than focusing on the product of the work. They disagreed, however, in their attempts to distinguish community arts from amateur arts and to differentiate the concept of "'music in the community' . . . [from] 'communal music-making,' where these terms relate[d] to a community being musical" (Higgins, 2008b, p. 232). Everitt (1997) questions the validity of such a distinction:

> Much amateur work (one thinks of brass bands in mining or ex-mining villages) is evidently concerned with the expression of individual creativity and social involvement. Likewise, many amateurs who are taking part in the remarkable revival of traditional Gaelic musics are doing so at least in part because it enables them to express their feelings about social development and democratic change. The best that can be said is that most, but not all, amateur activity emerges spontaneously for local communities or groups of enthusiasts and that most, but not all, community arts are the result of external intervention by professional artists. (p. 38)

Everett's view constitutes a reasonable starting point for a description of community music in the United Kingdom. It describes professional musicians carrying out interventions *intended* to have consequences other than musical, as opposed to laypeople (non-professional musicians) doing it for themselves, with results that *may* have consequences beyond the musical.

By the mid-1980s, as Joss (1993) explains, a number of initiatives followed this new, if tentative, description of community music. These included, for example, music collectives or cooperatives born out of the punk music movement and the London Sinfonietta's appointment of its first orchestra education organizer in 1984. But in general, dissatisfaction with formal music education persisted because it emphasized the re-creation of an established tradition instead of creativity. A broader canvas was needed, and community arts practices showed the way.

One such practice, artist residencies, contributed to a new form of cultural democracy. In these, professional artists worked together with members of a local community and empowered them to make their own art and their own cultural decisions. This demonstrates the ethic of self-reliance because it encourages people to complete artistic tasks themselves, rather than relying on more experienced or able people completing them. It promotes the idea that an ordinary person can learn to do more than he or she thought was possible. Central to this ethic is the empowerment of individuals and communities, encouraging the employment of alternative approaches when faced with bureaucratic or societal obstacles to achieving their objectives. In this spirit, the Lincolnshire-based Firebird Trust was constituted in 1985 to "benefit the community, especially disadvantaged groups, through the expressive and creative power of music" (Steptoe, 2009, p. 13).

A tipping point in the development of British community music was the first national community music conference, Making Connections, which attracted one hundred and thirty delegates—community music workers of all kinds, funders, lecturers, and students. It established the commonly held understandings of the practice: it is a non-exclusive activity, a human right that can be reintegrated into social life; it encourages participation in the fullest sense; it promotes community-led activities in which institutions and professionals serve as resources; and it facilitates group activity. The delegates also identified certain issues requiring further exploration: a generally accepted definition of community music; the debate about process (the act of creating music) versus product (the delivery of a finished piece of musical creation); the role of community music in agendas of social change; principles and procedures for assessing activity; and community music's relationship with other musical activity (in particular, formal education, music therapy, the music industry, and funding). Following this seminal meeting Sound Sense, the national association for professional community music workers, was formed.

In 1990, Sound Sense began publishing a quarterly journal, and early issues explored the foundational concerns for the theory, practice, and recognition of community music. These early issues offer valuable descriptions of community music work. They map the field and describe how people who defined themselves as community musicians viewed the practice of community music. The following examples illustrate the range of work, client groups, and approaches to community music described in the first four issues of *Sounding Board:*

- The world's first concert of one-minute pieces of music, written during a series of open workshops in Lincoln.
- Samba bands gathered to serve "as a symbol for local environment groups to increase public awareness of the destruction of the rain forests."
- A local authority arts development worker offered workshops with a musician, funded through the Gorbals Unemployed Workers Centre.
- Goldsmiths College University of London gave accreditation to a course training practitioners to work with "the mentally ill, inner city and rural youth, mainstream and special school pupils, and others described as having special educational, physical or social needs."
- The recently formed community/education department at the Royal Liverpool Philharmonic Orchestra ran a five-week project for women using a community center "in a working-class area of high unemployment" with crèche and childcare facilities provided.
- The Tibble Trust offered workshops to musicians who wanted to develop skills in music making with older people in residential settings.
- A housing estate in Bristol, southwest England, employed Pete Rosser as a full-time "musician in the community" working out of the youth center and organizing workshops and performances with schoolchildren, young people, women, those with learning difficulties, and elderly people.
- A community recording studio in Middlesborough, northeast England, focused on encouraging a wide range of groups to become involved in music in ways which did not depend on participants having musical or technical knowledge. They adapted and invented musical instruments for use with people with special needs.

Although the work listed above does not overtly appear to have the political purposes of the community arts movement of the 1960s and 1970s, it certainly embraces the principle of music with additional social purposes.

By the beginning of 1994, the Sound Sense organizing committee was confident enough in its understanding of the work to attempt to define the field. Its definition, reflecting the diversity of practice while identifying the fundamentals of the work, states that community music (1) involves musicians from any musical discipline working with groups of people to enable them to develop active and creative participation in music; (2) is concerned with putting equal opportunities into practice; and (3) happens in all types of community, whether based on place, institution, interest, age, or gender group, where it reflects the context in which it takes place (Macdonald, 1995, 29).[1] Sound Sense itself has never been dogmatic about this definition and largely eschews definitions for more examples of the work itself. The last four issues of *Sounding Board* illustrate that breadth of provision, which has changed little in the past twenty years.

COMMUNITY MUSIC AND SOCIAL POLICY

In 1997, the New Labor administration offered the next driver for the community-development end of a community musician's work. Its policy action teams challenged every government department to plan how it would implement the government's social policy aspirations; the arts were not to be excepted. *Use or Ornament,* a key 1997 report, argues: (1) participation in the arts brings social impacts; (2) benefits are integral to the act of participation in the arts; and (3) the resulting social changes can be planned for and evaluated (Matarasso, p. ix). Matarasso concludes that "the election of a Government committed to tackling problems like youth unemployment, fear of crime, and social exclusion is the right moment to start talking about what the arts can do for society, rather than what society can do for the arts" (p. iii).

By 1999, the policy action team examining arts activities recommended that participation in the arts should be seen as central to regeneration policies and practices. It recognized that the arts appealed directly to individuals' interests, development, and self-confidence and could thus improve conditions in deprived communities. Since the arts addressed not just the symptoms, but also the causes of social exclusion, the government associated them with its four priority areas of health, crime, employment, and education.

At this same time, Sound Sense commissioned research into the nature of community music. The report (Kushner, Walker, & Tarr, 2001) had no difficulty identifying a complex, but visible, path along which community musicians walked:

> Community musicians are boundary-walkers [inhabiting] public territories that lie between other professions. They take their music to health settings, schools, the voluntary sector, the criminal justice system—and while denying they are therapists, teachers, community workers or probation officers, they find themselves working alongside these people and often doing what those professionals do. (p. 4)

Community musicians themselves concurred. For example, Sound It Out Community Music, located in Birmingham in the West Midlands of England, provided a support service to help exiled musicians. Pete Moser, who runs More Music, in Morecambe (a seaside town undergoing regeneration in the northwest of England) says: "Almost all the work I do has a dual purpose. Community music, for me, has always been a mixture of being a social worker and a composer and finding ways of bridging that . . . I passionately believe that music has the ability to make communities pull together" (Moser & McKay, 2005, p. 68).

COMMUNITY MUSIC AND YOUNG PEOPLE

By far the greatest change in community music has been the increasing attention given to young people's music, both inside and outside the classroom. There has been a strong strand of young people's education work within community music practice for many years. Andrew Peggie's *Musicians Go to School; Partnership in the Classroom* (1997) explores the work undertaken by visiting musicians in schools during the 1990s. Written from the perspective of a "reflective practitioner," the book lays out its focus most carefully:

> The label "visiting musician" is used in a particular way. It is intended to be all-embracing and neutral in respect of musical specialization, culture or style . . . The label excludes work which would normally be described as peripatetic music teaching, lecturing or school classroom teaching itself; thus, anyone who finds him or herself visiting a school for the sole purpose of making music with pupils and teachers (as an adjunct to, not a replacement for, the latter) is considered a visiting musician. (p. 5)

"Visiting musician" also refers to a specific way of working—"Pupils, teachers, and visitors will undertake practical musical activities together, very often with an important element of musical creation involved"—and a specific issue of access—pupils "working generally in whole class groups (that is, not selected for particular music aptitude or commitment)" (p. 6).

A 1998 report on music projects from the National Youth Agency (Ings, 1999) describes a variety of music activities (essentially, rock and pop and what came to be called urban music forms) operating in a range of youth clubs, studios, and community centers across the United Kingdom. Consequently, *Sounding Board* devoted the majority of one issue to the role of young people's music work in community music (e.g., Deane, 1998). *Mapping Hidden Talent* revealed a vital, creative strand of music making that was at least as powerful as adult brass bands or orchestral outreach programs taking place in schools, although it was less well-known. Two-thirds of the two hundred or so activities identified particular groups of young people for reasons of unemployment, economic deprivation, at-risk status, or gender, and thus fall securely within the circle of community music.

Gavin Lombos (1998) went further in mapping the lineage from targeted youth music projects to success in the commercial music industry. He found that many community musicians inhabited the increasingly blurred boundaries between community music and the music industry. For example, the project Pulsation, set up by a north London arts development organization, targeted six young bands and ensembles on rundown estates. While this project aimed to improve the band members' quality of life, its work was pure music creation: developing and recording each band's music for promotional CDs that were launched with showcase performances. Lombos explained that the process came "straight out of the old school of community-music workshopping" (p. 13). Lombos then noted, for example, that the rap/reggae/punk band Asian Dub Foundation (ADF) started as a community music project in the late 1990s and remains commercially successful. Lombos tied the band's success to community music's ethos of equal opportunities. As ADF's guitarist Chandrasonic said, "if you give opportunities to people who don't have a chance, you'll not only get an increase in self-esteem, but new music: new sounds, new combinations, that will guarantee music's longevity" (quoted in Lombos, 1998, p. 12–13). While Lombos welcomed this extension of community music's orbit, he cautioned practitioners to take care in preserving "the traditional workshop ethos—whose benefits are as apparent in rock and pop projects as in other genres and types of work" (pp. 12–13)

In 1999 the new funding and development agency National Foundation for Youth Music began operations with a budget of £10 million a year generated from National Lottery money. It established four criteria for funding awards:

- *Access:* to help more young people develop through music making, especially those who had only limited access to music making before
- *Breadth:* to encourage the widest range of musical styles and cultural traditions
- *Coverage:* to improve provision for those isolated by geography, lack of facilities, or other circumstances
- *Quality:* to encourage young music makers to transform musical ideas into creating music that is inventive and vibrant (Davies, 1999)

Sound Sense's definition of community music met these criteria, and this type of youth music work fit naturally into the community musician's portfolio.

The community music approach has taken hold within school systems as well. "Music services" in England cover countywide areas and provide instrumental and vocal tuition to school pupils and develop young people's ensembles. Around the turn of the twentieth century, commentators denounced these services as too limited in scope in terms of both the number of students reached (typically only 8 percent of students) and the material covered (largely from Western classical canon). One answer to these criticisms was Rhythmix, a consortium of four music services offered in southeast England. This coalition was formed to reach young people who rejected the activities offered by the existing services, particularly those who were disaffected and disadvantaged because of social deprivation or learning difficulties. Rhythmix offered new areas of work (such as rock and pop, world and ethnic music) in new locations (such as youth and community centers), in and out of school hours. According to Holford (2003), "the facilitators were to be skilled musicians who would use an informal workshop approach to engage young people and act as role models, and the project would promote the development of partnerships between community music providers and the formal music education sector, encouraging the exchange of viewpoints and skills" (p. 11). In two years, the project increased the number of young people taking part in activities by 67 percent.

Two further developments in schools' music in England have also fused community music and traditional music education. At the primary level, so-called wider opportunities (sometimes called whole class instrumental or vocal tuition) schemes were developed, beginning in 2003, in response to a government pledge that "over time, all pupils in primary schools who wish to will have the opportunity to learn a music instrument" (p. 7). Evaluations quickly found the benefit of including community music approaches in the work (making music in ensembles from the outset, composition and performance, improvisation). When whole classes or large groups were taught, a greater number of pupils wanted to continue and issues of cultural and gender stereotypes were avoided (Deane, 2004a).

At the secondary level, a range of new approaches to classroom music work have been developed though the Musical Futures initiative. Beginning in 2004, this project took a radical approach to addressing the failure of music education in schools to excite young people. The lack of cooperation between formal education and the non-formal youth music activities described above often resulted in "an 'incoherent and confusing set of specialisms' that may not reflect young people's changing tastes, ambitions, and learning styles" (Holford, 2004, p. 11).

A report from Sound Sense (2003), *Towards a Youth Music Makers Network,* envisaged a partnership in which community musicians, youth services, music services, and classroom teachers would all be part of a single support and development network for young people's music making. Musical Futures saw a similar vision, with a synergy of methodologies giving a coherent direction to young people choosing music routes. According to Musical Futures project leader David Price,

> What's really exciting about doing this project at this time is that there's now a desire to informalize music education right across the board. The landmark achievement of the community music movement over the last 15 years is that people get it, and understand its attraction to young people . . . I would like to think that in ten years' times we're not describing participation in that informal/formal continuum; rather, community music practice will be recognized as a good way of working in any context. (Holford, 2004, p. 13)

Although a great deal remains to be done, there has been progress toward the realization of his vision.

The English government-initiated Music Manifesto aims to create a "set of shared priorities for music education . . . which will act as a focus for joint activity" (Department for Education and Skills, 2004). A wide range of music organizations have been involved from the start, including commercial, broadcasting, formal education, community groups, and naturally, Sound Sense. The Music Manifesto's initial report sets out the state of play (Rogers, 2005). It provides not only a thumbnail sketch of the range of non-formal and informal routes to music making, it also cites some three dozen exemplars of community music projects. Nonetheless, the report states

> We have no comprehensive picture of the number and quality of music activities, or of the level and type of participation, within the non-formal sector. Nor do we know, over-

all, how effectively they reach the intended participants and meet their diverse musical, personal and professional needs." (p. 30)

This lack of statistical information was partly remedied by a Youth Music survey in 2006 that showed that about three times as many young people (29 percent compared with about 10 percent) were making music in the informal sectors as compared to those involved in formal education.

A Music Manifesto report a year later (Rogers, 2006), subtitled *Making Every Child's Music Matter: A Consultation For Action*, contained sixty-nine recommendations for improving young people's music education. These included offering a more personalized approach delivered through a wide range of providers, a better and more broadly trained workforce, and more comprehensive local frameworks for music education.

The report argued for better coordination of provision, claiming that the wide range of pathways for young people was patchy, poorly understood, or simply unknown, either by the young people themselves or the adults who were supposed to guide them. Indeed, those pathways could appear to oppose precisely what the young people wanted to learn.

"Until music education providers work more closely together, more focused on what young people want and need—rather than prosecuting the case for what they can individually supply—this situation will not improve" (Jones & Deane in Rogers, 2006, p. 63).

COMMUNITY MUSIC, YOUNG PEOPLE, SOCIAL POLICY

Many of the sixty-nine recommendations of the second Music Manifesto report have now been implemented, but none with such an immediate impact as the ones calling for "group singing opportunities to be offered to every primary school child . . . backed by a national campaign [to] build a sustainable legacy of singing at the heart of all primary schools." These recommendations were swiftly turned into the Sing Up campaign in 2007.

Sing Up aimed to get *all* of England's primary school children singing. Moreover, it paid particular attention to those children whose life circumstances made it less likely that they would or could take part in the campaign. This attention led to the development of the "Beyond the Mainstream" strand of Sing Up's work. Beyond the Mainstream neatly encapsulates UK community music's approaches and so serves as the case study explored in the second half of this chapter.

Every Child Has a Voice: Reflections on the First Phase of the Beyond the Mainstream Strand of Sing Up's National Singing Program for English Children

The Projects

It was a cold, wet, overcast Monday morning in Bradford, a northern English town with widespread social problems. An all-day singing and songwriting workshop would kick-start musical activity and generate ideas and support for the staff at one of Bradford's five primary-age pupil referral units (PRUs). These special schools cater to children who cannot attend mainstream school for a variety of reasons, such as the absence of English language skills or psychological, developmental, or behavioral problems. These children have troubled lives and are likely to be underachievers. Some of them are in state care (labeled "looked after children," or LACs), no longer living at home with their parents. Bradford has five PRUs for primary-age kids: four of them are for children who have been excluded from school, and one is for children who have been excluded from the other PRUs.

The last group of the day is the "Willow class," for children excluded from the other classes within the PRU. All the furnishings in the classroom are soft (so they will not cause injury if they are thrown), and there are four adults with three children, all in close proximity to each other. The program begins with short, easy, fun, and engaging activities, designed to help the children maintain focus. No written material is used because many of these children have few, if any, literacy skills. If a teacher misjudges the complexity of the task, a student may lose his or her temper and have to be removed from the room. The project leader sang and played on the guitar the Toots and the Maytals' classic "Monkey Man." After a little help, the students joined in, singing along, learning to work in harmony, adding new verses, and even learning how to do a signed version of the song. Other songs, like "Jamawaile," a Wolof welcoming song from the Gambia, were added, and the children improvised voice percussion. These children, often violent and unable to function in traditional settings, had a chance to be children playing together, and for a day the school had been transformed. In the feedback session, the staff remarked on how well behaved almost all the children were and indicated their excitement about setting up a permanent music program. This was a fairly typical day in the Sing Up: Beyond the Mainstream program.

Another fairly typical day was set in a special school in the west of England. Nick, a singing leader, worked one-on-one with an eleven-year-old student with profound multiple disabilities. Helen is wheelchair bound, has limited movement (although she can hold things if motivated to), no speech, and major cognitive difficulties. It is difficult to know if Helen does things because she wants to or if her gestures and sound making are random. Nick had been meeting with her once a week for two or three weeks.

On this day, Nick wrapped a radio microphone inside a soft doll (so it would not be cold, metallic, and unattractive to hold) and gave it to Helen. She made a stream of seemingly random vocal sounds. In order to help Helen become aware that she was the sound-maker, Nick also set up a mirror in front of her face to allow her to see her own mouth move when she vocalized and connected the microphone to an amplifier in order to boost the volume of Helen's vocalizing. Finally, he added a digital delay sound effect so Helen heard any sound she made at least twice, if not several times over. The sounds in the room were clearly Helen's voice, but not in any way she had heard them before.

As the session continued, it became clear that Helen was fascinated with the sounds she heard. Her support worker told Nick that, from the look on her face, Helen loved what she was doing. She began to pause in her vocalizing to listen back to the sounds she made and then began experimenting with new sounds. Helen seemed to realize that she was the one creating the sounds and had the power to change them. In her own way, she had just become a composer.

The third fairly typical day occurred in the northwest of England with singing leader Tim and a group of "looked after children" (i.e., children in state care). Tim set the session up carefully, making sure there was a lot of space available for the children to sit out and do other things if they did not want to sing or make music. There were healthy snacks and crayons and doodling paper available and a big table to sit around. Tim and the children recorded a CD track about different places they had been. There was no sense of coercion, just encouragement, and the session rolled along smoothly. One young boy, about nine or ten years old, seemed unfocused and stayed on the edge of the group. Tim was patient and supportive, the boy became involved, and the track was successfully recorded. Afterward, Tim said that he was delighted that the boy got involved, as he had been bullied at school all week.

The Background

Sing Up, the UK's national singing program for primary-age children, was launched in 2007 and resulted from the UK Music Manifesto and a massive collaboration between the Department for Children, Schools, and Families and the Department for Culture, Media, and Sport, in partnership with a number of organizations and individuals involved in British music and music education. Youth Music, the UK's largest children's music charity, working in a consortium with three other partners—Abbot Meade Vickers, Faber Publishing, and the Sage Gateshead—leads Sing Up.

English education is inclusive, allowing every child to find his or her own form of excellence. Sing Up's Beyond the Mainstream initiative developed from the realization that many children were not regularly attending mainstream school and were falling through the cracks in terms of cultural provision, and that some children in mainstream school, because of their life or birth circumstances, were not likely to get the full benefits of the mainstream Sing Up singing program.

Sing Up promotes the idea that every child deserves the chance to sing every day and believes that singing improves learning, confidence, health, and social development and has the power to change lives and build stronger communities. It focuses on a number of different activities, including publications, an advocacy campaign, workforce development, direct delivery (programs for children), as well as a comprehensive web resource, which includes a song bank for children and teachers. Its approach has been flexible and creative, which meshes well with a school climate that values children's creativity and self-expression. Since its inception in 2007, Sing Up has been successful in working with over 90 percent of mainstream UK schools.

The Research Phase

Sing Up began the Beyond the Mainstream initiative and commissioned Rob Hunter and Phil Mullen to survey singing in Beyond the Mainstream situations with marginalized children under thirteen. They contacted seventy organizations and individuals involved in or connected to this field. Their survey found that:

- 4.1 out of 4.6 million primary-age children in England are in mainstream schooling.
- Fewer than 500,000 children are not attending mainstream schooling.
- Approximately 50,000 primary-age children attend special schools.
- Approximately 60,000 children are "in care" in England at any one time.
- Approximately 12,000 out of an estimated 70,000 to 80,000 Travellers[2] are not registered at any school.
- About 100,000 children and young people per year require education outside school because of illness or injury.

Additional research considered provisions for children who were homeschooled, caretakers themselves, children of servicemen and women serving in Iraq or Afghanistan, children of prisoners, and others who were in some way marginalized or vulnerable. It was found that Traveller children, children within the criminal justice system, looked after children, and children with chronic illness were all particularly prone to being moved on before satisfactorily concluding a music project.

Working with children Beyond the Mainstream requires different approaches from working with students in mainstream classrooms. Because many of these children have low educational achievement or complex problems and life issues, facilitators need to be cognizant of their personal, social, health, and emotional (PSHE) needs and development. Sing Up regards a child's well-being and holistic development as having equal value to his or her musical development. Since the program's inception two years ago, there have been indications of an emerging methodology of good practice, where singing leaders have developed ways to engage students in fun yet educational singing and vocalizing, adapting their approaches to the children's life challenges.

All music organizations and leaders involved with the program have emphasized the importance of the relationship with the music leader. Music leaders must understand both participatory leadership and a range of relatively instant engagement methodologies and have a commitment to a non-authoritarian approach. To gain this, they might begin a project with one or two sessions of reconnaissance to make contacts and build relationships with young people and other staff, learn the participants' names, identify young people's interests (which might inform the starting point), understand the culture of the project, and discuss the best way to begin with the staff and the young people. Leaders stress the importance of the centeredness and self-management of the worker. Managing challenging behavior is an integral part of the program, and a worker needs to be clear about boundaries. This strongly emotional work requires a corresponding emotional literacy.

Several problems prevent an ideal implementation of the program for the four-through twelve-year-olds. Research concludes that there are few adult-led singing activities with primary-age children in Beyond the Mainstream (with the noteworthy exception of those in special schools) at the time of writing. Organizations working with young people through Beyond the Mainstream are generally not closely linked to each other, and the work has tended to be fragmented. Funding for this work is problematic. There is more notable public and hence government acceptance of the importance of Early Years Music and provision for the thirteen- through nineteen-year-olds. While there is sympathy for the four- through twelve-year-olds, there are fewer psychological, sociological, or economic policy drivers channeling resources to this population.

In addition, some practitioners feel strongly that using the term *singing* alienates some young people and gives a limited impression of what might be offered. Rap and beatboxing have been strong parts of the Beyond the Mainstream program. For some boys in this age group, being seen and being heard, particularly in front of their friends, creates self-consciousness. Singing may be seen as uncool, and these young men often have few positive models of it. Even adults helping with the program often have some resistance to singing themselves.

It is also important to recognize the challenge in balancing the need for musical excellence with the need to engage as many young people as possible through the adults who already work with them in Beyond the Mainstream settings. Sing Up's approach, subsequent to 2008, was to teach motivated adults who worked with or had access to working with these children (care workers and teaching assistants, as well as trained singing leaders) a combination of singing, musical, and creative skills and give input on context, effective group work, and leadership.

Sing Up received several recommendations from an internal report's conclusions. These included:

- Set up a series of direct-delivery projects and include an element of inquiry within these projects.
- Develop the workforce to lead singing, rap, and beatbox performances.
- Focus on the systematic use of inclusive language.
- Highlight Beyond the Mainstream work in publications and on the web.
- Increase accessibility to Sing Up resources and develop new accessible resources where appropriate.
- Develop resources and structures to support the work and the evaluation.

The Implementation

From late 2008, Sing Up established singing programs in fourteen different Beyond the Mainstream settings around the country. These included work with children who have:

- Emotional and behavioral difficulties.
- Mental-health problems.
- Various forms of disability.
- Refugee status.
- State-care status.
- Traumatic experiences.
- A sick relative to care for.

Many different music education and community music organizations throughout the country delivered these projects. The organizations defined their own goals, and these encompassed:

- Ensuring young-people-centered singing and promoting participant leadership.
- Guaranteeing that, if songwriting becomes part of the singing process, young people naturally deal with their personal issues as subject matter.
- Using vocal looping technology to enhance singing and vocal practice in special education needs (SEN) settings.
- Developing a flexible repertoire and methodology which uses a wide range of verbal/non-verbal singing activities to attract and keep the children's attention.
- Determining the reception of different styles of music, such as rap or MCing, in the singing arena.

From January to September 2009, these projects successfully engaged 825 children in regular singing activities and trained 171 staff and novice singing leaders. Most of the work took place outside school in locations such as hospitals or community centers. By the end of nine months, all of the projects indicated that the children had made improvements in confidence and self-esteem, enjoyment and motivation, pride and achievement, and social interaction. A number of projects reported children "opening up" through songwriting, addressing difficult, often personal, topics. The children initiated exploration of issues. Some who found it difficult to socialize and make friends discovered it was easier to get along with their peers in the singing group than with other children their age. Thirteen out of the fourteen projects reported that the children improved focus and concentration. Many participants had become less disruptive, and this transferred to their school lives. They showed pride and motivation for the first time. And finally, they became more skillful singers. Part of Sing Up's success stems from the teachers and staff. Committed to reflective practice and evaluation, they shared their work and findings with others within the field. Part also comes from collaboration with other program strands and its central position within the Beyond the Mainstream program.

In addition to the fourteen programs, substantial workforce development has taken place with a range of Beyond the Mainstream professionals through a strand of Sing Up called Vocal Force. These professionals include special schoolteachers and clinicians working in mental-health environments, as well as those working with children with autism spectrum disorders, with behavioral issues, or living within the Traveller community. Vocal Force has offered both off-the-job training and on-the-job support and mentoring. In many cases, the most important support that was needed for workers to conquer their inhibitions about singing and leading singing was the encouragement to go ahead.

Sing Up has developed and disseminated a variety of resources. These include The Pyramid pack (a song and activity book for working with the more vulnerable children in mainstream schools), software and training for developing voice-work for children with profound and multiple disabilities (developed in partnership with the Drake music project), and a songbook for children experiencing mental-health problems. Online resources include a number of songs and activities uploaded on the organization's website that deal with children's personal, social, emotional, and health issues and a number of songs (developed in partnership with Music for the Deaf) that can be read in a Braille version as well as non-Braille and videos of songs being signed. In addition, Sing Up has established a dedicated manager, administrative support, and a national advisory panel for the Beyond the Mainstream initiative.

Current and Future Developments

In early 2010, Sing Up moved into a second phase of the Beyond the Mainstream program. This phase, in partnership with the National Children's Bureau and evaluated by Pat Petrie from the Institute of Education, focused on looked after children in a range of projects across the country. This concentration of focus allows partnerships to grow between music organizations and local Children's Services in a way that optimizes the potential for long-term sustainability by concentrating resources on working with a particularly hard-to-reach and low-achieving group of children.

Conclusion

Sing Up officially concludes its programs at the end of March 2011. This program's outcomes will be valued enough for its work to be continued in the future. With the conclusion of the program, a number of outcomes have been identified about children, leaders, and organizational partnerships.

Learnings about children include:

- All children can participate fully in voice/singing programs if the programs are properly designed and managed.
- Children find singing a pleasurable activity that makes them feel good about themselves both individually and collectively.
- Singing helps children become motivated and take pride in their work.
- With the aid of such programs, children become more skilled at singing and, by extension, at group performance and creative activities.
- Children develop positive relationships with adults and co-participants, learning to trust themselves and others.
- Singing and especially songwriting can help children address problems and challenges in their own lives.
- Singing can still be a strong form of communication for those children without speech.

Learnings about leaders include:

- Non-specialists can lead singing sessions well.
- Sessions require patience, enthusiasm, hard work, and support.
- The best singing leaders do not always have to be the best singers.

Learnings about organizations include:

- Singing can uplift institutions.
- Organizations working collaboratively can effectively embed singing.

- For partnerships to really work, there must be buy-in at every level—from management through to workers.
- Large, mainstream organizations can fully embrace the vision, thinking, language, culture, and activities central to working Beyond the Mainstream.

To conclude, community music in the United Kingdom is subject to lively negotiations as stakeholders seek to reach all citizens through meaningful music making. Although the United Kingdom encompasses a comparatively small geographic area, the terrain is rich and complex as both the broader historical perspective beginning this chapter and the in-depth case study of Sing Up demonstrate.

NOTES

1. The definition itself has seldom been contested in *Sounding Board*—except by the organization itself. In 2004, Sound Sense staffer Chinyelu-Hope wrote that the description was "helpful" for Asian, Black, and Chinese community music practitioners, but the language of equal opportunities was a bit old-fashioned, and the examples of "community" did not even mention ethnicities or faith.

2. In Ireland, the term "Traveller" refers to an ethnic Irish group who have maintained nomadic or seminomadic ways of life, as well as distinct language and customs. Similar groups may be called "gypsies" in other countries. Although significantly less economically advantaged than other Irish groups, Irish Travellers are keepers of rich musical traditions.

BIBLIOGRAPHY

Abbot Meade Vickers. Retrieved from www.singup.org/about-us/consortium-partners/amv-bbdo

Ashman, G. (2000). West Gallery Music. Retrieved from www.wgma.org.uk/Articles/intro.htm

Chinyelu-Hope, K. (2004). *Facing up: Overcoming barriers to employment for Asian, Black and Chinese community musicians.* Bury St. Edmunds: Sound Sense.

Craigmillar Festival Society. Retrieved from www.absoluteastronomy.com/topics/Craigmillar_Festival_ Society

Crummy, H. (1992). *Let the people sing! A story of Craigmillar.* Edinburgh: Craigmillar Communiversity Press.

Davies, J. (1999). Leading notes. *Sounding Board,* Summer, pp. 14–15.

Deane, K. (1998). Talent revealed. *Sounding Board,* Autumn, pp. 10–11.

Deane, K. (2004a). Wider opportunities? *Sounding Board,* Spring, pp. 10–12.

Deane, K. (2004b). *The music manifesto.* Retrieved from http://publications.teachernet.gov.uk/default.aspx?PageFunction=productdetails&PageMode=publications&ProductId=DfESD21–0604–72&

Department for Education and Skills. (2004). The Music Manifesto. Retrieved from www.education.gov.uk/publications/standard/publicationDetail/Page1/DfESD21-0604-72

Everitt, A. (1997). *Joining in: An investigation into participatory music.* London: Calouste Gulbenkian Foundation.

Higgins, L. (2008a). Growth, pathways and groundwork: Community music in the United Kingdom. *International Journal of Community Music. 1* (1), pp. 23–37.

Higgins, L. (2008b). *Safety without safety: Participation, the workshop, and the welcome.* Retrieved from http://cma2008.wikispaces.com/Paper+2+-+Higgins+-+Safety+without+Safety+ -+Participation,+the+workshop,+and+the+welcome

Holford, A. (2000). Music for a changing world: Community music and social inclusion. *Sounding Board,* Spring, pp. 16–18.

Holford, A. (2003). Common purpose. *Sounding Board,* Spring, pp. 10–11.

Holford, A. (2004). Musical futures. *Sounding Board,* Summer, pp. 11–13.

Hunter, J. (2009) *Beyond the mainstream: Report on funded programs 2009.*

Hunter, R., & Mullen, P. (2008). *Sing up beyond the mainstream: Sing up internal report.*

Ings, R., Jones, R., & Randell, N. (1999). *Mapping hidden talent: Investigating youth music projects.* Leicester: Youth Work Press.

Joss, T. (1993). A short history of community music. In T. Joss & D. Price (Eds.), *The first national directory of community music.* Bury St. Edmunds: Sound Sense.

Kushner, S., Walker, B., & Tarr, J. (2001). *Case studies and issues in community music.* Bristol: University of the West of England.

Lombos, G. (1998). Finding the community in youth music projects. *Sounding Board,* Autumn, pp. 12–13.

Macdonald, I. (1995). The Leiston statement. *Sounding Board,* Spring, pp. 29–30.

Matarasso, M. (1997). *Use or ornament: The social impact of participation in the arts.* Stroud: Comedia. Retrieved from http://web.me.com/matarasso/one/research/Entries/2009/2/19_ Use_or_Ornament_files/Use%20r%20rnament.pdf

Moser, P., & McKay, G. (Eds.). (2005). *Community music: A handbook.* Lyme Regis: Russell House Publishing.

Music Manifesto. Retrieved from www.musicmanifesto.co.uk

Music Manifesto Partners. Retrieved from www.singup.org/about-us/consortium-partners/ amv-bbdo

Nettel, R. (1944). *Music in the five towns 1840–1914: A study of the social influence of music in an industrial district.* London: Oxford University Press.

Peggie, A. (1997). *Musicians go to school: Partnership in the classroom.* Bury St. Edmunds: Sound Sense.

Rogers, R. (2005). *Music manifesto report no. 1.* London: Department for Education and Skills. Retrieved from http://publications.teachernet.gov.uk/default.aspx?PageFunction=productdet ails&PageMode=publications&ProductId=1–84478–533–5&

Rogers, R. (2006). *Music manifesto report no. 2.* London: Department for Education and Skills. Retrieved from http://publications.teachernet.gov.uk/default.aspx?PageFunction=productdet ails&PageMode=publications&ProductId=MM-03898–2006&

Sing Up. Retrieved from www.singup.org

Sound it Out. Retrieved from www.sounditout.co.uk

Steptoe, S. (2009). The secret of a long life. *Sounding Board,* 2009 (5), pp. 13–14.

Swingler, T. (1990). A new voice for community musicians. *Sounding Board,* 2.

Towards a youth music makers network. (2003). Bury St. Edmunds: Sound Sense.

Warning! This organization changes lives. (2004). Bury St. Edmunds: Sound Sense.

Youth Music. Retrieved from www.youthmusic.org.uk/news/youth_music_announces_2006_ omnibus_survey_findings.html

Chapter Four

Community Music in the Nordic Countries: Politics, Research, Programs, and Educational Significance

Sidsel Karlsen, Heidi Westerlund,
Heidi Partti, and Einar Solbu

INTRODUCTION

The aim of this chapter is to give an overview of the community music (CM) field and its educational significance in the Nordic countries[1], with a special emphasis on the current situation in Norway, Sweden, and Finland. While the Nordic countries appear to share a collective vision of musical access for all, this vision varies. It is our aim to examine similarities as well as differences in order to give a picture of Nordic community music actors, institutions, and researchers.

A central concern that runs throughout the chapter is the epistemological aspects of Nordic community music: participants' experiences of learning in CM, modes of construction and transmission of knowledge in CM, and the access to knowledge and knowing that exist within CM. In the first section, community music is defined and described from a Nordic perspective. The second and third sections give an overview of research conducted on CM activities and the current range of CM programs. In the fourth section, three case studies examine a higher education institution for the transmission of Norwegian vernacular music and dance, experiences of learning among festival audiences in a Swedish context, and the intertwined processes of identity construction and learning in a Finnish online music community. The fifth section discusses epistemological issues concerning CM settings and their relevance for music education. Finally, lines are drawn between the Nordic CM field and its empowering cultural role in Nordic societies.

PART 1: DEFINITION AND THE IDEOLOGICAL AND POLITICAL CLIMATE FOR COMMUNITY MUSIC ACTIVITIES

Wherever there is conjoint activity whose consequences are appreciated as good by all singular persons who take part in it, and where the realization of the good is such as to effect an energetic desire and effort to sustain it in being just because it is a good shared by all, there is in so far a community. (Dewey LW 2, p. 328)

Defining a Slippery Concept—A "Nordic" Attempt

While Bartleet, Dunbar-Hall, Letts, and Schippers (2009) recognize community music as a complex and slippery concept, Elliott, Higgins, and Veblen (2008), in their editorial in the first edition of the *International Journal of Community Music,* see community music as "a complex, multidimensional, and continuously evolving human endeavour" (p. 3). Recent attempts have been made at defining CM in order to explore what the term may mean from a Nordic cultural context.

Veblen and Olsson (2002) emphasize that all definitions of CM "concur that community music concerns people making music" (p. 730). The characteristics of community music activities include the multiple learner/teacher relationships often found in a variety of settings, a commitment to "lifelong musical learning and access for all members of the community," the importance of the participants' social and personal growth alongside their musical growth, and an awareness of the need to include "disadvantaged individuals or groups" in the activities (p. 731). These characteristics emphasize everyone's right to make music, the empowerment—on both individual and communal levels—that may come through engaging in community music activities, and the personal and communal expressions of "artistic, social, political, and cultural concerns" that such activities provide (p. 731). With CM programs nurturing participants' individual and collective identity and students taking more responsibility for their own learning and direction when they participate in community music activities, CM activities complement, interface with, and extend formal music education structures (Veblen, 2008).

While the term "community music" is not commonly used in the Nordic countries, the field exists in full. A Nordic definition of the term emphasizes that community music activities encompass a wide range of musics and music-related activities[2] and imply a focus on lifelong learning and an open-access attitude. Students elect to participate, and the act of participation is equally as important as the musical outcome. Community music activities and programs promote growth and enhanced confidence (e.g., Veblen & Olsson, 2002) by nurturing participants' identities and strengthening their agentic skills. By this standard, outreach programs, through which regional or national institutions contribute to such empowerment, may be considered as community music. Finally, community music activities, in a Nordic context, exist in and contribute to the extensive interplay between informal or formal learning situations or practices (Folkestad, 2006).

Mapping the Ideological and Political Ground

In mapping the specificities of the "Nordic cultural model," Duelund (2003, pp. 486–487) points out that while many similarities exist in today's policies, the Nordic countries' backgrounds for forming their policies have been quite diverse. The forerunners of the present national cultural policies in the Nordic countries were created after World War II, and while Denmark and Sweden had been independent states for hundreds of years, "with rich feudal and aristocratic traditions" (p. 481), Norway, Finland, and Iceland were new nation-states, created in the twentieth century, which had to invent national standards and cultural institutions without the touchstones of history and heritage upon which the older states could rely. Today, the similarities are more evident than the differences in the ideological and political climate for supporting culture and the arts, and thereby community music activities, among these countries. According to Duelund, the main objectives of the cultural policies formulated in the Nordic countries can be summarized by particular cultural goals (pp. 489–490):

- *The enlightenment perspective,* in which the consumption and creation of culture is seen as connected to education, training, and the individual's personal growth on his or her own terms
- *The element of liberty,* in which cultural institutions' autonomous status in relation to economic or political pressure or attempts at public or private regulation is emphasized
- *The egalitarian element,* which concerns "equal opportunities for access to cultural arrangements for the population" (p. 490)
- *The social welfare aim,* in which culture is seen as an integrated part of general social policies
- *The national aim,* in which nations' cultural heritage is protected

Even though claims can be made that a more "economic and business-oriented view of culture within culture policy" (p. 493) has developed in recent years, these five elements still play an important role in shaping the ideological and political climates in which Nordic cultural activities reside.

Although elitist traditions certainly exist in the field of music, a wide range of efforts have been made in the Nordic countries to make music and other arts accessible to all. The Danish Ministry of Culture's web page states: "Music has an important function as a carrier of cultural values and norms in all societies. The Ministry provides funding for the music field in order to secure its diversity and equal access to musical experiences for all" (Danish Ministry of Culture). Similar statements can be found on the web pages of most of the Ministries of Culture (or those that deal with cultural affairs) in the other Nordic countries (e.g., Swedish Ministry of Culture, Norwegian Ministry of Culture, Finnish Ministry of Education). These statements are not just political slogans but reflect that political, and thereby economic, priorities are set in order to facilitate a rich musical life for the countries' inhabitants.

Furthermore, community music activities are ascribed educational value and are financially supported at national, regional, and local levels. For example, the comprehensive systems of municipal music and art schools that exist in every Nordic country (for a broader explanation, see below) receive their funding from the state as well as from regional and local authorities. Amateur choirs and wind bands for adults, for example, traditionally receive some of their funding through state-generated adult-education money, and numerous institutions exist (the national Arts Councils, for example) through which one may apply for project grants for conducting different kinds of community music activities. Typically, there are specific funding opportunities for projects that address the needs of children and adolescents or utilize multicultural perspectives. However, although the conditions for CM activities in the Nordic countries might be considered favorable, most CM facilitators find themselves filling a variety of roles, including those of entrepreneurs and fund-raisers, in order to secure funding for their particular activities (Veblen, 2008).

PART 2: RESEARCH ON COMMUNITY MUSIC SETTINGS

While the field of music education research in the Nordic countries has, until very recently, been focused on formal school settings (Olsson, 2005), this research community leads in exploring processes of teaching and learning within community music-related environments. As theories of intentional and functional education and formal and informal learning situations and practices have preceded, underpinned, and occurred jointly with the development of this area of research (e.g., Benum, 1978; Folkestad, 2006; Ruud, 1983), investigators have directed their inquiries into how CM activities complement, interface with, extend, and sometimes collide with formal music education structures.[3]

One of the first studies to look into experiences of learning in CM settings in the Nordic countries was that of Heiling (2000), which investigated the sense of community and group coherence as well as the musical development that took place within the frames of an amateur brass band. The findings showed, among other things, that too much emphasis on developing musician skills and raising the quality of the band's performance was seen as a potential threat toward the band members' feelings of coherence and community spirit. The participants' social growth was perceived as equally or even more important than their musical growth.

The collective aspect of music making and learning was also strongly evident in Gullberg's (2002) study on rock musicians' learning and socialization. Along with Green (2002), she was one of the first researchers to shed light on the musical enculturation of popular musicians and how such musicians acquire skills and knowledge in informal arenas. While her findings in many ways resemble those of Green, she also shows how the musicians' non-institutional learning may collide with the more formalized requirements of higher music education.

While participating in brass and rock bands are two examples of established ways of making music, contemporary technologies have created new possibilities for collective musicking through Internet-based music communities. Investigating one such community, Salavuo (2006) found that the participants' motives for partaking were mainly connected to their own musical growth. He also discovered that, although the community's members were fairly active as musicians, they had very little formal training (for a more thorough investigation of the learning aspects of this particular community, see Part 4).

New musical styles can also trigger new modes of transmission of music-related knowledge with implications for the building of communality. While studying hip-hop musicians' artistic and educational strategies, Söderman (2007) revealed that these musicians often think of themselves as culture-bearers, fosterers, and educators, simultaneously taking the responsibility of giving voice to disadvantaged members of society. The musicians use their reputations to preach to younger music lovers about the importance of preserving their heritage and the significance of contributing to a community.

A number of recent studies investigate the development of music-related knowledge within CM settings; for example, Karlsen's study of learning among music festival audiences (2007); Knutsen's investigation of the use of music and dance in a Chilean immigrant community (2006); and Balsnes' study of the local choir as a medium for socialization (2009). Research has been carried out in municipal music and art schools in order to uncover instrumental music teacher typologies (Tivenius, 2008) and the motivations for immigrant parents to enroll their children into such schools (Hofvander-Trulsson, 2009). Studies, like Stige's (2003) investigation into the notion of community music therapy or Molin's (2009) examination of the use of music among adolescents with Asperger's syndrome, with relevance for community music have also appeared within the field of music therapy.

PART 3: COMMUNITY MUSIC PROGRAMS

Perhaps the most ubiquitous community music program within the Nordic countries is the comprehensive system of municipal music and art schools, through which children and adolescents can receive instrumental tuition and other kinds of music and art-related instruction from professionally educated teachers for a reasonable cost. While access to municipal music schools in Finland is regulated by entrance exams, the general approach within the rest of the Nordic countries is access for all,[4] at least within the limits of each school's financial ability. However, regardless of this official ideology, research shows that children from middle-class homes may experience greater access to such schools than, for example, children from working-class or immigrant families (e.g., Brändström & Wiklund, 1995; Hofvander-Trulsson, 2009; Väkevä & Westerlund, 2007). Municipal music and art schools are fully integrated with their communities, and the education that children and adolescents receive through this system helps to lay the groundwork for a flourishing musical life both for amateur as well as professional musicians.

While municipal music and art schools generally serve children during their school years, smaller targeted CM programs exist to serve other groups. In every Nordic country, parents bring their preschool children to intergenerational musical activities. These groups are usually led by professional music pedagogues with an emphasis on strengthening the musical bonds between parents and children by engaging in traditional children's songs and singing games (music from the Beginning of Life). At the other end of the spectrum, a project has been conducted since 1991 within Norwegian prisons to prepare prisoners to cope with freedom after they have served their sentences. The participants join music groups, both before and after their release from prison, and this continuity is intended to ease reintegration into society (Gotaas, 2006) and reduce recidivism (Norwegian Correctional Services, Oslo prison).

Throughout the Nordic countries, there is a long-standing tradition of choral singing, with a multitude of choirs that range from amateur community or church choirs to semi-professional or professional ensembles. A rather new phenomenon has arisen for people who claim to be non-musical or who have been labeled (or have labeled themselves) as non-singers—the so-called we-who-cannot-sing choirs. The underlying belief connected to these choirs is that everyone can learn to sing—"for some people it just takes more time" (Choir for All).

While the choral tradition may be thought of as essentially pan-Nordic, the tradition of amateur wind bands, especially bands for children and adolescents, is especially strong in Norway. This tradition is an outgrowth of the Norwegian custom of arranging national day children's parades, in which children march in school or class groups led by their wind band–playing classmates or peers. For decades, these bands have constituted an important CM arena, especially for working-class children who otherwise had limited access to any kind of music education.

Folk music groups are also an important part of the Nordic community music field, preserving and renewing musical cultural heritage. The transmission of time-honored tunes played on traditional instruments is still an important focus of regional and local groups. In recent years, these strains have undergone a transformation as instruments have become electrified and the melodies have been incorporated into non-traditional genres.

Nordic churches constitute an important setting for CM activities for all ages. Church-based choirs and ensembles offer a panoply of sacred music, which ranges from traditional church music and brass bands to urban contemporary gospel to, increasingly, modern pop/rock worship music.

While programs offering music therapy services can be found in every Nordic country (e.g., the Danish Association of Music Therapists, the Association for Music Therapy in Sweden, the Norwegian Music Therapy Association), programs also exist to empower underprivileged communities in various parts of the world by celebrating the musics of non-Nordic cultures. Since 2003, for example, a CM project has been based in a Palestinian refugee camp in Lebanon as collaboration between the Norwegian Academy of Music and two humanitarian organizations. This project seeks to empower the children and adolescents of the refugee camp, giving them "opportunities for alternative ways of perceiving of [their] own life" (Storsve, Westby, & Ruud, 2009) through music.

PART 4: THREE IN-DEPTH CASES—
NORWAY, SWEDEN, AND FINLAND

Norway: Folk Music in Norwegian Communities—
the Ole Bull Academy Effect

This study reflects on the consequences of an encounter between vernacular music, folk music, and institutional academic training. It is based on thematic interviews of five people with in-depth insight into the field of Norwegian folk music and its role in the society.

Paraphrasing a definition offered by the members of the International Folk Music Council in the 1950s (Aksdal & Nyhus, 1993), folk music is the product of a musical tradition that has developed through oral transmission processes. In the nineteenth century, during the so-called national romantic era, Norwegian music scholars, composers, and musicians—including Ole Bull and Edvard Grieg—took an interest in local oral traditions and utilized them in their compositions and performances.

Over the course of the past one hundred and fifty years, interest in local music traditions has been influenced by political occasions, such as the dissolution of the union between Norway and Sweden in 1905, World War II, and the struggle prior to the referendum on joining the European Economic Community in 1972. Furthermore, interest has been affected by the competition between rural and urban cultures and by cultural trends reinforced by the mass media.

In the 1970s, interest in national cultural expressions was high. In 1973, the first national, state-funded conservatoire, based on Western classical music traditions, was established in Oslo. This spurred into action one of the most prominent bearers of oral music tradition in Norway, the renowned player of the Hardanger fiddle, Sigbjørn Bernhoft Osa. He initiated the establishment of the Ole Bull Academy (OBA) in Voss, a small town on the west coast of Norway, with the intention of creating a national center for the transmission of folk music traditions (Mæland, 2006). From the very beginning, this academy offered one-week courses in folk music to students with backgrounds in classical singing, violin, or music education who had studied at a major Norwegian conservatory. It was not unusual for students to travel to Voss as skeptics and return to their alma maters as converts to the transmission of folk music after a week of working with some of the standard-bearers of Norwegian vernacular music.

The OBA has grown to become a resource center for folk music and now offers courses of various lengths, a bachelor's degree in folk music, and an annual folk music festival (Ole Bull Academy). It has become the hub for performers, researchers, and educators of Norwegian folk music, and, through its rather short history, has served approximately six thousand students.

The status of folk music in Norway ten years into the twenty-first century is far different from half a century before:

- Folk music is an important part of the curriculum at the local level of music instruction in many parts of the country, with approximately half of the municipal music and art schools offering training in this style (Aksdal, 2008).
- Applied folk music can be studied at the Norwegian Academy of Music at the bachelor's, master's, and doctoral levels.
- A continually growing number of highly skilled folk musicians perform locally as well as nationally, often in projects that explore hybrid genres in which folk music is one of several components.
- Folk music festivals draw large audiences.

Today, folk music is being performed again and listened to by an ever-increasing number of people in Norwegian communities. However, the cultural environment in which folk music exists has changed. In recent years, great changes have occurred in the ways in which Norwegian folk music is transmitted. Traditionally, the learner would sit at the feet of the master and learn by watching, listening, and repeating. The OBA builds on this tradition, as its teaching principle is "from ear to ear, string to string, and throat to throat" (Ole Bull Academy). Whereas traditional transmission occurred within a family or a local community, at the OBA, it occurs in a broader learning environment. Learners typically come from different backgrounds, study with several teachers, and attend seminars, lectures, performances, and workshops (arenas in which students and teachers meet, share with, and influence each other). Students also have opportunities to interact with various folk musics and musicians. Consequently, today's performers do not only carry forward their masters' traditions but also have at their disposal a wide reservoir of knowledge and traditions.

While most folk musicians traditionally would have seen fiddling or singing as a hobby or second profession, today's well-educated performers expect to make a living as musicians. They create their own professional platforms, which may include playing classical music, jazz, or rock; working with musicians from non-Western musical traditions; or teaching. Folk music no longer exists in isolation from other musical forms.

Traditionally, folk music has been the music of the people within a discrete cultural community. This music would be present at celebrations and parties to lead the dancing, at funerals to ease the mourning, and in homes, along with storytelling, to be enjoyed during the dark winter nights. Folk music is still utilized for these traditional purposes in parts of Norway; however, it has increasingly become stage or concert music. Professional fiddlers and singers, individuals or bands, attract large audiences to local culture houses, churches, and other arenas suited for concert performances.

Undoubtedly, by developing, over the years, into an established formal learning environment, the Ole Bull Academy has had a significant and sustaining impact on the musical scene of local communities in Norway. Norwegian folk music now plays an important thread in the fabric of musical activities, and while folk music lovers feared for its future half a century ago, it now thrives alongside many other musical styles and genres. The initiative taken by the founders of the OBA in the 1970s, and the work of the large number of excellent musicians and scholars who have taught at the Academy over the years, represent a turning point that has led to a revitalization[5] of folk music in Norway.

Sweden: The Music Festival as an Arena for Learning

While Veblen and Olsson (2002) lift "parades; fêtes; [and] festivals" (p. 730) to the fore as possible scenarios for community music activities, and Small (1998) also acknowledges the musicking that takes place during such events, both among audiences and performers, as legitimate ways of participating in musical activities, only a few investigations have been made into such arenas which in any way have concentrated on the participants' learning outcome (e.g., Pitts, 2005; Snell, 2005). However, in a recent Swedish study (Karlsen, 2007; Karlsen & Brändström, 2008) one particular music festival, the *Festspel i Pite Älvdal* (Festival in the Pite River Valley), was explored as an arena for learning. By looking into how the festival affected the audience's development of musical identity as well as the festival's host municipalities' local identity, connections between music-related identity and learning processes were explored and a deep and rich learning outcome revealed.

The *Festspel i Pite Älvdal* is an annual music festival held in Piteå (a small coastal town in the northernmost county of Sweden, North Bothnia) featuring a variety of musical styles from classical to folk, pop, and rock. The aim of the study was to explore the *Festspel i Pite Älvdal* as a source of informal learning by investigating its contribution to the formation of identity on both individual and collective levels. Sociological theories of modernity (Giddens, 1991) provided a ground for understanding identity formation in contemporary society, and theories of situated learning (Lave & Wenger, 1991; Wenger, 1998) were utilized to elucidate how processes of identity formation and learning are mutually dependent and deeply intertwined. Furthermore, within the latter framework, according to Lave and Wenger (1991), learning does not occur simply as an acquisition of knowledge but rather through legitimate peripheral participation in communities of practices, such as a music festival.

The exploration of the festival was designed as a case study with empirical data gathered through a survey conducted among the festival audience, audience interviews, interviews with official representatives from the festival's host municipalities, and participant observation of the festival's concerts. Documentation, such as program leaflets and newspaper clippings, was also utilized as data. The festival-related learning experiences reported by the survey participants and the interviewees revealed a deep and rich learning outcome, which was categorized as learning music, learning about music, and learning via music (Karlsen, 2009b).

In the category of learning music, outcomes, such as learning to be familiar with and enjoying new musical styles and learning listening skills and distinguishing between different instruments, were documented. One of the interviewees, for example, divulged that he had developed listening skills which enabled him to compare the festival performance with previously experienced live performances of the same piece of music and build what he called a live music experience library.

Reporting experiences of learning about music, the festival attendees emphasized acquiring knowledge about the history behind the music and facts about the music, such as the names of composers and pieces of music. One interviewee, Betty, counted such factual knowledge as crucially important for her continued listening to and love for the music. Learning names of pieces and composers allowed her revisit her concert experiences and widen her listening habits through recordings. For her, extending her knowledge was not just about learning music history; it was a way of getting behind the music that deeply affected the way she listened to and understood it.

The festival attendees also experienced a wide variety of outcomes that could be characterized as learning via music. Participants categorized this new knowledge, gained through their festival participation, as "general education," learning rules of behavior, widening their cultural horizons, and even learning to trust their own musical judgment. Another interviewee, Laura, brought her two young sons to one of the festival's children's concerts so they could develop a broader cultural understanding than what was offered through the TV-mediated *Swedish Idol* or the local ice hockey team.[6]

The study's epistemological foundation helped reveal how, and through what means, the festival audiences learned. By participating in the festival community of practice, the attendees learned through relating to identities, activities, and artifacts of the community, through identity work, and through the modeling of more experienced community members for newcomers or those more peripheral to the practice (for more elaborate explanations, see Karlsen, 2007; Karlsen, 2009b; Karlsen, forthcoming). In contrast to the study's epistemological framework, audiences reported learning through situations that resembled traditional teaching when, for example, music-related facts were mediated by a presenter prior to a concert.

The festival study also revealed broader social and communal aspects of music-related and community-based learning. Considering which attendees had access to the learning experiences provided by the festival community and whether or not there might exist an educational intention behind the festival, the findings of the study indicated that a community celebration, such as a music festival, might be understood as a community of practice which articulates the values of particular social groups and which might be used by those same groups to educate their members. Consequently, access to what was learnable within the festival context was, in many ways, reserved for those among the attendees who belonged to the social group in which the festival had its origin. Hence, the study of the *Festspel i Pite Älvdal* illuminated power dynamics and issues of access and social justice that might be found within open and informal CM settings.[7]

Finland: Making and Sharing Music as a Means of Identity Work in an Online Music Community

Modern technology has dramatically increased the possibilities for music-related activities, learning, and information sharing. For example, it has become increasingly common to join one or more online music communities. The breadth of the phenomenon is revealed in the fact that in a sparsely populated country such as Finland, thousands of people are actively creating, sharing, and discussing their own music in online music communities. The largest Finnish music portal, Mikseri (www.mikseri .net), is an open online community, specializing in music made by its members, with about 140,000 registered users. There are over eighty thousand copyright-free pieces of music available in this portal for anyone to download. In order to upload one's own music onto the site or comment on the music made by others, one has to be a registered member of the community. Registration is free, and once a member, one can create an artist profile and communicate with other members (usually identifying themselves by pseudonyms) in various ways.

Recent ethnographic studies of Mikseri (Partti, 2009; Partti & Westerlund, 2008) examined the appearance of the growth of expertise and the construction of music-related identity in this web-based community by studying the negotiations, with regard to defining the meanings of musicianship, that take place within this community. The study attempted to provide an in-depth description of the cultural system of Mikseri using a virtual ethnographic approach (Hine, 2000). The data consisted of field notes from an observation period of seven months as well as 1,329 selected messages from the message board of the online community. An exploration of the construction of both expertise and music-related identity in this amateur community was grounded on theories of sociocultural learning (Lave & Wenger, 1991; Wenger, 1998). As in Karlsen's (2007) study, the processes of music making, learning, and identity construction were seen as interrelated and mutually dependent.

An online music community offers an open forum for publishing, listening, and rating its members' own music. In practice, this means that the members of the community are creating the contents of their culture by themselves. This gives them a strong feeling of ownership and commitment to the community. The importance of the community and of making one's own music were shown to be the most important aspects of the culture of Mikseri, and the study shed light on the processes of learning and identity construction in an Internet-based reality.

The Finnish Mikseri is not necessarily the only music-related community of practice for its members; according to the data, the members may also belong to bands or various music groups and other online music communities. Nevertheless, Mikseri responds to the need of musicians to come together with their peers to share experiences, knowledge, and skills. A strong commitment to Mikseri, in particular, appeared in the members' narratives about their relationships with the community and the great effort devoted to the artist profiles. A common purpose—creating, sharing, rating, and listening to pieces of music—constitutes the core of the community and is therefore the most crucial factor in the vitality of Mikseri (see also Salavuo, 2006). Indeed, creating and sharing one's own music is a core practice in the community, even to the extent that musicians who only play other people's music are not equally appreciated. The members of Mikseri state that making one's own music is connected to the quality of life: creating music generates a sense of general well-being, significant life choices, and even the state of one's mental health. As one member put it: "The most important thing [in music making] is to have a chance to express oneself and to find a release." Furthermore, it is notable that, among the Mikseri members, the dominant emphasis in music making is not in the completion of musical pieces as end products but rather in the quality of the process of music making itself, including all kinds of musical experiments and sound adventures. In the Mikseri culture, instead of merely copying or reproducing something that has been done before, any musical style, piece, or sound bite can be detached from its original context and recycled to re-create something new for the members' own purposes. In other words, for the members of Mikseri, a piece of music does not necessarily possess aesthetic value in itself; rather, its value lies in its utility for the music maker.

The study shows that the members of Mikseri make flexible use of technology for self-expression, creating and strengthening social bonds, and constructing and mutually defining identities. Hence, Mikseri has had significant meaning for its members, not only in terms of learning and creating social interactions, but also in the processes of identity construction. For the members of Mikseri, creating one's own music, whether by using modern technology or more traditional instruments, is strongly connected to self-expression, and by sharing it with each other, the members are able to use the site to construct music-related identities within a virtual reality. Thus, today's online communities constitute arenas for identity work by providing spaces for displaying a web-based musical self, a platform for telling and sharing one's musical life stories, and, moreover, creating a social context for dialogues and negotiations of experiences and their meanings (Partti & Karlsen, forthcoming). As Wenger (1998) suggests, it is through negotiations in social communities that both individual and collective identities are constructed and defined. Online music communities and message-board discussions, as well as ratings and comments on each other's composi-tions and blogs, all provide opportunities for these vital negotiations of meaning.

PART 5: COMMUNITY MUSIC
AND THE FIELD OF MUSIC EDUCATION—
EPISTEMOLOGICAL CONSIDERATIONS FOR THE FUTURE

[M]uch of present education fails because it neglects this fundamental principle of the school as a form of community life. (John Dewey, EW 5, p. 88)

In the past decade, community music practices have become some of the most interesting phenomena for music educators worldwide. While formal music educa-tion, in many contexts, suffers from the lack of adolescents' interest (Green, 2002; Sloboda, 2001), various traditional or emerging practices, in which learning spurs identity construction, self-expression, social bonding, and empowerment, function as models for meaningful learning. In other words, formal music education may benefit from characteristic CM practices that acknowledge that there is more to learning than learning. However, since music education writ large is, above all, about learning, the epistemological aspects of community music practices are still its main interest and concern. Consequently, such practices should be investigated as learning through theoretical perspectives that enable such processes can be clari-fied and explained.

It is noteworthy that current educational theories support the perspective where learning is examined in the context of human practices and communities. The Finn-ish scholars Paavola and Hakkarainen (2005) have developed theoretical distinc-tions between various epistemological aspects in order to show how communities potentially create knowledge. Paavola and Hakkarainen distinguish three meta-phorical theories of learning: acquisition, participation, and knowledge creation. The acquisition metaphor, or monological view, rests on the idea that knowledge is the property of an individual mind. The participation metaphor, or dialogical view, asserts that knowledge is created through an interactive process of participation in various cultural practices and shared learning activities that shape any cognitive activity. Learning is seen as the situated process of becoming a member of a com-munity and acquiring the skills to communicate and act according to its socially negotiated norms. Learning is "located" in the relationships and networks of dis-tributed activities of participation rather than in individual minds (see also Ryle, 1949). Furthermore, the participation metaphor emphasizes the social character of knowledge: people have epistemological access and "know things because they act in certain ways" (Paavola & Hakkarainen, 2005, p. 547).

As the monological view of learning concentrates on the individual learner owning knowledge, the dialogical approach concentrates on the mastery of a specific commu-nity's inherent knowledge. The participatory aspect of learning was used, for example, in Karlsen's (2007) study, in which a music festival was examined as a community of practice, and its attendees' participation brought about experiences of learning.

According to Paavola and Hakkarainen (2005), however, neither the acquisition metaphor nor the participation metaphor sufficiently addresses the processes of deliberately creating, transforming, and advancing knowledge within innovative knowledge communities: "The role of social communities, larger networks, and research instruments has been left outside of these frameworks" (p. 539). The theories of innovative knowledge communities—the trialogical approaches—concentrate not only on individuals or community but also on mediated processes where common objects of activity—the artifacts—are developed collaboratively. The trialogical view of knowledge creation comes close to the participation model (the dialogic model) since it examines learning in terms of the creation of social structures and collaborative processes that support knowledge advancement and innovation primarily, with an emphasis on generating new ideas. When emphasizing conceptual knowledge, this model also resembles the acquisition, or monological, view. Yet, a trialogical approach opens new epistemological perspectives when, for example, one examines such innovative artistic practices as the online community Mikseri, in which the common objects of activity are the members' own or collaboratively created compositions.

Paavola and Hakkarainen see all three metaphors of learning as complementary and necessary when trying to understand the complex field of learning (see Table 4.1). They emphasize learning and knowledge advancement as a process of creating and articulating rather than simply assimilating existing knowledge or participating in prevailing communal practices. By combining the theories of Bereiter (2002) and Engeström (1987), as well as the research of Nonaka and Takeuchi (1995), they create an epistemological framework for knowledge construction that takes place in innovative knowledge communities. While Bereiter is interested in knowledge-building processes of dynamic experts who collaboratively develop new ideas, methods, or theories, Engeström emphasizes actions in collective activity systems that take place within larger socio-historical contexts. Nonaka and Takeuchi stress the importance of metaphors, analogies, and fuzzy intuitions in the emergence of innovation, focusing especially on the activities surrounding knowledge creation (Paavola & Hakkarainen, 2005, pp. 542–544). Although all of these theorists concentrate on innovative communities, Paavola and Hakkarainen's trialogical approach to learning focuses not only on interactions between people or between people and the environment, but also on specific objects of activity (such as musical outcomes) that are systematically developed within these communities. Hence, the trialogical (or artifact creation) approach to learning in communities addresses the mediational aspect of communal activities. In other words, groups are not seen as simply reacting to their musical environments; rather, they are created by using signs, sounds, and symbols, cultural and musical artifacts, as tools. Artifacts become common objects and are developed through joint activity. Such objects can, for example, be a musical sequence developed through the interaction between a music therapist and her client, the songs written by a garage band, or a joint composition sketched out in a virtual community by its members. The trialogical (or knowledge creation) metaphor focuses on the organization of collaborative processes in order to develop new common objects or activities, and on the combination of individual competences and initiatives within cooperative social networks that drive innovative processes (Paavola & Hakkarainen, 2005, p. 546).

Table 4.1.   The Ideal-Typical Characteristics of the Three Metaphors of Learning

	Acquisition	Participation	Knowledge Creation
Main focus	A process of adopting or constructing subject-matter knowledge and mental representations	A process of participating in social communities	A process of creating and developing new material and conceptual artifacts
		Enculturation, cognitive socialization	Conscious knowledge advancement, discovery, and innovation
		Norms, values, and identities	
Theoretical foundations	Theories of knowledge structures and schemata	Situated and distributed cognition	Knowledge-creating organizations
	Individual expertise	Communities of practice	Activity theory
	Traditional cognitivist theories	Sociologically oriented epistemology	Knowledge-building theory
	Logically oriented epistemology		Epistemology of mediation
Unit of analysis	Individuals	Groups, communities, networks, and cultures	Individuals and groups creating mediating artifacts within cultural settings

After Paavola & Hakkarainen, 2005, p. 541.

As researchers of learning theories are increasingly interested in the sociocultural aspects of learning and advancing skills for collaboration in professional communities (e.g., Bereiter, 2002; Brown & Campione, 1994; Bruner, 1996; Carey & Smith, 1995; Hakkarainen, Palonen, Paavola, & Lehtinen, 2004), community music practices should be investigated from the perspective of knowledge creation. Although benefits of learning through cultural practices, such as CM activities, is recognized (e.g., Duelund, 2003), more research is needed to understand the mechanisms that CM practices in the Nordic countries provide for individuals and how they create and sustain social relationships that promote learning, keeping, and knowing music. Such research, combined with the theoretical perspectives of participation and the artifact creation of learning, could aid in the development of innovative, participatory learning environments that could be utilized in formal music education.

We believe that there is a growing need in music education to look beyond the monological view of learning (Westerlund, 2002) and to explore what Paavola and Hakkarainen (2005) call "epistemic agency": "Epistemic agency does not simply arise from the participants' individual characteristics, but emerges through participation in sociocultural activities, and its manifestation is dependent on the nature of these collective activities" (p. 554). The authors further argue that epistemic agency entails that the students learn to take their own responsibility in terms of learning and making a community. The importance of this particular kind of agency was pointed out already by John Dewey (1938) and has more recently been addressed by Bruner (1996) and Wenger (1998). According to Bruner (1996, pp. 22–23), even modest collective products of joint efforts, or what he calls "oeuvres," are valuable in their channeling of the division of labor as they create pride and identity while sustaining a sense of continuity. Furthermore, learning environments that enhance such common objects and actions also create joint encouragement and interpersonal rewards (Slavin, 2004).

CONCLUSION

This chapter has offered a brief review of the Nordic community music field. By discussing the field's activities, programs, and research, we have shown the participants' experiences of learning, the different modes of construction and transmission of knowledge, and the matters of access, inclusion, and exclusion that are inherently tied thereto.

It is our impression that the Nordic CM field is accessible to many, including disadvantaged or marginal groups within Nordic societies and their educational institutions. This is representative of the broader Nordic cultural model (Duelund, 2003), with its emphasis on egalitarianism and social welfare. Community music activities that might not usually be thought of as being connected to learning (festival attendance in rural, sparsely populated areas, online community participation under a pseudonym, or senior citizens' popular music bands) have educational value, as well as wider cultural and societal significance, from this perspective. They are a vibrant part of the Enlightenment aims of the Nordic countries, cultural policies (Duelund, 2003). Moreover, persons who are not usually perceived as teachers (hip-hop musicians or the peers of an online music community member, for example) assume an educational role in their interactions with others. By strengthening epistemic agency (Paavola & Hakkarainen, 2005), CM activities may lead to the growth and the empowerment of non-professional participants (as with the projects run within the Norwegian prisons or among children and adolescents in a Palestinian refugee camp), and they may also let many people's voices be heard, both figuratively and literally (the latter illustrated by the choirs for the self-proclaimed non-singers).

Letting a diversity of voices be heard is not only a musical matter. It is also, according to the political theorist Mouffe (2005; 2009), a matter of maintaining and expanding the kinds of democratic practices that are needed in a twenty-first-century society. From such a perspective, the significance of the Nordic CM field, as well as underlying cultural policies, gains new value. A diverse education becomes an education in democracy. This mixing of the musical and the societal, the individual and the communal, places a great cultural, educational, and ethical responsibility on CM practices and practitioners. Looking at community music from the perspective of knowledge creation and potential innovation opens new educational vistas for studying present and future communities in formal education, the "anarchic mixed economy of out-of-school music provision," to use Sloboda's (2001, p. 243) words, that may lead to a more effective music education environment. The epistemological view may thus grant the diverse manifestations of the community music field the status they deserve within the larger context of music education.

NOTES

1. The Nordic countries make up a region in Northern Europe consisting of Denmark, Finland, Iceland, Norway, and Sweden and their associated territories, which include the Faroe Islands, Greenland, and Åland.

2. Drawing on Small's (1998) concept of musicking, we also include shared music listening—for example, the listening that takes place among the audiences in a festival community of practice—in the range of activities that can be counted as making music in a community music setting.

3. In this section, we have chosen to take into consideration only research conducted on the PhD-level and above. The most recent scholarly contributions, developed within the disciplines of music education, musicology, and music therapy and published from the year 2000 onwards are emphasized.

4. In Norway, each municipality is legally required to provide its inhabitants with access to music and art schools (the Norwegian Council for Schools of Music and Performing Arts). In the Norwegian government election in the fall of 2009, access to such schools for all children became an important issue for the Norwegian Labor Party.

5. According to Doherty (2002), a similar revitalization of folk music is occurring throughout the rest of Europe.

6. While the festival organizers facilitated such broadening and explorations by presenting more than one musical style within the same concert or combining styles and locations in unexpected ways, the findings of the study also showed that most of the audience members who took the opportunity to educate themselves in this way during the festival already thought of themselves as explorers or open-minded (Karlsen, 2008).

7. See Karlsen (2009a) for a broader discussion on this topic.

BIBLIOGRAPHY

Aksdal, B. (2008). *Folkemusikk og folkedans i kulturskolen: En undersøkelse av dagens situasjon* [Folk music and folk dance in the municipal culture schools. A review of today's situation]. Trondheim: Rådet for folkemusikk og folkedans.

Aksdal, B., & Nyhus, S. (1993). *Fanitullen: Innføring i norsk og Samisk folkemusikk* [The Devil's tune: An introduction to Norwegian and Sami folk music]. Oslo: Universitetsforlaget.

The Association for Music Therapy in Sweden (n.d.). Retrieved from www.musikterapi.se/index.html

Balsnes, A. H. (2009). *Å lære i kor. Belcanto som praksisfelleskap* [Learning in choir. Belcanto as a community of practice] (Unpublished dissertation). Oslo: NMH-publikasjoner 2009:6.

Bartleet, B-L., Dunbar-Hall, P., Letts, R., & Schippers, H. (2009). *Sound links. Community music in Australia.* Brisbane: Queensland Conservatorium Research Centre, Griffith University.

Benum, I. (1978). Musikkpedagogiske Aspekter [Aspects of music education]. *Norsk Musikktidsskrift, 3,* 121–130.

Bereiter, C. (2002). *Education and mind in the knowledge age.* Hillsdale, NJ: Erlbaum.

Brändström, S., & Wiklund, C. (1995). *Två Musikpedagogiska fält. En studie om kommunal Musikskola och musiklärarutbildning* [Two music education fields. A study on municipality music schools and music teacher education] (Unpublished dissertation). Umeå University, Umeå.

Brown, A. L., & Campione, J. C. (1994). Guided discovery in a community of learners. In K. McGilly (Ed.), *Classroom lessons. Integrating cognitive theory and classroom practice* (pp. 229–287). Cambridge: MIT Press.

Bruner, J. (1996). *The culture of education.* London: Harvard University Press.

Carey, S., & Smith, C. (1995). On understanding scientific knowledge. In D. N. Perkins, J. L. Schwartz, M. M. West, & M. S. Wiske (Eds.), *Software goes to school* (pp. 39–55). Oxford: Oxford University Press.

Choir for All (n.d.). Retrieved from http://www.korforalla.se

Danish Association of Music Therapists (n.d.). Retrieved from www.musikterapi.org

Danish Ministry of Culture (n.d.). Retrieved from www.kum.dk/sw700.asp

Dewey, J. (1938/1963). *Experience and education.* New York: Collier.

Dewey, J. The Early Works: 1882–1898 (EW). *The collected works of John Dewey 1882–1953.* (Electronic version). Toim. J. A. Boydston. Carbondale: Southern Illinois University Press.

Dewey, J. The Later Works: 1925–1953 (LW). *The collected works of John Dewey 1882–1953.* (Electronic version). Toim. J. A. Boydston. Carbondale: Southern Illinois University Press.

Doherty, L. (2002). *A needs analysis of the training and transmission of traditional music in university and professional level education throughout Europe.* Unpublished manuscript.

Duelund, P. (2003). The Nordic cultural model. Summary. In P. Duelund (Ed.), *The Nordic cultural model* (pp. 479–529). Copenhagen: Nordic Cultural Institute.

Elliott, D., Higgins, L., & Veblen, K. (2008). Editorial. *International Journal of Community Music, 1* (1), 3–4.

Engeström, Y. (1987). *Learning by expanding.* Helsinki: Orienta-Konsultit Oy.

Finnish Ministry of Education (n.d.). Retrieved from www.minedu.fi/OPM/Kulttuuri/monikulttuurisuus/?lang=en

Folkestad, G. (2006). Formal and informal learning situations or practices vs. formal and informal ways of learning. *British Journal of Music Education, 23* (2), 135–145.

Giddens, A. (1991). *Modernity and self-identity. Self and society in the late modern age.* Stanford, CA: Stanford University Press.

Gotaas, N. (2006). *Rocka stabilitet. En evaluering av prosjektet musikk i fengsel og frihet. Et tilbud for kvinner i oslo* [Rocked stability. An evaluation of the project music in prison and freedom. An opportunity for women in Oslo]. Oslo: NIBR-rapport 2006:8.

Green, L. (2002). *How popular musicians learn. A way ahead for music education.* Aldershot: Ashgate.

Green, L. (2008). *Music, informal learning and the school: A new classroom pedagogy.* Aldershot: Ashgate.

Gullberg, A. K. (2002). *Skolvägen eller garagevägen. Studier av musikalisk socialization* [By learning or doing. Studies in the socialization of music]. (Unpublished dissertation). Luleå University of Technology, Luleå.

Hakkarainen, K., Palonen, T., Paavola, S., & Lehtinen, E. (2004). *Communities of networked expertise: Professional and educational perspectives.* Amsterdam: Elsevier.

Heiling, G. (2000). *Spela snyggt och ha kul. Gemenskap, Sammanhållning och musikalisk utveckling i en amatörorkester* [Play well and have fun. Community, group-coherence and musical development in an amateur brass band] (Unpublished dissertation). Malmö Academy of Music, Malmö.

Hine, C. (2000). *Virtual ethnography.* London: Sage Publications.

Hofvander-Trulsson, Y. (2009, April 14–18). Music fostering in the eyes of immigrant parents. Paper presented at the Sixth International Research in Music Education Conference, Exeter, UK.

International Society for Music Education. (n.d.). Retrieved from www.isme.org/en/community-music-activity/vision.html

Karlsen, S. (2007). *The music festival as an arena for learning. Festspel i Pite Älvdal and matters of identity* (Unpublished dissertation). Luleå University of Technology, Luleå.

Karlsen, S. (2008). Why some go for the safe and others challenge the unknown: Music festival attendees' strategies when choosing events. In F. V. Nielsen, S. G. Nielsen, & S. E. Holgersen (Eds.), *Nordic research in music education. Yearbook vol. 10, 2008* (pp. 229–244). Oslo: NMH-publikasjoner 2008:6.

Karlsen, S. (2009a). Access to the learnable: Music education and the development of strong learners within informal arenas. In E. Gould, C. Morton, J. Countryman, & L. Stewart Rose (Eds.), *Exploring social justice: How music education might matter* (pp. 257–268). Waterloo, ON: Canadian Music Educators' Association/L'Association Canadienne des Musiciens Éducateurs.

Karlsen, S. (2009b). Learning through music festivals. *International Journal of Community Music, 2* (2/3), 129–141.

Karlsen, S. (forthcoming). Revealing musical learning in the informal field. In R. Wright (Ed.), *Sociology and music education.* Aldershot: Ashgate.

Karlsen, S., & Brändström, S. (2008). Exploring the music festival as a music educational project. *International Journal of Music Education, 26* (4), 363–373.

Knutsen, J. S. (2006). *Those that fly without wings—Music and dance in a Chilean immigrant community.* Oslo: Oslo Academic Press.

Lave, J., & Wenger, E. (1991). *Situated learning. Legitimate peripheral participation.* Cambridge: Cambridge University Press.

Mæland, J. (2006). Ole Bull Akademiet [The Ole Bull Academy]. In D. H Sæverud (Ed.), *Gamalt frå Voss 2006.* Voss: Voss Bygdeboknemnd.

Molin, M. (2009). *Hverdagsmusikk—En intervjuundersøkelse av ungdommer med høytfungerende autisme eller aspberger syndrom* [Everyday music: An interview study of adolescents with high-functioning Autism or Aspbergers] (Unpublished dissertation). Norwegian Academy of Music, Oslo.

Mouffe, C. (2005). *On the political.* London: Routledge.

Mouffe, C. (2009). *The democratic paradox.* London: Verso.

Music from the Beginning of Life (n.d.). Retrieved from http://www.musikkfralivetsbegyn-nelse.no/organisasjon

Nonaka, I., & Takeuchi, H. (1995). *The knowledge-creating company: How Japanese companies create the dynamics of innovation.* New York: Oxford University Press.

Norwegian Correctional Services, Oslo prison (n.d.). Retrieved from www.oslofengsel.no/nyhet-miff.html

The Norwegian Council for Schools of Music and Performing Arts (n.d.). Retrieved from www.kulturskoleradet.no/www/FOV1–0004E2DB/S00704735?Plugin=Mappe&dir=/www/FOV1–0004E2DB/S00704735

Norwegian Ministry of Culture (n.d.). Retrieved from www.regjeringen.no/en/dep/kkd/Selected-Topics/Culture/The-Cultural-Initiative/Implementing-the-Cultural-Initiative.html?id=592438

The Norwegian Music Therapy Association (n.d.). Retrieved from www.musikkterapi.no

Ole Bull Academy (n.d.). Retrieved from www.olebull.no

Olsson, B. (2005). Scandinavian research on music education—Its scope of ideas and present status. In B. Olsson (Ed.), *RAIME—Proceedings of the Eight International Symposium* (pp. 15–26). Göteborg: ArtMonitor, Göteborg University.

Paavola, S., & Hakkarainen, K. (2005). The knowledge creation metaphor—An emergent epistemological approach to learning. *Science & Education, 14,* 535–557.

Partti, H. (2009). Musiikin Verkkoyhteisöissä opitaan tekemällä. Kokemisen, jakamisen, yhteisön ja oman musiikinteon merkitykset osallistumisen kulttuurissa [Learning by doing in an online music community. The meaning of experience, sharing, music making and community in participatory culture]. *Finnish Journal of Music Education, 12* (2), 39–47.

Partti, H., & Karlsen, S. (forthcoming). Reconceptualizing musical learning: New media, identity and community in music education. *Music Education Research.*

Partti, H., & Westerlund, H. (2008, July 20–25). New meanings of composing in music education. Learning from re-mixing and re-cycling within informal online music communities. Paper presented at the International Society for Music Education 2008 World Conference, Bologna, Italy.

Pitts, S. (2005). *Valuing musical participation.* Aldershot: Ashgate.

Ruud, E. (1983). *Musikken, vårt nye rusmiddel?* [Music, our new intoxicant?]. Oslo: Norsk Musikforlag.

Ryle, G. (1949). *The concept of mind.* London: Hutchinson's University Library.

Salavuo, M. (2006). Open and informal online communities as forums of collaborative musical activities and learning. *British Journal of Music Education, 23* (3), 253–271.

Slavin, R. (2004). When and why does cooperative learning increase achievement? Theoretical and empirical perspectives. In H. Daniels & A. Edwards (Eds.), *Psychology of education* (pp. 269–293). London: RoutledgeFalmer.

Sloboda, J. (2001). Emotion, functionality and the everyday experience of music: Where does music education fit? *Music Education Research, 3* (2), 243–253.

Small, C. (1998). *Musicking. The meanings of performing and listening.* Middletown, CT: Wesleyan University Press.

Snell, K. (2005). Music education through popular music festivals. A study of the OM music festival in Ontario, Canada. *Action, Criticism & Theory for Music Education, 4* (2).

Söderman, J. (2007). *Rap(p) i käften. Hiphopmusikers konstnärliga och Pedagogiska strategier* [Verbally Fa(s)t. Hip-hop musicians' artistic and educational strategies] (Unpublished dissertation). Lund University, Lund.

Stige, B. (2003). *Elaborations toward a notion of community music therapy* (Unpublished dissertation). Oslo: Unipub forlag.

Storsve, V., Westby, I. A., & Ruud, E. (2009). Håp og anerkjennelse. Om et musikkprosjekt Blant ungdommer i en Palestinsk Flyktningleir [Hope and recognition. On a music project in a Palestinian refugee camp]." In E. Ruud (Ed.), *Musikk som Psykisk Helsevern.* Oslo: NMH-publikasjoner 2009:5.

Swedish Ministry of Culture (n.d.). Retrieved from http://www.sweden.gov.se/sb/d/3009

Tivenius, O. (2008). *Musiklärartyper: En Typologisk studie av musiklärare vid kommunal musikskola* [Music teacher types: A typological study of music teachers at municipal music schools] (Unpublished dissertation). Örebro University, Örebro.

Väkevä, L., & Westerlund, H. (2007). The "method" of democracy in music education. *Action, Criticism, and Theory for Music Education, 6* (4), 96–108.

Veblen, K. (2008). The many ways of community music. *International Journal of Community Music, 1* (1), 5–21.

Veblen, K., & Olsson, B. (2002). Community music. Toward an international overview. In R. Colwell & C. Richardson (Eds.), *The new handbook of research on music teaching and learning. A project of the music educators national conference.* Oxford: Oxford University Press.

Wenger, E. (1998). *Communities of practice. Learning, meaning, and identity.* Cambridge: Cambridge University Press.

Westerlund, H. (2002). *Bridging experience, action, and culture in music education* (Unpublished dissertation). Sibelius Academy, Helsinki.

Chapter Five

Community Music in Africa: Perspectives from South Africa, Kenya, and Eritrea

Elizabeth Oehrle, David O. Akombo, and Elias Weldegebriel

This chapter offers three different interpretations of community music from the continent of Africa. Elizabeth Oehrle details the case study of the Durban-based Ukusa program. *Ukusa* means "sunrise" in Zulu, and this thriving music project has provided many people access to cultural opportunities of all kinds. Elias Weldegebriel broadly details the Eritrean music-scape. Weldegebriel considers the Amsara Music School and its role in promoting various musics. A final section is offered by David O. Akombo, who considers tradition and change by examining the role of women *Isikuti* musicians among the Isukha people of Kenya.

UKUSA: A DEVELOPMENTAL COMMUNITY PERFORMING NON-PROFIT ORGANIZATION IN DURBAN, SOUTH AFRICA

During the dark days of apartheid in 1987, a member of the Community Arts Workshop approached me with the idea of starting a music program in Durban to be financed by the Shell corporation. Angered by Shell's investment in the South African government of the time, anti-apartheid activists were blowing up Shell offices in Europe. Thus, I refused their request.

In 1988, they approached me again. Following discussions with several potential teachers and a member of the Culture and Working Life Project involved with Community Organizations, I decided to take on the task of laying the groundwork for a music program with the following provisos:

- First, the program must be based on the musical needs and desires of people involved.
- Second, quality of music education must be put before quantity or numbers of students.
- Third, the content and form of the program must evolve by working with and through the students rather than prescribing for them.

Shell agreed to these provisos and thus began one of the first arts outreach programs in South Africa primarily for people living in the townships.

The Ukusa program started as a small local arts outreach project in a dilapidated shed of the old Durban Station building. The first task was to find musically competent teachers who were willing to establish a program based on the musical needs and desires of students. My hope was to develop a program based on music of Africa, but the students were more interested in Western music, primarily jazz, so that became our focus. Initially, there were only a few classes, but young people responded enthusiastically, and soon a nearby school allowed us to use their keyboard center. Student numbers grew, and as we had strong support from the head of the department, arrangements were made to move to the University of KwaZulu-Natal's music department. With the additional space and the assistance of students and staff from the music department as teachers, Ukusa's growth continued.

From its inception, the Ukusa program focused on helping the historically disadvantaged who never had an opportunity to study music, dance, or drama at school. Today Ukusa is registered as a Developmental Community Performing Non-Profit Organization in South Africa. People sixteen years and older are welcome to register. We do not exclude anyone through auditions or other selection criteria, and several hundred attend each year.

Essentially, Ukusa is a grassroots project with a positive sense of community. Many students return year after year as they wish to remain part of the Ukusa community and broaden their skills in a variety of instruments. Over the years, Ukusa has offered creative opportunities to hundreds of aspiring musicians, dancers, actors, and actresses. Some have gone on to achieve their dreams in careers of their choice.

During the apartheid years, classes were free. After 1994, students were charged a nominal fee in order to add value to our work as well as move students away from dependency. Currently, we charge R 400 for the year; however, no student is refused entry through lack of income. Funding for this program is essential. Initially, several funders, such as the Shell corporation, the Swedish International Development Association (SIDA), and various trust foundations, provided money for a few consecutive years. SIDA referred to us as their dream project because we have delivered on our proposals and our administrative costs are low. When funders shift their focus, however, their funding stops, and we have had to look for funding from other organizations.

Ukusa, or Sunrise—a word that symbolizes the promise and certainty of a new day, and which was chosen by the students—initially answered a need in a volatile situation. We are living out the legacy of apartheid education, and many South Africans still do not have the opportunity to develop their artistic skills. Ukusa continues to expand educational and employment opportunities through the arts for the historically disadvantaged, supporting social transformation and redressing the many wrongs of the past. As a testimony to the need for the options Ukusa offers, each year, without any advertisement, more than three hundred people come to register.

Ukusa's mission is to help students who show willingness to work, ability in the creative arts, and a desire to share with others in their community what they have learned at Ukusa. Ukusa provides an opportunity for self-affirmation, which is essential toward contributing to the social and economic advancement of South Africans, and skills developed at Ukusa improve students' self-respect and confidence. Students are also enabled to further their education at technikons (polytechnics) and universities and/or to be practically involved in the fields of music, dance, and drama.

Ukusa is located in the Ethekwini metropolis, and most of our students come from nearby townships. A considerable number, however, travel greater distances; some come from Pietermaritzburg, which is eighty-three kilometers away. Students must bring their own musical instruments, but Ukusa offers classes every Saturday, from March through November, in keyboard, trumpet, saxophone, *maskanda* (a genre of African guitar playing), lead guitar, bass guitar, drumming, traditional dance, contemporary dance, drama, choir, music theory, and basic arts administration. In addition to regular classes, special workshops in music administration, music technology, and guitar making are offered when sponsorship is available. Ukusa encourages the strengthening of African musical cultures by providing classes in traditional African music and dance and workshops that extend students' experiences of the musics of Africa such as "Ngoma Traditional Dance," Nigerian drumming, "Igba Joli Four," and Ghanaian Komla Amoaka's "African Music." There are twenty-three paid teaching staff, so classes are large and group teaching is essential. Teachers and students are held to a high standard of commitment and responsibility through a code of conduct.

Ukusa classrooms are widely spread around the University of KwaZulu-Natal (UKZN) Howard College Campus, which makes communication difficult, so we distribute a community newsletter called *Ukusanews*. In addition, the administration holds four meetings with student representatives from each class during the year to discuss relevant issues. The administration and teaching staff meet with the class representatives twice a year to evaluate the successes and failures of projects and initiate necessary changes.

There are four in-house Ukusa concerts each year and students perform in front of large audiences. We invite students of the African Music Project at UKZN to perform in the Ukusa concerts. Although our students have expressed their preference for so-called Western gospel, jazz, and popular music, *maskanda* and traditional African song and dance in the Ukusa concerts always elicit the most enthusiastic appreciation. Teachers are encouraged to perform with their classes. Students thus perform with well-known South African performers and Ukusa staff such as Feya Faku, Zim Ngqawana, Melvin Peters, Bongani Sokhela, George Mari, Llianne Loots, Mageshen Naidoo, and Burton Naidoo.

Over the years, former students and staff of Ukusa have joined the chorus line of the *Sarafina* movie and played on Broadway in hits of Jerry Pooe. Ukusa has also been a stepping stone into University Music School. Nontukuso Mlangeni, Paul Kock, Khethiwe Memela, Mduduzi Mbhele, and Lungani Gumede all began their musical training at Ukusa and have since graduated with music degrees from UKZN.

Ukusa admits older youth and adults in order to develop a reservoir of mature, skilled performing artists willing to share their talents and interests with their communities. In 1997, Ukusa students began to initiate youth outreach projects in their own communities. These projects receive seed money (R 300 per year), and if a project is successful, the amount increases to R 3000 per year. The number of projects has increased each year. Community project leaders meet four times a year with their co-ordinators to discuss problems, issues of development, and new ideas. Ukusa's plans for expansion focus on maintaining current projects and developing new projects.

Ukusa strives to meet specific objectives:

- To expose students to music, dance, and drama in various forms
- To train students in the theory and practice of music
- To give students the opportunity to take part in the concerts during the year
- To award certificates for passing examinations on music theory
- To award certificates of merit based on progress and the performance at the year's end

Budget

The annual budget of Ukusa is approximately R 400,000 and includes instruction in twenty-five classes; student transport from town to campus; concerts and workshops; publications; community youth arts projects; and administrative fees and office expenses. The Ukusa program has been continually subsidized for the benefit of students with financial needs, but fund-raising is an ongoing concern.

Stories of Students and Teachers

Hundreds of students have attended Ukusa over the years.

Sikhosiphu Mbongwa writes in *Ukusanews* (2002):

> I started hearing about Ukusa around the early 1990s. I thought, "This is like a dream come true for me," seeing as music was my passion ever since I was young when I used to make home-made guitars by collecting tins and strings. From where I live it takes about 2 to 3 hours of traveling by a taxi. Then to reach the school (Ukusa) you need another bus.

Mbongwa progressed quickly through music theory and keyboard to find his niche in guitar. He notes: "I am not stopping now until I become the best bass guitar player that can be . . . Seeing as I am the only person attending at Ukusa from my area of Inanda, my mission is to teach my community what I have learned. Especially the youth—I like taking them off the streets. I'd like to make a difference, do something for them through Ukusa."

Former student and now guitar teacher at Ukusa Lloyd Francis echoes the positive influence that Ukusa has provided:

> I first heard about Ukusa in the mid-90s, through my elder brother, who had in turn heard about it from a high school friend. At the time I was a self-employed electronic techni-cian. From a young age I always wanted to play the guitar, not to be the best or a super-star, but just to be able to strum along to a few songs. Unfortunately my parents couldn't afford to send us for music lessons . . .

Francis began classes and then went to the University of KwaZulu-Natal for music. After his guitar teacher invited him to substitute teach for him, Francis became a permanent guitar and music theory teacher for the program. Francis adds:

> Because of the impact Ukusa has had on my life and the direction it has taken, I cherish the opportunity to be a part of the teaching staff. Because now I am in a position to affect or influence the futures of my students in a positive manner, they too can realize the true potential that lies within them.

A third student, Nompumelelo Sibiya, reveals how varied her studies have been at Ukusa. She writes:

> I began classes in 1991. I heard about Ukusa from Radio Ukhozi FM. At first I studied Dance and Drama. The following year I moved into music and started Music Theory and Beginner Keyboard. In subsequent years I completed Music Theory through grade 6. At the same time I continued to study keyboard. Then I moved on to drumming and choir. Now I am enjoying learning how to play *Maskanda.* It is my third year of *Maskanda.* On top of all this I am involved in a Community Development Project. I started my own Music and Dance Project in 2000, and it is still progressing well. We help youngsters of 6 to 16 years develop performance skills. I teach staff notation and translating to Tonic-Sol-fa is not a problem anymore. And all this came about with the help of Ukusa. I have so much I could say about Ukusa and how Ukusa has grown me. Thank you, Ukusa.

The Basic Arts Administration course has been instructive for students who initiate Ukusa Community Projects in their neighborhoods. Ruth Thipe wrote:

> The course entailed financial management; how to budget for your project; implementing a plan for your project; fundraising and marketing. Everything we did during the course was exciting. We formed many discussion groups in which everyone had a chance to experience and share ideas together. This was an example of how valuable communication skills were . . . I feel that the knowledge I gained through Ukusa, I will use to best advantage with others. That was for me a precious and blessed time. (*Ukusanews,* August 2002).

Ghanaian Komla Amoaka, director of the National Theatre in Ghana, is an educator, musician, and traveler who views the world as a unit between the visible and invisible, and culture as the expression of life. For him, music making is part of a holistic approach to life. At the conclusion of his workshop, he said, "Ukusa students understand what I am saying." Amoaka (1995) explained:

> They understand that proverbs, riddles, and folktales are a means by which education takes place. They understand that the heightening and refining of one's intuition is more important than the development of the intellect. They understand that education requires the full integration of a person as an individual and as a fully responsible member of the society in the African context. (*Ukusanews,* August 1995)

Tholi Khanyi began as an Ukusa student in 1996 and in 1999 went on to become a highly respected and much loved teacher of traditional dance and drama. He was the project leader for the Sakhisizwe Arts Project for children five years and older in the informal settlements in and around Umlazi. Ukusa concerts were always enhanced with Tholi's innovative ideas. He not only danced; he sang songs and wrote poems about the merits of Ukusa. In his last praise poem to Ukusa, he tells us to go forward, or, in Zulu, *phambili:*

> The sun has risen;
> The clouds run away;
> The sky becomes clear and beautiful
> And there emerges the name
> Ukusa
> I hear about Ukusa
> I see development flowing to our communities
> I hear about Ukusa
> I see Artists realising themselves and their potential . . .
> Ukusa Arts Program you are a candle in the dark
> You give light to those who need it
> You are the rain in the desert
> You provide life where it never existed . . .
> We say "*Phambili* Ukusa Arts Program, *Phambili*
> *Phambili* for your good work, *Phambili*
> *Phambili* Ukusa staff and students, *Phambili*
> *Phambili* with dedication, *Phambili*
> *Phambili* with enthusiasm and determination, *Phambili*
> *Phambili* with the culture of learning and teaching, *Phambili*
> *Phambili* Ukusa Arts Program

COMMUNITY MUSIC IN ERITREA AND THE ASMARA MUSIC SCHOOL

Eritrea is situated in the northern horn of Africa, neighbored by Ethiopia and Djibouti to the south, by the Red Sea to the east, and by Sudan to the west. Though most parts of Eritrea are semi-arid, its climate varies from harsh, hot coasts to the mild highlands. Eritrea fought Africa's longest armed liberation struggle for thirty years until it gained its independence in 1991 after one hundred years of Italian, British, and Ethiopian colonial rule. Its population is nearly 4.4 million.

Historically, the land that has come to be known as Eritrea was a place of great civilizations, including the Axumite kingdom, due to its bustling trade activities with the Arabian, East Asian, and North African regions, and beyond. Before most African countries, it possessed its own unique script and has practiced modern religions since the fourth century CE.

Eritrea's Musics

Community music in Eritrea is mostly traditional or indigenous music: the music of the ordinary rural as well as the urban population. It is not only played as music for its own sake, but it is part of the daily communal life. It carries the values that are attributed to whatever social landmark or occasion is celebrated. With different ethnic groups, the evolution is varied from very little to considerable; the intensity gets weaker as the geographical proximity gets farther away from the capital city (Asmara), where the changes are influenced by the exposure to modernity. The closer to Amsara, the greater the influence of modernity; however, the national efforts to revive, celebrate, and popularize traditional music are centered in the capital city, and communal, traditional music is becoming part of the popular musical culture.

In the Tigrigna ethnic group, wedding songs are sung during the brewing of *suwa* (a traditional beer) and the baking of *miyess* (a honey bread) as they are made especially for the occasion, as well as during the wedding ceremony and when the wedded couple leaves the *das(es)* (venue of the wedding). The songs are repetitive, containing one, sometimes two strophes, and wish the new couple well.

In the Nara ethnic group, *Dada* is celebrated by singing in order to praise, bless, insult (tease), and welcome *Santortos* around a town called Gogne. *Dada* is a show of preparedness and fitness for the forthcoming fertile season's arduous work of plowing, sowing, and harvesting. A variety of songs and dances are fervently celebrated by male and female youths as they gather from several villages. The Nara also perform *Anandilo,* a wedding road song sung and danced to by the entire group as they fetch the bride to and from her village for the wedding.

In the Afar ethnic group, *Keke* is a general-purpose music and dance that is performed by males and females. The singing is antiphonal (the solo and chorus alternately repeating the same melody). The solo singing and drumming is done by men, and the chorus is sung by males and females.

Development of Modern Popular Music in Eritrea

As varied as its climate, so too are Eritrea's people, who belong to nine different ethnic groups and speak nine different languages. This cultural mosaic contributes to Eritrea's colorful musical diversity. Music is part of Eritrean community life. In the 1950s, due to the modernization of institutions in education, health, politics, entertainment, and religion, a wind of change breezed through the art of stage performance. What began in the cities as dramatic, educational, and propagandistic work soon developed into music and related performance arts and spread across the land. Contemporary music had a strong following among the youth, helped by its strong anti-colonial content, and the introduction of Western music felt relevant when global pop-rock carried an image of modernity. The songs, which are now regarded as classics, tactfully and sensually assimilated foreign elements. Groups like MATEDE, MATEAa, Zerai Derres, MeQalH Guaila, Rocket Police Band, and others came and went and had an enormous impact on the society and building the music performance experience.

However, in the 1970s, due to assumed hidden messages and the political polarization of the musical works and worsening Ethiopian colonial oppression, important members of the bands were forced to join the liberation movements or flee their country to become refugees abroad. Most continued their musical activities, helping the emerging music groups in the movements.

In the 1980s, *zemenawi*[1] (modern), *bahlawi* (traditional music), and traditional music with Western and local instruments (traditional pop) were played in three different contexts, namely in the diaspora, in areas under the control of Ethiopian colonialists, and in the liberation movements. Along with traditional music, popular music functioned effectively as the standard-bearer of the Eritrean aspiration toward freedom. These different environments brought about different tendencies, influences, and tastes.

In a post-liberation setting, popular music genres continued to grow in production and popularity with both *zemenawi* and traditional. However, the production of recordings of the different ethnic groups is disproportional due to the respective degree of urbanization among the ethnic groups. Most recording studios are centered in Asmara; thus, music production features mainly Tigrigna artists due to that ethnic group's geographical location.

Generally, Eritreans are widely practicing and enjoying folk, traditional pop, and modern/*zemenawi* pop, and are being exposed to international music through global media and, as émigrés, through their host countries' musics. Neighboring countries' and ex-colonizers' music are also widely enjoyed by and familiar to city and town people.

Though not promulgated yet, the government's drafted cultural policy is waiting for approval and implementation. Cognizant of the importance of community music in the development of the same and the country as a whole, the policy is geared toward encouraging and fostering it in different ways.

Festivals at national and regional levels are a milieu created by the local and governmental administrations to foster and explore the indigenous cultures and present them to the wider public. During these festivities, competitions showcase elements of culture and history from every community. Winners receive prizes in the form of trophies, lessons, contacts for additional work, and even considerable amounts of money. Six regional musical performances are the climax of the competitions.

A large budget is allotted to allow the groups to keep performing as groups, especially during the preparation for and participation in festivals representing the region. During the annual national festival that is held at the expo compound in Asmara, participants stay for ten to fourteen days. The number of activities carried on during the festivals calls for professional guidance and teaching, a role which is currently being played by amateurs. These activities create a positive atmosphere of understanding among cultures and friendship among different ethnic groups. Unfortunately, what one sees in these competitive performance is not necessarily a community's authentic music, but a performance that is modified for the sake of uniformity and choreography and the need for spectacle.

The Eritrean musical culture involves learning skills and techniques of singing and playing traditional instruments. The process of learning and passing on these skills to successive generations is important. Learning is accomplished through experience. It starts in the neighborhood as the musician establishes a reputation for entertaining. Then performers play small venues. If they are successful, they are established and ready to be invited musicians. This learning process bolsters the emergence of young talented players of musical instruments and singers. Schools form music groups composed of young students to perform at important events and national and public holidays for the community Most of these amateur musicians are self-taught youngsters or were once participants of short music courses.

At a national level, traditional musical instrument players and singers as young as ten years old are getting awards for exceptional performances. This is an inspiration for others to follow. At the 2009 national festival, a special prize was awarded for creativity and authenticity, as well as for the dedication and musicianship to traditional music, to a youth, Abadi Bahta, who produced a traditional music album titled *Qumenaa Shege.*

It is not only the national cultural festival that promotes community music. There are other groups and projects, such as students' music groups, Sbrit (the national folklore group), the Drum Ensemble, Arts Education, and the Abrham Afewerki Foundation for Music (AAFM).

In the capital city Asmara, besides Sbrit, other students and youth cultural groups carry out musical activities, some repeating classic songs, others preserving and revisiting liberation struggle songs, and quite a few more actively engaged in celebrating traditional music and dance activities. These groups are organized and administered by the Peoples' Front for Democracy and Justice, the Cultural Affairs Bureau (of the Ministry of Education), and the National Union of Eritrean Youth and Students.

Drums Ensemble Project

Another form of community music activity is the training and performance of a drum ensemble. This occurs during national festival and Independence Day celebrations. It is run by a drummer/violin player/teacher in Asmara Music School. Approximately sixty young students from junior secondary schools are given drum playing training for one and a half months. This activity adds spectacle and a sense of African culture to the festivities.

Arts Education

Arts education is being prepared to be introduced to Eritrean schools as an integrated subject for the first time and is likely to both have an influence on and be influenced by contemporary community musical practices. Arts education will include drama, music, dance, and visual arts and is based on a learner-centered approach. It will explore local as well as regional and international cultures and will attempt to influence . learners through empirical/experiential and cognitive means. This subject will also be a means of promoting the local musical culture via mass teaching—among students and the Eritrean populace at-large.

The Abrham Afewerki Foundation for Music

The Abrham Afewerki Foundation for Music (AAFM) is a foundation established in the United States by friends and family of the late famous Eritrean singer, songwriter, and arranger/composer after his passing. The foundation seeks to establish a community music school in Eritrea where the underprivileged, orphans, and children can study music for the benefit of Eritrean society. At present, during the summer school break, it is offering a three-month musical training course in basic musical theory and instrumental performance, called Wari, to a performing group of twenty students and plans to continue with similar courses in the future.

For many youngsters, playing indigenous musical instruments has not equated with being a complete musician; only playing Western musical instruments could validate a person's musicianship. This attitude is changing dramatically. The production of traditional music is evidence of this. These musical and cultural activities foster cohesion within a culturally diverse population, unifying a people through the creation and sharing of common values, celebrating their gains, and lamenting their losses.

Although the citizens of Eritrea appreciate the efforts of the groups and projects like the national festivals, Sbrit, and the AAFM, compared to education in other fields, music education and musically educated persons are almost non-existent. In addition, musical instruments are in short supply and unaffordable for most people. Although there is diverse local music and an abundance of foreign musical influences, for community music to flourish, a center of gravity is vital. In the absence of an educated knowledge base and expertise in arts, the correct and relevant path can lead to contributions that will preserve and enrich the indigenous community music.

Asmara Music School

There were no institutions that played leadership roles in the teaching of music, except for the informal training programs conducted by individuals and religious institutions to a handful of followers, until the Eritrean Peoples' Liberation Front (EPLF) established a school for the arts, the Amsara Music School (AMS), during the struggle in 1985. The EPLF, understanding the importance of fostering and making the indigenous art the base for any movement toward cultural enrichment and change, invested in cultural education, using the school to unite people in the war for liberation as well as in social transformation.

In the post-liberation era, because of the lack of arts institutions and national interest, there was no one who could authoritatively write, teach, critique, and research the musical performance practices, although these performance practices were and are abundant. It has been difficult for musicians and audiences to discern the "good" music and who the model musicians and musics are. This problem manifests itself in discussions in the few workshops and seminars conducted, where concerned people have been divided on whether Eritrean music is showing positive change, what positive change might be, and how to bring about that change or enrichment.

Amsara Music School has developed specific goals:

• Produce musicians who are skilled and knowledgeable in the art of music, contribute toward the national arts institutional growth, and influence the music arena (be it popular or traditional) in a way that reflects the communities' authentic musical practices.

- Act as a provider of a professional guide to community musicians and music practices to better serve as the communities' self-expression medium
- Preserve the indigenous musics and inspire creativity to stimulate an informed advancement and enrichment of Eritrean musics

AMS is a government/public school that gives music education for a nominal monthly fee of ERN 50, equivalent to 17 percent of the fee private schools charge (orphans and students who can't afford to pay are exempted from paying). Students use the school's musical instruments for free. The school exists to give Eritrean citizens with the talent and love for music, regardless of race, wealth, gender, or ethnicity, equal musical education opportunities. What is important to the school is the product of the process it has set in motion.

AMS teaches basic to intermediate music theory, harmony, general Western and local music history, general applied electroacoustics, and aural perception and instrumental performance on keyboards and piano, guitar, saxophone, trumpet, flute, clarinet, violin, and drums in three- and five-year courses on a semi part-time arrangement. Academic studies are addressed, as well as time for music learning, in four shifts of three to four hours three days per week. Theoretical teaching is minimal in order to provide the young learners more time to practice since most of them have no instruments of their own.

On the practical level, the school utilizes mostly Western classical music and a few other popular written musical resources. It has introduced playing by ear as an important method of learning local indigenous music. The criteria for judging good performances concerns the mastery of the technique, correctness, and articulation and mood as well as performance practice and style. In the past, this method of studying music had been considered as one that failed to contribute to the musicality of a learner. As a result, learners were discouraged from playing local musical material that was not notated or transcribed. This only encouraged learners to play foreign songs of unfamiliar tonalities (Eritrean tonality is pentatonic). Learning European scores in this way led to scorn for indigenous musical material as inferior to the Western music. This methodology did not match the realities of the Eritrean social musical environment. People who took years of musical training in the music school were struggling to play their culture's own indigenous songs with musicians who were self-taught or who had had little or no formal music education.

The performance of music at AMS is done either individually or in an ensemble. Ensemble practice sessions are conducted to ensure the participation of any music student at any level. Learners in Asmara Music School are ages thirteen to seventeen. They are from Asmara and its environs. The music school instills in youngsters that the community's musical culture is important, is the ultimate goal for their skills, and is the source of their creative musical work. To strengthen this outlook, the music school plans to form a resident music group to lead by example. Its repertoire will include Eritrean traditional, *zemenawi* (modern Eritrean pop), and international musics.

It is the music school's belief that every student comes with some musical experience and has something to give and take. Hence, creating an avenue for them to expand their experiences, to learn and improve their performance skills, and to simultaneously enjoy themselves is a way of making a community-like relationship in the school. This project will benefit the music of the country, Asmara Music School, and the musicians professionally, educationally, and financially.

AMS and its predecessors have produced more than seven hundred musicians. Some have risen to become singers and musicians at a national level. Asser, a musical group with two years of musical training at AMS, produced an album, *Ajibeni*, in 2008 and 2009. The title song has been widely sold as a single both locally and abroad. Efrem Andemariam, the song's writer and arranger, is a fine performer on the saxophone and keyboard and a teacher at Asmara Music School. Senait Amine, singer and wife of Andemariam, motherless and the daughter of a martyred father, is now entertaining tens of thousands of people and earning her living making music.

Numerous orphans have been beneficiaries of the school's training program by becoming musicians. They contribute their services to the public and take pride in what they do, which in turn benefits Eritrean society. They have proved to be financially viable, making their living and supporting others by making and performing music.

THE ROLE OF WOMEN IN *ISIKUTI* COMMUNITY MUSIC OF THE ISUKHA PEOPLE OF KENYA

The general social role of women in society, particularly in music making, has been disparaged in Africa for millennia. This section highlights the ideological and philosophical principles that have led to the struggles of the African woman despite the significant role she has played and continues to play in community music-making endeavors. Specifically, this section focuses on the musical roles that the women of Western Kenya's Isukha tribe have played in a male-dominated community music arena.

The Isukha are a sub-tribe of the broader Luhya ethnic group of Kenya, approximately 100,000 people comprising seven smaller sub-ethnic groups who live in the Western Province of Kenya, close to Lake Victoria, east of the Cherengani Hills. They occupy the entire plateau, living on five- to ten-acre farms in small villages. The higher elevation of the hills provides a panoramic view of the fertile farmland in the lowlands. Although Isukha women have been disenfranchised and socio-economically alienated by the men, for centuries they have continued to create music and fully participate in village community music-making endeavors.

Historical Roles of Women in African Societies

African societies have often been examined only from a masculine perspective. In contemporary Africa, where basic human rights are frequently violated, women have commonly been denied their dignity along with their rights (Dimandja, 2004). However, viewing women's roles in traditional music making among the Isukha people of Western Kenya from a feminine perspective can be richly illuminating.

Religious and philosophical factors come into play in defining gender roles. In many cultures, religion has been regarded as the main criterion for assigning gender its place in the social order. As a result, many scholars (Eliade, 1957; Danquah, 1968; Anti, 1978) have attributed gender inequality to religion. In the Arab world, women are kept behind a veil. They are a silent and invisible "beast of burden," born and nurtured to suffer the twin burdens of childbearing and heavy household chores (Rassam, 1984, p. 125). Scholars propose that because the husband is the breadwinner in a patriarchal family structure, he has more resources to contribute and gains more power in the community. The wife, on the other hand, is financially dependent and therefore has less opportunity for power and equality (Schwartz, Patterson, & Steen, 1995).

Anti (1978) observes that Jewish mythology did not regard women as a necessity, but merely as helpers to men. In fact, classic Jewish thought acknowledged only one masculine God, the God of Abraham, Isaac, and Jacob, but not the God of Sarah, Rebecca, and Rachel. Although in many parts of Africa God is conceived as male, in other locations there are feminine goddesses, and musical instruments are embedded with artistic images to honor them. For example, the supreme twin gods of the Ewe of Ghana are Mawu-Lisa. The goddess Mawu is represented by the moon, while Lisa, the male god, is represented by the sun. As husband and wife, Mawu-Lisa had seven pairs of twins who became the Ewe people's major gods.

It is difficult to ponder the meaning of myth, especially where the supernatural world of a deity is concerned. Anti (1978) further stimulates our inquiry by revealing that, according to St. Paul, women speaking in church was taboo. A woman had to ask her husband's permission to speak at the church or to communicate to the church in his absence. In Islamic traditions, women can only lead prayers for congregations of women. Within the mosque, women are not permitted to stand or sit in the same rows with the men but rather sit separately, behind them.

This situation is, however, not exactly the same throughout Africa. In the context of the *isikuti* community music of the Isukha people, African society must be carefully examined in order to apprehend the role of women in the traditional religion and understand the roles of women in the *isikuti* dance. *Isikuti* community music existed long before 900 CE, but the name *isikuti* was created early in the seventeenth century. Ethnographic studies have shown that the word *isikuti* originated from the English expression "it is good," a phrase that became synonymous with community music whenever white men watched or described the *isikuti* dancers. By the beginning of the nineteenth century, the Isukha transformed the expression "it is good" into *isikuti,* and the name came to be applied to community dance music. *Isikuti* is an ensemble consisting of idiophones, membranophones, a chorus, dancers, and soloists. The idiophones include *ikengele* (bell), *ebisala* (sticks), and *ifirimbi* (whistle). The membranophones include *isikuti* (male drum), *isikuti ikhasi* (female drum), and *isikuti mwana* or *mutindindi* (child drum).

The influences of Christian missionaries and the adaptation to a modern lifestyle have had a significant impact on Isukha traditions, including music making, and the role of Isukha women in the broader Luhya culture. Historical discourses have observed that the missionaries continually discouraged musical performance, including all social and shamanistic observances, and abolished ceremonial paraphernalia. The missionaries considered these antithetical to their religion. *Isikuti* community music was displaced, with women being discouraged from participating in public dances. The beginning of colonial rule in Kenya introduced a new European ideology, a philosophy of female societal roles that ran counter to African views of women as family nurturers and home caretakers. Since a woman's work was considered menial, it might be said that a woman was a man's chief domesticated animal, a beast of burden (Montagu, 1957, p. 150). This view corroborates Rassam's (1984) notion of women in the Arab world.

By drastically altering the roles of women, this ideology began to alter the African model of engendering the arts. By means of legislation, the colonial governments aimed to preserve colonial economies, in part, by restricting women to special duties at the expense of their cultural rights. Anti (1978) notes that the missionaries wanted to overturn not only spiritual beliefs but also key aspects of everyday life and community authority. Other scholars view the role of missionaries in Africa differently. According to Sharkey (2002), the missionaries did great good for Africa. They provided crucial services, like education and health care, that would not have otherwise been available to the Africans. In traditionally male-dominated societies, female missionaries provided women with health-care knowledge and basic education (Sharkey, 2002).

The Isukha, however, have continued to perform *isikuti* community music at almost every social event, ranging from birthdays to courtships to marriages to initiations. In the context of the *isikuti* community music performances, certain questions arise in regard to the women's historical space in community music-making ceremonies within the Isukha cosmology. First, is music making based more on gender dichotomies than on cultural beliefs of the sonic material? Second, are certain roles in *isikuti* dance music purely for women? Third, are these roles pertinent to performance among the Isukha people? Fourth, are some women's roles indispensable to the *isikuti* ensemble? Fifth, which instruments are for male performers, which ones are for female performer, and who makes these decisions? Sixth, do men or women compose the majority of the music?

One key issue that continues to hinder socio-economic empowerment among Isukha women is the lack of involvement and consultation with men in major decision making. Decisions affecting women's participation in economic activities and productivity and those relating to the introduction and development of new technology are frequently made without female involvement or consultation. Some technologies have increased the workload of women, especially when such technologies are targeted at men's roles in agriculture.

Another issue that limits women's freedom is the traditional social practice that denies women the right to commercialization of their intellectual property. These women are put at a disadvantage in seeking access to the global market for their music, marketing outlets, and the opportunities accruing from membership of women's community dance groups. Women are not, therefore, granted entrée to external market destinations because men are the custodians of all of the women's products, including their music.

The high level of illiteracy among rural Isukha women, who also make up the majority of community music groups' membership, is a great hindrance to their self-reliance and to sharing their music with the global markets.

Other Kenyan women have supported and continue to support the rural women by engaging in the commercialization of their music. Kenyan pop singer and composer Suzanna Owiyo was born and raised in Kenya's Luo ethnic community but has traveled and performed throughout Kenya, supporting women in their community music-making endeavors. Her current involvement with the Isukha women has seen her play not just the Luo *nyatiti* (a lyre with seven to eight strings and a large round resonating chamber), but also the *isikuti* drums of the Isukha people. Ms. Owiyo grew up listening to and watching her grandfather play the *nyatiti,* and she attributes her love of music to him. During her primary and secondary school years, she excelled in dance and music competitions and eventually made music her career. She began singing and playing the guitar at nightclubs and sought to meet members of community music groups. At first, her father was not pleased with her career decision and gave her no support, but this only fueled her determination to prove to herself and to her parents that she could succeed. Her cross-cultural musicianship has endeared her to the Kenyan public, as she has become one of Kenya's most celebrated community musicians.

Educational Goals and Musical Performance

Many songs sung during *isikuti* community sessions are songs of praise or commemoration of specific social events or seasons. If dances are held during the rainy season, the female soloists begin with an interlude of praise to the supernatural powers for the rain and ask the gods to protect the land from floods. At harvest time, women compose songs to thank the gods for the good crops. For other festivities, songs and dances begin by praising warriors for jobs well done, such as fighting a village enemy. In most of these instances, the women in the Isukha tribe are the main composers of these songs.

The traditional or tribal Isukha society expected women to be significant wage earners in the family. They labored in farming, fishing, poetry, commerce, and textile production while composing songs. These songs were later taken by the men for stage and community performances. The educational role assumed by women in Africa has underpinned the continued contribution of songs and dances by women in the Isukha community. By and large, these expectations conform to cultural goals for female children, who are the custodians of informal education in Africa.

Non-formal education, whose main medium of communication is through song and community music, is aimed at

- developing the child's latent physical skills for honest labor;
- developing character;
- inculcating respect for elders and authority figures;
- developing intellectual skills;
- developing a sense of belonging and participation in community building; and
- promoting cultural heritage.

The role of non-formal education led to increased socio-economic freedom where women could earn meager incomes as musicians to help support their families. This was much different from many western societies, especially at the beginning of the nineteenth century, when women had to fight for their right to gainful employment in white-collar jobs. Kenya, in particular, has progressed in terms of promoting gender equity from independence to the present day. This is reflected in Census Bureau data (KIHBS, 2005/6, pp. 9–11) that show women as major contributors to family income. The census found that female-headed households accounted for 33 percent of the nation's total, while 89 percent of the female population was in the labor force. According to the 2006 Report on National Policy on Gender and Development, women make up 52 percent of Kenya's population, with over 80 percent living in rural areas, and the majority engaging in cash-crop farming, livestock cultivation, and agricultural-based income initiatives.

Music Composed by Women

Songs for harvest and thanksgiving have been mainly composed by women. In the early part of the century, when modern health care was far from reach, midwives who helped deliver children in rural homes composed songs that are still performed in the community to help babies and their mothers in labor. Such songs have come to form the repertoire of the childbirth songs for the *isikuti* dance ensembles. Ironically, even though the bulk of the repertoire is composed by women (songs for working on the farm, fetching firewood and water, initiating their daughters into womanhood), the men take the credit. A good example is Ingosi Mwoshi, an *isikuti*

Figure 5.1.   Mwana Wa Mberi.
Transcribed by David Akombo.

performer born in 1939 in the Tiriki village of western Kenya. Mwoshi is praised for composing much of *isikuti* music for the public despite the fact that some of the music was actually composed by women. Mwoshi's unique style of contemporary *isikuti* storytelling spans more than four decades and has made him Kenya's best known neo-traditional griot. His most popular song, "*Mwana Wa Mberi Ni Shikhoy-elo* (The First Born Is an Apron)," is the quintessential birthday song for the entire Luhya tribe of western Kenya. But this call-and-response song was actually composed by the wife of Matasiyo, an elder in the Isukha community, who dedicated it to the first child in that community.

Customarily, Isukha women are not permitted to play the musical instruments they might choose because the instruments in an *isikuti* ensemble are gender-coded. For example, the *isikuti* (big drum) is considered to be a male drum and therefore can only be played by a male. As in other African traditions, the *isikuti* ensemble is a metaphor for the Isukha household, where the male is the head of the household as the *isikuti* drum is the head of the *isikuti* ensemble. The *isikuti ikhasi* (female drum) complements the *isikuti* drum as the wife supports the husband within the marriage and the family. As children bring vitality and joy to the family, the *isikuti mwana* (baby drum), or *mutindi*, not only marks the meter but also maintains the tempo that drives the entire *isikuti* dance. Even though there is a female drum in the ensemble (*isikuti ikhasi*), it is played by a male drummer. Women are considered the fragrance of the dance, and the female's role is to enhance the aesthetic value of the ritual, bringing sexuality to the dance, through innuendo and imagery, that is viewed as signs of fertility. In this regard, the female role is to choreograph the dance and musically vocalize poems, transforming them into song.

In Luhya mythology, it is disrespectful for a woman to perform with male musicians on fiddles and percussion. Even though these instruments perform a "feminine" role in the dance ensemble by producing lyrical, feminine melodies over undulating male drum patterns, this prohibition is still in force.

Isikuti community music is also performed during bullfights. In the bullfight dance, the women sing as the men send the bulls to war. The men play the *isikuti* drums while the women sing and dance, and the ritual is incomplete without the participation of women.

Conclusion

The role of women in the *isikuti* community music is of paramount importance. The Isukha people of Kenya have preserved the traditional role of women in community music-making endeavors despite the influence of Christian missionaries in the early twentieth century. It is clear that women have traditionally played a major role in the musical life of the Isukha people. They have not only composed dance songs, but they have also been the bedrock upon which the philosophical principles of *isikuti* community music are founded. Even though their role in community music is not usually openly acknowledged, women are indispensable in the *isikuti* dance; the music-making traditions of the Isukha people of Kenya depend upon the contributions they make.

NOTE

1. *Zemenawi* is defined as music that contains Western and Latin elements, in the form of musical instruments and rhythms.

BIBLIOGRAPHY

Adagala, K. (1992). Mother nature, patriarchal cosmology & gender. In E.M. Gilbert (Ed.), *God, humanity & mother nature,* (Nairobi, pp. 47–65). Kenya: Masaki Publishers.

Adegbite, A. (1988). The drum and its role in Yoruba religion. *Journal of religion in Africa,18,* 15–26.

Aidoo, A. A. (1981). Asante queen mothers in government and politics in the nineteenth century. In F. Steady (Ed.), *The black woman cross-culturally.* Cambridge: MA: Schenckman Publishing Co.

Anti, K. K. A. (1978). *The relationship between the supreme being and the lesser gods of the Akan* (Unpublished master's thesis). University of Ghana, Legon.

Appiah, P. (1979). Akan symbolism. *African arts, 13* (1), 64–67.

Arhin, K. (1983) The political and military roles of Akan women. In C. Oppong (Ed.), *Female and male in West Africa.* London: George Unwin & Allen.

Awolalu, J. O. (1972). The African view of man. *Orita 6,* 108–116.

Danquah, J. B. (1968). *The Akan doctrine of God.* New York, NY: Humanities Press, Inc.

Dimandja, A. (2004). *The role and place of women in Sub-Saharan African societies.* Retrieved from www.globalaging.org/elderrights/world/2004/subsaharan.htm

Eliade, M. (1957). *The sacred and the profane.* (W. Trask, Trans). New York: Harcourt, Brace & World.

Eliade, M. (1987). *Encyclopedia of religion* (vol. 8). New York: Collier MacMillan.

Idowu, E. B. (1962). *God in Yoruba belief.* London: Longmans.

Idowu, E. B. (1973). *African traditional religion, a definition.* London: S.C.M.

KIHBS (2005/2006). Kenya integrated household budget survey. Retrieved from www.knbs .or.ke/pdf/basic%20(revised%20edition)pdf

Montagu, A. (1957). *Man: His first two million years.* New York, NY: Dell Publishing Company.

Nketia, K. (1962a). The problem of meaning in African music. *Ethnomusicology 6* (1), 17.

Nketia, K. (1962b). *African music in Ghana: A survey of traditional forms.* Accra, Ghana: William Clowes & Sons Limited.

Nketia, K. (1979). *The music of Africa.* London: Victor Gollancz Ltd.

Rassam, A. (1984). *Women in the Arab world.* London: UNESCO, Frances Pinter.

Schwartz, P., Patterson, D., & Steen, S. (1995). The dynamics of power: Money and sex in intimate relationships. In P. J. Kalbfleisch & M. J. Cody (Eds.), *Gender, power, and communication in human relationships* (pp. 253–274). Hillsdale, NJ: Lawrence Erlbaum Associates.

Senoga-Zake, G. (1986). *Folk music of Kenya.* Nairobi: Uzima Press.

Sharkey, H. (2002). Religion in colonial Africa. *The Daily Pennsylvanian.* Retrieved from www.dailypennsylvanian.com/node/27491

Chapter Six

Community Music in Australia and New Zealand Aotearoa

Brydie-Leigh Bartleet, Shelley Brunt,
Anja Tait, and Catherine Threlfall

This chapter explores themes arising from diverse examples of community music making in the neighboring Pacific nations of Australia and New Zealand Aotearoa. These nations are located in the Australasian region of the southern hemisphere and are characterized by geographical isolation and cultural diversity. Almost 25 percent of Australia's population of more than twenty-two million people were born overseas and hail from two hundred different countries (Australian Bureau of Statistics [ABS], 2006). Just under 20 percent of New Zealand Aotearoa's population of four million people were born overseas (Statistics New Zealand, 2002), and both countries have significant Indigenous populations. In 2006, 2.4 percent of the population identified as Indigenous Australians of Aboriginal or Torres Strait Islander heritage (ABS, 2006). The 2001 census in New Zealand found that one in seven New Zealanders were of Maori ancestry (Statistics New Zealand, 2002). With this cultural diversity, community music in Australia and New Zealand is always "situated, contested, contingent," and difficult to reduce to any single definition (Elliott, Higgins, & Veblen, 2008, p. 3). These differences arise because community music (and its variations) is a complex phenomenon that is evoked and defined based upon the presence or absence, interpretation, and weight of a number of different elements (Mason, 2000, p. 19). Within the Australian and New Zealand context, common themes are found throughout the diverse range of community music activities in this region.

SITUATING COMMUNITY MUSIC

Within Australia and New Zealand, community music is widely acknowledged as a group activity where people join together to actively participate in the music-making process. Musical interactions include playing, listening, watching, moving, creating, and recording. Other interactions involve community members who provide the physical, human, and social resources (Tait & Falk, 2004) that enable community music making. Within this region, community music encompasses a wide and diverse range of cultural traditions, musical genres, and practices, which reflect and enrich the cultural lives of the participants and their broader communities.[1] These activities are reflective of a geographical community, a community of interest, or an imagined community (Anderson, 1991) and involve complex webs, networks, or pathways through which music making happens in person or online.

This chapter presents three case studies from the region: Sound Links (an Australian nationwide community music research initiative); ArtStories (in the remote Northern Territory); and the Cuba Street Carnival (Wellington, New Zealand).

Three common themes emerge from these very different stories: place-making, social inclusion, and inspired and inspiring individuals. Place-making is important as community music making is deeply connected to people and places as well as to the relationships and interactions between locations and communities of people. Closely related to the concept of place-making is the notion of social inclusion. The invitation to be involved in community music is inclusive of individuals, families, groups, organizations and communities, and people of all ages, cultures, and abilities. Inclusion is a widely upheld and celebrated value of community music making, and a commitment to social inclusion can be found at the heart of each of the three case studies discussed in this chapter. The work of inspired and inspiring individuals underpins these two themes. Individuals work with communities, often against considerable odds, to create and realize visions of vibrant musical communities by seeking out, recognizing, and nurturing the involvement and social cooperation of other energetic and passionate music makers. These three themes are the foundation of the activities featured in this chapter and, more broadly, reflect the unique elements of the community music practices of this region.

CASE STUDIES

Case Study One: Australia (Sound Links)

> As I sit in my demountable cabin in Borroloola's caravan park and reflect on my day of research activities, I can't help but notice the red dirt still stuck to the soles of my feet. It feels like a symbol of the remote Indigenous community in which I find myself, and I like the mark that it leaves on me. I decide to not wash it off tonight. Today, I received my Aboriginal skin name, Nungarrima. My marruwarra, the senior law and culture woman, gave me this name when my colleague Liz and I visited her and a group of women singers and dancers. Suddenly, the ways in which I am able to relate to the women in this community have changed. I seem to be related to everyone! This forces me to think about concepts of community, community music, relationships, and kinship anew. As I sat under the trees talking and eating with these women, I came to understand that, in this Australian context, concepts of community and community music cannot be separated from relationships, kinship, the land, and the spirit world. I thought that I knew what community music was before I came into this setting, but now, I'm not so sure. As I sit in my cabin and reflect on what I have just experienced, I realize that, up until now, my ideas of community music have been formed by Westernized notions of music-making (Adapted from Bartleet, fieldnotes, April 25, 2008).

This fieldwork experience emerged from the nationwide study known as Sound Links. Its goal was to understand the dynamics of community music in Australia and the models it represents for music learning and teaching in formal and informal settings.[2] For this project, the research team traveled to six diverse case study locations and interviewed and observed more than four hundred participants. These communities included a middle-class suburban location (Dandenong Ranges, Victoria), a large established regional city (Albany, Western Australia), a small rural town (McLaren Vale, South Australia), a culturally diverse urban city (Fairfield City, New South Wales), a remote Indigenous setting (Borroloola, Northern Territory), and an urban Indigenous setting (Inala, Queensland). An additional two hundred participants also contributed to a nationwide survey on the topic. The interviews, observations, and survey uncovered a revealing picture of musical activity in Australia which, previously, had hardly been visible outside the circles of its participants (Bartleet, 2008).

Sound Links provides insight into the dynamics of community music across Australia. Research at the Dandenong Ranges Music Council (DRMC), for instance, yields a vibrant model for creative and innovative community partnerships, both through the DRMC's ongoing activities and their successful school-community collaborations, which occur on both an everyday level and a flagship level. Our time in Albany provides valuable understanding of how community music operates in an Australian regional city. A striking community mindedness in this regional center has engendered a commitment to participating in and supporting community music making. The McLaren Vale case study provides a practical model of how a school-initiated community music program can take shape. The local Tatachilla Lutheran College nurtures a number of vibrant school-community collaborations that show a commitment to intergenerational learning and, in turn, enhance the school's curriculum and students' learning experiences.

The research in Fairfield City examines how community music programs operate in a culturally diverse urban location in Australia. In this case study, there is compelling evidence to document the connectivity between community music and cultural identity, particularly in migrant communities. In Borroloola, the research identifies how community music operates in a remote Indigenous context. These revealed notions of culture, kinship, and the land are deeply connected to Indigenous concepts of community and, by extension, community music. In Inala, Stylin'UP, a community-driven program strongly supported by a local council, engages young Indigenous people in an urban context and allows them to feel pride in their cultural identity.

Each of the six case studies represented very different circumstances and environments, and the characteristics of the community music activities were unique to their specific participants, facilitators, sites, contexts, aims, and infrastructure. However, strongly shared underlying characteristics of nine domains link the disparate community music activities observed across the country: infrastructure; organization and leadership; visibility and public relations; relationship to place; social engagement; support and networking; dynamic music making; engaging pedagogy and facilitation; and links to school (Bartleet et al., 2009).

Place-making is an essential component of many Australian localities. A striking example of this aspect of community is evident in the Dandenong Ranges, where the local music council is committed to developing projects, such as fire prevention, water conservation, local tourist attractions, and events for well-known poets and composers, that focus on issues that have significant local interest and deep connections to place. For example, in 2006, the Composers Connecting Community project involved more than four hundred schoolchildren in workshops and a performance of a suite, written by local composer Dr. Calvin Bowman, consisting of seven songs based on text from C. J. Dennis' (an acclaimed Australian poet who lived in the Dandenong Ranges) *A Book for Kids.* This project gave students and community members the opportunity to work with a living composer and gave them insights into the compositional process. In addition, the project reintroduced the works of C. J. Dennis to a new generation of readers. Teachers from local schools integrated this project into their music curricula. Bev McAlister, executive officer of the Dandenong Ranges Music Council, reflected on the importance of this work:

> The philosophy, I think, is about creating the opportunity for people of all ages and abilities to make music. And for music to be performed and integrated into the lifestyle of the community. And then the other part of that is in partnership with the local music teachers and schools and the professionals that actually live here so that we create work for them. (personal communication, September 14, 2007)

Alongside place-making, social engagement is also widely considered to be at the heart of many community music activities in Australia. Indeed, inclusion is one of the most widely upheld values, extending to those at the margins of society. In Fairfield City there is a strong connection between local musicians' social engagement and cultural identities and their chosen community music activities. Many people speak of the ways that music gives people, young and old, a means to express their cultural identity and feel pride about who they are and where they come from. Ramphay Chittasy, from the local Lao Temple Wat Phrayortkeo Dhammayanaram, puts this into perspective:

> In the Western society people are always rushing, but when we come here to the temple, the young people learn about being graceful. The minute they put the costume on, they don't run anymore . . . and they learn how to move their fingers to go along with the music, so it all synchronizes, the teacher, the drum, everything, the music, girls, and boys. It brings out the spirit of the music, and you can feel it with goose bumps, you know. It brings back something from our country, which is really needed. When you go out and say, "Where are you from?" I say, "I'm from Laos, and I'm very proud that we have something to treasure." (personal communication, February 21, 2007)

Some of the most vibrant community groups in Fairfield speak about their organizations in familial terms, discussing the ways in which a sense of social engagement, cultural community, and family is nurtured through making music together. Many of these community music groups, such as the Yauguru Uruguayan Drumming group, provide traditional food for their members, and this adds a social aspect to the rehearsals. Members of Yauguru describe the communality of their group:

> It's just a big family. We're all just a big family. We all care for one another. We go out on the weekend or whatever and . . . if people from our group are at the same club we all take care of each other and if one is in trouble we all go and say, "Are you all right?"

It's all a big family. If you have problems you just go to Anna . . . and they all advise, "When I was young!" [Everyone laughs.] (personal communication, February 20, 2008)

When the community musicians in this study were asked to enumerate the factors that contribute to the vibrancy of their activities, the first response was often a description of the inspiring leadership of an individual community musician or educator who directs the activity with which they are involved, referring to the person's leadership capabilities, musical and administrative expertise, pedagogical skills, inspiration, or encouragement. The most respected community music leaders show a deep understanding of how music connects people not only in their own groups, but also within the broader community. This is strikingly shown in McLaren Vale in the guidance of community music leader Greg John, head of Performing Arts at Tatachilla Lutheran College. His learning and teaching philosophy, which is centered on community engagement and intergenerational interactions, plays a significant role in all the music activities he leads:

It's about community building and relationship building and the underpinning thing in all of this is . . . the music . . . The thread that goes through all this community building around here, where you can get people from the stiff accountant through to the hippie performing together, from an 87-year-old to a 13-year-old, and the little kids and the mums and dads performing with each other and cheering and saying, "Isn't this wonderful?" and seeing where they can go . . . all of that is only possible because of the music. I don't know any other medium that could do it. (personal communication, December 9, 2007)

A leader such as Greg John is deeply attuned to the unique needs and concerns of the people in his or her local area and has an overarching vision of how music can assist his or her community to grow. These are highly creative people who have the ability to find a multitude of ways to engage people in music.

As the Sound Links study shows, community music is a vibrant and widespread phenomenon in Australia. In each of the settings, loose but effective community music structures and practices have evolved. These practices have almost always been led by visionary individuals committed to nurturing a strong sense of place-making and social engagement and to structuring activities that are highly responsive to change, challenges, and opportunities.

Case Study Two: Northern Territory (ArtStories)

The Northern Territory (NT) is one of six states and two territories in Australia. The capital city of the Northern Territory is Darwin, the most northern city in Australia, with a population of more than 120,000 people. It has close geographical proximity to Southeast Asia and is a strategic defense location.

The Top End is the most northern part of the Northern Territory. It is both multicultural and multilingual, with more than fifty Indigenous Australian languages and more than sixty migrant languages spoken. For more than 30 percent of children ages five to seventeen, the home language is not English. Almost 45 percent of Northern Territory school-age students identify as Aboriginals or Torres Strait Islanders (i.e.,

Indigenous Australians), and more than half of the schools in the Northern Territory are located in remote areas.

Some remote Indigenous communities have acknowledged third and fourth world conditions of housing, sanitation, and nutrition, while other communities are recognized centers of culture and innovation in two-way education, health and well-being, and arts practice. The Top End is the wet/dry tropics, and for at least six months of the year, travel to many remote school communities in the Northern Territory is only possible by single-engine light aircraft or off-road vehicles. Schools experience a high turnover of staff and must contend with limited resources. The Northern Territory has the lowest English literacy and numeracy levels in Australia.

The Northern Territory population is highly mobile, with short-term government contracts common for large numbers of defense personnel and public servants in health, education, and infrastructure. The Aboriginal population, too, is highly mobile, responsive to family and cultural obligations that may require travel throughout the region. The transient nature of the Northern Territory population in urban, rural, and remote areas adds complexity to both workplaces and schools. Across the Northern Territory, music is valued as a medium for personal and cultural expression and renewal, a conduit for learning, and a pathway to employment in the music industry (Hesser & Heinemann, 2010, p. 85).

Arising from this intricate mixture of cultures and peoples, a participatory educational research study was conceived by Anja Tait. Tait then collaborated with Catherine Threlfall and Edel Musco to design and deliver what came to be known as ArtStories. Tait, Threlfall, and Musco are qualified primary teachers (elementary school), with broad experiences in Indigenous education. Musco is a literacy specialist and visual artist, while Tait and Threlfall are registered music therapists, music educators, and community musicians. All three practitioner-researchers work and live in the Northern Territory of Australia. ArtStories began as an arts-based response to teachers asking for support to make learning purposeful for disengaged students, and policy-driven demands that students attain academic benchmarks on a par with their same-age peers across the nation.

ArtStories emerged in five urban, rural, and remote schools as a participatory educational research initiative lasting from January 2006 to December 2008. ArtStories demonstrates the point where community music, music therapy, and education intersect, collide, and are ultimately bound together. New learnings, ideas, and concepts emerge at this nexus of education, therapy, and community practice and practitioners, who include and involve people in their local community. ArtStories has influenced practice in many more schools as well as in health and community settings throughout the Top End of the Northern Territory.

ArtStories became a model of transdisciplinary practice characterized by intergenerational involvement and learning with the arts. It remains a framework for participatory arts-based initiatives in educational, health, and community settings, where participants create and tell stories of self, family, community, and dreams. ArtStories practitioners are drivers of change within schools, communities, and workplaces, advocating, modeling, and celebrating the impact of learning and involvement with the arts. ArtStories' four core principles are:

1. Connecting people, ideas, and purpose
2. Sharing stories of people, place, and practice
3. Exploring the past, the present, and future possibilities
4. Being inventive and open to learning from the unexpected (ArtStories website)

Each manifestation of ArtStories' work is visibly different and responsive to place, with its practice and practitioners continually adapting to context but sharing essential elements. ArtStories is a model of practice led by inspired and inspiring individuals who promote social inclusion, specific to place. In each iteration, ArtStories provides a framework for practice rather than a prescription for action. Lead practitioners locate community members who display energy and drive and then provide the impetus, support, or provocation that guides these people's energy, skills, and knowledge to include and involve everyone around them.

What follows are two examples of practice that demonstrate ArtStories' core principles in a community music context. The first takes place in a special needs setting in Darwin. The second is located in a remote Indigenous community education center in Arnhem Land.

The story of Christine Carrigg, a teacher in a secondary special school in the regional city of Darwin, demonstrates how practitioners can work together to enable community music making in a school context.

> In the humid heat of midday, kids and staff wander out of their classrooms for lunch break. A smiling woman sings rhythmic dance tunes as she leads a young man into the leafy yard. He energetically waves his arms to the beat and picks up the melody in his feet. A group of teenage boys sit glued to a portable stereo booming out reggae, singing and daring each other to beat box. A young girl places her ears and head on the speaker amidst the boys, feeling the vibrations through her skull. They share her pleasure and comment to the teacher on duty about her enjoyment of the music. A teenage boy, recently arrived from a bush community, loudly drums a strong rock rhythm on the ramp handrail. In the shade of the mahogany trees, a student seeking solitude sits, humming quietly. The teacher walking past briefly joins the song and then wanders to the next group of students. Music is the life-blood of this school. (personal communication, 2011)

Henbury School is a government secondary school for students with disabilities, located in Darwin in the tropical north of Australia. The school serves seventy-seven special needs students, ages twelve to eighteen, with a main campus for high-support students, four outreach classrooms in mainstream secondary schools, and a school opportunity shop- and work-training center. An ArtStories lead practitioner, Catherine Threlfall, was employed in 2008 at Henbury School as a special education teacher. At this time, as teacher Christine Carrigg explains, music was not central to teaching and learning.

> Music was widely regarded as being something that happened on one-off occasions, such as school assemblies or end-of-year productions. Music was otherwise delivered by visiting music teachers. While these visits were entertaining, they didn't create ongoing opportunities to build further student learning. (personal communication, 2011)

Christine wanted Henbury School to be a musical place where music making was inclusive of the whole school community.

> I began to dream that Henbury School could become a place where music and the arts flourished, where students with high-support needs especially, had teachers with the skill base to prioritize music and the arts in their education. I hoped for . . . better working relationships among staff as we learned and had fun together. To perhaps break down the sense of isolation and insulation which had developed. (personal communication, 2011)

The success of any community music activity depends, in large part, on the presence of an inspired and inspiring individual. Two important challenges, professional isolation and the lack of opportunity for ongoing musical life, provided Christine with the impetus to emerge as an inspired and inspiring individual in the school community. With support, encouragement, a partner in risk taking, and some provocation, Christine was able to include and involve the whole school community, people of all ages and abilities, in creating a musical place.

Key to Christine's approach were the staff learning opportunities offered early in the process. Funds from the Australian Government Quality Teaching Program were used to involve all staff in seminars, workshops, arts experiences, and creating shared resources for classrooms. School staff requested arts learning groups—guitar, dance, singing, sewing, scrapbooking, watercolors, and mosaics. High-quality instruments were purchased, and teaching artists found from within and outside of the school community to share their knowledge and skills. Once staff members were included and started to become involved, other enthusiasts emerged and became deeply involved in the transformation of the school as a musical place.

With energy, commitment, and encouragement from Christine, music began to creep into the daily life of the school. Christine inspired others by her example, which included guitar playing, drumming, and singing as part of her daily routines in and outside the classroom. She also introduced music at break times. A CD player, microphone, and instruments were supplied at recess and lunch times, acting as a key point of contact.

Staff with musical skills were invited into classrooms to share their musical ideas and repertoire. The sounds of sing-along tunes such as "In the Jungle" and students crooning along to the blues were heard around the school. Dance, theater, and musical artists were invited to work on a weekly basis in classrooms across the school, including a class of boys at risk of leaving school, learning, and jamming to electric guitar, bass, and drum kit and inclusive drumming circles for students and staff. Due to the tireless, inspirational action of Ms. Carrigg, community music thrived at the school.

Community music activities here were also characterized by place-making. As Henbury School's musical sense of identity grew, the school community began to reach out to the Darwin community's musical life. Christine and her class of young men (with a range of significant disabilities that included autism, Down syndrome, sensory integration disorder, and intellectual disabilities) performed in the 2009 Darwin Festival. They shared a homegrown blend of striking vocals, wild instrumental sounds, and songs composed by Indigenous students with the Darwin community. Henbury students also joined with eight hundred other young voices for a performance at Parliament House. The music created and confidently shared by students and staff in these extracurricular performances not only demonstrated the uniquely inclusive nature of this school community but also enabled young people with disabilities and their supporters to find a place in the broader Darwin community.

Community music activities are underpinned by strong principles of social inclusion. Christine began her journey with a strong vision of complete inclusion of the whole school community, regardless of ability. The validity of this approach was epitomized when a young percussionist was recruited to work as a casual assistant at the school. Christine recognized and nurtured his musical and leadership abilities, encouraging him to create and lead a large African drumming group that included staff and students with a diverse range of abilities, including those with very high-support needs:

> This young man . . . helped to consolidate our musical community. It was an exciting year for us. We became the H Berries and began to be asked to perform both within the school and at special functions to promote our school. (personal communication, 2011)

The H Berries became the bellwether of true inclusion for the school, performing an intoxicating blend of African rhythms, hip-hop sounds, and wild, improvised vocals. Christine's vision of breaking down barriers between staff members and between students of differing abilities was realized through everyday shared music making, both within and outside the classrooms, as part of the teaching and learning process at the school. The dynamic combination of an inspired and inspiring individual, place-making, and social inclusion enabled the transformation of the school into a musical place. As an ArtStories lead practitioner, Ms. Catherine Threlfall recognized Christine as an inspired and inspiring individual in the community whose passion and energy to make a musical place included every individual, regardless of ability. Christine clearly describes this metamorphosis:

> Changes in the use of music for learning since then have been phenomenal! Teachers are now much more likely to work together, whereas before they would not have foreseen a way to successfully combine their classes. Making music together has provided that context . . . Making music together has given us a way to engage both staff and students in learning while embracing our individual differences. Students have blossomed over time; THEY know THEY make the music. Some are less engaged than others, but they have learned it's OK to participate when they are ready and in the meantime to remain with us in our music circle. Others have grasped the chance to perform or to lead within a piece. We all experienced a lot of fun and shared moments of sheer joy every time we played together. (personal communication, 2011)

Christine's story illustrates the impact of an ArtStories lead practitioner who works with a classroom teacher without fanfare or fuss. The confidence and competencies of Christine, the classroom teacher, increased over time until she too was inviting others to be included and involved in new initiatives. This professional development was not necessarily visible to Christine, but in this way, she became visible in the school community as an inspired and inspiring practitioner.

While Christine's experience at the Henley School emphasizes the contribution of an inspired and inspiring individual in a special education teaching environment, the purpose of ArtStories, located in a remote community in Arnhem Land, is to support the revitalization of an Indigenous language. This practice example illuminates a lead practitioner surrendering the boundaries of an initial vision in a rich collaboration involving community members across gender, generation, and culture.

> In this indigenous community, the rhythm of life is palpable. Life is lived outdoors. Music wafts and sometimes blasts onto the street through the open doors and windows of people's homes. Opportunities for education through music are a part of life and embraced by community members, from the elders to babies carried on their mothers' hips. (Tait et al., 2010, p. 137)

In ArtStories, early childhood teachers, teacher-linguists, music educators, community linguists, and local musicians collaborate to design and deliver an arts-based bilingual language and culture program. Together, the program leaders identified target language and cultural knowledge about kinship, nutrition, health, and well-being that skipped generations of young Indigenous Australians in the region. To invite people in a remote Aboriginal community, across gender, generation, and culture, to be included and involved in a shared community music initiative is a risk.

Over time, a diverse but inclusive group of practitioners gained the confidence of the community and collaboratively designed and produced inventive audiovisual materials that bring together Indigenous and non-Indigenous ways of teaching and learning. At the local school, ArtStories was embedded within both the language revitalization program and the daily early childhood bilingual literacy program. An impact evaluation conducted by Slee (2008) reported that ArtStories became an important part of students' literacy learning and that this successful pedagogical approach should become part of Northern Territory school curricula.

In this remote community, ArtStories continues to be supported and led by the passion and commitment of an inspired and inspiring individual: a senior Aboriginal woman[3] who is a community linguist and Indigenous language teacher and an active musician and composer of songs and chants. She is committed to working with young children so they will have a strong foundation in language and culture. In specially composed chants and songs, the stress, rhythm, intonation, and phrasing of language is learned and anticipated through repetition—in both English and Indigenous languages. The music and lyrics are original. Some of the material is sung or chanted acappella and accompanied by body percussion, while other songs are arranged as energetic Indigenous rock backed by contemporary guitar, bass, drums, and keyboards.

ArtStories has produced two CDs and a DVD of original songs with video narratives to aid in teaching language and culture to children and families. All materials are created and produced by community members onsite and distributed to families in the community. These and other creative outcomes, such as publications, community exhibitions, and performances form an important part of an ongoing local community culture. This process of language revitalization brings together community members across gender, generation, and culture. ArtStories is a potent example of social inclusion and place-making which has grown independently of the creator of the original idea.

ArtStories practitioners continue to be included and involved in professional extension activities such as joint presentations and co-authorship of publications (Musco

& Tait, 2005; Tait & Murrungun, 2008; Tait et al., 2010). There are now many ArtStories lead practitioners who contribute to a web of interactions, ideas, and actions. Community music initiatives become self-sustaining when the body of people involved share the responsibility of acting on the shared ideas. ArtStories is a community of interest and practice that has become self-sustaining because it is flexible, inventive, and responsive to context.

Case Study Three: New Zealand Aotearoa (The Cuba Street Carnival)

Community musicians, ensembles, and events occupy an important place in the vibrant musical landscape of New Zealand Aotearoa. Although this small country is geographically isolated, its proximity to neighboring Australia, Fiji, Samoa, Tonga, and other Pacific Islands has resulted in a unique cross-fertilization of musical ideas, practices, and expressions of culture. Music spawned outside this region has also surged into the New Zealand Aotearoa archipelago through the global process of cultural flow (Appadurai, 1996) and traveled with migrants as aural memory, notated scores, instrumental practices, and traditions. This mélange has resulted in a burgeoning multiculturalism in New Zealand Aotearoa (Johnson & Moloughney, 2006) despite its government-sanctioned status as a bi-cultural nation of Maori (traditional land owners) and *pakeha* ("others," or white Europeans residing in New Zealand Aotearoa).

Even a cursory glance at community music making in New Zealand Aotearoa (Keam & Mitchell, 2011; Johnson, 2010) reveals the diversity of musics and cultural groups within this nation. New Zealand Aotearoa's ethnic communities often find expression through musical performance, ranging from weekly impromptu folk gigs by Irish immigrants in rural bars to highly organized Cantonese karaoke-style song performances during Chinese New Year celebrations in major cities. Community music making is not, however, limited to groups united by culture. It also extends to citizens wanting, for example, to learn new instruments by playing in local guitar ensembles or to school students jamming on ukuleles. Indeed, community music making in New Zealand Aotearoa varies based upon a variety of factors:

- the geographical location of performances (North Island, South Island; urban or rural),
- the physical location (indoor or outdoor),
- the audience (attending a private or public event),
- the degree of organization of the performances (informal, planned, impromptu),
- the structure of the performance group (self-governed or externally regulated),
- the links with educational institutions (universities, polytechnics, colleges, or schools), and
- the links with cultural institutions (embassies, trusts, etc).

Perhaps the best understanding of community music in New Zealand Aotearoa can be gained through an investigation of the Cuba Street Carnival, hailed as the nation's largest community music festival. This event features community musicians performing alongside professionals. Food and craft stalls, art displays, roving buskers, and a night parade, all taking place indoors and outdoors in the city's streets (which are closed to traffic for the carnival), create a festive atmosphere. Since 1999, the Cuba Street Carnival has been formally staged in the Cuba Street precinct in the city of Wellington—the nation's capital located at the bottom of the North Island—although there have been several informal festivals held in the vicinity prior to this date. The longevity of this event is a testament to the precise planning undertaken by an inspiring leader, founder Chris Morley-Hall, his small team of workers, and their association with a board of trustees from a non-profit trust. A free event, the carnival relies on financial support from the Wellington City Council and several corporate sponsors.[4]

This event demonstrates a dynamic synergy, at a local level, between organizers, the council, corporate sponsors, performers, and audiences. Moreover, the carnival offers a unique illustration of the role of community music in New Zealand Aotearoa.

> Standing on the footpath of Cuba Street, pressed against a street barrier along with the rest of the crowd, I can hear the percussive sounds of Brazilian samba, droning Scottish bagpipes, and the bright melody of Caribbean steel drums well before I can see the musicians themselves. As the first of many spectacular illuminated floats turns the corner from Taranaki Street along with their accompanying musicians and dancers in bright costumes, the visual spectacle of the night parade also comes into view. The crowd cheers when glitter is thrown into the air. The sky is alight with fireworks, and the sounds of the Carnival continue to echo throughout Wellington's streets . . . (fieldnotes, February 21, 2009)

The Cuba Street Carnival allows community musicians to construct, negotiate, and maintain a sense of connection to place. For these musicians, place has multiple meanings, be it Cuba Street and its surrounding precinct, Wellington as a city, or, more broadly, the country of New Zealand Aotearoa. Cuba Street is a colorful, vibrant, hip area that is far removed, both physically and spiritually, from the serious end of town where Parliament resides. The street was named after an early settler ship (named after the island nation), and since the 2000s, the businesses in the precinct have adopted a "Cuba" branding. The popularity of cafés, bars, and pubs with Cuba-themed names such as "Fidel's Café" do not point to the presence of a Cuban migrant community; rather, they indicate a bohemian aesthetic inherent in the street. It is a zone where tattoo parlors stand alongside vintage clothing stores and trendy eateries, and artists, writers, musicians, and students congregate in a hub of creativity. Many Carnival musicians have emerged from this environment, and the Cuba Street precinct has become the prime location in which to hold an event. According to the Carnival founder, Chris Morley-Hall, the street has a remarkable status within Wellington:

> A street like Cuba Street is so unique . . . It's where new ideas, new designs, new concepts come out of. And it's often the place where the "creatives" hang out and treat as their sort of hub for collaborations and stuff. And so that's what Cuba Street is to Wellington. (personal communication, 2009)

The staging of musical events in this precinct has helped to solidify Cuba Street's identity. At the tenth anniversary Cuba Street Carnival in 2009, for example, there were ten outdoor stages located throughout the precinct, in neighboring streets and alleyways. Each stage was elevated and housed lighting rigs and professional sound systems. While the stages' main purpose was to group similar musicians together, many were given specific names that were in keeping with the Cuba Quarter's Latin American theme (Cuba Street Carnival, 2009). The "Havana Club Square" stage, for example, featured "music, mojitos, and all things Latin American" including the semi-professional Afro-Brazilian-influenced local band Zirigidum. Other stages, such as the smaller "Zeal Street Culture Stage," specialized in "Wellington's hottest up-and-coming acts," such as the Charm School Rejects, the Stray Dogs, and the Pawn Shoppe Boys, many of which featured teenagers in rock bands from local high schools. The largest stage at the Carnival held place of pride in a vacant single-level car park on Cuba Street among a flock of cafés and bars. Called the "Cuba St. Main Stage," it primarily featured established acts from the city's close-knit music scene. In 2009, one such group was the Wellington International Ukulele Orchestra, a popular music ensemble that formed following friendly jam sessions at Wellington's Delux Café in 2005.

The geographical location of the stages was important in creating a sense of place at the Carnival. Stages were well-spaced throughout the streets, from the top of Cuba Street to the intersection of Cuba Mall and Manners Mall, to the far end of the Courtenay Place nightlife strip. Moving from one stage to the next provided an opportunity for audiences to take in new Carnival experiences, such as shopping at a clothing stall, pausing to join in a communal knitting project on Cuba Mall, or enjoying a theme-park ride at the fairgrounds on Ghuznee Street. Even if one's main objective was to see specific community bands performing on particular stages, the placement of the stages around Wellington ensured a fluid atmosphere of celebration that enabled fresh urban experiences in a city with which most attendees were already familiar. Indeed, the Cuba Street Carnival contributes toward the larger goal of marking Wellington as the center for creative and cultural activities in New Zealand. Indeed, this event, along with others in the city, has enabled the branding of Wellington as the "creative capital" and "culture capital" and "events capital" for tourists (Positively Wellington Tourism, n.d. and Wellington City Council, 2006). For residents, however, there is the more immediate goal of creating a vibrant and inclusive city. This intention is articulated in Wellington City Council's mission statement:

> . . . [by] developing closer partnerships with ethnic, religious and social communities, supporting their events, festivals, and visual and performing arts that reflect their traditions and diversity; encouraging greater tolerance and acceptance of difference and diversity; [and] recording the history of the city and community groups and sharing their stories. (Wellington City Council, 2006, p. 7)

The second theme of this chapter is social inclusion. An event such as the Cuba Street Carnival creates a socially welcoming environment for its participants, relying on the support of local networks to get off the ground. In the early years of the Carnival, support from local professional and creative networks and building and nurturing cooperative social relationships was crucial if the Carnival was to succeed. Bands were suggested by friends of friends, so there was a broad range of local, amateur, and semi-professional acts, such as the Roots Foundation Sound

System, Fat Freddy's Drop, and Crackheads. The early Carnivals were community-driven, rather than commercially driven, with the small amount of money raised to fund the project being used for hiring sound equipment and printing programs. As Morley-Hall notes: "Nobody got paid, but nobody seemed to worry as it was just great fun" (White, 2007, p. 24).

The Illuminated Night Parade—the grand finale of the Carnival—is a noteworthy example of social inclusion. This event is based on the South American carnival tradition and features a procession of community groups and musicians on purpose-made floats, marching through the street. In 1999, the first Parade was not organized in an especially strict manner but rather began with a "spontaneous collection of random individuals and community groups" who casually came to a Cuba Street café and began marching from there (MacDonald, 2007, WM4). It was not a matter of delineating the kinds of musicians or musics that were sought for the Carnival; it was simply a case of finding "any friend of a friend of a friend that could play an instrument" (MacDonald, 2007, WM4). This approach to enlisting performers is less concerned with quality control than encouraging a sense of inclusiveness that was already present in the creative world of Cuba Street in 1999 (and, arguably, remains so today). The fact that there is no admission fee to the Carnival underscores this explicit sense of community building. Morley-Hall is well aware that keeping the event free helps to build a sense of place for the attendees and the performers:

> [Keeping the Carnival free] means you have the total spectrum of a society or a community who attend . . . And it's so obvious that you would want to allow as many of those community groups to have an involvement in it. And the more that take ownership and say "Yes, we really want to be part of this," then that's good. (C. Morley-Hall, personal communication, 2009)

Indeed, the long-term involvement in the Carnival by some of Wellington's community music groups means that, according to Morley-Hall, "the ownership of Carnival is being taken over by the community" (personal communication, 2009). One such community group is Wellington Batucada, a Brazilian samba percussion ensemble that formed in November 2001 expressly to perform in the Cuba Street Carnival's Illuminated Night Parade. Since then, the group has performed in the Carnival five times (in 2002, 2004, 2005, 2007, and 2009) and has developed its own sound to reflect the broad range of cultural and musical influences found in New Zealand Aotearoa. Composed mainly of New Zealanders, but featuring some Brazilian migrants, the group's participation makes an implicit connection between the Illuminated Night Parade and the competitive parades (*carnaval desfile*) between samba schools found in Brazil. Drawing its name from the rhythmic patterns (*batucadas*) played by samba school members (*sambistas*), the Wellington Batucada specialize in urban street band performance. The ensemble is a Cuba Street institution; their home is the community venue Thistle Hall on upper Cuba Street where their loud percussive beats can be heard as they rehearse on Sunday afternoons. This dedication is an integral part of their community spirit, as longtime member Gordon Cessford observes:

We're a community group, so we're all volunteers; we do it for fun. We are an incorporated society, so we're a bit organized, and we get funds for some of the events that we do. Some of them are band gigs, and then some of them are voluntary ones . . . just a freebie, we just do it for fun. And the whole thing is that it's a community group. (personal communication, 2011)

This attitude is in keeping with the formal vision of Wellington Batucada, which relies on a creating community and encouraging social inclusion for participants regardless of their musical ability. The group's goal is to:

continue the growth of Wellington Batucada, the samba percussion group dedicated to creating community through the learning and sharing of samba, [and] provide expertise, instruments and opportunities for anyone, regardless of experience, to learn and share percussion music. (Wellington Batucada, 2011)

This perspective goes beyond the immediate members of the group. Wellington Batucada see a broader role for the ensemble: to play a role in the musical soundscape of Wellington and educate New Zealanders about their music.

[Our vision is to] take our music to the street and stage so that musicians can experience performing and New Zealand audiences can experience the sound of samba, contribute to the arts and cultural scene in Wellington, and inject it with sound, color, and energy! (Wellington Batucada, 2011)

In recent years, the Wellington Batucada's regular involvement in the Parade has encouraged other community samba groups around New Zealand to participate. This has, in turn, broadened the scope of the Parade so that it is no longer solely about a particular street, or even the city of Wellington itself, but about representing the cultural and musical diversity of New Zealand.

The final theme to be considered here is that of inspired and inspiring individuals. Clearly, there are many individuals that play important roles in making the Carnival a success. These range from band managers to sound engineers to soloists to ensemble conductors and, most certainly, founder Chris Morley-Hall. While it is impossible to outline the importance of all of these individuals, one individual who has helped to bring a new dimension to the 2009 Carnival is Murali Kumar. Kumar acted as the curator of the Asian music stage known as the Asia Corner, which was a new addition to the 2009 Cuba Street Carnival.

Kumar's connections with the various communities, and his prior experience coordinating other Asian cultural events in Wellington, made him the perfect impresario to persuade performers to appear without performance fees, which was necessary for a free event such as the Carnival. Kumar also acted as MC, introducing each act and encouraging people passing by to stay and watch. Since the footpath only allowed a limited space for an audience of perhaps forty people to congregate, only the most experienced fans were able to glimpse the performances as they walked along Dixon Street in the steady stream of pedestrian traffic between Cuba Mall and Courtenay Place.

The Asia Corner performances were designed to display the cultural activities of communities from China, Korea, Vietnam, India, Thailand, and the Philippines.

Kumar's selections were based purely upon his contacts rather than an attempt to represent the full breadth of Wellington's Asian communities. The performances ranged from a Chinese lion dance and a traditional Filipino dance to an Indian woman singing along to a pre-recorded backing track (karaoke-style). The performances were billed on Kumar's makeshift signboard alongside the stage. To indicate the Asian countries they represented, most performers wore traditional clothing and sang in their native languages. The supportive, non-threatening environment meant that there was a diverse range of performance abilities, with some performers clearly singing off-the-cuff while others were well-rehearsed. The most formal demonstration was of samul'nori, a neo-traditional South Korean percussion genre, by the all-male ensemble Man-dang-ha-nu-ri as part of a collaborative sponsorship deal between the Korean Association in Wellington and the Korean Embassy. Although the performers themselves were Korean migrants from the Auckland area, their inclusion in the event was deemed an effective way of including the Wellington Korean community in the Carnival.

Unlike the other Carnival stages, which were all well-equipped, of considerable stature, and well-signed, the Asia Corner was a very small, knee-high stage positioned to the side of the street on the Dixon Street footpath. Aside from a diminutive PA system and a few microphones and stands, there was no signage or other indication that it was a formal component of the Carnival. The absence of a backstage area meant that performers and Kumar stood on the footpath and mingled with the crowd while they waited for their turns onstage. This was in keeping with the low-key ethos of the performance space that was designed for informal as well as formal performances by amateurs representing the various Asian communities of Wellington.

CONCLUSION

Even the brief survey presented in this chapter demonstrates the eclectic variety of community music initiatives in this geographical region. From the Sound Links program across Australia to the education-oriented ArtStories in the Northern Territory to the festive atmosphere of the urban Cuba Street Carnival in New Zealand Aotearoa, community music affects people's lives. In addition to being a joyful and creative activity, music making plays an essential part in the complex formation of individual and collective identities. For musicians (and even those who think of themselves as non-musicians), community music initiatives assist with this formation and serve to establish a sense of belonging within a group, a community, and a place. The three themes of place-making, social inclusion, and inspired and inspiring individuals demonstrate that community music is for all.

NOTES

1. Such ensembles are inclusive of, but are not limited to, large ensembles, music therapy programs, Indigenous Australian bands, contemporary Maori music groups, festivals, regional conservatoriums, country music clubs, samba schools, folk clubs, taiko drumming groups,

thistle pipe bands, hip-hop groups, studio recording projects, ukulele ensembles, and electro-acoustic music projects.

2. Sound Links was a project of Queensland Conservatorium Research Centre Griffith University in partnership with the Music Council of Australia, the Australian Music Association, and the Australian Society for Music Education. It was supported by the Australia Research Council's Linkage scheme. The research team for the project consisted of Professor Huib Schippers (Queensland Conservatorium Research Centre), Associate Professor Peter Dunbar-Hall (Sydney Conservatorium of Music), Dr. Richard Letts (Music Council of Australia), and Research Fellow Dr. Brydie-Leigh Bartleet (Queensland Conservatorium Research Centre).

3. Not named due to cultural protocols.

4. This has become an event that has battled a variety of logistical nightmares widely played out in the local media—from problems such as seeking resource consents for traffic management, rubbish removal, and public toilets from Wellington City Council to issues over the requested closure of State Highway One (a major arterial road intersecting Cuba Street) to concerns over pedestrian safety on Cuba Street to competing against Wellington's New Zealand International Arts Festival (Gruschow, 2002; Jacobson, 2003, 2004; Johnson, 2002a, 2002b; N.A., 1999b; Pierce, 1999). The issues faced by the Carnival have seen the event cancelled on more than one occasion so that the 2009 Carnival—on the occasion of its tenth anniversary—was actually only the seventh time it had been staged. These historical difficulties continue today with uncertainly remaining over financial support for the 2011 Carnival, possibly resulting in the cancellation of the event.

BIBLIOGRAPHY

Anderson, B. (1991). *Imagined communities: Reflections on the origin and spread of nationalism* (2nd ed.). London: Verso.

Appadurai, A. (1996). *Modernity at large: Cultural dimensions of globalization.* Minneapolis: University of Minnesota Press.

Art Stories, www.artstories.cdu.edu.au/

Australia Council. (2001). *Planning for the future: Issues, trends and opportunities for the arts in Australia.* Surrey Hills, NSW: Australia Council.

Australian Bureau of Statistics. (2006). *Cultural diversity overview.* Retrieved from www.ausstats.abs.gov.au/ausstats/subscriber.nsf/0/C724250359785DC6CA25754C0013DC0A/$File/20700_cultural_overview.pdf

Australian Bureau of Statistics. (2010). *Population clock.* Retrieved from www.abs.gov.au/AUSSTATS/abs@.nsf/Web+Pages/Population+Clock

Bartleet, B. L. (2008). Sound Links: Exploring the social, cultural and educational dynamics of musical communities in Australia. *International Journal of Community Music, 1* (3), 333–354.

Bartleet, B. L., Dunbar-Hall, P., Letts, R., & Schippers, H. (2009). *Sound Links: Community music in Australia.* Brisbane: Queensland Conservatorium Research Centre.

Bendrups, D., & Johnson H. (2011). Migrant music and cultural identity. In G. Keam & T. Mitchell (Eds.), *Home, land and sea: Situating music in Aotearoa New Zealand* (pp. 73–88). Auckland: Pearson.

Breen, M. (1994). Constructing the popular from public funding of community music: Notes from Australia. *Popular Music, 13* (3): 313–326.

Brunt, S. (2009a, October 13). *The ukulele in New Zealand.* Radio New Zealand Concert FM, Upbeat.

Brunt, S. (2009b). Uke'an be serious: Placing the value of the ukulele in New Zealand popular music. Paper presented at the conference for the International Association for the Study of Popular Music, Australia and New Zealand Branch (IASPM-ANZ), University of Auckland.

Brunt, S. (2010). Tracking the jumping flea: The ukulele as a transnational instrument of change. Paper presented at the conference for the International Association for the Study of Popular Music, Australia and New Zealand Branch (IASPM-ANZ), Monash University.

Cahill, A. (1998). *The community music handbook: A practical guide to developing music projects and organizations.* Sydney: Currency Press, in association with the Music Council of Australia.

Coffman, D. D. (2006). Voices of experience: Interviews of adult community band members in Launceston, Tasmania, Australia. *International Journal of Community Music.* Retrieved from www.intljcm.com/index.html

Cuba Street Carnival. (2009). Ephemeral pocket program, n.a.

Elliott, D., Higgins, L., & Veblen, K. (2008). Editorial. *International Journal of Community Music, 1*(1), 3–4.

Gruschow, Kim. (2002). "Jumping on Bandwagon." *Dominion Post*, October 21.

Harrison, G. (1996). Community music in Australia. In M. A. Leglar (Ed.), *The role of community music in a changing world: Proceedings of the International Society for Music Education, 1994 seminar of the commission on community music activity* (pp. 39–45). Athens, GA: University of Georgia Press.

Hawkins, G. (1993). *From Nimbin to Mardi Gras: Constructing community arts.* St. Leonards, NSW, Australia: Allen & Unwin.

Hesser, B., & Heinemann, H. N. (Eds.). (2010). *Music as a natural resource: Solutions for social and economic issues compendium.* New York: The International Council for Caring Communities (ICCC).

Jacobson, J. (2003). SH1 to be closed for city carnival. *Asia Africa Intelligence Wire*, November 6.

Jacobson, Julie. (2004a). "Fears Carnival Party May Gridlock Traffic." *Dominion Post*, February 25.

Jacobson, Julie. (2004b). "Motorists Not in Party Mood." *Dominion Post*, March 2.

Johnson, Ann-Marie. (2002a). "Road Fears Stop Cuba St Carnival." *Dominion Post*, October 12.

Johnson, Ann-Marie. (2002b.) "The Party that Pooped." *Dominion Post*, October 30.

Johnson, H. M. (2007). "Happy Diwali!" Performance, multicultural soundscapes and intervention in Aotearoa/New Zealand. In T. K. Ranarine (Ed.), *Musical performance in the diaspora* (pp. 71–94). New York: Routledge.

Johnson, H. M. (2008). Why taiko? Understanding taiko performance at New Zealand's first taiko festival. *Sites: A Journal of Social Anthropology & Cultural Studies 5* (2): 111–34.

Johnson, H. M. (Ed.). (2010). *Many voices: Music and national identity in Aotearoa/New Zealand.* Newcastle upon Tyne: Cambridge Scholars Publishing.

Johnson, H., & Moloughney, B. (Eds.). (2006). *Asia in the making of New Zealand.* Auckland: Auckland University Press.

Keam, G., & Mitchell, T. (Eds.). (2011). *Home, land and sea: Situating music in Aotearoa, New Zealand.* Auckland: Pearson.

Lave, J., & Wenger, E. (1991). *Situated learning—legitimate peripheral participation.* New York: Cambridge University Press.

MacDonald, N. (2007). The little fair that could. *Dominion Post*, March 24, 2007, p. E4.

Mason, A. (2000). *Community, solidarity and belonging: Levels of community and their normative significance.* Cambridge: Cambridge University Press.

Mitchell, T. (2006). Blackfellas rapping, breaking and writing: A short history of aboriginal hip hop. *Aboriginal History,* 30: 124–137.

Musco, E., & Tait, A. (2005). creating magic and meaning: Looking at the potential of arts-infused learning. *Music in Action, 2* (4), 12–14.

NZ Trust Ukulele. (2009). *Information. Mission Statement.*

Pierce, David. (1999). "Last-Ditch Deal Saves Fair Banner." *The Evening Post*, February 19.

Positively Wellington Tourism (n.d.). Retrieved from www.newzealand.com/int/plan/business/positively-wellington-tourism/

Slee, J. (2008). *ArtStories: An impact evaluation of an arts-based approach to teaching and learning in five Northern Territory school communities.* Retrieved from www.australia council.gov.au/research_hub/arts_rippa/arts_rippa_projects/artstories_participatory_research_in_northern_territory_school_communities_2006–2008

Statistics New Zealand. (2002). *Census snapshot. Cultural diversity.* Retrieved from www.stats.govt.nz/browse_for_stats/population/census_counts/census-snapshot-cultural-diversity.aspx

Tait, A., & Falk, I. (2004). Professional learning communities: Connecting teachers' practices and student outcomes through the arts. Paper presented at the International Educational Research Conference, Australian Association for Research in Education, Melbourne, Australia.

Tait, A., & Murrungun, L. (2008). Art stories: Partnerships for learning and well being. Paper presented at the Charles Darwin University Symposium: Art Works—Communities Thrive. Educating for Social Cohesion: What Works and Why? Alice Springs, Australia.

Tait, A., & Murrungun, L. (2010). ArtStories: Early childhood learning in remote Indigenous Australian communities. *Imagine, 1* (1).

Tait, A., Musco, E., Atfield, M., Murrungun, L., Orton, C., & Gray, A. (2010). Weaving new patterns of music in Indigenous education. In J. Ballantyne & B. L. Bartleet (Eds.), *Navigating music and sound education: Meaningful music making for life* (pp. 129–160). Newcastle upon Tyne: Cambridge Scholars Publishing.

Wallace, R., & Tait, A. (2006). Community control and knowledge management: Practitioners and community working together. Paper presented at the Connecting Intergenerational Communities through Creative Exchange Conference, Melbourne, Australia.

Wellington Batucada. (2011). *About us.* Retrieved from www.batucada.org.nz/about_us.html

Wellington City Council (2006). Cultural wellbeing strategy. Retrieved from www.wellington.govt.nz/plans/strategies/pdfs/cultural.pdf

Wenger, E. (1998). *Communities of practice: Learning, meaning and identity.* Cambridge: Cambridge University Press.

White, Mike. (2007). "Party On." *North & South*, February 1.

Chapter Seven

Community Music in East Asia

Chi Cheung Leung, Mari Shiobara, and Christine Yau

Community music in East Asia is popular, plentiful, and protean. This chapter focuses on three examples of this diversity from Hong Kong (China), Kokubunji (Japan), and Shenzhen (China). Chi Cheung Leung shares his personal experience of the operation of a modern Chinese orchestra in Hong Kong and discusses ways to survive strategically under limited workforce and funding provisions, stressing the importance of continual growth and sustainable development of an orchestra. Mari Shiobara focuses on one of the traditional Japanese singing art forms, *min'yō*, explaining how the practice of oral tradition survives in transmitting the art form in modern society, the supporting system in the community, and provisions in the school sector. Christine Yau describes the promotion of the Red Songs to maintain a harmonized society by the Chinese government and explores the transformative and representative functions of the Red Songs in their historical and modern contexts.

GROWTH OF A MODERN CHINESE ORCHESTRA IN HONG KONG: A CASE OF STRATEGIC SURVIVAL BIRTH OF THE MODERN CHINESE ORCHESTRA

The birth of the modern Chinese orchestra can be traced to the early twentieth century, when a group of enthusiastic Chinese music lovers, led by Yaozhang Liu, founded the Datong Music Society in Shanghai in 1920, followed later by Tianhua Liu's Society for Improving National Music in Beijing in 1927 (Tsui, 1998; Wu, 2006; Yeung, 2009). This development was an extension of the advocacies of the 1919 May Fourth Movement, which called for modernizing China, including its music, in order to catch up with the West. The modern Chinese orchestra, which was modeled on the structure of the Western orchestra, is one of the cultural products that resulted from this modernization. Modern Chinese music abandoned its original practice of improvization and adopted the practices of Western music, which articulates notated scores for different instruments in the orchestra (Yu, 2005). With the encouragement of the Chinese Communist Party, beginning in 1949, new Chinese instruments were

invented to extend the versatility and range of Chinese music, modern Chinese orchestras and conservatories were set up in major cities, and new music was written
for these modern orchestras. This music gradually found acceptance among Chinese
music lovers in mainland China, Hong Kong, Taiwan, Singapore, Malaysia, and other
places with Chinese immigrants. Recently, it has begun to appeal to Western and
Japanese audiences.

Emergence of the Yao Yueh Chinese Music Association

The first well-established modern Chinese orchestra in Hong Kong was believed to
be the South China Film Workers Association Chinese Folk Orchestra founded in
1957 (Chow, 1999; Tsui, 1990; Wu, 2006). This was followed by the establishment
of a number of Chinese music groups and orchestras in the 1960s. Among them was
the Diocesan Boys' School Chinese Music Society founded in 1961, where Chinese
instrumental lessons had been provided since 1960 (Fung & Chan-Yeung, 2009).
Graduates of the Diocesan Boys' School (DBS) were founders or co-founders of three
Chinese orchestras: Yuk Kwong Ho founded the Wang Kwong Chinese Orchestra in
1962, Chi Cheung Leung and Kam Hung Ng founded the Yao Yueh Chinese Music
Association (YYCMA Orchestra) in 1974, and Chi Hang Leung founded the University of Hong Kong (HKU) Chinese Music Society in 1975.

The Birth of the YYCMA Orchestra

In 1974, I was encouraged by my brother to form a Chinese orchestra, which was
later named the Yao Yueh Chinese Music Association (*Yao Yueh* means "enthusiastic
about music"). My brother was studying at HKU at that time, and I had just finished
high school. That summer, my brother asked me to gather a group of players to give
a performance at the HKU, and I received the enthusiastic support from schoolmates
and friends.

My brother and I had studied at DBS, a traditional British missionary school
founded in 1869. During the first week of class, he brought me to the Chinese music
storeroom. He had learned to play the *dizi* (a horizontal Chinese bamboo flute) and the
pipa (a four-string Chinese lute). I was fascinated by the Chinese instruments there,
particularly the *yangqin,* a trapezoid-shaped hammer dulcimer sounded by striking
two pieces of thin bamboo stick (around eight inches long) on over fifty strings (later
versions of this instrument utilize over 140 strings) on the sound box, and I began to
learn the instrument from a schoolmate, Yiu Shan Chan.

During the 1960s and 1970s, very few young people were interested in learning
Chinese instruments. Most of them were fond of listening to songs sung by Elvis
Presley or the Beatles at that time (Leung, 1999). They played guitars and sang
Western popular songs and folk songs. In school, Western classical music was taught
and Chinese music was almost neglected (Lam, 1999; Liu, 1999; Mittler, 1997). At
that time, most Chinese people had a low regard for Chinese music, an idea inherited
from the May Fourth Movement. Western music was perceived as high art, played in
concert halls, while Chinese music, except for *guqin* and *xiao* music practiced among

the traditional scholars, was of low social status. This lack of respect began at the end of the nineteenth century when the Qing Dynasty began its downfall. The Chinese studied Western knowledge and technology in order to strengthen and empower their motherland (Tsui, 1998). In Hong Kong, which had been a British colony since 1841, the perception of Western culture as being of high status was simply accepted by people. The low status of Chinese music was a result of Western political and cultural domination, the long-lasting impact of colonialism.

Kam Hung Ng (my classmate) and I formed an orchestra of around thirty players, consisting of our schoolmates, friends, relatives, and neighbors. After its first appearance, where the orchestra performed two demanding contemporary works for the HKU Student Union, the response was very encouraging. On October 7, 1975, the YYCMA Orchestra gave its official debut concert at the Lok Yew Hall of HKU. Around the same time, the orchestra performed in a joint concert with the Wang Kwong Chinese Orchestra, the Pui Sing Music Institute (founded in 1970), and the DBS Chinese Orchestra at the Hong Kong City Hall Concert Hall. In 1977, the YMCMA Orchestra drafted its ordinances and registered as a non-profit organization in Hong Kong. After four years of looking for a permanent rehearsal venue, the orchestra finally settled in a seven-hundred-square-foot Chinese Music Storeroom at DBS (where it still rehearses, in the same room, after thirty years), with the permission of the principal, S. J. Lowcock, J. P.

Since the birth of this orchestra, all the administrative and organizing work for concerts and financial matters has been completely conducted by its members. There has been no regular external support for any of its expenses, such as rentals of concert venues, poster and concert program printing, and musicians' fees; most of the income has come from the sales of tickets and advertisements. It has been a difficult task for members to maintain and continue the development of the orchestra.

A New Era for the Orchestra

The two major elements of success for a community orchestra are the stable attendance of its musicians and the standard of the orchestra. In October 2007, I was appointed the music director of the orchestra (at that time, there were only twelve to fifteen regular players). A concert had been scheduled for December 2007. I recruited fifty new members, barely enough for the concert, and most of these temporary players left the orchestra after the concert. The real challenge was to build an orchestra that was sustainable.

In Hong Kong, amateur musicians participate in different ensembles whenever there are concerts. This unusual practice prevents groups from being able to recruit stable members. Attracting musicians who will stay in an orchestra as regular members is not an easy task. The most fundamental approach, a harmonious collaboration emphasizing quality rehearsals, attracts musicians by enhancing their musicianship every time they come for rehearsal. By assiduously preparing for rehearsals, after six months I was able to secure around thirty musicians. Compared to the fifty temporary musicians who gathered for the December 2007 concert, the number was still fewer than was needed, but compared with the original twelve to fifteen players, it was an improvement.

The orchestra began a series of ten concerts with six different programs for the 2008/2009 music season. This was a huge challenge for the orchestra and its members because the orchestra had never before performed so many concerts in a season. Any performing group should have frequent and well-planned performances in order to

1. provide visible goals for the musicians,
2. encourage musicians to attend the rehearsals and internalize their musicianship,
3. widen the performing repertoire from traditional to contemporary and from chamber to orchestral,
4. collaborate with renowned and professional musicians and facilitate soloists within and outside of the orchestra, respectively,
5. build a professional and active public image for the orchestra, and
6. attract sponsors and donors.

First, the concert series provided a clear and achievable target for the orchestra within a timeframe, which helped planning to recruit musicians, especially those who were well sought after by other orchestras. With confirmed concert dates, musicians could schedule in advance when accepting invitations. At the same time, the orchestra could schedule rehearsals, conduct promotions, and operate all administrative aspects of the ensemble in an effective manner.

Second, the continuous performances of the concert series pushed players to attend rehearsals regularly. With more consistent attendance, the conductor could communicate better with the musicians and further improve their ensemble skills and musicianship.

Third, the concert series provided different music programs, featuring works which embraced varied styles and regions, such as traditional works like Cantonese music and *Jiangnan sizhu,* classical and avant-garde works, works written by contemporary composers from mainland China and Hong Kong, and works for Chinese and Western instruments as well as solos, chamber music, and full orchestral works. This wide-ranging repertoire provided a good platform for the players to improve their musicianship and their ability to adapt to different musical styles.

Fourth, through collaboration with professional players and composers, players were exposed to high standards of performance and the expectations of living composers, thus deepening their understanding of music. At the same time, players were also given chances to perform solo pieces and play in chamber works, which helped to sharpen their skills so they could perform at a higher level.

Fifth, frequent concert appearances, collaborations with professional musicians, quality performances, well-planned programs, and publicity combined to build a professional, active, well-organized, and promising image for the orchestra among music lovers and the public. The results of this concert series led to further concert engagements with different performing groups within and outside Hong Kong.

Sixth, the positive image of the orchestra, engendered by the concert series, also facilitated attracting donors and sponsors and resulted in the group receiving sponsorship from the Hong Kong Arts Development Council and other private donations.

To help the members adapt to the new focus of the orchestra and to compensate for the heavy performance load and the pressure faced by the amateur players, the concert series had to be explained and conducted after consulting with and getting endorsement from members and the committee. It was crucial that the initiative had been openly discussed before it was launched because without the members' support and managerial and administrative approval and assistance from the committee members, the success of the concerts would have been impossible.

Viewpoints of the Member Musicians

Currently, the number of players in the orchestra has grown to seventy, and many professionally trained musicians and freelance musicians have joined. On average, the orchestra performs three major programs during each music season at different public venues. Members range from teenagers to players in their seventies.

The viewpoints and feelings of the member musicians reflected in a focused group discussion show that the primary interest of amateur musicians is music, and their passion about Chinese music is the key to motivating them to stay in the orchestra. The enjoyment of music is very important to them. One of the members said:

> The initial purpose of setting up this orchestra is to let [Chinese] music lovers make music, and hence our name "Yao Yueh" . . . Basically [because of] music . . . people will come for good music. Music is what brings us together. (Player A)

At the same time, they treasure their friendships and relationships in the group. Two of them explained:

> I have a group of friends here . . . which makes me feel very comfortable. (Player B)

> Many members, concertmasters, and guest performers have become our friends after performing with us. I feel very happy and privileged to make friends with those distinguished artists. Since then I have accumulated a lot of friends. (Player C)

Players treat the orchestra as their second family. Besides their friends, classmates, and schoolmates, many members have brought their family members and relatives to the orchestra. The feeling of being a part of a family is very strong in this orchestra. They stated:

> They (the member musicians) stayed in the orchestra and supported it unselfishly for such a long time that they even bring their next generation to participate. [I believe] the orchestra must have a very strong attraction. (Player D)

> Most importantly, I grew up in this orchestra since my teens. My best friends, my husband, and the friends I know today are all here . . . perhaps some of my friends would think it is a tough job for me, to work so hard for the orchestra, but in fact I find a lot of pleasure in the orchestra as part of my social life. (Player E)

We are all equal. We treat music seriously. No one thinks one is a maestro, and no one competes for the principal seat. If we enjoy music, what is the point of fighting? So, "Yes," we are like a big family. (Player A)

The close friendship and the sense of being part of a big family have been a result of the harmonious atmosphere naturally created among members. There has been no hierarchy among the senior and junior members. These musicians are helpful to, unselfish with, caring for, and tolerant of players who are technically less capable. As they articulated,

I received a very warm and friendly welcome when I first joined the orchestra. I was worried when I came for the first rehearsal. I did not know anyone there. I was welcomed with different food prepared by the orchestral members. Oh! How could [members of] an orchestra be so warm? I am not just talking about the generosity of the members; I mean I have a very comfortable feeling being with them. The members are very tolerant and unselfish . . . They are willing to help with different things [for the orchestra] regardless of how senior they are. (Player D)

The second reason [for staying in the orchestra] is the fact that I was not expelled, which means they (the core players) have been very toleratant. This can also be seen from the great diversity of ages and standards of the orchestral members. (Player F)

It was Yao Yueh that made me stay [in the ensemble]. Actually I had thought about leaving twice . . . The feeling [of playing in the orchestra] was very warm. (Player G)

Apart from the good feeling of playing in the orchestra, the high standard and the wide range of repertoire performed are two important elements influencing players to stay. They reflected:

The overall standard (of musicianship) is very high, and I am led by some skillful musicians here whose playing enables me to truly enjoy the music. (Player G)

Very high standard . . . there are many skillful musicians surrounding us. (Player F)

The second reason is the diversity of the music played. The orchestra has the ability to invite different musicians to perform various types of music, and to a high standard . . . The variety of music has also given me the opportunity to improve my musicianship. With all these, I feel much rewarded. (Player D)

Last, a sense of satisfaction is gained from good rehearsal experiences and performances. Three members shared:

All of us have different levels of desire to perform [on stage]. (Player H)

Performance itself is very enjoyable. I do enjoy the rehearsals but somehow not to the same extent [as having performances] . . . Satisfaction . . . I often find this feeling here [in this orchestra]. (Player G)

We want to come back [to the orchestra for rehearsals] if we gain satisfaction. (Player A)

Remarks

Running a community orchestra is no different from running a professional one. With limited resources and manpower, the survival of a community orchestra must rely on professionalism and strategy. Nevertheless, it is important for music directors and conductors to make a concerted effort to enhance the performance standard of the orchestra and, at the same time, provide a variety of concert programs, which are equally valued by the players, for the audience. It must be noted that a music director should not overemphasize musical quality and ignore the feelings of the players. A balance between the demand for a high standard and tolerance of a lower standard will help to soothe hard feelings. For the musicians, the performance standard is as important as having their voices heard. Sincere consultation with the members and support from them for major initiatives are crucial. Even though the members aspire to have performance opportunities and to work with professionals, they also treasure their friendships, and they value the feeling of being in a family. If harmonious growth of the orchestra is to be sustained, all of the above aspects should be taken into consideration.

COMMUNITY MUSICIANS OF *MIN'YŌ*: A CASE OF KINSEIKAI— "VOICES OF GOLDEN BROCADE SOCIETY"—IN TOKYO

Min'yō Singing in Kokubunji

Three Friday evenings each month, a group of *min'yō* singers gathers in a small conference room in one of the five community centers in Kokubunji, a suburban city to the west of Tokyo. The group is named Kinseikai, which literally means "the voices of golden brocade." The ages of the members range between fifty and the early eighties, and among them are prizewinners of the national and regional contests organized annually under the patronage of the *Nihon Min'yō Kyōkai* (Japan Folk Song Association). The group welcomes not only experienced singers, but also beginners who are encouraged to learn with the group. Several members are *natori,* diploma holders from particular schools of *min'yō*, and have professional names associated with the schools to which they belong.

Min'yō literally means "folk song." Expressions such as "folk song is the heart's hometown" or "folk song is the hometown's heart" are vocalized by folk song enthusiasts (Hughes, 2008). "Hometown" in Japanese—*furusato*—conjures up images of one's old village, home community, or native place. Hughes (2008) concludes that "my old country home" is the best English translation for the word *min'yō* (pp. 8-15). It is closely linked to local places, specific locations, landscapes, and even histories. For example, a name card of one of the members has a small photograph of a mountain landscape reflected onto a lake. The name card holder explained that it was a place in Hokkaido, the northernmost place in Japan, where she was born and raised.

Asano, a historian of Japanese music, defines *min'yō* as songs that were born naturally, without lyricists or composers, within local folk communities and have been transmitted aurally. The songs have undergone unconscious and unintentional alterations and have become songs that reflect, in the simplest manner, the sentiments and feelings of the common people (Asano, 1966). Newly composed folk songs (by known composers and lyricists), which comprise part of the repertoire of Kinseikai, are known as *shin min'yō* [new folk songs]. There are two different categories of *min'yō,* which can be differentiated by their rhythmic structures: metric songs in duple meter and songs in free rhythm (Koizumi, 1984). Usually, one person sings the main part of a verse and the others give a unison choral response (Koizumi, 1973). An expert singer is considered one who can elaborate or ornament the vocal melody line in his or her own way within the range of a traditionally expected standard. This singing technique, called *kobushi,* is the barometer of good singing.

Friday Evening Gatherings

Around a quarter past six on a Friday evening in late November 2009, the members of Kinseikai started arriving at the small conference room of the community center. There were sixteen members, eight men and eight women, including three *shamisen* (three-stringed plucked lute) players, a drummer, and four *shakuhachi* (end-blown bamboo flute) players who accompanied the singers when they were not singing. The leader of the group, Mr. Komatsuda, a brilliant singer/teacher in his sixties, was sitting next to the drummer, making sure that everybody settled down and was ready to start.

Kinseikai is not a *min'yō* school per se, and there is no vocal or instrumental instruction taking place. Rather, it is a time for professional and non-professional *min'yō* lovers to get together and sing to each other for enjoyment. These singers look forward to these meetings because they can have real *shamisen* and *shakuhachi* accompaniment instead of practicing their singing with karaoke at home.

Someone called out, ". . . san (mister), please sing for us . . ." A male singer stood up and said, "As I am not in the best condition today, I may spoil your ears but . . . well . . . I will still sing . . ." He mentioned the title of the song, one of his favorites from the Tsugaru region in the north of Japan. He started singing after making sure that the *shamisen* players were ready, and, later, the *shakuhachi* players joined in. These processes went smoothly, without any words or cues. He was an excellent singer and everybody listened to him attentively. Some of them closed their eyes, concentrating on his *kobushi,* and the others sang along with him, moving their lips quietly.

Everybody in the room was asked to take turns singing a song that he or she had prepared. About halfway through the session, a male singer with a very good voice but still going through the beginner's stage, was singing a song from the Tsugaru repertoire. A professional singer/teacher, Mr. Harada, who was also a brilliant Tsugaru *shamisen* player, stopped his accompaniment after hearing the singer struggle with the same line of the verse with every repetition. Since the accompaniment stopped, the singer had to stop, and because the singer realized the difficulty, he was ready for advice. Everybody in the room was curious about what Mr. Harada would say to the singer. Mr. Harada said that the singer should be careful with his pitch in the problematic section; it was too low, and therefore the song finished unsatisfactorily, without a climax. Mr. Harada explained how it should be done and demonstrated what he meant by using his own voice. The singer followed him by imitating his singing several times but still could not get the point right. Mr. Komatsuda then joined in the demonstration and gave similar comments. The two senior members, who were both renowned *min'yō* teachers, tried to get the singer to sing *kobushi* at a particular point, bringing his amateurish expressions to a more sophisticated level. One by one, the others in the room were drawn together and started singing in low voices, practicing the points that had been made by the two teachers. While the singer was trying to master the *kobushi,* the others started giving comments like "Not yet . . . wait!," "Higher! Oh, well, it's better though . . . ," and "Listen to yourself . . . !" The members of Kinseikai were learning together important aspects of singing *min'yō* with first-class performers. While giving the singer moral support, the members listened to and carefully watched what was going on and understood the differences in musical expressions.

Through the incident described above, the founder and the chair of Kinseikai, Master Endo, had been quietly observing what was happening and playing *shakuhachi,* whenever appropriate, to accompany the singing. It seemed that he was simply supporting the singing with his presence. He is now seventy years old and is still very busy, so it is not possible for him to attend every Friday evening. However, he is a key person connecting a small local music community like the Kinseikai to the much wider community of *min'yō* through the close ties of professional organizations in Japan, where he still plays an important role.

Background Organizations and Supporting Systems

Master Endo was seventeen years old when he first heard a traditional ensemble piece performed with *koto* (a plucked zither with thirteen strings) and *shakuhachi* called *Haru no Umi* (Spring Sea). He was deeply moved by the music and started learning *shakuhachi* soon after. Throughout his career, he lived a sort of double life as a businessman in one of the largest electric companies as well as a *min'yō shakuhachi* player and teacher/master. When he was thirty-five years old, he founded a *min'yō* school and society called "Shōfūkai," named after his professional name, Shōfūzan, while still working in the electric company as a section chief. He retired from the company when he was fifty-five years old in order to fully dedicate himself to teaching all levels of *min'yō* and transmitting the tradition of *min'yō* to young people. It has been thirty-five years since Master Endo started Shōfūkai, and in this time it has spawned thirteen branch schools all over west Tokyo, with ninety-four diploma holders whom Master Endo trained.

Kinseikai is an offshoot of one of the Shōfūkai's branch schools, Kinsei, where the teachers of the school come and sing together, but it is also open to outsiders. Beginners, if they wish, can take lessons with one of the teachers at the Kinsei school. Kinsei's parent organization, Shōfūkai, is a branch of an incorporated foundation, *Nihon Min'yō Kyōkai* (Japan Folk Song Association). The association has fifty-five main branches throughout Japan, two branches in Brazil, and one in the United States. In Tokyo alone, there are eleven main branches (Shōfūkai is one of the fourteen sub-branches under the Tama-South main branch). Master Endo has served as a member of the board of directors of the association for many years, and now, as an advisor, he still handles some administrative and managerial work for the association.

The Japan Folk Song Association was founded in 1950 to preserve, develop, and popularize folk songs and dances and to contribute to the advancement of Japanese culture (Japan Folk Song Association, 2007). It does this by researching and transcribing folk songs and dances, publishing, organizing regional and national contests, arranging outreach activities, and qualifying diploma holders. Its headquarters are associated with a concert hall and a library in central Tokyo, which are open to the general public. In recent years, the association has been actively involved in outreach activities to teach children in schools and has established a system of qualifying its members for this purpose. This movement has been further acknowledged in the 2008 Course of Studies Music for Lower Secondary Schools put forward by the Ministry of Education, which specifies that teaching materials include "traditional songs such as *min'yō* . . . songs that have characteristics of traditional voices" (The Ministry of Education and Science, 2008).

Outreach Programs at a Local Lower Secondary School

In 2002, much sooner than the Ministry's course of study required, Master Endo started an outreach program with members of Kinseikai at a local lower secondary school. In the following year, the program received grants from the Ministry of Culture and initiated a project to teach local children Kokubunji traditional performing arts, as well as *min'yō* and other genres of traditional arts, on Saturdays.

In the *min'yō* elective music classes at the school, taken by the second- and third-year students, there are fourteen students (eleven girls and three boys) attending the second-year *shamisen* class, and they are jointly taught by a visiting teacher and the music teacher of the school. For the third-year students, there are three classes of one hour and forty minutes from which to choose, like the advanced *shamisen,* and for the second-year students, there are choices such as *tsugaru shamisen* (taught by a member of Kinseikai) and *shakuhachi* (taught by Master Endo).

Tsugaru shamisen is a special genre of *min'yō shamisen* that is often played purely as instrumental music. It originated in the northernmost region of the main island of Japan and has recently become popular among young people, in large part thanks to the Yoshida Brothers, who hit the top of the charts in the recording industry in 2003. There were three boys and three girls in the class who were taught in the traditional way, without any written scores. They watched the teacher play and then imitated his music and technique as best as they could. Since they did not have the musical instruments at home, they had done all their practicing during school recesses.

Master Endo taught four female third-year students *shakuhachi* by starting the lesson with a scale and then a few simple pieces. Because of the nature of the instruments, it was sometimes difficult for the students to produce the right notes although everybody was very patient and there was a warm, trusting relationship between the teacher and the students. Master Endo said that on their graduation day at the end of the year he would give his handmade *shakuhachi* to those students who wish to continue learning the instrument and make it their lifelong companion.

Remarks

Kinseikai is one of the numerous community music activities that exist in Japan that are open to anybody interested in *min'yō* and the musical instruments associated with the genre. My introduction to the group, which is mostly composed of senior citizens, occurred when a neighbor and current member of the group invited my husband, who plays *shakuhachi,* to visit the gathering on a Friday evening, after which he eventually joined the group. It is crucial to recruit more young people in order for the group to continue acting as an invaluable bridge connecting local amateur folk song lovers to the national organization.

CREATING COMMUNITIES THROUGH RED SONGS IN MODERN URBAN CHINA

Red[1] Songs were revolutionary songs originally composed as a new artistic genre to promote political campaigns and the doctrine of communism after the establishment of the People's Republic of China (PRC) in 1949. Sixty years later, in 2009, Red Songs were revived and made popular again as a means to promote a harmonized society by the Chinese government for the ongoing celebration of the nation's sixtieth anniversary. Within both historical and modern contexts, Red Songs serve the two functions of transformation and representation. On the one hand, they are used as a tool as part of the transformative processes to alter the way Chinese people see themselves, their relationship to others, and their nation. On the other hand, there is no other musical genre that uniquely represents the traditional Chinese musical, socialist, nationalist, and consumerist values that modern China embraces today. In other words, Red Songs form part of the "mutually transformative process of making music national and of realizing the nation musically" (Tuohy, 2001, p. 108). In this part of the chapter, such transformative and representative functions of the Red Songs are explored in relation to their historical and modern contexts. A local singing competition is discussed to illustrate how this form of community music is operationalized to achieve these functions in an urbanized Chinese city.

Historic Contexts: To Revolutionize, Popularize, and Nationalize

The use of music for social and political control in Chinese history predates the Chinese Communist Party (CCP). Confucius regarded music[2] as an indicative activity of the ethical level of people as it "provides enhanced possibilities for disclosing personal style, spirit and consequence" (Hall & Ames, 1987, p. 276). In recent centuries, the practice of using music as a political tool was documented in the Taiping Rebellion period (1851–1864) (Bryant, 2007, p. 89). This social and political function of music in modern Chinese history was developed extensively under Mao Zedong's[3] direction. Red Songs, in their original intention and like all arts created in a totalitarian society, were primarily aimed at transforming the Chinese people by affirming the ideology and practice of the CCP and musically representing the proletariat (the workers, peasants, and soldiers).

According to Mao, as China entered into the new political era brought by the CCP, it should have its own "new cultural force" facilitated by "the theatre, the cinema, music, sculpture and painting" (Perris, 1983, p. 6). Building on Mao's ideologies about the arts and literature, Premier Zhou Enlai[4] presented a cultural policy in 1963. As a framework from which to begin exploring revolutionary arts, this policy aimed to transform and represent Chinese people via a "Three Processes of Transformation" strategy (*sanhua*) (Bryant, 2007, p. 91). These three processes were "revolutionize" (*geminghua*), "popularize" (*qunzhonghua*), and "nationalize" (*minzuhua*) (Bryant, 2007, p. 91).

To revolutionize was to use Mao's understanding of literature and art as the "cultural army" in terms of both modifying the content and function of music (Bryant, 2007, p. 91). Mao's 1942 "Talks at the Yan'an Conference on Literature and Art" is one of the most important documents that provides his guiding principle about the role of the arts as a revolutionary tool for the PRC:

> . . . to ensure that literature and art fit well into the whole revolutionary machine as a component part, that they operate as powerful weapons for uniting and educating the people, and for attacking and destroying the enemy, and that they help the people to fight the enemy with one heart and one mind. (Mao, 1965, p. 70)

To popularize was to promote a socialist society without "any elite or intellectual bourgeois class" (Bryant, 2007, p. 91). To some extent, this also served the function of representation. Thus, revolutionary literature and art were to be in simple forms and fully distributed throughout the country.

Finally, to nationalize was to represent the Chinese people inclusively through music. The Chinese characters *minzu* consist of concepts of race, ethnicity, nation, and nationality (Bryant, 2007, p. 91; Tuohy, 2001, p. 108). This meant that to nationalize was to employ forms and styles from different ethnicities in China so that music would "[be] base[d] on, reflect, and serve 'the people'" (Tuohy, 2001, p. 115). This also meant that music was to be strategically presented to place ethnic and minority groups who might not consider themselves "Chinese" within the concept of the "nation" (Tuohy, 2001, p. 91). In order to ensure that the new revolutionary art represented the Chinese people, Mao recommended that composers and performers learn from folk and other popular forms, such as village operas and song and dance shows (Perris, 1983, p. 8). During the Cultural Revolution,[5] in particular, composers were sent into the rural areas to collect the songs of the people while they performed manual labor alongside the working class "so that the composers could develop a realistic understanding of the worker's needs and could accurately reflect these needs in their compositions" (Wong, 1984, p. 130). In 1937, the Lu Xun Arts Academy[6] was established for the purpose of "the rectification of the people in the arts" (Perris, 1983, p. 2). In this academy, composers revised local folk songs with new political ideas before passing them on to the masses for dissemination (Tuohy, 2001, p. 113). According to the American anthropologist Clifford Geertz, images and metaphors (such as Red Songs) could be considered the "cultural devices designed to render one or another aspect of the broad process of collective self-redefinition explicit, to cast essentialist pride or epochalist hope into specific symbolic forms" (1973, p. 252). In other words, these songs were used as a tool to enable the broader process of nationalism, which involves the association of preexisting local sounds and identities into national ones (Tuohy, 2001, p. 109). Figure 7.1 visually shows how the functions of transformation and representation of the Red Songs were achieved in the historical context.

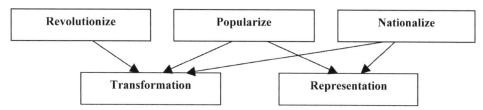

Figure 7.1. Ways of transformation and representation of Red Songs in the historical context.

Modern Contexts: To Harmonize and Consumerize in the Urban City

After sixty years, the meanings of the Red Songs have taken on different dimensions of representation and transformation in modern contexts from both the political and commercial perspectives. After the death of Mao, Deng Xiaoping[7] and his supporters took control of the CCP (Garnaut, 2001, p. 2). Many of Mao's political goals of utopian egalitarianism were abandoned in favor of the economic reforms championed by Deng (Perkins, 2001, p. 36). Socialism was quickly redefined as "raising people's living standards through developing 'the forces of production'" (Zhao, 1997, p. 46). Since the economic reform process began in 1978, China has become one of the world's fastest-growing economies.[8] It is predicted that it will continue to enjoy impressive economic growth in the coming years and has the potential to become the world's largest economy within a decade or so.

Despite the fact that many segments of society in China are considerably better off than before, the economic reform policy left a large number of social issues unresolved. The CCP is now confronted with increasing social unrest resulting from issues such as loss-making state-owned enterprises, urban-rural wealth disparity, widening income disparities, corruption by government officials, and growing inflationary pressures. In 2005 alone, there were over eighty-seven thousand protests reported, many of which stemmed partly from the frustrations of many Chinese who "are not benefiting from China's economic reforms and rapid growth, and the perception that those who are getting rich are doing so because of their connections to government officials" (Morrison, 2006, p. 23). Many of the frustrated poor are former workers of state-owned enterprises and peasants, who were the original support base of Chinese industries (Zhao, 1997, p. 51). In 2006, in order to tackle these issues, the Chinese government officially introduced its goal of building a "harmonious socialist society" for the purpose of promoting "more balanced economic growth and address[ing] a number of economic and social issues" (Morrison, 2006, p. 5).

Under this broader agenda of building a harmonized society, an official notice[9] titled "The Launch of 'Patriotic Songs We Sing' Mass Singing Activities" was disseminated for the celebratory campaign of the nation's sixtieth birthday in 2009 (Source Juice, 2009). This official notice[10] was issued to the general public as well as to all public and private organizations calling for the revived performance and appreciation of the Red Songs by featuring them in television programs, concerts, and community music activities. This official notice specifically claimed that these music activities were aimed toward the "grass roots and the masses . . . within community and cultural centers" to ensure that these activities were "widespread" to "reach" the people. In this sense, the key to harmonization lay with representation through inclusive participation of Chinese citizens, especially those from economically deprived groups and those groups who had not benefited from China's new economic reforms and rapid growth. The Red Songs were revived by the Chinese government in these contexts with an aim to harmonize the people and to lower the effect of social unrest through music.

In this modern context, the political intention of the Chinese government is reflected in the commercial sector. Red Songs are utilized in the commercial sector as a transformative tool of commoditization and consumerism. After opening its retail market in 1992 in five special economic zones (SEZs),[11] along with other major cities and foreign investors "to accelerate the country's tertiary industry growth and create more job opportunities" (Wong & Yu, 2003, p. 62), China entered through another kind of revolution in the age of consumerism. Large-scale shopping centers, stocked with expensive consumer goods, rapidly transformed the SEZs throughout the 1990s and 2000s (Zhao, 1997, p. 47). In this commercial climate, many major shopping centers utilize all kinds of community activities with the aim of promoting the widespread consumption of products and reaching target consumers on a local basis. Given that the Chinese value system places emphasis on the power of music in bringing people together and forming harmonious and meaningful relationships (Hall & Ames, 1987, p. 276), it is not surprising to find that an increasing number of marketing activities foster local communities through musical activities by linking their promotional message to music (Fan & Pfitzenmaier, 2001, p. 13). The community music activity described below illustrates how the Red Songs are utilized for the purpose of harmonizing and consumerizing in the Chinese urban city Shenzhen.

In September 2009, a local singing competition themed "Red Songs Bring the Brightest Sound" was launched in the Kingkey Banner Shopping Center[12] in an affluent area of Shenzhen.[13] The competition was held on a stage with the audience seated near the main entrance of the shopping center on the ground floor. Specifically built as cultural community and performance space, this stage was designed to be the focal point of the shopping center and to be visible from all its floors. With the aim of bringing local consumers together into the shopping center through the arts and nurturing a local collective identity, this singing competition provided a cultural platform for people to actively participate in their Red Songs performance, regardless of age and singing ability. The seemingly inclusive nature of this competition called for participants of all ages and singing ability by advertising in newspapers.[14] There was great diversity among the participants who entered this competition as a result of this inclusive advertisement. In total, twenty-six groups (soloists, choirs, duets, and trios) were formed from sixty participants who showed a wide range of vocal training. Approximately one-third of the participants were male and two-thirds were female, with the youngest participant being four years old and the oldest seventy-eight. Many participants embraced their cultural identity and ethnicity (Han, Mongolian, Tibetan, and Uyghur) by wearing traditional Chinese costumes (*qipao*, for example) for their performances. The twenty-two Red Songs performed in the competition were of a great variety in lyrical content. On stage, some participants proudly spoke of their joy in the nation's economic success while others dedicated their songs to the audience with best wishes for their country. The familiarity of these songs provided a sense of unity for the participants and audience, who seemed to be bonded by their shared pride and joy in how far the nation had come in the past sixty years.

Besides celebrating China's birthday, the shopping center aimed to use this competition to create a neighborhood community center by attracting affluent consumers to centrally located cultural activities, entertainment, dining, and luxurious shopping. Apart from transforming the people's national identity, the competition also targeted the consumer purchasing behavior by creating a local, collective identity. Shopping discounts, promotional gifts, and vouchers were offered as part of the competition to prizewinners, audience members, and adjudicators to stimulate sales volume during the National Day holiday season. Messages about promotional discounts at the shopping center were also announced at the beginning and the end of the competition. Regardless of whether this event achieved its purpose of harmonization or consumerization, this community activity reflects the dichotomy currently facing modern China in regard to the conflicting values of harmonization and consumerization.

For the harmonization process to succeed in the modern Chinese context, Red Songs must reach economically deprived groups. The extent to which economically deprived participants were included in this competition is highly debatable, given its affluent location. Would the disenfranchised feel comfortable enough to visit a luxury-goods shopping center filled with expensive brands? And, if this competition *did* attract participants from all levels of the social classes, it failed in its purpose of consumerization, as it intended by locating the competition in a shopping center that targets affluent consumers. This community music activity highlights the issues surrounding China's current social condition: a constant friction between the competing values of harmonization and consumerization beneath a veneer of growth and prosperity. Figures 7.2a and 7.2b visually show the relationships in this dichotomy. The question remains—can the process of harmonization and consumerization really co-exist in modern China?

Remarks

Musical genres such as the Red Songs provide a wealth of materials essential to the process of transformation and representation. These Red Songs are composed, performed, reproduced, and reorganized daily in diverse settings to portray the chronological and spatial dimensions of the Chinese nation. They give tangible form to the abstract concepts of harmony, historical continuity, and national identity through sounds that have infused the daily lives of Chinese citizens for the past six decades. While the older generations might relate the Red Songs to the wars with Japan and the Cultural Revolution, the younger generations relate them to the social issues surrounding consumerism. One might wonder what the Red Songs would represent for future generations on the nation's 120th birthday. Only time will tell.

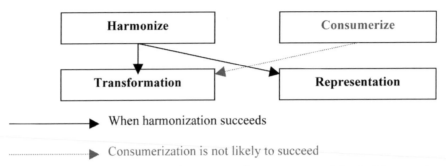

When harmonization succeeds

Consumerization is not likely to succeed

Figure 7.2a.   Harmonization—transformation and representation of the Red Songs in the modern political context.

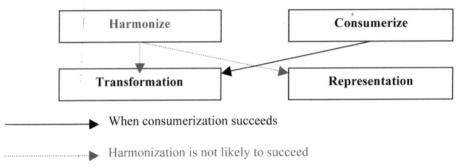

When consumerization succeeds

Harmonization is not likely to succeed

Figure 7.2b.   Consumerization—transformation of Red Songs in the modern commercial context.

CONCLUSION

This discussion highlights three different scenarios that exist in the context of community music in Japan and China. The story of the Yao Yueh Chinese Music Association Orchestra in Hong Kong highlights the competitiveness of running a modern Chinese orchestra, which demands high standards and frequent public performances. At the same time, inclusiveness of different standards, continuous consultation at times of change, support, friendship, and performance opportunities are important elements which are required if there is to be harmonious and sustainable growth for the orchestra. The Voices of Golden Brocade Society (Kinseikai) in Kokubunji portrays a harmonious picture of the transmission of *min'yō* singing, offering an opportunity for any *min'yō* lovers to meet with like-minded individuals to sing traditional music with live instrumentation. This practice occurs in many communities in Japan and has been extended to school education. The Red Songs competition in Shenzhen illustrates the dichotomy inherent in the attempt by the Chinese government to harmonize society through promoting the Red Songs to economically deprived groups and the result of consumerization in shopping centers that target affluent consumers. The transformation of the Red Songs and its resultant representations among the old and younger generations contradicts, and is diverting from, the initial intention of economic reform amid rapid growth. These three distinct instances of musical transmission illustrate the range of community music activities in Japan and China.

NOTES

1. The color red is commonly related with communism and revolution.

2. By "music," he referred not only to instrumental music but also to poetry and dance (Hall & Ames, 1987, p. 276).

3. Mao Zedong, CCP chairman for forty years, led the PRC from its establishment in 1949 until his death in 1976. He was also a Chinese revolutionary and political theorist whose contribution to Marxism-Leninism, military strategies, and Communist policies were later collectively known as Maoism.

4. Zhou was the first PRC premier, serving from 1949 until his death in 1976. His was one of the fundamental figures in facilitating the CCP's rise to power, and, subsequently, in the development of the economy and restructuring of Chinese society.

5. Also known as the Great Proletarian Cultural Revolution, this ten-year political campaign movement was launched by Mao Zedong in 1966 in the PRC. In the name of ideological cleansing, Mao closed schools and encouraged students to join Red Guard units with the aim to attack so-called intellectuals and to remove bourgeois influences. Millions of Chinese were forced to go into rural areas to perform manual labor, and tens of thousands were executed.

6. The Academy was named after the late revolutionary author Lu Xun.

7. As the leader of the CCP from 1978 to the early 1990s, Deng was a reformer who led China toward a market economy.

8. Between 1979 and 2007, the real gross domestic product (GDP) in China increased at an average annual rate of 9.8 percent.

9. This official notice was disseminated by the Central Propaganda Department and Central Civilization Office of the Chinese central government (Central Propaganda Department and Central Civilization Office of the Chinese Central Government, 2009).

10. The call states: "[P]raise the good of communism, socialism, economic reform, the great motherland and people of all ethnicities . . . to inspire passion for nationalism, to unite the power of the people, to express the people's joy and heroic emotions for the nation's birthday . . . to reveal the harmony of the people of all ethnicities and the positive spirit of enthusiasm . . . to create a strong sense of community . . . to maintain economic growth, the people's livelihood and stability." (Central Propaganda Department and Central Civilization Office of the Chinese Central Government, 2009)

11. Among other economic reform initiatives, Deng established four special economic zones (SEZs) along the coast "for the purpose of attracting foreign investment, boosting exports, and importing high technology products into China" (Morrison, 2006, p. 3).

12. The major shopping center, Kingkey Banner, was built in 2008 in the NanShan district—one of most affluent residential areas in Shenzhen (Kingkey Limited, 2009).

13. Among the five Chinese SEZs, Shenzhen is the most successful and experienced city in terms of the influence of consumerism and commercial advertisements.

14. The newspaper advertisement read: "Both old and young members from the family are welcome to apply. Regardless of whoever you are, come and express your true joy (for the nation's birthday) from the bottom of your heart. Free entry" (Huang, 2009).

BIBLIOGRAPHY

Asano, K. (1966). *Nihon no min'yō* [Japanese folk song]. Tokyo: Iwanami Shoten.

Bryant, L. O. (2007). Flowers on the battlefield are more fragrant. *Asian Music,* Winter/Spring, 88–122.

Central Propaganda Department and Central Civilization Office of the Chinese Central Government. (2009). *Official notice*. Retrieved from www.wenming.cn/zt/2009–06/05/content_16723555.htm.

Chow, F. F. (1999). Benshiji de Xianggang Yinyue Yanchu Huodong [Hong Kong music performance in the 20th century]. In S. B. Chu (Ed.), *Xianggang Yinyue Fazhan Gailun* [The development of music in Hong Kong]. Hong Kong: Joint Published (HK) Co. Ltd.

Fan, Y., & Pfitzenmaier, N. (2001). How to reach 1.3bn consumers in China? *Deutsch-Chinesisches Wirtschaftsforum 5*, 13–19.

Fung, Y. M., & Chan-Yeung, M. W. M. (2009). *To serve and to lead: A history of the Diocesan Boys' School Hong Kong*. Hong Kong: Hong Kong University Press.

Garnaut, R. (2001). Twenty years of economic reform and structural change in the Chinese economy. In R. Garnaut & Y. Huang (Eds.), *Growth without miracles: Readings on the Chinese economy in the era of reform*. New York: Oxford University Press.

Geertz, C. (1973). *The interpretation of cultures*. New York: Basic Books.

Hall, D. L., & Ames, R. T. (1987). *Thinking through Confucius*. Albany: State University of New York Press.

Huang, Lina (2009). *Hongbian Shenzhen, Secai Jianrong* [Redness among Shenzhen, the color becomes denser]. Retrieved from http://jb.sznews.com/page/1161/2009–09/03/C05/20090903C05_pdf.pdf

Hughes, D. W. (2008). *Traditional folk song in modern Japan*. Kent: Global Oriental.

Japan Folk Song Association. (2007). *Aramashi* [An outline]. Retrieved from www.nichimin.or.jp/

Kingkey Limited. (2009). *Shenzhen Kingkey Banner Commercial Management Co. Ltd.* Retrieved from www.kingkeybanner.com

Koizumi, F. (1973). *Nihon Ongaku no Onkai to Senpō* [Scale and mode in Japanese music]. Tokyo: Ongakunotomo-sha.

Koizumi, F. (1984). *Nihon Dentō Ongaku no Kenkyū 2: Rizumu* [Research in Japanese traditional music 2: Rhythm]. Tokyo: Ongakunotomo-sha.

Lam, C. W. (1999). Xianggang Yinyue Jiaoyu de Fazhan [The development of Hong Kong's music education]. In S. B. Chu (Ed.), *Xianggang Yinyue Fazhan Gailun* [The development of music in Hong Kong]. Hong Kong: Joint Published (HK) Co. Ltd.

Leung, B. Y. (1999). Xianggang di Liuxing Yinyue [Popular music in Hong Kong]. In S. B. Chu (Ed.), *Xianggang Yinyue Fazhan Gailun* [The development of music in Hong Kong]. Hong Kong: Joint Published (HK) Co. Ltd.

Liu, C. C. (1999). Zaonian Xianggang de Yinyue Jiaoyu, Juodong yu Chuangzuo [Music education, activities and creation in the early days of Hong Kong]. In S. B. Chu (Ed.), *Xianggang Yinyue Fazhan Gailun* [The development of music in Hong Kong]. Hong Kong: Joint Published (HK) Co. Ltd.

Mao, T. T. (1965). *Selected works of Mao Tse-Tung*. Peking: People's Republic of China: Foreign Languages Press.

The Ministry of Education and Science. (2008). *The course of study for lower secondary schools*. Tokyo: Tokyo Shoseki.

Mittler, B. (1997). *Dangerous tunes: The politics of Chinese music in Hong Kong, Taiwan, and the People's Republic of China since 1949*. Wiesbaden: Harrassowitz.

Morrison, W. (2006). *China's economic condition: Foreign affairs, defense, and trade division*. Retrieved from www.fas.org/sgp/crs/row/IB98014.pdf

Perkins, D. (2001). Completing China's move to the market. In R. Garnaut & Y. Huang (Eds.), *Growth without miracles: Readings on the Chinese economy in the era of reform*. New York: Oxford University Press.

Perris, A. (1983). Music as propaganda: Art at the command of doctrine in the People's Republic of China. *Ethnomusicology, 27* (1), 1–28.

Source Juice (2009). Extensively carried out on the "patriotic songs we sing," mass choir activity. Retrieved at www.sourcejuice.com/1191781/2009/07/15/extensively

Tsui, Y. F. (1990). *Amateur Chinese orchestras in Hong Kong in [the] 1970's* (Unpublished master's thesis). The Chinese University of Hong Kong.

Tsui, Y. F. (1998). Ensembles: The modern Chinese orchestra. In R. C. Provine, Y. Tokumaru, & J. L. Witzleben (Eds.), *The Garland encyclopedia of world music, volume 7: East Asia: China, Japan, and Korea.* NY, London: Routledge.

Tuohy, S. (2001). The sonic dimensions of nationalism in modern China: Musical representation and transformation. *Ethnomusicology, 45* (1), 107–131.

Wong, G. K. M., & Yu, L. (2003). Consumers' perception of store image of joint venture shopping centres: First-tier versus second-tier cities in China. *Journal of Retailing and Consumer Services, 10*, 61–70.

Wong, I. K. F. (1984). *Geming Gequ:* Songs for the education of the masses. In B. S. McDougall (Ed.), *Popular Chinese literature and performing arts in the People's Republic of China.* Berkeley: University of California Press.

Wu, G. B. (2006). *A sketch history of traditional Chinese music in 20th century Hong Kong.* Hong Kong: International Association of Theatre Critics.

Yeung, W. K. (2009). The modern Chinese orchestra. In C. F. Wong (Ed.), *Listening to Chinese music.* Hong Kong: The Commercial Press (HK) Ltd.

Yu, S. W. (1999). Xianggang di Zhongguo Yinyue [Chinese music in Hong Kong]. In S. B. Chu (Ed.), *Xianggang Yinyue Fazhan Gailun* [The development of music in Hong Kong]. Hong Kong: Joint Published (HK) Co. Ltd.

Yu, S. W. (2005). *Such are the fading sounds.* Hong Kong: International Association of Theatre Critics.

Zhao, B. (1997). Consumerism, Confucianism, communism: Making sense of China today. *New Left Review, 222* (March–April), 43–59.

Zhou, Chang. (2003). *Zhongguo Xian Dangdai Yinyuejia yu Zuopin* [Chinese contemporary composers and compositions]. Peking: People's Music Publishing House.

Part II

INTERCONNECTIONS

Chapter Eight

Intergenerational Music Learning in Community and Schools

Carol Beynon and Chris Alfano

The term *intergenerational* can be defined as groups of people from different generations interacting with each other. An abundance of literature has shown that when senior citizens are involved in learning experiences with youngsters, benefits are accrued by both young and old (Alfano, 2008; Loewen, 1996; Mitras, 2009; Strom & Strom, 1995). Many of these studies have focused on increased literacy development in primary children, with older adults gaining a sense of satisfaction and well-being when working with children. The primary benefit of intergenerational activities for children has been documented as increased individualized learning opportunities, while for seniors, it is feeling valued and making an important contribution.

In the community music setting, there are discrete organizations for children, youth, young adults, middle-aged adults, and seniors. However, there are also a number of community music settings where the young learn alongside adults, a situation that challenges the traditional notions of adult as teacher, role model, or expert, and child or adolescent as novice learner. In most of these types of intergenerational activities, common practice is to rely upon the notion that the older person is more knowledgeable than the younger student, which supports the traditional interactive roles of teacher and student linked to age.

This chapter reports on two case studies where music learning, performance, and individual well-being have been enhanced by the blending of younger and older learners studying and performing together. The concept of Reciprocal Relations Interaction (Loewen, 1996) suggests that each student, regardless of age, can act as teacher or learner by either receiving or giving help in the forms of musical knowledge and personal support. The cases in this chapter look specifically at

1. How community music can influence music programs in schools as well as how school music can influence community music
2. How participating in singing in an intergenerational setting might not only alter how music is learned, but also inform opinions and stereotypes of a different age cohort by fostering multi-age friendships

Each of the authors of this chapter works in musical performance situations where the interaction of young and older learners is critical to the outcomes of their musical setting. Carol Beynon is co-director of the community-based, intergenerational Amabile Boys & Men's Choirs in London, Ontario, Canada. This organization has been described as a highly successful male choral organization in terms of the number of males involved in singing, the intergenerational impact of each choir on the others, the consistent exceptional quality of performance, and the creation of models of leadership development among youth and men. Chris Alfano is a music teacher in a traditional secondary school in Ontario, Canada, where adults, most of whom are between the ages of fifty-five and eighty-five, take high school instrumental music courses alongside the youth of the school. In Beynon's case, the original participants came to the community choirs from the school system, while in Alfano's case, the community—specifically the seniors and members of the community—came to the school, each having a significant and synergistic impact upon the other. In this chapter, Beynon and Alfano each provide a brief description of their respective programs and summarize the findings into themes that arise from their individual studies of these programs.

BEYNON CASE STUDY: THE AMABILE BOYS & MEN'S CHOIRS

In 1990, Carol Beynon was one of two artistic directors who founded the community-based Amabile Boys Choirs in London, Ontario. Their sister organization, the Amabile Youth Singers and Junior Amabile Singers, provided music education and performance opportunities for girls and young women in the region. However, no such choir existed for boys who might like to sing. What began almost twenty years ago as a traditional boys' choir organization for about thirty unchanged voices has grown dramatically into a large community-based choir organization with about 150 members for unchanged and changing voices, called the Amabile Boys & Men's Choirs (AB&MC). There are four choirs—the Amabile Treble Training Choir; the Amabile Treble Concert Choir; the Amabile Young Men's Ensemble; and Primus, the Amabile Men's Choir. Many of the members have been singing with the organization for ten years or longer, and, in fact, some of the men now singing in Primus began with the original treble choir in 1990. The ages of the members range from eight to sixty-eight, and the choirs have gained not only international status for artistic excellence, but have also earned an equally renowned reputation for using singing as an agent for character development. The choirs are invited as featured guest artists nationally and internationally and are also frequently invited to give workshops on singing as leadership development, as well as vocal training for boys and young men, to teachers, community leaders, and students.

There are numerous community choirs where there is a range in age span of twenty-five or more years among the member, but normally the participants are all adults, sharing adult interests and life habits. What is unusual about the AB&MC is that the ages of the singers span child, youth, young adult, middle-aged, and senior adult males. And while the various AB&MC choirs rehearse and perform independently, they also work together on a regular basis on the same vocal techniques and repertoire. One of the primary mandates of the men's choir, Primus, is its responsibility in rehearsing, mentoring, teaching, and performing on a regular basis with the younger choirs, especially the Young Men's Ensemble. As the Young Men observe and receive mentoring in singing from the oldest choir, so too do they learn to become mentors to the younger treble choirs, and, eventually, senior mentors themselves.

As artistic director, researcher, and participant-observer in this organization since 1990, Beynon has had the opportunity to take a firsthand experiential approach to the questions about how community music can influence music programs in schools and how participating in singing in an intergenerational setting might not only alter how music is learned, but also inform opinions and stereotypes of a different age cohort. She lists two important contributions that this community-based musical organization has created:

1. The increase in the number of boys' choirs that have developed in the elementary and secondary schools in the region as well as the general increase of the number of males involved in singing in the community, which is a phenomenon in and of itself in current society
2. The intergenerational associations that have emerged through the development of the organization, from one traditional boys' choir for unchanged voices to four choirs that range from children- to adult-based

Influence of Community Music in the Schools

In times of financial restraint when educational programs are targets of budget cuts, or when political issues about standards of education become concerns, music and other peripheral subjects are often affected first as key resources are redirected toward core subject disciplines. Such has been the case in many schools in North America for the past twenty years. Because of political lobbying and intervention in difficult economic times, music programs in schools have suffered losses of specialist music teachers and music program cuts. When school choral music programs decline, community choral music programs for youth grow, filling a need and providing new opportunities for youth to experience music (Beynon, 2004). Perhaps coincidentally, the AB&MC program was founded at about the same time as cutbacks began to impact the music curriculum in London's schools.

The Choirs were first designed as a traditional boys' choir program for about thirty unchanged voices. However, the response and demand from the community and the boys themselves caused it to grow from a small children's program into a large program, initially for youth, but ultimately for young men. Teachers who had exceptional boys in their classes in schools recommended that these young men join the choirs, and many parents chose this venue for their sons' music education. What began as a treble choir transformed into a youth and then an adult choir because, as the boys' voices matured and changed, they said they wanted to keep singing, not wanting to leave this choral organization. The young men enjoyed the experience of singing together in a male ensemble at exceptionally high artistic levels and felt that they were making an important contribution to the success of the choirs. Although sometimes ridiculed by their peers for singing, choir members felt safe and productive in this environment, and many of their best friends were members of the choirs. The expansion of the treble choir into the youth and men's choirs was a serendipitous grassroots development initiated by the boys themselves.

As the boys in the choir developed into young men, some began to think of studying music at university as voice majors. There is now a long list of current members and alumni who have chosen professional singing or acting careers or who have become graduate students in music, university professors of choral music, or most importantly, teachers in the local public schools. Some have degrees in music education and some do not, but all are developing vocal music programs for young men in their schools. For example, four members of Primus, who are local music teachers, have now developed their own high school young men's choirs. They bring their choirs together at least three times during the school year to rehearse and perform, building confidence and musical competence and reinforcing the notion that male singing is an acceptable way of learning music despite societal norms and stigmas. One young teacher and longtime member of Primus, who has developed a men's choir of about forty-five singers in his school, comments:

> I knew there were many students in the school with an interest in vocal music but [who] stayed away from the program. My goal was to help bring those students back into music as well as to help foster an environment for others to feel welcome and have fun while creating music . . . The camaraderie between the guys carries through the school's social circles [and] . . . provides an environment for students who may be afraid to sing (though they enjoy it) to try it out and find themselves become a leader both musically and socially . . . I've seen firsthand the huge difference that can come for many guys who have never felt accepted or had a place where they belonged.

As a direct result of the community choir organization, there are more boys and men singing in this region than before. A symbiotic relationship developed. The Amabile boys' choirs needed students to sing, and many of the boys returned to their schools to sing and encouraged their friends to sing as well, increasing the number of new programs within the schools and increasing the membership of the community choirs. The success of these community choirs has had a role in increasing the numbers in choral programs and extracurricular choirs as well as increasing the number of boys and young men singing in the schools.

At the same time as the number of males singing increased in schools, one elementary teacher involved with Amabile confirms that the same societal stigmas associated with male singing are prevalent even in the early years.

> I started a boys' choir to try to dispel the stigma of elementary school boys singing in my school. Many boys were too afraid to join the choirs that were mainly [made up of] girls for fear that they would be ridiculed. I knew that once the boys started to sing they would become some of our strongest voices, and I wanted to improve the level of all of our ex-

tracurricular music groups, as well as the singing in regular classes. Also, I realized that many boys did not realize that their voices were in the same treble range as girls, so they were trying to sing notes outside of their range, because that is where they thought that they should sing. Therefore, many boys used their talking voices to sing. When the boys sang in their treble range with girls they felt they were singing too high, [but] when they sang in their treble range with just boys, more of them were comfortable with their sound.

This teacher goes on to note that school music programs promote more learning than just musical literacy:

Of course, the boys that sing in boys' choir attain a higher level of music reading and vocal technique than they would if they were not part of the choir. Many of them improve their language skills as well. There are a lot of social skill lessons that are taught incidentally throughout the choir rehearsal and teamwork is a big part of learning in any musical group.

Singing and Learning in an Intergenerational Setting

In the AB&MC, there are now fathers and sons singing in the various choirs; however, the concept of intergenerationality occurs between other different-age groups who work together for the mutual benefit of self and each other. As the organization transitioned into a series of choirs of children, teenagers, young adults, and then older adults, the older members automatically assumed a sense of responsibility for the younger members in the organization in terms of musical learning and development as well as character development.

Musical Development

Singing in a boys' choir is a unique challenge due to the complex nature of the changing male voice. Whereas female voices experience small and usually unnoticeable changes in quality throughout life, the male voice changes dramatically at the onset of puberty and then continues to change as the individual ages. In the case of the AB&MC, the male voice change process has actually supported both musical and intergenerational development. This change can be a worrisome part of growing up, and the older singers support and reassure the younger members during this process. For many men, the fully mature adult singing voice is not settled until the early thirties, causing many of those who are interested in singing to become impatient with the process and give up. To learn to sing well with an unchanged voice and to then lose it can be a somewhat traumatic experience for many young men, and trying to find a brand-new voice that has a totally different placement while one is feeling the insecurities of approaching adolescence is difficult. To be a male singer in a society that devalues singing for men only compounds the situation. With this in mind, it has become an expectation that the older singers mentor the younger singers, and not only in musical development and vocal technique.

Those who have gone through the voice change as singers have far more empathy and credibility with the frustrated and embarrassed younger singer. However, an important mentoring understanding and relationship develops between younger and older singers. In the Amabile Young Men's Ensemble, a boy with a changing voice, trying to read the bass clef for the first time, realizes that only some notes in the first or second tenor, baritone, or bass parts are within his current range on a particular day. He is placed between two men whose voices have changed, and these men point out notes to him in the score that are within his limited range and sing along with him, providing a model of sound as well as a model of sight-reading that may pivot from part to part depending on his changing voice. The older singers provide mentoring in several areas, including musical development (vocal technique, breathing, reading, and performance technique) as well as social development. Hence, the boys with changing voices look up to the men singing around them with great respect. These are men who have been invited to perform at elite international events or who are the winners of the CBC (Canadian Broadcasting Corporation) national radio competition for amateur choirs in Canada and who garner respect from and are recognized in the community. As boys and young men learn to sing with new voices while sitting beside experts who once walked in their shoes, they develop non-threatening, mutually valuable relationships that result in a camaraderie among these singers as learning peers. They realize that learning a new voice need not be intimidating within the security of a multi-age group. Most importantly, there is sincere mutual respect and appreciation for each other's learning accomplishments among singers of differing ages. The younger singers learn the mentorship roles that they will extend to the next group of younger singers as they develop new voices.

Breaking Down Stereotypes

The older singers in the AB&MC report that they learn as much about music and life from the younger singers as the younger singers say they do from the older members. Normally these groups would not associate socially, but as the older singers interact with the younger singers in choir in rehearsals and in social settings, such as pick-up soccer or cards, the boundaries of age are blurred. They realize that the stereotypes of the younger generation that they subconsciously develop are challenged by their conversations and musical sharing; likewise, the intimidation that the younger singers feel about communicating with the older singers is broken down. In rehearsal, the older singers encourage the younger singers to try solos and applaud enthusiastically when they finish. Older singers will work with groups of young singers on pieces to help them develop the notes as well as the musical phrasing. They may sing in double quartets, combining four young singers and four experienced singers, and comment openly that some of the younger singers are equally or more capable than some of the older singers. Some young singers say they feel more comfortable asking older peers for help than they do asking one of the artistic directors. As these developments help to break down the traditional stereotypes that each group may have held about each other, the musical and non-musical outcomes become obvious—better choral singing and a healthy cross-generational social environment. There is a natural and apparent synergy in this particular intergenerational learning environment that develops in the rehearsal and performance settings and spills over onto sports fields or card tables during free time. Blending various ages into musical learning and social environments has benefits for all participants, whether the setting is choral or instrumental.

ALFANO CASE STUDY: LEARNING TO PLAY IN THE BAND IN THE SECONDARY SCHOOL SETTING

In January 1994, Chris Alfano initiated a music instruction program for seniors (retired men and women) and middle-aged adults, teaching them to perform on woodwind, brass, and percussion instruments in a concert band setting. The program is housed at LaSalle Secondary School in Kingston, Ontario. The course runs for two hours each morning, five days a week, for the entire school year and has been in continuous operation since its inception. There are more than seventy adult students enrolled, most of whom are between the ages of sixty-five and eighty-five. It is a fully funded program sponsored by the Ontario Ministry of Education through the local school board. The adults are registered as daytime high school students in the same manner as adolescent students. The curriculum of study is based on the same Ministry of Education guidelines that are in place for the delivery of performance-based instrumental music courses at the high school level.

Many of the adult learners in this program start from scratch. That is, they have never played the instrument that they are learning or they have never played any musical instrument. Those in the program learn to read and apply music notation as well as develop competent practical skills on a wind instrument in the same manner as any adolescent would when enrolled in an instrumental music course. In addition to receiving instruction, the class functions as a concert band and performs during the academic year. Many of the musicians continue to perform in this band during the summer months by meeting at another location outside of LaSalle School and hiring a conductor to lead their rehearsals and summer concerts. The Adult Band (as it is known in the secondary school) frequently performs with the adolescent band in class and concert settings. The band also acts as a pit orchestra for the high school musical productions.

This site is rich with information concerning seniors as active learners and provides insights regarding intergenerational learning and associations. Interviews with some of the participants in this program (Alfano, 2009) provide the basis for the findings presented at the end of this case.

Julian[1] describes his experiences as a music learner in this environment and comments that his high school peers are effective teachers.

> To me, the interactions that are more interesting are when the kids play with us. The musicianship is the great equalizer, so in that circumstance I have no problem accepting the fact that Charlie [a high school student] plays better than me and reads better than me. And I think he showed me an alternate fingering for something, so I've actually learned something from him.

Julian talks about how playing music together with seniors may actually help those adolescents who are experiencing difficulties with adults such as their parents. He tells how performing music with his son many years ago was a positive experience for their relationship.

He starts by saying that their identities as "father and son" were overshadowed by their identities as collaborating "musicians."

There are certain ages that kids go through [when] they are not getting along with their parents terribly well, and certainly mine went through that. So my son . . . went to the university where I was [teaching], and that was problematic in itself, and he was surly and he was just going through that hormonal stuff, but we both played in the clarinet group and he's a much better player than me. And that really made it possible for us to talk because we could talk about music, have equal footing.

Many of the adult learners expressed the belief that their age and the age of the adolescents is somehow less visible and less important when they frequently interact with each other while they are engaged in music learning. The identity of being a student is reinforced by the fact that the music classes are in a high school, while it is in session, which allows the adult learners to participate with the adolescents as part of the high school student body. Perhaps this role shift is similar to that of adolescents who are "students" while in school, but while at a part-time job, they are "employees." At one point, adult music students La Verne, Maxine, and Patricia were discussing their role as students.

Patricia: We're all students. We're having the same music. We're having the same difficulty, the same problems, you know, and we need the same amount of time with the teacher. So, really, we are the same.

La Verne: That's right. We have a common focus.

Maxine: That's right. When it came to parceling out clarinet parts, I mean, we weren't playing first clarinet. The hotshot kids were. We were playing second and the [teacher] was rotating some parts so, on a couple of things, we were third and uh, kids who were third were second, but you know I mean, when they have the opportunity to be with adults as peers, with absolutely no authority, in place, it's just . . . it's astonishing.

Patricia explains that being a music student in the school music program is different from being a performer in a community band.

One of the things I like about going to school—and that's what I say—I don't say going to band, I don't say going to music—I say I'm going to school in the morning. And it sort of gives me . . . I go as a student so not as much is expected of me . . . I've never been to [Town] band or [Community] band, but I would be very intimidated to go into those two bands at the same level of competence or incompetence where I'm at right now with my music. I would expect that they would expect me to be better than I am, but going to school gives me . . . I'm a student, so I'm still learning. I don't feel nearly as intimidated about learning.

The notion of being a student in a school led to conversations with the participants about their thoughts of being an adult student in a building that caters, almost entirely, to adolescent learners. Hubert describes his concerns of being a senior citizen in a school during his first few days as a student.

Well, when I first joined the class, I was, quite honestly, I was a bit leery of walking through the hallways and encountering the kids because I didn't know what type of reaction I would encounter from the kids. Here is somebody, who is, you know, who is somebody who doesn't have practically any hair whatever or has white hair.

He realized that his identity as a member of a different age cohort would make him more identifiable to the majority of adolescents. As his time as a student increased, he explained that this uneasy feeling of "sticking out" because of his physical age differ-ence dissipated. His experience became more positive.

> [B]ut once you get immersed into the class, you find . . . that the kids go their own way, you go your own way, and they are very respectful. Actually, you find it very pleasant, and there are no examples of friction whatsoever . . . The kids that come to the class are quite joyful and are very nice. The ones that I've met are very, very nice.

As an adult and teacher in the school, Alfano's role is that of teacher, albeit younger than many of the adult students. Students regard him as someone knowledgeable who has credentials and experience supporting his position. Loewen (1996) describes the importance of having a qualified instructor in a recognized learning institution such as a high school, college, or university as "curriculum-based learning." Loewen explains that a key component of an intergenerational association in a classroom is the notion that a learning activity has value because it is recognized as a course. There is a per-ception that having organized learning material delivered by a teacher gives greater value to the activities than if it were through a group organized in a non-school-based program. "For better or for worse, the institutional value of student assessment is stamped in this project, thus legitimizing it in the same way as a unit in history, French, or math" (p. 26). Whether the program is interest-based, credit-based, or non-credit-granting, or even if a person is only auditing a program, the structure of the learning environment as a course gives an impression of importance and legitimacy.

The classroom setting provides an atmosphere where all learners can interact with each other as friends regardless of their ages. The older participants recalled some sig-nificant events where they felt accepted by the adolescents as friends even in the wider venue of the school and not just in the music classroom. Maxine shared this story:

> I've not talked to you about this before, but, you know, you take the [walk] down to the girls' washroom. And of course the girls, they're so cute, they're always [primping] in front of the mirror, you know, and they're fluffing their hair and, ah, one day I walked in and one of the girls was putting eyeliner on eyes. And mascara. And I said to her, "Oh, you're really going to look hot after that's done," and she said, "Well, you know, I can't really quite get it." So we ended up talking about how to put eyeliner on . . . how to put mascara on. You know . . . the proper kind of way that you use hair spray. And it was so—not anything music.

> CA [Chris Alfano]: Was she a musician?

> Maxine: No. No. She was just a kid in the washroom. But, it was—here's a sixty-four-year-old woman—talking to a sixteen-year-old kid about putting eyeliner on. Using hair tones and just getting beautified. It was . . . it was so fun. I wondered the first few times that I went to use that washroom, I wondered if some of the kids wondered why this per-son—this older person—was coming into their washroom. Well, I told them why.

CA: It's not your environment. Like, they're not comfortable . . . because if you were staff, you would go into a staff washroom.

Maxine: Right. The first time that I went in there I said, "I'm a student."

Billy had some reservations about his daily associations with adolescents in the high school and their social behaviors.

Well, I think about how it was when I was in high school. The first thing, being honest, the first thing I noticed was, ah, in general, the lack of a certain amount of respect and discipline from the younger people, and I don't say that with any disdain or nothing like that . . . it's just that it was so different when we went.

However, after he became more acquainted with the adolescents as music students and engaged in music learning with them on a daily basis, his original perceptions of their behavior was modified.

But I don't think that way at all now. I don't. And I realize, what do they think of us? They probably figure, look at those old white-haired, silver-haired old buggers in there trying to blow a horn and all this and all of the sudden within a few days you're respecting each other. That thought just left my mind . . . because they don't think that way. You know? One lad sat down beside me there. I don't know, this was only about six months after seeing this band, they were all sitting beside me, he's looking down at my feet. I said to him, like this, "What's happening, man?" He says, "I'm just looking at your boots, man, they're cool." I had bought these neat boots I thought were pretty good. He liked the boots and I thought, OK, that broke the ice right there, you know. This guy's all right.

The experiences shared and comments provided in the interviews about interacting with adolescents in a daytime high school band program were highly positive and provide the following summations.

1. Being involved in a music-learning program in an active high school puts older adults in contact with adolescents on a daily basis, a scenario that does not present itself in any other part of their lives. Likewise, adolescents are in contact with older adults as peer learners in the high school setting, another uncommon scenario.
2. The act of learning with adolescents has contributed positively to the lives of adults by immersing them in learning with a group of young people who are energetic, joyous, and exciting by the very nature of their youth.
3. The adults can share their life experiences and reminisce about their own youth as well as share in the lives of the adolescents through conversation and daily interaction. This frequency of association fosters intergenerational friendships and conversations.
4. Adults have learned that their frequent daily interaction with adolescents has changed their views and stereotypes of adolescents. This interaction produced a more realistic and positive awareness of this younger age group as intelligent, caring, and thoughtful people who are, in many ways, no different in their beliefs, goals, and ambitions from the adults with whom they associate. The frequency of

association between adolescents and seniors has positively affected seniors' perceptions of their social group identity and their own personal identities.

CONCLUSION

While the literature (Alfano, 2008; Loewen, 1996; Mitras, 2009; Strom & Strom, 1995; see also Bowers, 1998; Dupuis, 2002; Farkas & Hogan, 1995 Manheimer, 1997; Russell, 2001) has clearly shown that intergenerational learning experiences benefit both young and old, this chapter describes two music education situations in which significant learning and interaction is occurring, impacting both community and school music. Several pertinent findings emerge from the data:

1. Elders learn as much from youngsters as the youngsters learn from their elders in intergenerational community and school music settings.
2. Younger and older learners develop non-threatening, mutually valuable relationships, and the age differences between learners are blurred and, at times, almost invisible.
3. Learning is not as intimidating when working with others in multi-age groups.
4. Youngsters and seniors learn how to interact with each other inside and outside the musical learning environment without the traditional stereotypes of each other.
5. There is sincere mutual respect and appreciation between youngsters and elders for each other's learning accomplishments.
6. A natural and obvious synergy develops in the intergenerational learning environment.

Breaking down age stereotyping of one age group toward another is a significant non-musical but important social outcome of intergenerational association. These studies show that learning music in an intergenerational situation can be a great equalizer. In fact, some authors recommend that public schools be added to the list of sites where the participation and association through learning by multi-age groups takes place. The frequent association that occurs between young and old in a curriculum-based, intergenerational program can be beneficial to all age groups in sharing cultural and experiential differences for a richer understanding, acceptance, support, and respect of themselves and others.

NOTE

1. All names are pseudonyms to provide anonymity.

BIBLIOGRAPHY

Alfano, C. (2008). Intergenerational learning in a high school environment. *International Journal of Community Music Education, 1* (2), 253–266.

Alfano, C. (2009). Seniors' participation in an intergenerational music learning program (Unpublished dissertation). McGill University, Montreal, Quebec, Canada.

Beynon, C. A. (2004). The rise and fall and rise and fall and rise . . . of choral music in Canada. *Canadian Music Educator, 45* (2).

Bowers, J. (1998). Effects of an intergenerational choir for community-based seniors and college students on age-related attitudes. *Journal of Music Therapy, 35* (1), 2–18.

Dupuis, S. L. (2002). Intergenerational education programs in leisure and aging courses: Older adult and student experiences. *School Journal of Leisure Studies and Recreation Education, 17*, 73–86.

Farkas, J., & Hogan, D. (1995). The demography of changing intergenerational relationships. In V. Bengtson, K. Warner, S. Schaie, & L. Burton, (Eds.), *Adult intergenerational relationships* (pp. 1–18). New York: Springer Publishing.

Loewen, J. (1996). *Intergenerational learning: What if schools were places where adults and children learned together?* Retrieved from http://eric.ed.gov

Manheimer, R. J. (1997). Generations learning together. *Journal of Gerontological Social Work, 28* (1/2), 79–91.

Mitras, D. L. (2009). Strengthening student voice initiatives in high schools: An examination of the supports needed for school-based youth-adult partnerships. *Youth & Society, 40* (3), 311–335.

Myers, D. E. (2009). Lifelong learning: An emerging research agenda for music education. *Research Studies in Music Education, 4* (1), 21–27.

Russell, J. (2001). Born to sing: Fiji's "singing culture" and implications for music education in Canada. *McGill Journal of Education, 36* (3), 197–216.

Stebbins, R. A. (2009). *Personal decisions in the public square: Beyond problem solving into a positive sociology.* New Brunswick, NJ: Transaction Publications.

Strom, R. D., & Strom, S. K. (1995). Intergenerational learning: Grandparents in the schools. *Educational Gerontology, 21* (21), 321–335.

Chapter Nine

Music Learning as a Lifespan Endeavor

David Myers, Chelcy Bowles, and Will Dabback

Access to music experience and understanding—whether through performing, listening, or creating—is more widely available to more people today than at any time in history. Increasing user-friendly technology and a shrinking global society have combined to broaden the range of opportunities. People can compose, perform, and record music instantly in the comfort of their homes, without prior training or the pressure of others listening. Long-standing forms of access remain, such as family and recreational music making, in-person music lessons and classes, community ensembles, rituals and customs, radio and television broadcasts, and commercial recordings. However, these avenues are expanding to include Internet streaming, music games, real-time music interaction with teachers and others next door or thousands of miles away, global travel to and from formerly remote regions, and personalized digital playlists to accompany working, sleeping, or traveling.

Broadly defined, access is not only about availability. It is also about acquisition of knowledge, understanding, and skill, which, logically, ought to further engagement, make music experience more meaningful, and inspire continued learning. The National Center for Creative Aging publishes an arts and aging toolkit to help service providers understand how and why elders benefit from professionally conducted community arts programs. Clearly, many people, regardless of age, are actively pursuing music-related activities as education, recreation, and avocation.

In the midst of such unprecedented access, is a discussion of lifespan music learning necessary or even relevant? Levitin's (2009) blanket assertion that "music is important in the daily lives of most people in the world, and has been throughout human history" (p. 2) raises many potential questions as to the manifestations of music's relative importance and meaning in daily life, particularly in an increasingly digital and commercialized music environment.

It is relatively straightforward to study the lives, interests, choices, and pursuits of those who actively engage with music and to illuminate the relevance of music to the human condition. What is difficult to understand is the apparent dichotomy between the universal human affinity for music and the relatively low stature music holds as a socially and politically important dimension of society at-large. To what extent is music truly valued by most people, in terms of having fundamental social and expressive import? To what extent is music fascinating as a superficial activity, primarily as recreation, diversion, or hobby, and to what extent is it an internalized, essential source of meaning and value? In the words of Sean Gregory (2005), "Contemporary culture is no longer limited to handing down a tradition, and a belief in the integrity and transformative potential of 'local' traditions must now be aligned with the development of skills, attitudes, and outlooks that encourage connections within different contexts of our cultural evolution" (p. 19).

Issues surrounding the topic of music learning as a lifespan endeavor go well beyond the availability of and access to personal music making and learning throughout life. While these are important, it is also important to identify the ways in which change across a person's lifespan influences the learning process and how delivery systems may meet the needs of diverse learners. But the larger view of lifespan music learning focuses upon the potential values of a musically engaged society in which the expressive qualities inherent within music are essential. In such a society, the professional music and music education communities must ensure equitable and responsible music learning for all people as the embodiment of the creative, nuanced, and sensitive interrelationships that secure a healthy society. Elliot Eisner (2005) has suggested that the forms of thinking that the arts stimulate and develop relate to our "ability to deal with conflicting messages, to make judgments in the absence of rule, to cope with ambiguity, and to frame imaginative solutions to problems we face . . . We need to be able not only to envision fresh options, we need to have *feel* for the situations in which they appear" (p. 213, emphasis added).

This chapter urges a lifespan vision of music learning and music education oriented toward the kind of musically engaged society suggested above. Evidence suggests that school music programs, and the music teacher education programs that support them, rarely emphasize learners' essential confidence and independence for a lifelong musical endeavor. It is important that community music education provide opportunities to nurture a continuity of musical growth and development across the lifespan. A lifespan perspective challenges us to ask "how systematic music education . . . embraces organic musical proclivities of humans, empowers musical choices of value, provides for independent and social engagement across the lifespan, and enhances the quality of the human condition and the societies in which we live" (Myers, 2007, p. 55).

MUSIC ENGAGEMENT IN A LEARNING SOCIETY

The average life expectancy in the United States has increased from the mid-1940s to the mid-1970s, with significant implications for lifelong learning. Ongoing professional and career learning as well as leisure, health, and self-help learning are now recognized as important dimensions of a positive and productive adulthood. Some learning represents a continuation and upgrading of current knowledge, while other learning delves into new areas for the first time.

The term "learning society" was introduced in the latter half of the twentieth century by authors such as Hutchins (1970) and Cross (1981) to suggest that continuity of learning over a lifetime is essential both to personal and societal well-being. Such learning may be formal or informal, self-regulated or obtained through formal program delivery, and related to professional and career development or diverse areas of personal fulfillment.

Continuity of music participation and learning beyond the traditional years of schooling has been a concern in American music education for decades. As far back as the 1920s and continuing through the 1960s, music education leaders, including Gordon, Dykema, and Gehrkens, expressed the view that music in the schools ought to relate to community life and music participation through adulthood (Myers, 2008, p. 51). The final report of the Tanglewood Symposium (Choate, 1968) eloquently argued that "continuing education should offer an opportunity to move as far in depth or breadth as each [person] can, through a comprehensive program of music that will equip him [or her] to live in the modern world" (p. 115). The report went on to advocate that "music should be offered to adults both for instrumental purposes, to satisfy psychological, religious, and vocational needs, and for expressive purposes, to help each individual find means for self-realization, either as creator or as participant audience" (p. 115). In 1974, the National Association for Music Education (MENC) produced a position paper on adult and continuing music education that listed self-realization, human relations, enrichment of family life, sustaining and improving health, and improvement of occupational competence as objectives. And in 1996, the Music2Education Research Council affirmed the importance of adult and community music by approving the formation of a special research interest group in adult and community music education.

Envisioning music learning as lifespan endeavor, rather than as something that occurs during childhood and adolescence as a precursor to lifelong participation, is consistent with the concept of a learning society. Music, like all other disciplines, is fluid, dynamic, and evolving. Among those who pursue music avocationally, or for enhancing the quality of their lives, the opportunity to increase understanding, skills, and expressive capacity through music can be a continually unfolding process of inquiry and discovery that yields motivation to continue, a sense of achievement, inherent aesthetic fulfillment, and positive socialization within and across age groups. In addition, music learning affords opportunities in areas such as creativity, dexterity, and aural perception that may positively influence other cognitive, affective, and behavioral domains. Such benefits accrue, however, in relation to the nature and quality of the learning experience, which is what generally affords the strongest impetus for individuals to participate in ongoing education (Cross, 1981). In general, principles of sound music learning for adults do not differ dramatically from those for children. However, in the context of maturity represented by adult learners, strategies and techniques for realizing these principles will be employed with cognizance regarding the needs, interests, and age-related traits of adults.

Adult Demographics and Historical Perspective

Demographic data for the United States depict a society with an ever-expanding adult population. According to the 2000 census, adult cohorts outnumber children under eighteen years old for the first time in history. The 2007 Summit on Global Aging issued a report that estimates that people over sixty-five years of age will account for one in every eight of the earth's inhabitants by the year 2030 (Dobriansky et al., 2007). By the middle of the twenty-first century, approximately seventy-nine million senior adults will make up 20 percent of the total population of the United States. Our society currently lacks a comprehensive policy to prepare citizens to understand, much less address, the issues and choices related to aging that they and society will soon face (Krout & Wasyliw, 2002). The call for social reforms will increase commensurately as the baby boom generation ages and adult populations demand new services, seek increased civic engagement, and search for access to cultural and learning opportunities across their lifespans (*A Blueprint for Action*, 2007).

Historically, the music education profession in the United States has largely focused on work in Pre-K–12 school systems. Society should always hold the education of children as one of its central priorities, but at what point in the life course does the music education profession's responsibility end? Given society's rapidly changing demographics and the corresponding emergent issues, American music education must examine its foci to not only better serve traditional school-age populations but also further the cause of music and music education in adult populations. Lawrence-Lightfoot (2009) believes "that the designers of childhood education need to consider the developmental tasks of adulthood and old age as well as those of childhood when they construct curricula, develop effective pedagogies, and build school cultures" (p. 238).

In addition to the history of concern for continuing music participation cited above, the National Association for Music Education (formerly MENC) has long called for a more prominent position for adult teaching and learning in the mission of the organization. An early MENC *Yearbook* (1938) promoted a dual conception of school music educators that included community music leadership as well as appropriate remuneration and scheduling to support such efforts. In 1955, Morgan called for collaborative planning approaches to community programs, activities that featured informal, recreational qualities, and empathetic teaching and learning interactions. Likewise, Kaplan et al. (1958) encouraged dialogue regarding specific techniques and attitudes that teachers might find useful or necessary in their work with adults, the relation of adult music learning to home interests and family, exploration of the special learning needs of populations such as elders, and the connections of school music experiences and music in adults' lives.

To date, researchers have not identified a single explanation for continued engagement in music activities through adulthood, but Coffman (2002) categorizes professed reasons into three areas: personal motivations (such as creativity and leisure), musical motivations (that include love of music and performing), and social motivations (related to group participation and friendship). A close look at participation studies reveals that people who continue to participate in music programs represent a fairly small percentage of those who participated in school music programs and an even smaller percentage of the total population.

The National Endowment for the Arts (NEA) regularly conducts studies of adult participation in the arts. In its latest study (2009), NEA reports that the highest level of participation is in performing choral music, where about 5 percent of adults had participated at least once in a twelve-month period. This statistic, however, represents a decline of 6.3 percent since 1992. For the first time, the 2008 NEA study surveyed Internet usage related to the arts. Of those adults going online at least once a day for any purpose, nearly 40 percent used the Internet for some arts-related purpose. Of these, about 30 percent pursued these activities at least once a week.

Trends suggest that attendance and participation data may not be fully reflective of adults' artistic pursuits. Ivey and Tepper (2006) have written about a growing renaissance of personal art making and creative practices made possible by new technologies, the explosion of cultural choice, and the growth of a do-it-yourself ethos. Tepper and Gao (2008) contend that data on artistic practice show a less negative relationship to barriers of age, income, and education when compared with attendance data. In music, examples of high levels of adult interest in music learning include the New Horizons Band programs, the growth of adult participation in programs sponsored by community music schools, the number of music programs offered through community divisions of universities and public schools, and classes offered by older-adult programs (such as Road Scholar, formerly Elderhostel).

The context of history perhaps provides at least some directions for future work. The profession needs to explore issues of attrition in music participation, not only through school, but through life as well. What resources do music educators require to create opportunities for adults seeking musical outlets? Does the profession offer flexible programs that interest adults enough to dedicate time to them? Perhaps most important, with respect to connections between Pre-K–12 music programs and participation after graduation, do students learn the skills in school programs that will enable them to continue to meaningfully engage with music throughout their lives? What shape might alternative music education take if the profession peers beyond the predominant and hierarchical performance ensemble paradigm found in most middle and high schools?

Facilitating Music Experiences with Adult Learners

Though the term "adult development" is controversial, researchers agree that adulthood should not be viewed in terms of stasis and decline but rather as a time of continuing growth influenced by life experiences, education, and many other variables. Most individuals adapt efficiently to the typical declines of adulthood, such as those experienced in perceptual and motor-sensory functions, and remain competent into their eighties. In fact, it now appears that some faculties, earlier believed to experience inevitable declines and thus subjected only to maintenance, are actually capable of being enhanced with appropriate activities. Agencies such as the National Institute on Aging and the Society for the Arts in Healthcare have concurred that the brain adapts throughout adulthood for continued learning and creativity.

From a cognitive perspective, it is apparent that adults may carry increasing ability to incorporate knowledge from various spheres in solving problems and to tolerate greater ambiguity in problem-solving tasks in comparison to young learners (Labouvie-Vief, 1985). The interplay between life experience and learning is a developmental trait that may enhance knowledge development in adults as they draw on accumulated experience in developing new concepts and skills. Adults tend to be more aware of their own learning styles, better able to articulate their learning goals and needs, and generally more self-directed in terms of how to approach learning.

The limited research on adult and older adult learners in music suggests that there is no identifiable decline in music-learning ability or achievement throughout adulthood (Myers, 1988; 1990; 1995). To the contrary, adults who are given appropriate support and strategies are likely to be successful music learners and participants, and they may provide excellent role models for younger music learners.

If we are to realize a music education system with the pursuit of and engagement in music across the lifespan as its overarching goal, how can we develop and implement this perspective among those in the profession whose backgrounds and practices reflect the historical Pre-K–12 construct? What are issues specific to adult music learners that should be explored in our teacher education programs, and what changes are needed among practitioners to effectively provide experiences across the lifespan?

Characteristics of Adult Music Learners

Although there are certainly principles of teaching and learning that are applicable across age levels, there are characteristics that are specific to particular age groups that affect the planning, development, and evaluation of learning experiences. Brookfield provides a detailed summary of the major studies related to adult learning principles in *Understanding and Facilitating Adult Learning* (1986, pp. 26–39). Although researchers have formulated lengthy lists of principles, there are five characteristics that are typically associated with adult learners across studies and should be taken into account when planning experiences for adult learners: self-defined needs, goals, and motivations; problem-solving applications; self-direction in learning; cognitive and physical changes; and life experience, background, and self-worth. It is appropriate to examine these five general principles in relation to teaching and learning strategies and applications in the context of music-learning experiences.

Self-Defined Needs, Goals, and Motivations

Adults generally enter a learning experience knowing what they want to learn and are highly motivated to achieve their goals. By the time adults get to the point of engaging in a learning experience, they have pinpointed a specific need or desire for particular skills and knowledge and have self-selected a learning experience that they feel will help them reach their goal. Their motivation for learning is self-initiated, and they are ready to plunge into the experience without having to be convinced of its value. Even so, adults may experience heightened anxiety associated with learning—especially related to music performance. Because adults have individualized goals in mind, sometimes a challenge exists in aligning the goals of the student with the time allotted for fulfilling the goals. Especially in learning experiences related to the development of music skills, facilitators and adult learners should engage collaboratively in priority setting and progress evaluation in the context of the level of effort required for successfully realizing goals. Learning strategies should be varied and paced to match individual learning styles and prior levels of music experience and understanding.

Problem-Solving Applications

Active experiential learning that is life-centered—applicable to real-life settings, problems, and interests—is consistent with adulthood. Adults should participate in activities that have immediate application to the problem they have defined. Psychologists have found that adult learners often demonstrate an ability to move beyond solving existing problems to become problem identifiers; that is, adults with the benefit of education, life experience, self-confidence, and competence begin to structure problems they want to solve. Therefore, adult music-learning experiences should involve both constructing and solving musical problems within a framework of performing, creating, and listening to music that connects with life-centered concerns and interests and should transfer to music opportunities available in and through the community. Even in those cases in which the learner's self-identified need is a philosophical exploration, activities can be designed that have application to the learner conceptualizing about and experimenting within an experience of music, regardless of the form that it takes for the individual. An investigation-action-reflection cycle may be used to engage adult learners in active learning, irrespective of the problem to be solved. There should also be immediate real-life application at some level toward the self-defined goal; busy adults need to know that they are making obvious progress on an incremental basis.

Self-Direction in Learning

Self-directed learning is the most commonly cited characteristic of adult learners in the literature and should be recognized as the actual motivation for participation in many cases. An important aim in adult learning experiences is to nurture independent choice making and critical reflection leading toward new understandings, attitudes, and skills, especially when the opportunities outside of the learner's current experience are limited. Learners should be given opportunities to extend their knowledge and skills and to apply them in new contexts once the structured experience is completed. A goal of adult music learning should be to foster self-direction and empowerment to engage actively in music, to think in new ways by reflecting critically about music, and to develop self-confidence and competence, leading to greater independence in future learning.

Cognitive and Physical Changes

Physical and sensorimotor declines associated with aging are typically compensated for with cognitive maturity, socialization, prior experience, self-knowledge, and understanding of personal learning style. In terms of cognition, many researchers now consider adulthood to be a period of continuing development rather than a time of maintenance or inevitable decline and deficit. People who engage or re-engage in music activities in maturity do so with a developed cognition that understands and accepts limitation, with the patience and will to persist in the face of difficulty. With maturity come abilities to process and appreciate expressive aspects of the arts, regardless of skill level, prior knowledge, and experience.

Life Experience, Background, and Self-Worth

Adults have a lifetime of musical experience, whatever their levels of expertise, and they have experienced prior learning, either through structured experiences or through exposure and reflection. Adult learners may possess musical insight as well as performing or listening skills. They have perhaps thought about music intensely and reflected on its meaning in their lives. Thus, music learning may be a matter of applying labels to what adults already know so that they can express their ideas, discover their current capacities, and expand their knowledge and skill. Novice adult learners may require convincing, but introducing and reinforcing this recognition generates communication and assists greatly in collaborative goal setting.

Prior experience may, however, carry both positive and negative connotations and may enhance or impede present learning. Teachers of adult music learners rate changing learned habits or preconceived ideas as the most challenging aspect of teaching adults (Bowles, 2010). Self-concept is a key factor in successful learning, and it is the role of the facilitator to utilize life experience to help develop confidence and competence. Recognizing and relating the importance of life experience to the adult learner is clearly significant in enhancing a learner's self-concept and sense of efficacy about learning new concepts and skills and in developing self-confidence for pursuing future learning and musical engagement.

Motivation for Adult Music Learning

What motivates adults to engage in music learning? A decision to engage in musical activity indicates both an interest and a willingness to spend valuable time away from other life pursuits. How can we better serve those with interest and retain those who join our programs? An important step is to acknowledge that not all musicians and potential musicians have the same motivations for musical engagement. One size does not fit all.

Community Ensembles

Most towns claim at least one community music ensemble, and many have a variety of volunteer vocal and instrumental groups. People in such programs obviously have interest, and much academic and anecdotal evidence exists to suggest that music activity itself serves as the prime motivation for participation. While, on a fundamental level, individuals want to make music with other people, social and environmental factors also affect decisions to join and remain in community ensembles. Ryan and Deci (2000) state that activities that hold novel or aesthetic value for people can elicit intrinsic motivation for those activities given proper conditions. Ensemble participation can satisfy the human needs to seek challenges, learn, and explore; however, music leaders must provide environments that satisfy the fulfillment of these needs.

Competence Participants must perceive themselves as competent in musical action. Leaders must present challenges to participants or else risk boring them. Conversely, challenges that are too great will result in frustration. When members believe that they possess both the strategies and capacity to apply to an appropriate challenge, they will feel competent in their musical activity.

Music offers almost limitless potential for skill building and challenges at all levels. Leaders must first know their musicians' capabilities and then determine materials and activities that will interest performers in their learning. In traditional ensembles, literature selection demands a primary focus. Consistent repertoire choices beyond participants' capabilities risk sub-par music making at one end of the spectrum and high attrition on the other. Alternately, music that does not contain enough substance to engage a participant's critical thinking and existing musical skills can lead to similar results. While an occasional piece that pushes musicians to develop new abilities certainly has its place, choosing literature that participants may sight-read ensures success. This allows both the director and musicians to focus on music making in rehearsal and performance rather than sacrificing quality for the sake of technique.

Even relatively simple pieces offer opportunities for challenge. Musicians at all levels strive to perfect tone, articulation, dynamic contrast, phrasing, and all the other characteristics that musicality comprises. A successful adult music director understands that challenge often lies in the minutiae of parts rather than in overt compositional complexity. Good performance literature repertoire exists at all levels, and it is up to music leaders to find appropriate pieces, lead their ensembles to fully engage with substantive music, and successfully facilitate perceptions of competence.

Autonomy Adult music learners must perceive a measure of autonomy in their musical activities. Instructors can provide structure but should avoid coercion or controlling approaches. Participants must feel that they have choice and input into their own contributions and learning within the parameters set by the program.

Many traditional ensembles utilize a hierarchical leadership model. Professional groups embrace this structure for its efficiency; one director can realize a unified musical vision with a group. However, at the professional level, each musician still contributes a unique voice and interpretation to the final result; they retain their autonomy in the musical choices they make from moment to moment.

Less accomplished ensembles may experience better learning and music making when the director shares some of the leadership responsibility with players. Co-creation of musical interpretation in dynamics and phrasing, for example, encourages participants to think beyond their own parts and embrace a larger role in ensembles. Insight into musical decision making can help individuals understand how their voices contribute to the whole, and, consequently, empower them to make their own musical choices. When appropriate in a program, instructors should encourage individual goal setting, giving members both responsibility and accountability for their own music learning.

Chamber groups and less structured ensembles (certain jazz ensembles, for example) offer even greater flexibility regarding participant roles and choices. Small ensembles challenge musicians to play independently, as each person must manage his or her own part. These opportunities magnify the importance of each voice and, therefore, the musical choices of each moment. Musicians communicate in a much more intimate fashion in such settings, and choices become a matter of group dialogue. For this reason, many large ensemble programs encourage small ensemble formation. Many musicians will seek these opportunities to engage with others in ways that large ensemble structures make difficult.

Relatedness Ensemble members must feel a sense of relatedness. Music groups often develop camaraderie and closeness between participants that emerges from shared activities and peer interactions. Leaders should promote an atmosphere that enhances opportunities for members to engage with each other in supportive roles and extends the sense of social and musical connectedness.

Instructors can provide space and time within rehearsals to enhance opportunities for social exchange. Sectional work can promote both musical improvement and enhance esprit de corps among players as they communicate with each other about music. Breaks (with or without refreshments) release participants from their musical focus to engage with each other in different ways. And performances themselves create group memories and shared history that help to bind people to one another.

External Motivation Individuals' motivations vary, and not everyone will find every activity intrinsically motivating. Participants often engage in such pursuits due to their desire to emulate others whom they respect, to whom they feel related, and who prompt or value specific actions. Peer models and the actual culture of an ensemble have especial importance to motivation. The more ensemble members assimilate the values of these significant others, the more they perceive greater autonomy in their actions.

Directors and music leaders set the tone for music engagement, but participants create the actual contexts through their interactions. The importance of peer models highlights the significance of relatedness within a group. Successful programs promote strong participant leadership. Perceptions of competence and autonomy encourage individuals to participate in music, yet group interactions ultimately lead to trust between the director and among members and, therefore, to motivation for both personal and group musical success.

Other Programs

Many individuals find value in community performance ensembles. The ubiquity of such bands, choirs, and orchestras attests that people may indeed "vote with their feet." However, the numbers in these groups represent a relatively small percentage of the total populace. Community groups usually consist of members with school ensemble backgrounds. Examples of entry points for adult novice musicians are less common. Increasing numbers of communities offer such programs as the Late-Starters Orchestra in London, England, and New Horizons bands, choirs, and orchestras (which feature instruction for beginners) in the United States and Canada. But evidence suggests that most members of these programs are returning to participation rather than beginning for the first time. This situation attests to the fact that, as in school settings, the music education profession has yet to develop programs that reach and interest the majority of society.

Gates (1991) proposes a model of music participation in which he notes that once people become socialized into either participant groups, spectator/audience groups, or groups not involved with music activity, they find difficulty in changing their affiliation. Gates further differentiates the motivations of people who do participate. Professional models of music participation prevail in schools and community groups, where hierarchical structures and an emphasis on public performance mirror those found in professional bands, choirs, and orchestras. Professionals and the amateurs who emulate them view music as work, whereas others may profess a similar work ethic and level of appreciation for music yet wish for looser structures and little to no emphasis on performing. Such "hobbyists" can frustrate music directors who perceive those individuals' abilities and potential yet cannot convince the players to commit to an organization as others do. Such learners may need a different kind of program that deemphasizes aspects they find burdensome or simply offers greater understanding and compromise from directors. Yet another class of participants prefers to briefly sample music activities and move on to other pursuits, both musical and non-musical. Often dismissed from traditional music education approaches, these groups, as well as those with a less performance-oriented mindset, may best be served through programs that stress informal adult education approaches that do not require an extended commitment.

Leaders seeking to increase music participation in a larger population need to explore alternative programs that match these disparate motivations. Opportunities for theory, composition and songwriting, improvisation, and appreciation all hold the potential to expand music engagement in society. Some people may only require opportunity, space, and resources; formal instruction may not suit their preferences or modes of music learning. Informal approaches, where the instructor serves more as a guide or coach, may be appealing to those pursuing music interests as hobbyists. Astute music leaders must understand adult participants' motivations, offer appropriate levels of guidance and resources, and, ultimately, communicate with individuals to craft the most effective music engagement strategies.

Shift from Teacher to Facilitator

Educators engaged in formal and non-formal adult music-learning contexts should reflect on the roles they play and the goals they promote for participants. Members demonstrate their willingness to engage with music within formal systems through their presence in voluntary groups. Directors of such community ensembles can easily continue patterns of replication that produce consistent performances yet fall short of assisting learners to increase their reflective skills and self-directedness. These practices may fail in and of themselves to broaden the view of music learning across the lifespan and the promotion of a true music-learning society.

Research suggests that adults who participate in music activities perceive benefits in their health, quality of life, mental well-being, and social connections (Coffman, 2002; Coffman & Adamek, 2001; Dabback, 2007). Some find these benefits through participation in organized community groups and programs, and others seek them through informal experiences somewhat or entirely divorced from professional music education. How can the music education profession serve those people who do not necessarily wish to participate in formal or non-formal programs yet desire more guidance than they might find in informal settings? How can music educators serve as resources and facilitators for people involved in informal music making who may seek information or advice? Further, how can instructors of community music groups promote principles of self-direction integral to theories of adult learning?

Collaboration lies at the heart of adult learning interactions. Deliberation and action can and do occur in group settings; participants negotiate roles and understandings in the process:

> Facilitators and learners are engaged in a cooperative enterprise in which, at different times and for different purposes, leadership and facilitation roles will be assumed by different group members . . . This collaboration is also constant, so that the group process involves a continual renegotiation of activities and priorities in which competing claims are explored, discussed, and negotiated. (Brookfield, 1986, p. 10)

The role of teacher-as-facilitator shifts and promotes learner autonomy, the core of self-directed learning.

To serve in flexible roles requires conscious effort and practice. Music teacher candidates usually experience socialization processes throughout their educations that create a perception of normalcy regarding music participation. Their familiarity with hierarchical systems, both in their own activities and in their observations of peer experiences, do not often challenge assumptions of music participation and the authoritarian place of teachers. As with adults engaged in music learning, music teachers should also utilize critical reflection to examine the contexts in which they teach and the roles that they occupy in learning interactions.

Implementing a Lifespan Perspective in Music Education

Ostensibly, programs and curricula of Pre-K–12 educational systems prepare people for learning throughout life. In the best possible scenario, schools help students to develop skills and attitudes that foster critical thinking, problem solving, and knowledge application. Too often, however, formal education approaches student learning as preparation for life rather than preparation for learning *through* life. Whereas the former mindset absolves the education profession of responsibility once its charges leave school, the latter offers potentially uncomfortable implications regarding the roles teachers and institutions should play in adult teaching and learning.

If the music education profession is to realize its core value of enhancing both personal and societal well-being through musical participation and growth throughout life and is, therefore, to be viewed as essential by those who make decisions about its worth, we must seriously examine the functional results of almost a century of our work. We can start by exploring what it means to be a musically engaged person. We must then continue by examining the responsibility of the music teacher in this expanded perspective and how music educators are perceived as a profession by those who should benefit from guidance of musically knowledgeable others.

Examine the Lifespan Perspective in the Pre-College Classroom

In order to explore the aspects of a lifespan perspective in music education, it is first important to examine, specifically and realistically, what implementing a lifespan perspective might mean in the pre-college school experience. Teaching from a lifespan perspective means recognizing that "the teaching process involves not only teaching toward musical goals to be met as a youth, but teaching toward musical goals to be met as an adult" (Bowles, 1999, p. 15).

For the pre-college student, a lifespan perspective also means that music experiences are both in preparation for their future engagement in music and inclusive of their current realm of life experiences. These two experience arenas can be highly interactive. Several points will help teachers develop a perspective on classroom activities and a classroom environment that is inclusive of and interactive with the total musical life of young students.

Envision the Child as an Adult and Plan Music Activities That are Similar to Adult Behaviors

In order for the music teacher to develop a lifespan perspective, it is essential to "transcend the view of the student as a child or youth and to choose goals, methods, activities and evaluation procedures that will function effectively for the student as an adult" (Bowles, 1999, p. 15). The teacher should try to give students at every level a variety of activities on which to build an experience base that resembles that of musically engaged adults and that will seem familiar once they are adults. Students need practice and familiarity with the variety of activities they are most likely to do with music as adults—not only the behaviors that we would like for them to do.

A first step in visualizing the child as an adult is to explore the reality of what actually happens in the adult world of music. We know that many adults do what we ultimately train them to do—play and sing in bands, orchestras, and choirs in which most decisions are made by a director. However, it is interesting to review adult music behaviors for which we may or may not give them practice. Many adults

- determine what type of music they want to play or sing and seek out opportunities on their own;
- form their own ensembles, choose the players and singers and the music, determine their own rehearsal schedules, and set up and promote performances;
- play music alone and for themselves;
- pursue music lessons, find an appropriate teacher, and determine their own practice schedules and techniques;
- compose their own music and perform it for themselves and for others;
- make music with people of all ages—with their own children and/or with other family members, at informal community and gatherings, and in ethnic groups;
- go to concerts and informal performances and discuss and critique music with their families, friends, and similarly interested adults—even people that they don't know;
- select recordings and radio programs and seek out opportunities to learn more about the music they listen to;
- make musical decisions for their children, choosing and interacting with their teachers;
- teach music and lead community music groups;
- coordinate music festivals and concert series;
- sit on boards and committees that choose artists and teachers; and
- select music for all kinds of social events, both private and public.

Strive for Independence When Setting Goals, and Plan Activities That Will Result in Some Degree of Independence at Every Stage

It is critical to keep in mind that adults initiate their own musical pursuits and guide their own experiences. At every stage, whether a class, a grading period or term, or a school year, students should be able to *independently* do whatever the goal or objective has been. This means taking learning beyond guided progress toward a long-range goal to functional use of knowledge and skills without guidance (i.e., adopting independence *as* the goal).

View the School Experience as an Opportunity to Empower and Encourage Current and Future Pursuits of Learning and Engagement in the Community

Encouraging students to pursue their own musical learning, formally or informally, helps young students understand that learning does not occur only within the school walls, the school day, or the school years, and develops familiarity with the way it is for adults who pursue musical learning.

While it is wonderful to bring music professionals into the schools, it is also important to have students interact with the people most of them are likely to become— music amateurs and people in other professions who have rich musical lives. It is important to give students the opportunity to share their personal musical experiences with their families and community members or on their own. Activities such as bringing in community members, both professional and amateur, to talk about their musical lives and make music with students, and planning both school-day and after-school assignments that take students out of the classroom to explore and interact with music makers and enthusiasts of all ages promotes an enlarged perspective. Such activities make the lifespan perspective integral to the school experience and interactive with learning objectives.

Reevaluate the Role of the Music Teacher in the Community

Teachers might consider how to best engage community adults in musical activities and encourage adults with whom they come in contact to participate. Teachers might also explore the various opportunities in the larger community for adults to engage in music, and serve as a resource for those expressing interest, developing a list of musical organizations and teachers in the community to which adults can be referred. It is worth considering what the role of the professional music teacher might be from the external community perspective.

Embrace a Lifespan Perspective in the Teacher Education Curriculum

It reasonable to assume that the development of the lifelong learning perspective in teaching should begin with the teacher education program and implementing strategies that will encourage pre-service teachers to explore broadened interpretations of their roles and responsibilities and empower them to initiate change within the profession. The teacher educator may be the key figure in moving the profession toward a lifespan perspective in music education.

It is important to understand that the implementation of a lifespan perspective is achieved through *infusion* rather than *addition.* There are several ways in which an existing curriculum can be enhanced to effectively promote a more comprehensive and inclusive teaching vision.

Expand the Learning Continuum and Broaden the Scope of Professional Music Teaching Opportunities

Teacher educators can promote the perception of teaching music across the lifespan as the norm by referring to the learning continuum as Pre-K through adulthood. The inclusion of readings that address adult learning characteristics and learning across the lifespan introduces students to adult-specific learning characteristics as well as those that are common for all ages.

Exploring careers beyond Pre-K–12 school teaching with prospective teachers can widen the perspective on what it means to be a music teacher. Good music teachers are needed in a wide variety of settings, and pre-service teachers should be aware of every opportunity. In addition, knowing about teaching opportunities beyond those in traditional Pre-K–12 may attract potential students to the teacher education program who cannot envision themselves in that particular setting.

Encourage Curiosity about the Musical Lives of Others

Teacher educators might incorporate activities in which prospective music teachers explore the music experiences of their university peers—beyond their music major colleagues—as well as the professors, family members, and community members with whom they interact, and to talk with non-traditional community musicians, both amateurs and professionals.

Encourage Students to Observe Informal Teaching and Learning and Engage in Adult and Cross-generational Teaching Through Field and Research Experiences

Informal music teaching activities happen in a variety of settings, and students should have the opportunity to observe and analyze teaching techniques and ways of learning in which they themselves may not have been trained. Effective teaching is not exclusive to the school music classroom, rehearsal, or formal lesson, and the school experience should be interactive with music learning that occurs informally.

In addition to in-school field experiences, it is important to engage pre-service teachers in activities with post-12, cross-age, and intergenerational learners through field experiences, service learning, and action research that will give pre-service teachers a variety of experiences in working with people of all ages and all levels of musical involvement.

Implement an Individual Lifespan Perspective

Finally, a critical step in introducing a lifespan perspective into the teaching environment is to implement an expanded and inclusive view of the learning continuum and to explore readings and research related to adult music learners and the relationship of early experiences to continued interest and functionality across the lifespan.

An important aspect of implementing an expanded perspective is to take interest in the musical lives of those with whom one interacts in various life settings by inviting them to share their musical backgrounds, current activities, preferences, and pursuits, even in casual conversation. Talking with those for whom music may have a different meaning than it holds for the school-trained musician may help strengthen the connection between what we, as music educators, think we prepare people to do and what they eventually do with music as adults.

CONCLUSION

The Music Education Profession

This chapter has explored lifespan music-learning issues in relation to the work of those involved in facilitating music learning and participation among adults, as well as of those involved in developing skills, knowledge, and attitudes in early life stages that lead to independent adult engagement. It is important to the realization of a musically engaged society that music leaders in the community, including school teachers, take a long view of learning and engagement across the lifespan and incorporate language, knowledge, skills, and experiences into the formal or informal learning curriculum that reinforce the expectation of engagement at every age and education level.

The change of orientation from preoccupation with music for Pre-K–12 to a lifespan music perspective requires a sweeping change in the music education profession in the United States. Historically, while there have been lifelong learning promoters and torchbearers in the music education profession for over a century, as well as professional symposia, position papers, journal articles, and research efforts devoted to lifelong music learning, the professional proclamation of "Music for All" has not produced an adult population who actively engages in music.

Although music teacher education programs cannot assume full responsibility for facilitating the sweeping change in perspective that is required to realize a musically engaged society, it is a reasonable place to start the process. It is essential to implement strategies that encourage pre-service music teachers and community leaders to explore broadened interpretations of what it means to be musically engaged and of their roles and responsibilities as music educators. Within a lifespan perspective, attention to the systematic teaching of music for young learners and the success of early performing experiences that help to inspire music engagement for some individuals across the lifespan should not be abandoned. A lifespan perspective calls for pre-service music teacher programs to move beyond their predominant emphases on traditional goals, objectives, and methodologies, and to incorporate attention to the skills, knowledge, and inclinations necessary for independent adult engagement.

A Musically Engaged Society

Lawrence-Lightfoot's (2009) investigation of learning among those in the fifty- to seventy-five-year age group includes an account of a retired journalist and newspaper executive who pursued the study of jazz piano. In endeavoring to describe the difference between music learning and the higher-order finance and mathematical modeling he had learned for his prior profession, he spoke of the relationships between structure and creativity, technique and improvisation, physicality and cognition, expectation and surprise, and verbal and aural expression, summing up by saying, "[Music is] a different way of knowing" (p. 185)

Music learning as a lifespan endeavor may be continuous or periodic, personal or social, formal or informal, goal-oriented or achievement-neutral, and diversified or persistently focused. Music offers participants a host of physical, psychological, and social benefits. Regardless of context, content, or approach, however, music development and growth embody distinctive ways of knowing that expand and inform our perceptual awareness, our sensitivity and responsiveness to others, and our creative potential. Ultimately, to the extent that lifespan learning nurtures a musically engaged society, music becomes a metaphor for the humanizing values that enhance the quality of life for all people.

BIBLIOGRAPHY

A blueprint for action: Developing a livable community. (2007). Washington, DC: MetLife Foundation, National Association of Area Agencies on Aging, Partners for Livable Communities, International City and County Management Association, National Association of Counties, National League of Cities.

Bowles, C. (1999). Teaching for adulthood: Transcending the child. *General Music Today, 12* (2), 15–16.

Bowles, C. (2010). Teachers of adult music learners: An assessment of characteristics and instructional practices, preparation, and needs. *Update: Applications of Research in Music Education, 28* (2), 50–59.

Brookfield, S. D. (1986). *Understanding and facilitating adult learning.* San Francisco: Jossey-Bass.

Choate, R. A. (1968). Documentary Report of the Tanglewood Symposium. Washington, D.C., Music Educators National Conference.

Coffman, D. (2002). Adult education. In R. Colwell & C. Richardson (Eds.), *The new handbook of research on music teaching and learning* (pp. 199–209). New York: Oxford University Press.

Coffman, D. D., & Adamek, M. S. (2001). Perceived social support of New Horizons Band participants. *Contributions to Music Education, 28* (1), 27–40.

Cross, K. P. (1981). *Adults as learners.* San Francisco: Jossey-Bass.

Dabback, W. M. (2007). *Toward a model of adult music learning as a socially embedded phenomenon* (Unpublished doctoral dissertation). University of Rochester, Eastman.

Dobriansky, P. S., Suzman, R. M., & Hodes, R. J. (2007). *Why population aging matters: A global perspective* (Publication No. 07–6134). Washington, DC: US Department of Health and Human Services, National Institutes of Health, National Institutes on Aging.

Eisner, E. (2005). What can education learn from the arts about the practice of education? In *Reimagining schools: The selected works of Elliot W. Eisner* (pp. 205–213). New York: Routledge.

Gates, T. (1991). Music participation: Theory, research, and policy. *Bulletin of the Council for Research in Music Education, 109,* 1–35.

Gregory, S. (2005). Creativity and conservatoires: The agenda and the issues. In G. Odam & N. Bannan (Eds.), *The reflective conservatoire* (pp. 19–25). London: Ashgate Publishing.

Hutchins, R. M. (1970). *The learning society.* Harmondsworth: Penguin.

Ivey, B., & Tepper, S. (2006). Cultural renaissance or cultural divide? *The Chronicle of Higher Education,* B6.

Kaplan, M. (1958). *A report for music in American life commission VIII: music in the community.* Washington, DC: MENC.

Krout, J. A., & Wasyliw, Z. (2002). Infusing gerontology into grades 7–12 social studies curricula. *The Gerontologist, 42,* 387–391.

Labouvie-Vief, G. (1985). Intelligence and cognition. In J. E. Birren & K. W. Schaie (Eds.), *Handbook of the psychology of aging* (2nd ed.; pp. 500–530). New York: Van Nostrand Reinhold.

Lawrence-Lightfoot, S. (2009). *The third chapter: Passion, risk, and adventure in the 25 years after 50.* New York: Farrar, Straus and Giroux.

Levitin, D. (2009). *The world in six songs: How the musical brain created human nature.* New York: Penguin Books.

Morgan, H. N. (1955). *Music in American education: Music education source book #2.* Washington, DC: MENC.

MENC (1938). *Thirty-first yearbook of the Music Educators National Conference.* Chicago: Author.

MENC (1974). A program for adult and continuing education in music. *Music Educators Journal, 61* (3), 66–67.

Myers, D. E. (1988). Aging effects and older adult learners: Implications of an instructional program in music. *Transactions of the Wisconsin Academy of Science, Arts, and Letters, 76,* 81–89.

Myers, D. E. (1990). Musical self-efficacy among older adults and elementary education majors in sequential music learning programs. *Southeastern Journal of Music Education, 2,* 195–202.

Myers, D. E. (1995). Lifelong learning: An emerging research agenda for music education. *Research Studies in Music Education, 4,* 21–27.

Myers, D. E. (2008). Freeing music education from schooling: Toward a lifespan perspective on music learning and teaching. *International Journal of Community Music, 1* (1), 49–61.

National Endowment for the Arts. (2009). *2008 survey of public participation in the arts research* (Report Number 49). Washington, DC: NEA.

Peterman, W. J. (1954). *An investigation of influences contributing to the post-school musical activities of adults in the city of Milwaukee, Wisconsin* (Unpublished doctoral dissertation). Northwestern University.

Ryan, R. M., & Deci, E. L. (2000). Self-determination theory and the facilitation of intrinsic motivation, social development, and well-being. *American Psychologist, 55* (1), 68–78.

Tepper, S., & Gao, Y. (2008). Engaging art: What counts? In S. Tepper & B. Ivey (Eds.), *Engaging art: The next great transformation of America's cultural life* (pp. 17–48). New York: Taylor & Francis.

Terdiman, D. (2007). *Is tomorrow's Clapton playing "Guitar Hero"?* Retrieved from http://news.cnet.com/Is-tomorrows-Clapton-playing-Guitar-Hero/2100-1043_3-6220398.htmlart

Chapter Ten

Community Music through Authentic Engagement: Bridging Community, School, University, and Arts Groups

Sylvia Chong, Debbie Rohwer, Donna Emmanuel, Nathan Kruse, and Rineke Smilde

This chapter considers the importance of intersections between community, school, university, and arts groups. Sylvia Chong documents several partnerships between schools and tradition bearers in Singapore as enabled by the Singapore National Arts Council (NAC). Debbie Rohwer, Donna Emmanuel, and Nathan Kruse discuss university outreach ensembles in one Texas community, with particular focus on the Águilas mariachi initiative. Rineke Smilde reports on the Netherlands experience "Opera in the Bus."

THE CASE OF SINGAPORE: PARTNERSHIPS BETWEEN SCHOOLS AND COMMUNITY MUSICIANS

With the demographic changes and technological advances of the twenty-first century, the world has become a small and crowded canvas. On this canvas, people share their knowledge and practices, and, one hopes, learn to accept and appreciate differences. As a country whose population is made up of generations of immigrants, Singapore's vision of nationhood involves a sense of shared destiny based on multiculturalism. Its cultural and creative vibrancy can be seen in terms of the economic, political, and social conditions governing the production and distribution of expression. Many co-ordinated efforts among government and arts leaders have taken place to ensure the development of the arts community and culture industry.

Singapore, a former British colony, is culturally and demographically an extension of the United Kingdom, Malaysia, Indonesia, China, and India, with a population mix of 76.8 percent Chinese, 13.9 percent Malays (including those of Indonesian and Middle Eastern descent), 7.9 percent Indians (including Pakistanis, Bangladeshis, and Sri Lankans), and 1.4 percent other races (World Factbook, 2010). The confluence of ethnic communities in this small nation has enriched the country with both traditional and cosmopolitan outlooks. The joint aims of preserving the diverse spectrum of cultural heritages as well as providing for a conducive environment toward the growth and development of the arts form the cornerstone of Singapore's cultural policy.

Singapore's arts and culture are in a constant state of flux, dynamic and continually evolving. Arts and culture reflect and serve both the community and individual needs, as both assure us of who we are and inspire us with intimations of our future goals. Singapore's cultural policy pursues the twin goals of democracy and excellence: (1) to make the arts and cultural life accessible to all, and (2) to create the conditions under which creativity can be enjoyed by both Singaporeans and the world community (National Arts Council, 2009).

Community music projects contribute enormously to Singapore's cultural and societal landscape through strategies such as engaging disenfranchised members or producing valuable resources. Increasing value is being placed on community activities that have positive impacts on the society. The strongest and most sustainable projects not only foster links between the artists and community members, but also create links with local organizations such as educational institutions.

Partnerships between Educational Institutions and Community Musicians

Arts partnerships have developed to expose students to the arts. Strategic partnerships between education institutions and arts communities are important for developing and sustaining the arts industries. The National Arts Council (NAC) consciously works with schools as well as corporate sponsors to develop arts partnerships. Many ethnic music communities have recognized the need to go out to the audiences of the future, to the schools, and bring their musics to those audiences.

At the turn of the twenty-first century, there has been a blossoming of arts partnerships between schools, arts organizations, and music communities. Schools and arts organizations have begun to collaborate, developing mutual respect for and an understanding of the value each can bring to the partnership. One of the strategies by which schools are able to offer music to students is the establishment of partnerships with community music providers. Partnerships may provide support and complement current music programs. Understanding the different values and goals that partners bring is crucial to the success of the partnership.

The Arts Education Program (AEP)

In the 2009 Renaissance City Report, the Ministry of Information and the Arts reviewed ten years of arts development in Singapore. Both the music community and governmental body recognize that these partnerships are fundamental if performing artists are to continue to form fruitful relationships. In Singapore, the relationship is described as a symbiotic partnership between the private sector, the individual citizen, and the arts community (Ministry of Information and the Arts, 2009).

Since education is a major means of socialization of a community, one primary strategy outlined in the report is to

> expose students to the arts as an aesthetic experience as well as to broaden their understanding and appreciation of the creative possibilities in our world. One key partnership program in Singapore is the NAC-Arts Education Program (AEP), which connects the arts community with schools. With this, additional and expanded funding was allocated

to the NAC-Arts Education Program (AEP) to support arts education at all levels in schools. (2009, p. 5)

Another important issue that has arisen in Singapore since 1997 is the Ministry of Education's initiative that requires the teaching of national music of the local Chinese, Malay, and Indian communities in the music curriculum (Ministry of Education, 2002). Many music teachers struggle to conduct lessons in these musics without the background, knowledge, or resources to do so. The NAC-Arts Education Program (NAC-AEP) has been the major promoter of local ethnic communities in an effort to garner interest and support for local arts. Aimed at developing arts appreciation among young students, the Arts Education Program (AEP) facilitated the involvement of local arts groups in creating and developing special performances or workshops for schools. Music is one of the six main art forms supported by the program.

The AEP receives generous sponsorship of up to 60 percent of the cost from the Singapore Totalisator (Tote) Board[1] schools. The AEP features a large number of performing groups, offering a diverse range of educational presentations to schools, and, through this program, schools enjoy a wide variety of performances not only in music, but also in literature, drama, film/media, and visual arts. In 2008, schools booked some 3,247 arts programs under the NAC-AEP, benefiting more than 330,000 students. The AEP assesses and endorses arts education programs offered by Singapore arts groups and arts education providers for schools. Endorsed programs are then eligible for the Tote Board Arts Grant subsidy. Assessment of the arts education programs are conducted by a panel of arts and education experts, principals, and officials from the Ministry of Education and the National Arts Council. Endorsed programs cover literary, performing, and visual arts and are categorized into three types: Arts Experience, Arts Excursion, and Arts Exposure.[2]

The AEP program includes a number of introductory appreciation sessions on Indian classical and folk music, Chinese orchestra, and Chinese opera, as well as on several Malay traditional music groups. While inviting these community musicians into schools assists the music teacher in exposing and familiarizing students in musics of the various communities, some of the community music groups have gone a step farther by packaging their performances with added educational emphasis, such as more detailed narrative commentary and explanations during the ensemble performances, or suggestions for further follow-up activities for teachers to carry out in class.

The following section presents three NAC-Arts Education Programs highlighting diverse musics of Malay, Chinese, and Indian communities: Nanyin—music of South China; Zapin—a Malay traditional dance and music; and mridangam and tabla—South and North Indian percussion instruments.

Nanyin (Music of South China) Nanyin, which literally means "the Music of the South," can be traced back to the Han Dynasty (206 BCE–220 CE). Originally palace music, it has preserved the characteristics of ancient music. Civil turbulence forced court musicians to migrate south. One group settled in Sichuan, in southwest China, while another group moved to the southeastern coastal province of Fujian. It was in the historical city of Quanzhou, China, that Nanyin flourished and evolved into the form we know today. Musicologists suggest that Nanyin is among the oldest and best preserved of musical art forms in the world, having a complete musical system and a unique set of notation of its own (Chong & Chia, 2003).

The chief musical instruments used in a Nanyin performance have not changed in form or appearance for hundreds of years. They are the *erxian* (a two-string fiddle), the *dongxiao* (a vertically held six-hole bamboo flute), the *pipa* (a pear-shaped four-string lute), and the *sanxian* (a long-necked three-string fretless string instrument whose sound box is covered with python skin).

The singer usually takes her place at the center of the ensemble, holding a clapper in her hands to mark the first beat of every measure. A full array of Nanyin musical instruments would include handbells, gongs, cymbals, and woodblocks, as well as a set of short hand-held bamboo pieces known as *sibao*, which are made to vibrate against each other at high velocity. Nanyin can be grouped into instrumental ensemble music, music which may either be played or sung, and songs. The Arts Exposure program in schools by the Nanyin community musicians includes learning about the instruments, notation, and percussion.

Zapin (Malay Traditional Dance and Music)   The Sri Warisan Som Said group recognizes its important role in nurturing new talent and audiences for the Malay arts through dance and music courses and competitions. They are committed to providing quality programs that not only entertain their participants, but also engage them in the arts to foster a healthy appreciation for Malay culture. The Sri Warisan group continues in its effort to reach the community of young people through education and strives to develop even better programs to communicate their vision of a Singapore where arts and culture are an integral part of life (Chong, 2003).

One of their school outreach programs introduces the Malay Zapin dance, a form of traditional Malay dance brought to the Malay Archipelago by Arab traders. The music for Zapin comes from an ensemble of traditional instruments, which include the *gambus* (lute), *marwas* (gypsy-type bongos), and the violin. The Arts Experience program provides teachers with a follow-up lesson right after watching a Sri Warisan ensemble performance. The activities include basic Zapin dance movements and listening for the various traditional Malay instruments.

Mridangam and Tabla (South and North Indian Percussion Instruments)   Mridangam and tabla are the basis for the rhythmic accompaniment for classical percussion in India. South India prefers the mridangam while North Indian music favors the tabla. The tabla is used for the rhythmic support of Indian and Hindustani classical music, while the mridangam provides the rhythm in Carnatic classical music. In addition to being introduced to the instruments, students are taught the various drum syllables used in Indian music in this Arts Exposure program. While learning them, students understand the execution of the tala, the rhythm, or time signature as well as the mathematics involved in the rhythm.

Challenges of Bridging the Worlds of School and Ethnic Community Musicians

A number of studies have examined arts partnerships involving schools. Undercofler (1997) reviewed different partnership models to conclude that partnerships between schools and the community organization offering the outreach programs provided experiential education opportunities, but did not really contribute to a program of music study. Remer (1996) identified elements that the schools and arts organization focused on when considering partnership: intensity, nature and mode of instruction, needs assessment and planning, artist training, type, documentation, evaluation, and student assessment. Moses (1994) concluded that artists, in this case, community musicians, need more training in education to make their outreach programs more effective.

Eustis (1998) found that emphasis on entertainment through simplification detracted from the educational benefits of outreach programs; similarly, Smith (2004) concluded that education was a more important focus than appreciation. Both highlighted concerns about the weak philosophical underpinnings for such programs, tendencies toward entertainment or appreciation over substance, and a lack of relevance to sequential programs.

Myers (2001) suggests that outreach programs have the potential to have a greater effect on the students if there is consultation with the teachers to align the presentation with the school music curriculum. Letona (1999) notes that partnership success comes from open contractual relationships where collaborations benefit both consumers and communities and where partnerships are established to solve problems such as inefficiency, diffuse public accountability, and a lack of responsiveness.

Eurocentric formal design elements and principles are predominant methods of teaching music in the classroom and these pedagogical expectations may make it more difficult for the ethnic community musicians as teachers. Issues of content integration, diverse voices, sources and materials, positive attitudes, and the recognition that knowledge is socially and contextually constructed pose frequent challenges.

In the community music partnership classroom, it should be clear that community musicians and classroom teachers work as a team in establishing a learning community. Outreach can be further enhanced with the involvement of experts in pedagogy to support community musicians. The duality of conceptual and technological revolutions that offer prospects of transformative pedagogical models in community music plays a key role toward improved engagement. The roles of youth leadership and constructivism, peer learning, and informal learning have significant implications for community music activities. As teachers and community musicians respect one another, students will participate in environments that encourage exploration and risk taking, mutual appreciation, and interest in learning.

THE PLACE FOR SMALL ENSEMBLES:
AUTHENTIC COMMUNITY ENGAGEMENT IN NORTH TEXAS

The processes of building community through music making, particularly when the process is initiated by a university, are best understood when the combined interactions of outreach, engagement, and service learning are considered (Gordon & Manosevitch, 2011; Hart & Northmore, 2011; Knapp, Fisher, & Levesque-Bristol, 2010; Schmidt, Marks, & Derrico, 2004; Scull & Cuthill, 2010; Timmermans & Bouman, 2004).

These interactions can be considered a spectrum, with outreach lying at one end and authentic community engagement (ACE) at the other. Depending on the context of the interaction, both are valuable and appropriate. At one end of the continuum, outreach activities tend toward time-honored formats in which academic music professionals share their music and/or research with interested community members, using delivery systems most comfortable to the presenters. At the other end of the outreach-engagement continuum, ACE activities contain elements of shared benefit and reciprocity, in which all parties learn from one another over time. Every interaction that falls on this spectrum is vital and necessary but differs in the manner in which the interaction is carried out.

The definition of "authentic community engagement" comes from the work of Ricchiuto (2010), who has been a community designer for over thirty years. He writes: "When a community is authentically engaged in conversations that matter, the conversation engages their assets in the realization of their dreams. In authentic engagement, the community becomes the author of its own future" (p. 1). What differentiates this type of interaction from outreach is the mindset of the participants. Stakeholders in outreach interactions may consider the "others" as deficient in some way, questioning them concerning identifiable problems and how they might want to be helped; these questions imply victimhood and entitlement. On the other hand, ACE is based upon an abundance-based perspective; ACE assumes that community members have gifts and dreams that should be valued by all participants.

While there are many instrumental community groups that resemble traditional band ensembles in the public schools, smaller instrumental groups also exist in our communities. These ensembles have a different feel, structure, and purpose than their larger counterparts, so it is important to develop a contextual understanding of small ensemble cases in order to envision the complexity of instrumental community music.

Within a five-mile radius of one growing community in North Texas, there are many community organizations. Some of them are iconic community institutions, such as the community theater or the community band, while others present a novel perspective, such as the Young at Heart Big Band, the Denton Dulci Doodlers' Dulcimer Ensemble, and the Mariachi Águilas.

The Young at Heart Big Band

The Young at Heart Big Band began in 1998 with three members of a New Horizons Beginning Band who wanted to get back into playing the instruments they had played in their youth. In addition to their participation in the New Horizons group, they decided to start a small side group which would allow them to play dance band music at a level of difficulty where they felt comfortable.

Since 1998, the group has grown in numbers to between twelve and fifteen members who play clarinet; alto, tenor, and baritone saxophone; trumpet; trombone; euphonium; piano; guitar; bass; or percussion. Some of the members play more than one instrument. The group includes both Caucasian men and women, aged fifty to eighty. The musical background of the members varies greatly. As one band member stated: "We have one member who has had a musician's union card for almost seventy years and has been playing continuously. He plays every reed instrument, improvises at will, and has a very good knowledge of theory." Other members played in high school, and one member began playing in the New Horizons Band as a beginner.

The group plays a number of engagements each year, including dances at senior centers, grand-opening functions, birthday parties, Christmas, Mother's Day, and Fourth of July celebrations, fund-raisers, church events, and retirement-home concerts. Some of these performances are paid gigs, paying from $250 to $550, while other gigs solicit donations, and still other gigs are fund-raising events for others' benefit. As the director said, "We have done many things that I am proud to have been a part of. We have served many charitable functions."

The director is a retired pilot who says that he was "appointed to run the rehearsals by default since no one else has the time or energy it takes to plan programs." Rehearsals are held twice a week, for an hour and a half each, year-round. The rehearsals are structured as preparation for the next engagement. "I make out the program, and we practice those particular songs until we feel ready." Most of the music that is played is from Fake Books: "Mostly we will play the tune (either the whole band or featuring one player while the rest of us chord). The second time around is generally a vocal. Usually, the third time through we start with the rhythm section, taking it down to the bridge where the vocal comes back to finish the tune." Some of the musicians in the group improvise on the chord changes, while the less experienced stick to the chords provided in the Fake Book.

As the most novice member of the group commented:

> I began in the group through my love of singing the melodies. Later, I started learning the chords of the music in order for me to better understand the overall approach to improving my musicianship . . . and I could support the solos behind the scenes, much as the rhythm section does. I began to do this, starting with the triads and copying the chords of the various pieces of music until I memorized the more common chords and could play them without thinking too much about it. In the process, I learned about the emphasis on the fifth part of the chord and arranging the tones to match the notes being played . . . the beginning of improvisation, I later learned. I slowly [expanded] my efforts to include the seventh and the ninth of the chords, and along with that, the chromatic scale and the various major scales. Along with that, I have been studying blues and the pentatonic scales, hoping one day to enlarge upon my techniques of improvisation in order to make music more interesting as I succumb to Father Time. I am now at the point where I can play some of the easier harmonies with joy, which is very ego-satisfying.

No matter the learning technique, the philosophy is the same for all the members. As one member said: "We *always* have a good time making music. That's the most important thing."

The Denton Dulcimer Club

The Denton Dulci Doodlers began in July 2003 as a group whose purpose was to learn and to share mountain dulcimer (also known as the Appalachian or lap dulcimer) music for all to enjoy. The group has approximately fifty people on the membership rolls now, but usually between fifteen and twenty attend rehearsals each month at a retirement facility. The dulcimer instruments sitting across the laps of the members range from basic models to ornate works of art. All members are Caucasian, one-third of the group is male, and two-thirds are female. Most of the members are retired, and the rest are past middle age but are still working.

The group meets for five hours, once a month, on the third Saturday of the month, with breaks for talking and lunch. The group organizer usually runs the meetings ("the first two hours are usually spent working on current music or learning new pieces, and after lunch we like to just jam"), but other individuals fill in when she is gone. The group is normally organized in three rows, with the most experienced members sitting up front with their dulcimers on their laps, facing forward, able to turn around to discuss rehearsal strategies with the other players.

The musical levels of the group's members vary from beginner to intermediate. The more experienced members offer assistance to those who are just beginning. Most members have learned to play their instrument though attendance at various festivals, some are self-taught, and others have had private lessons.

Rehearsals are characterized by low-key banter, laughter, and discussions of musical choices and historical information pertinent to the pieces. Members choose their parts based on musical balance and appropriate difficulty level. As the group goes through familiar tunes, requests are made by the members. The group learns new music, "mostly by [reading] music, but we still have a few that learn primarily by ear. Even those have now learned to follow the music and make notes as needed." One group member noted that "learning by ear is the most difficult thing for me, since I knew notation already and I rely on that too much." The new music is played line-by-line, multiple times, so that the less experienced players can master a little more each time. Mistakes are taken lightly with friendly, comfortable exchanges.

The group uses a series of portfolios of traditional music put together by a retired music teacher in East Texas as their primary written music source. The organizer of the group added that "there are also several nationally known players who love to share their arrangements, and we take full advantage of that. These are mostly multi-part ensemble pieces that take on a whole new sound." Group members also attend festivals around the country and learn new songs. The four-part pieces have dulcimer tablature as well as chord progressions and traditional notation. The tab includes fingerings that let the newcomers learn to play quickly.

The group performs from two to six concerts per year for Christmas and special celebrations at museums, nursing homes, and private parties. The group plays from sheet music in concerts "mainly because some people have learned different arrangements of the same piece, and if we use the music, we tend to stay together better." As a non-profit group, they do not charge a fee for concerts but welcome donations, and note, "We will always play for food!"

The organizer of the group believes that this group has provided for the community "a common format in which to learn about the instrument and the music it can produce." The lap dulcimer is a major emphasis for this group, but the social component of playing music together is clearly evidenced by friendly discussions at rehearsals and at the social hour over lunch. While the group members tend to limit their socialization with the other players to the five hours of rehearsal on Saturdays, the social connections of the members are evident.

The *Alegría* of Mariachi Águilas

Community music making is often discussed and examined within particular cultural groups, with culture encompassing more than simply race or ethnicity. If music is an expression of creating community as well as expressing community, the engagement of stakeholders across a variety of populations as co-creators of community is more likely to occur. As of 2010, Latinos make up the fastest-growing segment of the US population (U.S. Census, 2010). Music is a vital part of life in many Mexican-American families, particularly genres such as mariachi ensembles. The Mariachi Águilas (Eagles) began in 2004 as a university-based ensemble. While on the surface the Mariachi Águilas looked like any other performing ensemble in a college of music, the goals for this ensemble were different. Musical performance was indeed part of the equation, but culture was a much more significant component than is usual in a concert band.

An example of authentic community engagement (ACE), the mariachi program at the University of North Texas (UNT) is evidence of the three vital characteristics of relationships, reciprocity, and sustainability. Mariachi is inherently relational. Relationships are formed and nurtured through the lens of cultural identification and focused by the lyrics of the music among the musicians and between the musicians and the audience. Among the Águilas, the most valued attributes of membership in the mariachi are the bonds that have been formed and the relationships that have been created. These relationships extend beyond rehearsals and performances. Members celebrate birthdays together, cook out at one another's homes, take care of each other when they are ill, go to movies together, study together, and transcribe new pieces together.

The organizer of the ensemble hoped that the group would serve as a home for Latino students so that they might learn about their own culture through music, gain self-efficacy, and increase their retention rates in college. These students' success might become a favorable model for at-risk Latinos in the public schools. In addition, the ensemble could be used to recruit non-Latinos who were interested in Latino culture. Every participant could benefit from the small, interactive, mariachi style of musical engagement.

The group commonly consists of as few as twelve to as many as twenty Latino, Anglo, and international student members. Even in semesters when the group is predominantly Latino, there may be only a few students who actually speak or understand Spanish. Among the Latinos, there are some recent immigrants, but most are second-, third-, or fourth-generation American citizens. Some of the members of the mariachi have begun minors in Spanish because they want to understand what they are singing and want to sing it authentically.

The musicians vary in skill level. Some of the guitarists are doctor of musical Arts (DMA) candidates, and others are learning the guitar as a second instrument by watching and interacting with the more advanced members of the group. Most of the trumpet players and string players are music majors. The group rehearses for one hour, three times a week. The group also gets together for ad hoc sectional rehearsals at each other's houses. The rehearsals focus on repertoire with vocal warm-ups and technique building. Depending on what performances are coming up, some rehearsals are spent just playing songs the group members want to play, but most practices are focused on learning new repertoire, new styles, and new techniques. The members are given the freedom to provide input into choosing music, arranging pieces, or writing/transcribing new arrangements.

The Mariachi Águilas' repertoire is a mix of traditional mariachi songs and contemporary and classical music that is arranged in mariachi style. The music is learned from a score and then put to memory. The Mariachi Águilas have memorized between two and three hours of music for their concerts. There is no standard set of music for mariachi since mariachi is an aural tradition. As the organizer stated:

> Because it *is* an aural tradition, this is one of the challenges—how does the ensemble keep true to the tradition with music students who only read notation? So what we do isn't actually authentic because they learn the music from the score, although, as they stay in the group over time, they start learning more and more by ear.

The Mariachi Águilas perform one formal concert at the university and as many as fifty informal concerts off campus each semester. The success of the ensemble has changed one aspect of the group's musical experience, which went from searching for opportunities to perform to having to turn down gigs so the members will not be distracted from their studies. The cycle is further fed by a professional mariachi who emerged from Águilas. As members of the group graduated, they did not want to stop performing in a mariachi. Several former students and current students then formed a professional group, Mariachi Quetzal,[3] which performs all over the Dallas/Fort Worth metropolitan area.

In addition to their internal social bonds, group members reach out to students in the public schools. The university students mentor young mariachis after school. They work closely with mariachi/band directors, give performances at the schools, and act as the showcase group at public school students' concerts, sometimes as instructors side-by-side with mariachis from Los Angeles, Las Vegas, and Mexico. Consequently, the public school students aspire to be like these university student musicians. An event with even more impact on community building is the mariachi summer camp.

The first mariachi summer camp was offered four years ago with enrollment limited to twenty-five students. Full scholarships covered room, board, tuition, and materials. Nearly seventy middle and high school students, predominantly Mexican-American, and representing seven school districts, came to UNT's campus for the 2010 camp. Most of the campers were identified as at-risk. Coincidentally, in fall 2010, for the first time, four incoming freshmen at UNT (all at-risk, Mexican-American, and the first in each of their families to attend college) were summer camp alumni. All of these students credit mariachi camp for bringing them to UNT. They are currently members of Águilas and will be counselors and teachers for this year's summer camp.

When the university students discuss why they participate in mariachi, the following consistent themes emerge:

1. interacting with the audience and with the members of the group,
2. experiencing the novelty of different performance venues,

3. having their input valued and having ownership over musical decision making,
4. playing passionate, fun, and expressive music, and
5. having multiple opportunities to perform.

Because of these shared pivotal experiences, a formal mentoring program is being implemented for incoming students as a required part of Águilas.

The key to the success of this program and the summer camp started with the perspective that the Mexican-American community is culturally rich and has many gifts to offer. Rather than being part of a community that needs help, community members are collaborators in creating a thriving program that continues to engage members from students to parents to university graduates to professionals. In Ricchiuto's (2010) words:

> So it becomes important for institutions to start small, [then] create quick and compelling success stories. And then as the community develops both faith in itself and its institutions, everyone becomes more willing and adept at larger engagement opportunities. When this happens, institutions become authentic sources of their own transformation and the transformation of their communities. (p. 1)

The cycle is continuous in the North Texas region with music education graduates starting new mariachi programs in the public schools, and high school graduates enrolling in a music education program as well as becoming members of Águilas. When authentic community engagement occurs, communities thrive and make differences together. Through the avenue of mariachi, this evolving community is thriving, growing, and experiencing the joy and happiness, the *alegría*, of creating and building connections that engage and transform each other and our community. And the transformation continues.

"OPERA IN THE BUS:" A CASE STUDY OF A COMMUNITY PROJECT IN THE NETHERLANDS

The research group Lifelong Learning in Music & the Arts (LLLMA), of the Prince Claus Conservatoire in Groningen and the Royal Conservatoire in The Hague in the Netherlands, is engaged in examining the concept of lifelong learning and its consequences for musicians. It conducts pilot projects that aim to create new audiences and embrace innovative practices. One of these pilot projects explored the competences, skills, and attitudes of an *animateur*, and the critical reflection and reflexivity that are necessary for acting as an animateur. Its case study is described below.

Community Musicians and Animateurs

Community musicians devise and lead creative workshops in very diverse venues within health care, social care, prisons, and the like. These creative workshops are underpinned by the notion that the improvisational nature of collaborative music making in these workshops can lead to people expressing themselves creatively, instilling a sense of shared ownership and responsibility both in the process and in the final product of the workshop (Gregory, 2005). The exchange of ideas and skills among the participants in the form of participatory learning is an integral part of the process.

In the United Kingdom, the profile of the *animateur*, in addition to the community musician, has been strongly developed for some time. An *animateur* can be defined as "a practicing artist, in any form, who uses her/his skills, talents and personality to enable others to compose, design, devise, create, perform or engage with works of arts of any kind" (Animarts, 2003, p. 9). The word *animateur* is French and means animator, an artist who gets things going or sparks things off in a creative sense. Animateurs can be considered informal educators (Smith, 2009). They can work as catalysts between musicians and audiences. Orchestras, for instance, can use animateurs to create closer contact with their audiences. Animateurs can also facilitate musical or cross-arts workshops in community settings and help devise new formats for concerts.

Workshop-leading skills are essential for an animateur. Sean Gregory, a skilled creative workshop leader who was involved in the project that is studied in this chapter, refers to the multifaceted role of the animateur by describing her or him as "a skilled musician who can perform many diverse roles, such as composer, arranger, facilitator, improviser, performer, conductor, teacher and catalyst" (Mak & Kors, 2007, p. 75). In short, an animateur needs artistic, educational, and generic skills that can be applied to a variety of contexts.

Vocal Students as Animateurs: A Pilot Project

As part of a Community Opera Festival, organized by Yo! Opera Festival & Laboratory,[4] which took place in the city of Utrecht in October 2005, a project called "Opera in the Bus" was created, where, during one weekend, in a number of bus lines, various small musical events would take place, for instance, mini-operas and creative workshops. On the invitation of Yo!, the research group LLLMA had "adopted" bus line five, where singers would perform the role of animateur. Vocal students from the Royal Conservatory in The Hague took part in this pilot project.

The project started with a training day for the students, organized by the research group LLLMA and led by experienced leaders. The training focused on aspects of creative workshop leadership. At the end of this day, the students and trainers gave a presentation at the Hague Central Station, aiming at engaging the (traveling) audiences.

One month later, nine students worked for three days in Utrecht under the guidance of a community musician who had been contracted by Yo! to prepare the musical events that would take place during the bus rides on line five. Apart from workshops in the studio, there were also tryout sessions in various contexts and venues throughout the city. The students worked intensely with the community musician, where mutual expectations were not easily met. This made the students reflect on the relationships and balance between the artistic quality and the quality of connecting to different contexts, which led to reflections about their *identity* as musicians (Mak & Kors, 2007).

Finally, during the November weekend of the Community Opera Festival, the students, in groups of three, acted as animateurs on the city bus rides on bus line five. During each thirty-minute ride, three students tried to engage bus passengers into a participatory musical event by singing, improvising, and creating musical games. Some passengers would participate; others would not but would still leave the bus with a smile. The other students served by turn as peers traveling in the buses. Critical during the rides was the reflexive approach of the animateurs through leading while doing or reflection-in-action (Schön, 1983); the bus was on the move, passengers got on and off, and the animateurs had to keep the event going without stopping or explaining the process.

The Research[5] and Its Outcomes

The core research question was: What are the key competences of a music animateur? From there, a new step could be taken with regard to the training and development of animateurs in the music college.

The students reported comprehensively on the interventions they used and the skills needed while performing as animateurs on the bus, including:

- making a flexible plan, being proactive with respect to conditions that could be encountered, and offering variation;
- giving attention to musical and verbal bridges between the activities;
- concentrating on people who wanted to join in immediately and keeping an inviting attitude toward those who did not;
- striving for good cooperation and communication between the animateurs, shared leadership being at the core.

The ability of the animateur to "read the audience" appeared fundamental, and balance between intervention and non-intervention of the animateurs was extremely subtle (Mak & Kors, 2007). Individual decisions were constantly made, often on a tacit level of implicit knowledge and understanding (Polanyi, 1966).

Students' Experiences

The students reported that they enjoyed the challenge of working creatively, especially as it related to their professional identity. They were strongly motivated as soon as they were required to devise interventions connected to musical repertory with which they felt ownership. Teamwork was highly valued, and the collaborative aspect was experienced as inspiring. Interestingly, students reported that the shared ownership they perceived was quite new for them, giving them space as musicians. They felt free to improvise and experiment, coming close to a feeling of joy while making music they recalled from childhood; the fear of failure sometimes experienced in the music college was absent (Mak & Kors, 2007).

Student feedback through the evaluations included the following issues (Smilde, 2006):

- Renewing personal motivation
- Strengthening courage, confidence, and self-esteem
- Understanding the importance of teamwork and cooperation
- Becoming more aware of roles and responsibilities in a team

- Grasping the challenges of leadership and shared leadership
- Building up trust in oneself and in the group
- Thinking on one's feet and acting in the moment
- Becoming aware of the need for quality
- Seeing the need to create new forms of music making

Key Competences of the Animateur

As one of the outcomes of the project, a number of key competences of the animateur could be defined (Mak & Kors, 2007). They include the following artistic, educational, and generic competences:

- Artistic competences
  - Relating and responding to a range of musical styles and genres
  - Using the musical expertise present in the group
- Educational competences
  - Knowing how to teach the group; while learning a song together, pitching at the right level, and not getting into details
  - Engaging physically and aware of the voice/body coordination
  - Leading reflexively by keeping the event going without stopping or explaining
- Generic competences
  - Knowing how to work effectively and creating a safe atmosphere
  - Using the creative energy of participants and realizing shared ownership of the musical process and product
  - Switching between various roles of composer, facilitator, improviser, and catalyst within the process' momentum
  - Reflecting on one's role

Reflections on What We Learned

Partnerships, Training, and Quality

Relevant partnerships are of crucial importance for a dynamic synergy between the music college and the outside world. Strategic alliances and partnerships are important to help reinforce the learning environment of the music college (Smilde, 2006). Such partnerships require integrity of intentions of all partners, shared understanding of possible different agendas, shared values, shared understanding of modes of learning, and collaborative forms of practice and shared understanding of possible outcomes (Renshaw, 2010)

Training animateurs requires that music colleges provide challenging learning environments where students experience feelings of self-worth, excitement, and challenge. This can be created by establishing crossovers within musical disciplines and encompassing informal learning in non-formal learning contexts.

It is, however, of critical importance to ensure that the college's definition of quality is *not* a narrow one, limited to quality of performance and failing to take into account the contextual variables when making qualitative judgments arising from various processes, projects, and performances in different contexts.

Leadership and Learning Styles of Animateurs

Students displayed leadership in the project. Leadership is dependent on authority and the ability to exercise authority. Within the musical events in the bus, we can speak of *shared authority* through collaborative artistic practice, which is underpinned by qualities like informed decision making (often tacit), adaptability, flexibility, and committed values and attitudes (Smilde, 2009a). In order to function in a community context like this bus ride, the animateur has to display *artistic, educational,* and *generic* leadership.

Artistic leadership is constituted by an implicit understanding of the kind of "artistic laboratory" that took place in the bus. Examples of artistic leadership skills include the ability to make decisions about the musical language and structure, knowing how to enable the audience to understand, and creating a balance of "pace" that allows time and space for artistic development and creative momentum (Renshaw, 2007, p. 34).

Educational leadership refers to the many roles an animateur can perform reflex-ively: a guide, a mentor, an artistic leader, and an educator. Generic leadership can be described in the context of this project as the ability to create an inspiring and enabling environment which is encouraging and confidence building, where the animateurs have the skill and understanding to work effectively in different teams, the capacity to listen and respect, and the ability to display strong communication skills (Renshaw, 2007, pp. 34–35).

These forms of leadership are closely connected to musicians' learning styles (Smilde, 2009a). Students reported on renewing personal motivation, strengthening courage, confidence, and self-esteem, and building trust in themselves and in the group. These outcomes act as incentives, which are fundamental to the process of shaping musicians' motivation and sense of self-identity, and include singing and informal music making throughout childhood, improvisation, and engagement in high-quality performance (Smilde, 2009a). Moreover, an important aspect of musi-cians' informal learning is *peer learning,* which takes place in a setting of trust among friends. Musicians learn in a reflexive way—by playing together and improvising, by listening and observing. Informal, experiential learning within non-formal contexts strengthens musicians' feelings of ownership of their learning.

Finally, musicians learning to be animateurs clearly need an adaptive learning envi-ronment in the music college that gives them space for their own artistic laboratories where they can develop their skills and professional identities. The work of animateurs reflects the different forms of leadership and the roles they require, drawing on expe-riential learning styles. The animateur has to have an antenna, so to speak, for what is fit for a purpose for a particular moment. Hence, musical leadership in community contexts does not require unique or special methods or recipes, but it does require interconnected artistic, educational, and generic skills and an awareness of reflective and reflexive practice. Gregory reflects on the role and experience of the animateur:

> The roles can differ. You can be a leader, a facilitator, a composer, arranger, a support-ing instrumentalist, you can be the person who just makes it happen; you can shift roles. Artistically it comes back to this, trying to capture both the essence and the practice of this work, what it actually is, without putting it into a box, and at the same time defining

it enough so that it stops being just called "outreach" or "educational and community work." The principle is the notion that you are with a group of people, that you encourage them to come out with their own ideas . . . The key part is that *together you develop something into something else.* That can go for young children with no skills whatsoever or a highly trained dancer or a West African musician, searching and exploring new meeting points, new languages and possibilities. (Smilde, 2009b, pp. 278–279)

NOTES

1. The Totalisator Board manages the funding activities from the gaming surpluses generated from the operations of Singapore Turf Club and Singapore Pools, and from the casino entry levy. This sponsorship has enabled schools to afford many of the arts partnership programs for their students.

2. Arts Experience programs provide students hands-on participation in the various art forms. These programs are highly interactive and suitable for smaller groups of students. Arts Excursion programs refer to students' attendance at performances at performing venues, and students' visits to museums, art galleries, art centers, artists' studios, and theaters. Arts Exposure programs introduce students to a particular art form. Ranging in duration from thirty to forty minutes, each is presented by an arts practitioner. Each program is accompanied by an explanation on the background and development of the art form or a workshop demonstration. This is probably the most popular of the three. (National Arts Council, 2009)

3. The name for this group comes from the name of a colorful long-tailed bird of Central America.

4. Yo! Opera Festival & Laboratory was founded in 2001. Its goal is to introduce young people to opera. Yo! organizes a bi-annual youth opera festival in Utrecht, the Netherlands, which entails community projects. New operas are created together with youngsters and opera makers, aiming to connect to today's world. Yo!'s mission is threefold: education, talent development, and repertoire development.

5. The methods employed included the observations of two researchers and of the students themselves, as well as evaluations that were held throughout the process. Self-assessment by the students took place by their keeping a reflective journal throughout the process. Peer assessment took place among the students, based on observation of each other's work during the bus rides, by means of a number of questions given beforehand.

BIBLIOGRAPHY

Alapana Arts. (2011). *Mridangam traditional Malay music—educational kit.* www.alapana .org/lesson/mridang.htm

Animarts. (2003). *The art of the animateur: An investigation of the skills and insights required of artists to work effectively in schools and communities.* Retrieved from www.animarts .org.uk.

Chong, S. with Sri Warisan Som Said Performing Arts. (2003). *Traditional Malay music.* National Ails Council, Singapore.

Chong, S., & Chia, W. K. (2003). *Music of the south.* Handbook commissioned by National Arts Council, Singapore.

Eustis, L. E. (1998). *Educational outreach programs at regional opera companies: Guidelines for effectiveness* (Unpublished doctoral thesis). Florida State University.

Gordon, E., & Manosevitch, E. (2011). Augmented deliberation: Merging physical and virtual interaction to engage communities in urban planning. *New Media & Society, 13* (1), 75–95.

Gregory, S. (2005). The creative music workshop: A contextual study of its origin and practice. In G. Odam & N. Bannan (Eds.), *The reflective conservatoire.* London: Guildhall School of Music & Drama/Aldershot: Ashgate.

Hart, A., & Northmore, S. (2011). Auditing and evaluating university-community engagement: lessons from a UK case study. *Higher Education Quarterly, 65* (1).

Knapp, T., Fisher, B., & Levesque-Bristol, C. (2010). Service-learning's impact on college students' commitment to future civic engagement, self-efficacy, and social empowerment. *Journal of Community Practice, 18* (2–3), 233–251.

Letona, M. (1999). *The government non-profit relationship: Towards a partnership model.* Washington, DC: Non-profit Sector Research Fund.

Mak, P., & Kors, N. (2007). Vocal students as animateurs, a case study of non-formal learning. In P. Mak, N. Kors, & P. Renshaw (Eds.), *Formal, non-formal and informal learning in music.* Groningen/The Hague: Research Group Lifelong Learning in Music & the Arts.

Ministry of Education, Singapore. (2002). *A guide to the primary music syllabus.* Singapore: Curriculum Planning & Development Division, MOE.

Ministry of Information and the Arts. (2009). *Renaissance city report. Culture and the arts in renaissance Singapore.* Retrieved from http://app.mica.gov.sg/Portals/0/2_FinalRen.pdf

Moses, M. (1994). *A case study analysis of the impact of the Wolf Trap Institute for early learning through the arts on select classroom teachers' abilities to integrate the performing arts into their educational curriculums.* (Unpublished doctoral dissertation). Union Institute, Washington, DC.

Myers, D. E. (2001). *Excellence in arts teaching and learning: A collaborative responsibility of maturing partnerships.* 2001 Fowler Colloquium Papers, University of Maryland.

National Arts Council. (2009). *Developing a distinctive global city for the arts.* Retrieved from www.nac.gov.sg/edu/edu01.asp 2/23/2010

Polanyi, M. (1966). *The tacit dimension.* New York: Doubleday.

Remer, J. (1996). *Building effective arts partnerships with schools and your community.* New York: ACA Books, American Council for the Arts.

Renaissance City Report. (2009). Retrieved from www.nac.gov.sg/sta/sta02.asp

Renshaw, P. (2007). Lifelong learning for musicians. Critical issues arising from a case study of "connect." In P. Mak, N. Kors, & P. Renshaw (Eds.), *Formal, non-formal and informal learning in music.* Groningen/The Hague: Research Group Lifelong Learning in Music & the Arts.

Renshaw, P. (2010). *Engaged passions: Searches for quality in community contexts.* Groningen/The Hague: Research Group Lifelong Learning in Music & the Arts.

Ricchiuto, J. (2010). *The practice and power of authentic community engagement.* Retrieved from http://www.designinglife.com/Jack/AuthenticEngagement.html

Schmidt, M. E., Marks, J. L., & Derrico, L. (2004). What a difference mentoring makes: Service learning and engagement for college students. *Mentoring and Tutoring, 12* (2), 205–217.

Schön, D. A. (1983). *The reflective practitioner: How professionals think in action.* Aldershot: Ashgate.

Scripp, L. (2003). Critical links, new steps: An evolving conception of music and learning in public school education. In L. Scripp, & Keppel (Eds.), *Journal for Learning through Music* (pp. 28–31). Boston, MA: New England Conservatory.

Scull, S., & Cuthill, M. (2010). Engaged outreach: Using community engagement to facilitate access to higher education for people from low socio-economic backgrounds. *Higher Education Research & Development, 29* (1), 59–74.

Smilde, R. (2006). Lifelong learning for musicians. *Proceedings of the 81st Annual Meeting of the National Association of Schools of Music.* Reston, VA: NASM.

Smilde, R. (2009a). *Musicians as lifelong learners: Discovery through biography.* Delft: Eburon Academic Publishers.

Smilde, R. (2009b). *Musicians as lifelong learners: 32 biographies.* Delft: Eburon Academic Publishers.

Smith, M. K. (2009). Animateurs, animation and fostering learning and change. *The Encyclopedia of Informal Education.* Retrieved from www.infed.org/animate/b-animat.htm

Smith, R. A. (2004). Aesthetic education: Questions and issues. In E. W. Eisner & M. D. Day (Eds.), *Handbook of research and policy in art education* (pp. 163–186). London, UK: Lawrence Erlbaum Associates.

Texas Education Agency. (2009). *Enrollment in Texas public schools 2007–2008.* Retrieved from http://ritter.tea.state.tx.us/research/pdfs/enrollment_2007–08.pdf

Timmermans, S., & Bouman, J. (2004). Seven ways of teaching and learning: University-community partnerships at baccalaureate institutions. *Journal of Community Practice, 12* (3–4), 89–101.

Undercofler, J. (1997). Music in America's schools: A plan for action. *Arts Education Policy Review, 98* (6), 15–19.

U.S. Census. (2010). *2010 census shows nation's Hispanic population grew four times faster than total US population.* Retrieved from www.ida.org/images/stories/IDRA_Attrition_Study_2010.pdf

World Factbook. (2010). Retrieved from www.cia.gov/library/publications/the-world-factbook/geos/sn.html

Chapter Eleven

Digital Communities: Sharing, Teaching, Exploring

Stephen J. Messenger

This chapter explores the worldwide connection and community created and sustained by avid listeners and collectors of live performance. Although similar threads may be found in other musical genres, I focus on jambands, the men and women who record their work, and the people throughout the world who make this music their own. The jamband community embraces the Internet, enabling this community to flourish and create a new musical paradigm where the members share, teach, and explore music in a manner that could not have existed before.

In addition to connecting (in novel ways, thanks to media innovations), members of these deliberate communities find common ground in notions of sharing and music as culture as opposed to music as commodity. This practice of spreading or gifting music intentionally began with Grateful Dead followers and continues unbroken through the community of enthusiasts who follow performances by Gov't Mule, among others.

First, I explore the earliest jambands, beginning with the Grateful Dead. Then, I examine the phenomenon of tapers and taping, as enabled by the Internet, at concert and festival events. Themes of creative musicking, social capital, gifting, resistance to hegemonic commercial systems, and deliberate community building emerge.

> *He took his knife and he cut her down*
> *And on her bosom these words he found:*
> *"Go dig my grave both wide and deep,*
> *Put a marble stone at my head and feet,*
> *And on my breast, put a snow white dove*
> *To warn the world that I died of love."*
>
> *—"Railroad Boy"—traditional*

Warren Haynes notes:

> I learned that song from some folk music friends of mine when I was 14 or 15, growing up sneaking into these folk clubs in North Carolina. It's a traditional folk song, and . . . we turned the band loose on it to see what would happen from an arrangement perspective, and . . . it turned out like it is. (Waddell, 2009)

Gov't Mule first played "Railroad Boy" on August 5, 2009, at the Wellmont The-atre in Montclair, New Jersey, and according to bt.etree.org (2009), the show was taped by Frank D'Auria ("furtherest [sic] taper from stage 4th row balcony," uploaded on August 6, 2009, and downloaded 385 times). Within twenty-four hours of the per-formance, the music had been transmitted worldwide and remains available to anyone who chooses to access it.

Jamband communities may well be a pure extension of the ideas that have fostered community music (CM) and its development in that the music making and social activities are intertwined. Issues such as self-expression, networking, and both self-identity and group identity weave through the community's interactions. Jamband communities (and the tapers who provide them with aural artifacts) exist in virtual space that extends to real-time experiences with music. Hundreds of thousands of people from all walks of life from five continents go online to

- discuss a show,
- document songs played and songs "teased" at shows they have attended and/or col-lected,[1]
- instruct each other in computer techniques and programs,
- share song arrangements, discuss (and argue about) music, politics, and sports, or
- give support to community members who are ill or grieving over the loss of a loved one.[2]

This music may start with one band's repertoire, but within the jamband community, the constant infusion of new, unlikely, and serendipitous influences keeps the musical melting pot vibrant.

The thousands of people participating in jamband communities are more than, as photographer and eMuler Rachel Naugle (personal communication, 2004) puts it, "the cheesiest of teenage fan clubs." Jamband communities can be seen as musical communities, families of people "who share their knowledge and expertise in observ-ing, participating, creating, and leading in music knowing, music keeping, and music making" (Veblen, 2008, p. 1).

THE GRATEFUL DEAD AND THE
PATCHWORK QUILT THEY BEGAN

The musicians who were to become the Grateful Dead came to the table bringing diverse backgrounds and interests. Their early performances combined Kentucky fiddle tunes, traditional hymns, folk songs, bluegrass standards, driving blues, Ozark and Appalachian stringband classics, and protest songs, and then took off on swirling, jazz-based improvisations.

It was a heady time for making and learning music. American concert stages (no-tably the Fillmore East, Fillmore West, and Winterland) thought nothing of booking acts as seemingly incongruous as Lawrence Ferlinghetti and the Jefferson Airplane (Fillmore Auditorium, San Francisco, CA, April 7, 1966); The Nitty Gritty Dirt Band,

Blue Cheer, and B. B. King (Fillmore Auditorium, San Francisco, CA, November 30, 1967); Led Zeppelin, the Bonzo Dog Band, and Rashaan Roland Kirk (Winterland, San Francisco, CA, November 6, 1969); and Ornette Coleman and the Grateful Dead (Fillmore Auditorium, San Francisco, CA, February 3, 1993). These disparate musical expressions allowed musicians to play with experts in genres they might never ordinarily have met, learn and perfect their improvisational skills, and pave the way for the jambands of today.

The term "jamband"[3] was coined in 1937 in a glossary of terms stating that "a 'jam band' depends entirely on improvisation, using no written music" (Nye, 1937, p. 45). Probably not coincidentally, in April of that same year, Coleman Hawkins recorded with a band named "Coleman Hawkins and His All Star Jam Band" (Nye, 1937).

Jambands incorporate a passion for and a love of diverse musical influences in their original songs, improvisations, and covers. Duffy (1998) writes:

> A good jamband . . . can play the same song five times in a row and never play it the same way twice. A good jam is quite often not even a tune but a compilation of sound with one note feeding off the last until the final result is a "soundscape" of sorts. When a jamband runs four songs together in medley and finally pull(s) out to finish the first song of the night (total run time of about an hour) and the guy standing beside you at the show says "What song was that?!?" . . . there, now you've got some jammin'!

Jamband performances often feature extended musical improvisation (jams) over rhythmic grooves and chord patterns and long sets of music that cross genre boundaries played to audiences that follow every note and phrase.

> Please cast aside any preconceptions that this phrase may evoke. The term, as it is commonly used today, references a rich palette of sounds and textures. These groups share a collective penchant for improvisation, a commitment to songcraft and a propensity to cross genre boundaries, drawing from a range of traditions including blues, bluegrass, funk, jazz, rock, psychedelia and even techno. In addition, the jam bands of today are unified by the nimble ears of their receptive listeners. (Jambands.com, 2007)

Jamband fans revel in a band's "runs," a series of concerts in cities close enough for fans to attend four or five shows in as many nights. The Grateful Dead began the tradition, but it continues to this day. Steven Harrison recounts:

> My favorite run was a two-night run in 1988 (August 26 and 27) on the west coast. . . The first night (August 26) was in the Tacoma Dome near Seattle . . . First Santana played, and he lit the room up. The Dead and Jerry came out with a serious grudge after that— they would not be outplayed. I remember an emphatic change in "Uncle John's" where I actually thought they were trying to hurt us . . . via chord changes and loud playing. In the meantime everyone was dying of thirst and some were passing out down on the floor from the heat. It was the worst logistics of any show I saw. The next show was in Eugene, Oregon. The outdoor show was definitely kinder and like a giant party with Jerry calling the shots just like he always did. I think we stayed right in the parking lot with 20,000 other people. A close second was three nights in Utah (February 19–21) immediately followed by the three-night Mardi Gras run in Oakland (February 24–26) in 1995; my best friend was surprised I could survive that! (personal communication, 2011)

The Allman Brothers Band (ABB) traditionally spends two or three weeks in New York City every spring, playing nearly every night of the run[4] with a total of sixty-two different guest musicians sitting in (Hollems, 2009). Fans post their opinions about songs, setlists, and guests, not to mention suggestions and requests, on the listserves. Since every show is taped, both by the band for commercial distribution and by tapers for "spreading," and setlists are posted to the listserves by audience members via text and email as they happen during the performances, the members of the community have an almost instant record of the music and are able to discuss and reflect upon what has been played.

For a jamband, playing a repertoire that is constantly evolving, each concert is a session. The improvisations and the accompanying "teases" (quoting a riff, verse, or chorus that allows the musicians to make a cultural, emotional, or even political state-ment) allow for a special communication between the players, the audience, and the tapers. On September 28, 1998, in Birmingham, Alabama, Gov't Mule began their show with an improvisational medley: "Intro" > "Afro Blue" (Mongo Santamaria) > "Third Stone From the Sun" (Jimi Hendrix) > "Norwegian Wood" (John Lennon/ Paul McCartney) > "Third Stone" > "Afro Blue." Gary Nagle, an eMule list mem-ber, describes his reaction to this first "song": "In my opinion, the masterpiece is 9/28/98—44:30 of bliss" (personal communication, 2010).

> When a jamband plays, it has a great deal in common with an Irish session in that a session is both an occasion for playing and a gathering with friends and family. For jam-bands, every performance requires intention, awareness, and diligence. The audience and guest musicians take each other on as friends and, over time, share a metaphor of family and an appreciation of a bounded community, of belonging to a unique assemblage.

A jamband's raison d'etre is to challenge the listeners' expectations through impro-visation and an eclectic repertoire. Athens, Georgia's, Widespread Panic's musical philosophy of "Pay attention. What's going to happen is going to happen, so keep your eyes open" may be the defining explanation of jamband music. The New York band moe.'s longest jam lasted three hours. Atlanta's Derek Trucks Band's sound includes, according to guitarist Derek Trucks, "All the pure musics of the world" (Kemp, 2000). For Truck and his bandmates, each concert is one continuous jam which can include "Greensleeves," Sun Ra's "Rocket No. 9," the spiritual Qawwali music of Nusrat Fateh All Khan, and Curtis Mayfield's "Freddie's Dead" (from the score of the classic Blaxploitation film *Superfly*) (Kemp, 2000).

Along with those bands have emerged a jamband culture and communities whose focus is music. Members of this culture tape the live performances, compile them, dis-cuss them, trade them (and give them away) in person and through online listserves, and legally upload them to websites where the only payment required to enjoy the music is the unspoken dictum "Spread it!" Bove (1996) notes that

> The jamband culture is closely modeled on the Dead caravan-like tours . . . The jamband community has embraced the internet, enabling this community to flourish and create a new musical paradigm where the members share, teach, and explore music in a manner that could not have existed before.

The Tapers' Section

The Grateful Dead and their fans (also known as Dead Heads) began taping the band's performances in the mid-1960s. However, Grateful Dead Productions did not officially allow taping and, by extension, tape trading, until 1984, when it established a "taper section" at concerts. The sheer volume of Grateful Dead tapes is remarkable. From the early Grateful Dead days, legendary tapers like Rob Bertrando spread the word and the music, and in later days, Charlie Miller shared over two thousand audience tapes and SBDs (soundboard recordings) with the community (Haugen, personal communication, 2011). Other bands, especially in the jamband community, have since adopted this model through a focus on live performance and the open support of tapers and the non-commercial exchange of recordings (Harvey, 2009, p. 93).

The "tapers section" is a fixture at any jamband concert and generates live shows that are traded throughout the jamband community:

> [A]n amazing aspect of the Dead is the availability of their music free of charge . . . it has the largest trading market of its kind, fully sanctioned and encouraged by the band itself . . . No money changes hands in this process . . . just tapes . . . Admirably, this truly is about "getting the music out there." To mention or believe in a large-scale for-profit "bootleg tape industry" is to seriously offend any true Deadhead (or jamband community member) and show yourself to be an outsider . . . (Tapes) are a gift from the band. (Pattacini, 2000, p. 6)

In the early days of tape trading, these gifts were difficult to obtain. Sony Corporation introduced DAT (digital audio tape) in 1987. It never caught on in the consumer market, but over the next few years was adopted by professional users and advanced amateurs for taping possibilities. Al Booth (personal communication, 2004) explains that

> [b]efore the internet, tapers/traders got in touch mainly by ads posted in the back of magazines, newsletters, etc. The first tapes I ever got were back in the mid 70s. I think I found that person through an ad and for the longest time had no idea that any other show tapes existed . . . The first show I recall receiving that was mastered on DAT was the 3/3/92 ABB show from Boston. I got it on cassette, a first- or second-generation copy off the DAT master . . . . Before DAT, analog cassette was the most common form.

Today, there are thousands of tapers worldwide who tape a multitude of musicians playing a diverse repertoire, from grunge superstars Pearl Jam to the jamband favorite Gov't Mule to (before their performing hiatus) Riot Grrl founders Sleater-Kinney. Kurt Kemp and Mike Wagner's BTAT (Bands That Allow Taping) site (btat.wagnerone .com) lists over a thousand bands who are "taper-friendly."

One current taper, Steven Ziegler (Z-Man), has taped and uploaded nearly five hundred shows (as of July 5, 2010) to bt.etree.org since May 2008. Every one of these shows is available free for downloading and includes detailed information about the show and the recording.

> Been taping heavy since '95. You learn by taping with others and trial and error. There are boards such as Taperssection where you have forums you can ask and learn. I love

sharing my great shows with others too! It is a natural high! I am OBSESSED! (Ziegler, personal communication, 2011)

Sanders (2003) summarizes the experience of collecting live music:

What is it about these tapes that I am drawn to? . . . The intimacy of the moment. These tapes define a particular place in time, musicians putting their hearts and souls on the line for that audience . . . an exchange of ideas and emotions between each musician on the stage and the musicians with their audience . . . The show allows me to share a particular kind of joy that can be expressed in few ways other than music, the wordless language . . . It is at these moments that I feel a connection to the whole, I know that I am part of something much larger. They are moments of contact that are irreplaceable and unforgettable.

One common thread, echoed by both tapers and tape traders, is finding a sense of belonging in the jamband community:

The Internet gave me a chance, for the first time in my life, to truly learn about music . . . Through the online community that I encountered . . . I found myself loving music that I normally would have had no exposure to . . . being a fan in the midst of this musical revolution extends further than a mere love of the music. A family atmosphere is created online, e-mail discussion groups becoming places for friendships to be made, and music to be loved. Music becomes the linking force between the thousands of people who gather online to discuss and share issues and ideas that sometimes diverge far from the music itself . . . All fans of all jambands do indeed exist in a culture to their own, but they communicate with the help of something that superficially seems very different from music. After a closer examination, the Internet does resemble music in many ways. Just as when a band forges ahead into a jam late at night, the Internet forges ahead into regions of technology that mankind has never been. Perhaps it is this similarity that draws jambands and its fans to this fledgling medium: both foster the unknown and innovation. (Pennelli, 1998)

The eMule "Famuley"

A community is "place" where one feels a sense of belonging. Straw (1991; 1997) examined musical "scenes" to hypothesize that the musical communities that were forming (and of which the jamband communities are prototypical) were

a population group whose involvement in music takes the form of an ongoing exploration of one or more musical idioms . . . [a] cultural space in which a range of musical practices co-exist, interacting with each other within a variety of processes of differentiation, and according to widely varying trajectories of change and cross-fertilization. (Straw, 1991, p. 373)

Furthermore, Straw (p. 374) suggests that the "cosmopolitan character of musical scenes" may give such groups a powerful and affective unity, the feeling of family. For many jamband community members, a listserve is the "place" on the Net where the community meets. And while every jamband fan has his or her favorite band, a prototypical jamband might well be Gov't Mule. Gov't Mule has performed since 1994, playing its own music and jamming with the cream of the jambands (Phish, moe., Widespread Panic) and seminal figures in rock, jazz, and roots music as disparate as Leslie West, Little Milton, James Blood Ulmer, Ben Schenk (from the New Orleans Klezmer All-Stars), and John Scofield.

eMule, the Gov't Mule fan listserve, was begun in 1995 as an unofficial Internet gathering place for fans of the band. In its first decade, eMule's subscriber base grew to over 1,800, including members on five continents. There was never a central leader who dominated the list or the conversation. The fans who subscribed were the ones who maintained the feeling of family that flowed through this community, making eMule a home on the Net.

In 1979, ". . . back in the day of the 8088 processors . . ." (Booth, personal communication, 2004), there were local, dial-in bulletin boards (BBs). In order to maintain a BB, three people had to post per day or the forum was deleted until there was space to start it again. Kirk Anderson met the band and, in 1994, dedicated one of his AOL screen names to MULEemail@aol.com. All of the posts to MULEmail were held; once a day a single email, which contained all of the day's posts, was sent out to all the subscribers. Probably the largest concentration of jamband related listserves was concentrated at NETSPACE.ORG. According to the list archives at LISTS.NETSPACE.ORG,[5] approximately 37,000 subscribers were signed up on thirty-two jamband listserves.

The online community of Phish fans, led by Lee Silverman[6], and other student groups at Brown University, helped finance the purchase of a 486 computer to serve as the host for all of the student and Phish online forums. Brown University provided the seed money to help make the self-sufficient project Netspace. Netspace is a non-profit 501(c) corporation that existed through funds charged for hosting mail lists and websites as well as donations (Anderson, 2005a).

Anderson inaugurated the eMule list on Netspace in December 1996. "NETSPACE was the free online way for bands to stay in touch with their fans. The band opened up to these fans and asked about eMule" (Anderson, 2005b). When Netspace shut down on May 26, 2010, eMule moved its listserve and joined with Mulebase (a searchable database of Gov't Mule setlists and songs) in a new website, www.mulebase.com.

The new technology available on the Internet is changing the taping and trading of the live music that spawned the jamband community. In addition to taping music and then trading or spreading it by sending blank discs and postage to a community member who has offered to burn a show (B&Ps), it is now possible to download shows from official band sites for a fee (Gov't Mule's Muletracks or the Allman Brothers Band's Instant Live) or using BitTorrent (a software program that allows legal peer-to-peer [P2P] file sharing) for free.

> Plenty of music available online is not just free but also easily available, legal and—most important—worth hearing. Recording companies have tried and failed to shut down decentralized file-sharing networks . . . (and) countless musicians are taking advantage of the Internet to get their music heard. (Pareles, 2004)

With the widespread availability of broadband Internet service throughout the United States and abroad, more and more members of the jamband community are simply downloading the shows they choose to collect. BitTorrent is probably the predominant method of distribution. Bt.etree.org (a BitTorrent hosting site) gives the new torrent user helpful information as well as establishes the canon by which tapers and traders live within the community.[7]

Even the technology of disseminating shows relies upon a community working toward a common goal.

All of these communities endorse trading or seeding files in Shorten (.shn), Free Lossless Audio Codec (.flac) or Monkey's Audio (.ape) lossless formats, not permitting trade or seed in "lossy" formats like .mp3 (a "lossy" format is a data-encoding method which discards [loses] some of the data as it converts a signal with the result that decompressing the data yields content that is different from the original even though the data is still similar enough to be useful in some way). This technology ensures that music that is traded is always of the highest quality, and, as trader Joel Davies puts it, ensures that there is "no pee in the pool."

In its mission statement, Etree describes itself and the community it serves:

> The Net revolutionized the old tape-trading market, in which super-dedicated fans swapped bootleg recordings of live concerts. Many groups support taping—jambands like the Grateful Dead are famous for it—as long as fans agree not to sell the recordings . . . The site focuses on lossless-compression recordings of live shows (not MP3s), and it's hooked into BitTorrent, which helps you download faster . . . a not-for-profit venture, run by a hardworking community of volunteers . . . who love the music and simply want to see it spread. Etree.org is truly a community effort and without the support of all involved, we simply could not exist. (db.etree.org, 2005, "Who We Are")

The taper or trader in the jamband community adheres to a strict code of behavior in his or her recording and dissemination of recordings. Mark Klecka (2002) addressed the importance of taping to the community in a post to the eMule listserve:

> It's not a question of which mics were used, how the sample rate was converted, who remastered the show, etc. The purpose behind all these details is simply to identify a particular instantiation of an archived show. Whether or not an extraction was involved is not as important as the fact that the extraction is documented and you can determine exactly what you're getting.

Jamband culture and communities have evolved over time. Members tape music, compile it, discuss it (and a myriad of other topics), and trade it in-person and through online listserves. The jamband community has embraced the Internet, enabling this community to flourish and create a new musical paradigm where the members share, teach, and explore music in a manner that could not have existed before.

Kik Anderson, the creator of the eMule listserve, expresses his belief that he is part of a community and culture that is unique: "Yes, we are a funny breed . . . [being] online has shown me as much as being on the road about how we all have a point of view that's just a tad bit different from the next Joe. Use exponents on the 'tad' and the whole spectrum really comes out" (personal communication, 2004).

"When Giving Away the Arm Band, You Get to Keep the Arm Band"

Hyde (2007) describes two types of economies: (1) a commodity (or exchange) economy, in which status is accorded to those who have the most, and (2) a gift economy, in which status is accorded to those who give the most to others (Pinchot, 1995, p. 49, citing Hyde). A gift economy is a society where valuable goods or services are given without any explicit agreement for immediate or future rewards (Cheal, 1988, p. 1). Giving serves to circulate and redistribute valuables within the community. Informal custom governs exchanges (Kranton, 1996, p. 835).

A well-known gift economy is found in the potlatch ritual. As practiced by the Kwakiutls of the Pacific Northwest, leaders give away large amounts of goods to community members, thus securing a position of societal leadership and strengthening ties within the community. The principles of a gift economy work in many other contexts. Another example of a contemporary gift economy might be a knowledge community. Every scientist freely offers a presentation at a symposium, knowing that scientists are deemed most important by the contribution that they make to the field (Pinchot, 1995, p. 49, citing Hyde).

Similarly, traders have the most credibility and respect depending on what they give away. Harvey (2009) notes: "Traders respect one another as collectors, as archivists, seeking more music than they could possibly listen to in order to enhance or 'complete' their collections. Possessing a vast collection of tapes conferred status and power on the collector" (p. 111). According to Grateful Dead publicist Dennis McNally, the decision to openly support tapers and tape trading actually expanded the band's fan base and increased long-term profits. McNally comments,

> If you ask, "Did tape trading cut into the band's profits?" the answer's probably, "A little." But, overall, going back into the . . . late '70s and early '80s, it far more extended them because it added [to the fan base]. It brought in Dead Heads. It created new Dead Heads. (Harvey, 2009, p. 92)

This policy proved to be a pioneering, revolutionary, and lucrative decision. Fan taping functioned as free advertising and a key factor in building fan following and loyalty. Other bands have since adopted this model through a focus on live performance and the open support of tapers and the non-commercial exchange of recordings (Harvey, 2009, p. 105).

The tapes served as exchangeable artifacts that enticed and inducted new members into the world of Dead Heads. By reproducing tapes, Dead Heads reproduced culture. By circulating the music, tape traders and collectors forged new relationships between Dead Heads and became evangelists for the band. They created a network that created a means of connecting to the music and other fans independent of the concert experience.

Instead of placing a cash value on tapes through a commercial bootleg system, Grateful Dead tapers and tape collectors were morally opposed to buying and selling these recordings. Dead Heads endowed this system with a "principle of the exchange-gift" (distinct from a money-oriented marketplace). Dead Heads self-regulated the system, comparing and ranking recordings according to a value system that considered the musical performance within the history of the Grateful Dead, the quality of the recording within the limits of technology, and scarcity of the tape (Harvey, 2009, p. 118).

Many tapers and collectors freely produced and shared copies with other Dead Heads, thus spreading the music as much as possible. This generated an informal

economy with a circular flow where "brothers" took care of one another by recipro-
cally gifting tapes.

> The sharers . . . have always found that prosperity comes not from denying others what
> they want, but from spreading the wealth . . . There is a great joy also to be gained in the
> act of sharing. Passing the music on makes the circle complete—we give others the op-
> portunity to find joy, which was given to us when we received the tapes. Ultimately, the
> music is meant to be shared. (Dwork & Getz, 1998)

The importance of trading in the jamband communities cannot be overstated. Refer-
encing anthropological studies of gifting and their application to tape trade, taper Jerry
Moore stated: "When giving away the arm band, you get to keep the arm band" (Harvey, 2009, p. 109). Instead of actually giving away the material artifact, the collector
gives away a copy of the music and "transfer[s] [the] aura" of the master recording to
each subsequent copy (Zak, 2001, p. 19).

Tape trading, therefore, offered a special structure for gifting: tape traders could
adhere to a "social code of rules" mandating exchange without having to fight the
natural, human "acquisitive tendency [where individuals] love to possess and therefore desire to acquire and dread to lose" (Malinowski, 1953, p. 96). Traders can acquire, share, and reciprocate without depleting or diminishing their own artifacts and
engage in a culture of sharing. Within this system of exchange, sharers place others in
debt by giving away reproductions of the music. Recipients repay this debt by sharing
with others or acquiring new tapes from another source and sharing copies back to the
original giver. Tapers and traders are able to share the music, increase their collection,
and cultivate "kinship ties."

Initially, non-commercial tape (and later CD) trading was unique to the Grateful
Dead and their fans, but as jamband music and culture spread, so did the spreading
of the music. Markus Giesler (2006, p. 287), in his ethnography "Consumer Gift
Systems," sees music downloading and, by extension, tape trading and "spreading
the music," as a system of social solidarity based on gift transactions. In the jamband
community, one important aspect in the transmission of music is the "gifting" of the
shows that tapers record. Jamband culture and the social capital of both performers
and tapers/audience is based, to a large extent, on a gift economy.

"Just Couldn't Leave It Alone"

For members of the jamband community, and jambands' eclectic mix of traditions
and genres, melodies and improvisations, interspersed with "teases," the idea of
tunes being drawn closer through structural memories and commonalities rings true.
The jamband musician, in musical conversation with fellow players, draws closer to
the other players and the tapers and traders who spread the music, creating a vibrant
community.

These thousands of people scattered across the world are a community, a family, united by their love of music and their intense desire to "spread it." By sharing
what they love, they observe, document, and learn by keeping the music; by utilizing
cutting-edge technology, they create a family that knows the music. The community

grows through sharing, and the members of the community who are most respected within the community and most vital to it are those who record the music so they may give it away. The creativity of the musicians who make this music and the resourcefulness of the jamband community members who find new ways to recognize and honor this creativity are shining examples of improvisation. And while this remarkable mix of musical styles and genres that is jamband music began with the Grateful Dead nearly fifty years ago, its spirit of community remains vibrant, leading more and more people to experience the heady joys of music.

> Copyright law is fast evolving. Be aware when encouraging taping and distributing music that there may be licensing issues involved.

NOTES

1. Like modern-day Alan Lomaxes (thanks to sites like db.etree.org, "The Trader's Database," collectors can add almost infinite detail—musicians playing at the show, placement of microphones during the recording, brand and model of recording hardware used by the taper, hardware and software used in tape transfer and conversion, format—about a show to an online database that can be accessed by anyone willing to sign up).

2. A series of Memorial "vines" were created and distributed on eMule, a fan-created "gathering place," with " . . . the ideal of enlightenment through the music" (eMule, 2005) for followers of Gov't Mule, in the wake of September 11, 2001, to honor family and friends who had died in the attack, by sharing and spreading music, but always return to the music.

3. This term may be written as one word ("jamband") or two ("jam band").

4. During the 2009 Beacon Run, from March 9 to March 28, the ABB played a total of fifteen shows, totaling 244 songs played—of the 100 different songs that were played during the run, forty-seven songs were played only once, and the most-played song, "Statesboro Blues," was played nine times.

5. *Wired* magazine has hailed LISTS.NETSPACE.ORG as "one of the Internet's largest hosting services" (Manjoo, 2001).

6. Netscape was created at Brown University. The online community of Phish fans, led by Lee Silverman, and other student groups at Brown University helped finance the purchase of a 486 computer to serve as the host for all of the student and Phish online forums. But since the University required that all resources be shared, human-rights watch forums, software bug-alerting forums, and forums for other jam-oriented bands were also initiated. Phish.net, before the band broke up in 2004, had over 15,000 subscribers. Brown initially provided the seed money to help make Netspace a self-sufficient project, and now Netspace is a non-profit 501(c) corporation that exists through funds charged for hosting mail lists and websites as well as donations (Anderson, 2005).

7. BitTorrent only works if everyone uploads their share. There's no central server uploading the files to you—it's other people like you, who are using their upload bandwidth to get you the show, and expecting you to share what you have with them or pass it on to another person. So your goal should be to upload as much as you download. Somebody has to *upload* every byte that gets *downloaded.* You need to do your part, or the whole thing falls apart . . . a BitTorrent "swarm" is just a group of users running a single torrent—using their own ISP upload and download bandwidth . . . (bt.etree.org, 2006)

BIBLIOGRAPHY

Anderson, K. (2005a, February13). Message posted to eMule listserve. Netscape is no longer providing *** lists.

Anderson, K. (2005b, March 5). Jambands.com http:www.jambands.com/fan-sites/2005/03/05/emule

Bove, T. (1996). *Unlimited devotion: A brief history of the Grateful Dead.* Retrieved from www.rockument.com/grateful_dead.html

Bt.etree.org. (2006, May 8). *BitTorrent 101—Sharing Live Music.* Retrieved from http://audio-hub.org/bt/bt101.htm

Bt.etree.org. (2009). *Gov't Mule 8/5/2009 Wellmont Theater.* Monclair, NJ. Retrieved from http://bt.etree.org/details.php?id=527315

Budnick, D. (2003). *Jambands.* San Francisco: Backbeat Books.

Cheal, D. J. (1988). *The gift economy.* New York: Routledge.

Db.etree.org. (2005). Retrieved from http://db.etree.org/lookup_show.php?shows_key=35

Db.etree.org. (2005). *Who We Are.* Retrieved from www.etree.org/whoarewe.html

Db.etree.org. (2009). *Shows by Allman Brothers Band—2009.* Retrieved from http://db.etree.org/ bs_d.php?year=2009&artist_key=51

Duffy, C. (1998). *What is a "jamband" anyways?* Retrieved from www.jambands.com/oct98/features/duffy.html

Dwork, J., & Getz, M. M. (1998). *The Deadhead's taping compendium.* New York: Owl.

eMule. (2005, February 4). Retrieved from www.netspace.org/~emule

Giesler, M. (2006). Consumer gift systems. *Journal of Consumer Research, 33,* 283–290.

Harvey, K. A. (2009). *Embalming the dead: Taping, trading, and collecting the aura of the Grateful Dead* (Unpublished master's thesis). Tufts University. UMI 1460178.

Hollems, B. (2009). *Hittin' the web with the Allman Brothers Band: The sweet river ABB beacon set lists and stats 2009.* Retrieved from www.allmanbrothersband.com/modules.php?op =modload&name=News&file=article&sid=734

Hyde, L. (2007). *The gift: Imagination and the erotic life of property.* New York: Vintage Books.

Jambands.com. (2007). *What is a jam band?* Retrieved from www.jambands.com/jamband.html

Kemp, R. (2000). Fresh catches. *Rolling Stone.* 854, 42.

Klecka, M. (2002, February12). Message posted to eMule listserve.

Kranton, R. (1996). Reciprocal exchange: A self-sustaining system. *American Economic Review, 86* (4), 830–51.

Malinowski, B. (1953). *Argonauts of the Western Pacific: An account of native enterprise and adventure in the archipelagoes of Melanesian New Guinea.* New York: E. P. Dutton.

Manjoo, F. (2001). Netspace moves its net space. *Wired.* Retrieved from www.wired.com/culture/lifestyle/news/2001/05/43801

Mulebase.com. (2010, October 7). Setlists. Retrieved from www.mulebase.org/year.php?y=2004&q=e

Nye, R. B. (1937). A musician's word list. *American Speech, 12* (1), 45–48.

Pareles, J. (2004). *No fears: Laptop d.j.'s have a feast.* Retrieved from www.nytimes.com/2004/09/10/arts/music/10INTE.html?ex= 1095849682&ei=1&en=49d3aee624735d29

Pattacini, M. (2000). Deadheads yesterday and today: An audience study. *Popular Music and Society, 24* (1), 1–14.

Pennelli, P. (1998). *The new muse.* Retrieved from www.jambands.com/oct1598/features/pennelli.html

Pinchot, G. (1995). The gift economy. *Business on a Small Planet, 41*, 49. Retrieved from www.context.org/ICLIB/IC41/PinchotG.htm

Sanders, J. (2003). *Setting levels. Searchin' for the sound: Why I collect live tapes*. D. Budnick (Ed.). Retrieved from www.jambands.com/oct98/levels.html

Straw, W. (1991). Systems of articulation, logics of change: Scenes and communities in popular music. *Cultural Studies, 5* (3), 361–375.

Straw, W. (1997). *Collected work: The subcultures reader*. United Kingdom: Routledge. Previously published as "Systems of articulation, logics of change: Communities and scenes in popular music" in *Cultural Studies, 5* (3) (1991).

Traders' Den. Retrieved from www.thetradersden.org/

Veblen, K.K. (2008). The many ways of community music. *International Journal of Community Music, 1* (1), 5–21.

Waddell, R. (2009). Warren Haynes Q & A. *Billboard*. Retrieved from www.billboard .com/features/warren-haynes-q-a-1004004812.story?page=2#/features/warren-haynes-q -a-1004004812.story?page=2?

Zak III, A. J. (2001). *The poetics of rock: Cutting tracks, making records*. Berkeley: University of California Press.

Part III

MARGINALIZED MUSICS AND COMMUNITIES

Chapter Twelve

Marginalized Communities: Reaching Those Falling Outside Socially Accepted Norms

Sheila Woodward and Catherine Pestano

Marginalized individuals and groups who have experienced a breakdown in their relationship with society and those who have been identified as being at imminent risk of doing so present unique needs in community music programs. Besides simply offering these participants a healthy diversion from criminal and other destructive behaviors, efforts should be aimed at successfully reintegrating into society those who have become disconnected. This chapter focuses on music diversion programs for juvenile offenders, at-risk students, and those suffering oppression as a result of their ethnicity. Two unique programs are described: a program for juvenile offenders in South Africa and the United States (which offers participants marimba and djembe ensemble experience and cross-continental communication between the groups), and a UK program focused on students who have been diverted out of mainstream schools and on a creative participatory outreach to Serbian youth.

Individuals and groups marginalized by society present unique challenges for community music programs. Participants who may have no illness or disability, but who fit in to societal norms, may be excluded from opportunities as a result of their ethnicity, sexual orientation, age, disability, or gender. Social situations may also contribute to children making bad choices and moving through the legal system. Whatever the contributing factors that led these young people to have been excluded from other opportunities, community music can make a great difference in these populations (Veblen & Olsson, 2002). This chapter highlights several programs across continents that have addressed the needs of those who might otherwise be excluded from engaging in social musical activities, providing a means for healthy self-realization while actively engaging them in the process of social reintegration. In the first section, Sheila Woodward describes her work with juvenile offenders in both the United States and in South Africa. Catherine Pestano then recounts her work with ethnically oppressed populations and marginalized, disabled students in Serbia and at-risk students in the United Kingdom who do not attend traditional schools.

SHEILA WOODWARD'S PROGRAMS FOR JUVENILE OFFENDERS IN THE UNITED STATES AND SOUTH AFRICA

Background

In order to reach out to juvenile offenders in both the United States and South Africa, an international partnership was established in 2001 between the University of South Florida (United States) and the University of the Western Cape (South Africa). The key component in this three-year-long project was its collaborative nature between the disciplines of music, law, and psychology. Institutions and organizations in each country, including departments of juvenile justice, joined the many individuals involved in this program to work toward one common goal: to connect with children who had fallen outside of their societies' traditional supports.

Diversion into Music Education (DIME) came into being to provide juvenile offenders with musical skills that offer healthy alternatives to criminal activity while assisting in their successful reintegration into society. DIME initially focused on two groups: incarcerated American children and South African children within the court systems who were facing possible imprisonment. Later, this program reached larger numbers of children and expanded to include American juveniles assigned to diversion programs and other teenagers who were considered at-risk.

Programs that divert children from criminal prosecution and trial have historically been viewed as having a range of benefits such as helping children avoid criminal records and contact with prisoners, alleviating demands on court time and costs, improving the offender's function within the family and adaptation to society, being cost-effective, and preventing recidivism (Muntingh, 1998; Sloth-Nielsen, 2001; Sloth-Nielsen, 2003). Furthermore, these programs also indicated benefits to high-risk children (Steyn, 2003). Community-based initiatives have provided the means for juvenile justice systems to expand the range of their offerings and to incorporate a far greater number of juveniles than otherwise would have been possible.

The importance of families and communities in providing resources and being invested in the success of their young offenders is at the heart of the philosophy underpinning the support for community diversion options (Skelton, 2008). A new Child Justice Bill, which was based on numerous earlier recommendations, such as the 2002 Law Commission's *Report on Juvenile Justice,* was signed into South African law in 2009. Objectives of diversion programs were identified as meeting the child's needs, fostering accountability, and promoting reintegration into the family and society, while preventing future consequences of a criminal record, including social stigmatism, and reducing recidivism (South African Law Commission, 2003).

Providing educational and skill-building programs for young prisoners that prepare them for transition back to life in the community serves the interests of the offenders and promotes social welfare (Scott & Steinberg, 2008, referring to *Roper v. Simmons,* 541 US 1040 [2005]). Access of incarcerated youth ". . . to appropriate educational and vocation training . . . may make all the difference between successful reintegration into society and reoffending" (McCord, Widom & Crowell, 2001, p. 186).

At the time this project was being formulated, programs were being sought in South Africa that would divert children from court systems, be geographically accessible, offer practical skills as an alternative to criminal activity, and assist in social reintegration (Sloth-Nielsen, 2003). In the United States, Bay Area Youth Services had approached the University of South Florida, seeking support in their endeavors to meet the needs of incarcerated juvenile offenders. Both scenarios offered ideal opportunities for local universities to join in community music outreach programs.

Participants and Types of Music Programs

In its early stages, DIME targeted ten- to sixteen-year-olds and focused on about thirty children, half from the city of Tampa, Florida, and half from an informal squatter settlement, Khyalitsha, which is located close to the city of Cape Town, South Africa. One of the distinctive aspects of DIME was the selection of instruments. The African marimba and drum instruments were chosen as the medium of instruction because of their uniquely energetic sound, their suitability to beginner group performance, and the natural hitting motion that these instruments demand. There was no prerequisite of previous musical training or minimum grade level. Once referred to the program, each of the children was accepted based on the premise that all children are musical (Gardner, 1983). As a Tampa schoolteacher remarked: "They all started out on an equal basis; nobody could play the marimbas, so they felt equal. They didn't feel like somebody had the head start. It was just 'OK, here we are!' And they had no clue they were talented!" From the first teaching sessions, the children in both settings appeared to have a natural identification with the instruments and a positive connection with the rhythms. This experience provided the South African children with an opportunity to explore traditions suppressed by massive urbanization and to embrace their cultural heritage, and for the Americans, it offered an enriching intercultural experience.

Goals of the Program

Because music is a means by which a child's cultural, emotional, aesthetic, and intellectual needs can be met, it was chosen as the focus of the program. The goal of the program was to develop participants' musical skills in order to divert them from joining gangs. This was undergirded by a strong commitment to successfully reintegrate juvenile offenders into the community. It was anticipated that the participants' self-confidence and sense of self-worth would rise through their musical achievements, fostering healthy social relationships. As these young people became motivated by musical engagement, they would develop a strong level of focus and what Csikszentmihalyi (1990) describes as "flow." It was further anticipated that the active teamwork of performing in a musical ensemble, combined with positive interactions with teachers, administrators, and mentors within the program as well as successful performances in public, would impact broader family, school, and community relationships.

Motivational Challenges and Triumphs

Working with children with histories of resistance to social norms in communities rife with gang activity, violence, and crime presents many challenges. For example, one difficulty for the Cape Town group of children diverted from the courts was implementing the sessions during recreation time instead of within the regular school schedule. The children responded positively and dedicated their free time to the program, maintaining their commitment to this alternative to court procedures. In contrast, the incarcerated population of the Tampa group had no choice in its referral, and participation was offered as a privilege. For the program to be successful, the program would have to attract the participants' attention and become important to them. To those working on the project, it became evident that the musical experiences themselves became self-motivating, as was evidenced by the participants' engagement, focus, and emotional growth. A teacher reported: "We couldn't believe the change in their behavior. Because this was something (we) would hold over their heads—'if you don't do your homework, tomorrow is going to be DIME day and you're not going to be there.'"

Service Learning for University Students

In higher education, engaging students in field service closes the gap between theory and practice, offering future professionals exposure to working in real-life scenarios. In addition to involving music students as teachers, a strong mentoring component, based on positive indications of mentoring on high school students (Herrera, Sipe, McClanahan, Arbreton, & Pepper, 2000; Jekielek, Moore, Hair, & Scarupa, 2002), was established. Psychology and law students from the University of South Florida (USF) and the University of Western Cape (UWC), many of whom came from the same communities as the participants, played a strategic role as listeners, guides, and positive role models. They attended many of the music rehearsals and interacted with the participants outside of the sessions in order to encourage the participants. One mentor explained: "We are just playing a role of being models and being there for them, whenever they need us . . . we are giving them an ear to listen whenever they are having problems . . . to be a friend." The success of this modeling was evident in statements made by some participants about how they would like to study someday at university and direct programs like DIME to help other children. Furthermore, the researchers observed that the synergy and empathy between the children and the young university students aided the children in establishing robust, positive social connections.

Process in Achieving Goals

For the people who initiated DIME, it was important to create a program where children did not just learn about music but where they could be actively engaged in making it (Elliott, 1995). Acquiring musical skills was seen as the first essential ingredient of the program, offering the participants a healthy diversion from crime. A parent of a Cape Town participant described his son's involvement in the program: "He likes this music . . . he's living this music! . . . The crime is too high in South Africa; it [DIME] is taking him away from the streets, from roaming the streets. Every weekend I know that he is busy doing something good somewhere in this project."

These sentiments were echoed by one of the Cape Town participants who explained her perspective on the DIME program: "I think it is good for me. It gives me a better chance of playing marimba. Marimba could be my future. One day, I could become a very good musician. And it distances me away from many things. Because, by the time I play marimba, there are many outside things that are bad that are happening, and I'm being avoided by it [sic]." Although not all the children (especially not the Americans) might have had access to marimba or djembe bands after this experience, they were encouraged, upon discharge, to remember their success as musicians and to seek other musical groups (such as popular groups, jazz bands, and choirs) to join.

The second objective was to help them successfully reintegrate into society. This began as the students developed strong levels of self-confidence through their musical achievements. A schoolteacher at one of the juvenile facilities in the Tampa program recounted:

> I was just thinking in all of my years of teaching, thirty-three years, the DIME project just stands out. It was just so awesome to take these adjudicated kids that were really troubled and to see them blossom! Because, they really had not succeeded! And then along came the DIME project. You could stand back and watch the growth week by week. They felt good about themselves, their self-esteem just soared.

Making music within an ensemble requires social cooperation and offers a practical means for acquiring skills in team-peer interaction. During the early training sessions, there was occasionally some hostility among the participants. Participants who entered the program feeling lonely and isolated in an aggressive, non-trusting environment soon became acclimated to the community, showing positive expressions of self- and team-achievement and mutual respect. The musical activities fostered a sense of self-fulfillment and belonging through peer teaching. Having each learned one of the musical parts, the students then taught the others until everyone gained a level of proficiency on each part. The students helped each other, gaining a sense of mastery and ownership as they realized that they knew something that they could pass on to others. The researchers observed again and again how group ties were strengthened by sensitivity, hard work, and focused, "flowing," active behavior. These elements were essential factors in facilitating the creation of a musical product and a musical group that was united in its common goals.

A teacher in Tampa observed:

> They began to even work better together because they were helping each other out, trying to show each other this part or that part . . . You wouldn't think that music would be that important in social skills. But they learned very quickly that "I have this part and you have that part, but if we don't work together it doesn't sound right." In the beginning, there was a lot of, maybe, pushing at each other, or put-downs, you know, negative comments. But then it wasn't long before they realized that "we're not getting anywhere unless we're working together."

One ingredient of the participants' success was an ability to develop inner strength in order to overcome their individual hardships and circumstances. A Cape Town music teacher reported that he sometimes would need to suggest that the child forget about everything bad that was happening at home and to try to concentrate on the music. The musical experiences touched the children's inner spirits, enriching their appreciation of the arts, fostering cooperative peer relationships, and offering a further dimension of social cooperation.

In addition to the active class sessions, performance opportunities were set up in order to provide a strong motivational goal (O'Neill & McPherson, 2002). The fact that these children had been in trouble with the law indicated a breakdown in their relationship with society. In these experiences, parents, neighbors, departmental officials, and community leaders were invited, and as the children received public affirmation, they grew emotionally, they developed self-confidence, and there was evidence of some repairing of those relationships with society.

A teacher in Tampa stated:

> When they put on the program, parents showed up, and they were amazed that their little kids were actually up there on stage in front of a large audience, playing an instrument when they had never played anything but the radio! They were just amazed, and they would come back, several of them with tears in their eyes. They couldn't believe what their kids could do.

In addition, parents of the Cape Town children testified to improvements in their children's circumstances: "It's good for my child because it helps him, it keeps him busy." Another stated: "He is no longer drinking and smoking now. He comes back home in time. He is often at home. He does his homework well. I am no longer receiving complaints from the school. He is, indeed, a good child."

Intercultural and Intercontinental Connections

One element that makes this program unique is its international connection, which includes an exchange of directors and music teachers visiting each other's sites across the globe. The initial stage of the program was developed simultaneously on the two continents and documented on film, making sure that the identities of the children were not revealed, with some of these films being exchanged between the two groups. The children were able to talk on film to each other: "Hi, Cape Town, how you doing? I hope you enjoy our video and our presentation that we did for you all and all the other fun stuff. Hope you all get a chance to send us a video so we see how you all are doing." The children proudly shared their cultures, their roots, and the moment: "I like to play soccer, read books, and be with my family. Right now, I'm reading *The Firm.* It's by John Gresham [Grisham], my favorite author."

The children exhorted each other to improve themselves. This was a powerful influence especially when compared with similar words from adults. For example, a South African participant exclaimed: "Hello, America, I'm playing marimba music. I saw your video, you are improving. But I want to leave a message with you guys. You must carry on with your music. Stop doing bad things, you know. Be yourself and do what you're supposed to do." The children created virtual relationships. The periodic exchange of videos provoked a positive, competitive setting and inspiration. The motivation appeared to be mutual as participants exhorted one another to improve musically and to make better life choices. As one American child stated: "I suggest you stay in school and don't get in trouble. If you're already in trouble, get out of trouble and don't get back in it." It is a goal of the program to be able to have the groups communicate through video conferences, a process that requires infrastructure that is gradually developing in schools in both the United States and South Africa.

Final Reflections

After three years of continued development, a significant number of the initial Cape Town participants have remained as voluntary teachers, and some continue to perform regularly with the instruments, earning an income for their families. In America, for privacy reasons, the incarcerated children who had been encouraged to join musical groups could not be contacted after their discharges. With continued support, DIME will be able to continue and offer a model for expansion worldwide. As a Tampa teacher expressed:

> I can feel it in my heart. Wow, what an opportunity for these kids . . . they probably didn't realize it then, but I'll bet you now, three years later, five years later, ten years later, that's something they'll never forget, they'll tell their grandkids about "the time I played marimbas, I put on a production." They'll do it!

CATHERINE PESTANO'S PROGRAMS FOR AT-RISK STUDENTS IN THE UNITED KINGDOM AND ETHNICALLY OPPRESSED POPULATIONS AND MARGINALIZED DISABLED STUDENTS IN SERBIA

At-Risk Students in the United Kingdom

A small community music organization, the Croydon Intercultural Singing Project (CRISP) is based in South London, England. CRISP exists to enhance the lives of individuals and to build a sense of community by using community music activities to counter the marginalization and isolation of these individuals. Drawing on Small's (1998) idea of "musicking," CRISP provides opportunities for people of all ages to take part in creative and expressive music making, whether or not they have any prior experience or training, in order to have fun, experience creativity, and feel connected with others. There is no educational progression agenda, and while participants may or may not learn something technical about music or go on to study music, CRISP will help people to find what they desire. The program's goal is for participants to experience increased self-confidence and an enhanced sense of well-being. The project focuses on people who are in the most excluded parts of the community or who are at risk of exclusion: people with a variety of challenges who may experience discrimination and exclusion due to racism, homophobia, mental-health needs, disabilities, poverty, social isolation, crime, or bereavement, as well as being in the role of caregiver, refugee, or immigrant.

In England, schools known as pupil referral units (PRUs) educate children who cannot easily be taught in regular schools. All of these young people have been excluded from mainstream schooling and are at risk of exclusion from broader society. These are not places of punishment, but are intended to provide support. The emphasis is on core academic skills, with the result that there is little provision for creative and expressive arts, especially music. Many feel that they learn better or feel safer in the PRUs.

CRISP was invited by the local authority to deliver a medium-term range of music sessions (ten sessions lasting two hours per week with the program continuing for a second year) with three PRUs. The short-term nature of the projects is challenging for the program leaders and difficult for the groups because, just as strong relationships and a positive working ethic have been formed, the sessions end.

CRISP is centered on Mullen's (2002) maxim: "We don't teach, we explore." The organizers select musical styles with the young people in mind. These are adjusted to participants' expressed musical wishes and tastes, ranging from urban and pop music to world music, film music, and even more abstract pieces. Although the children often need a measure of encouragement to join, participation is by choice, without any coercion. Activities focus, at first, on MCing, singing, playing, and joining in on pieces taught by ear, and extend to participants creating their own songs using technology, instruments, and/or vocals. Developing the ability to work together and to tolerate feelings of finding things difficult, while having fun, is important.

One PRU, with young mothers and pregnant schoolgirls, makes a distinction of activities between singing with their babies/bumps and then being girls, singing together without their children. Participants work toward performing and recording original music (and covers of well-loved songs).

One of the PRU teachers vividly expressed her feelings about the impact of this program:

> Thank you for the music projects that you have initiated at Cotelands. It has been a wonderful opportunity for all our pupils to have this experience. For the schoolgirl mothers, it has equipped them with the confidence to sing with their babies, and this, in turn, has resulted in much joy from the little ones. The "choir" has developed musically, and it has been great to see even the reluctant pupils responding positively, writing and performing their own compositions.

The goal of these projects is to help build young people's creativity and self-esteem by expressing their ideas, working together, and persevering at an activity. For young, disenfranchised people who feel that their voices are not valued by society, denying them a means for full and complete expression may be seen as a form of oppression, so words are never censored, no matter how offensive. Creating a diversity of options and modeling alternatives, while looking at how successful artists express or alter their messages, helps the program participants to express unpleasant thoughts articulately, although not necessarily more positively. There are discussions about language, which help the young people to reflect on their ways of channeling and expressing ideas, and using a thesaurus and a rhyming dictionary is encouraged to extend word power and expand vocabulary and information skills. In a recent project, lyrical content was discussed with the school head because she wanted the group to perform in public. She felt that engagement of the young men involved in the project and the work that they had done was commendable. Since the language and ideas used in the songs were used in the group's everyday lives, she agreed to allow them to perform some quite uncomfortable lyrics for the entire school population.

Perhaps the most important aspect of community in this program is that, as well as emphasizing inclusion and creativity, the work supports, in each of the young participants an inner realization, that their voices are unique, that they are able to become part of a community, that they have something to offer society, and that they are welcome and acceptable just as they are.

Serbian Project with Marginalized Youth

The Serbian project was generated by a request from a colleague from former Yugoslavia who felt that the principles of community music were greatly needed in his homeland in order to provide access to music making and to help bring people together as they continued to emerge from civil conflict. CRISP received an award from the International Society for Music Education (ISME) and the Gibson Foundation to fund a year of exploratory visits and create short-term music projects to support an awareness of community music principles in Serbia.

Serbian young people did not have many organized opportunities to create music of their own choosing. In the province of Vojvodina, social problems could be addressed through shared music activities. These social problems included a need for diversionary activities to reduce risk of criminal offenses and alcoholism, a need for ways to help people to interact socially and work creatively both within and between ethnic groupings, and a need for social integration of the Roma community, which is disregarded by the broader community.

The Serbian state had made a commitment to provide an excellent technical music education for those who are able to pass entry aptitude tests. However, few students pass these examinations, so participation in music making is not widespread. With a strong focus on technical training for an elite group of musicians, a small part of the nation has very high levels of technical music capability, while a much larger part of the nation has less access to music making. Organized cultural societies are concerned mostly with preserving the diverse ethnic traditions, which involves the learning of "received" songs and dances.

The project team determined that the community music model of open access and creative participatory music making might be of value to the young people and the adults working with them. The principles of community music practice (mixed ability, group communication, skill sharing, active participation, and valuing diversity) lend themselves to supporting the idea of inclusion in wider society. In Serbia, a country with many ethnic and political divisions, this inclusive approach might be a valuable tool for encouraging the expression of children's ideas and using the medium of music to foster communication between people.

The work involved introducing the inclusive and accessible creative, improvisatory, and compositional approaches of community music making. Improvisation and songwriting were the main modes of work. Various dance and action songs incorporating diverse world music genres were explored through percussion and voice.

The program was centered on three main sites, across three language communities: a school for children with diverse disabilities in a regional city and kindergartens and schools in two rural village clusters. Children from kindergarten (ages five and six) through secondary school, as well as adults, were involved. A key feature throughout the programs was the integration of diverse communities, including the Roma population and people with disabilities. This social inclusivity has provided a new experience for many participants. Since the program had limited access to instruments, junk instruments (constructed from discarded materials), as well as some world percussion instruments, were used.

Teachers and musicians reported finding the sessions valuable but challenging at times, as they presented a very different way of working. What appeared to make the most difference to them was having to release their own creativity in workshops and training seminars. They understood that there was something other than music education being offered. Several adults initially gave the impression that they found it improper to see music being made for fun rather than concentrating on excellence. However, this prejudice quickly dissipated. In fact, a tutor who had initially found this work unacceptable saw the reactions of other students and staff and took part in further training. The children, on the other hand, almost universally seemed to love the activities and to experience great connection, joy, and release during the sessions. Furthermore, subsequent feedback from disabled children, who later recalled and sang the songs for their own pleasure, seemed to reveal the broader value of their work.

The purpose of this program was one of initiating and sowing seeds. The school for disabled children was most interested and welcoming from the start. Villages and individuals have responded differently, ranging from walking out in boredom, irritation, or disapproval to rushing up and exclaiming that this program was exactly what their communities needed. Educators and community members have begun to incorporate this community music approach into their work, and a new community music group has started in one village. Opportunities to speak about the work on local, regional, and national radio and television have created a ripple effect of interest and awareness of the possibilities available through creative, future-oriented music work.

A visiting group of young Bosnian Serbs, who live under very tight constraints, had moments of glorious and carefree fun filled with playful exuberance and high spirits as they created songs together. When the Serbian teachers first understood the value of waiting for the children's input rather than the musical activities being adult-directed, the magic of the pause in improvised music making, where the young person is able to improvise into a sound space while finding ways to express him- or herself and be fully part of the group in that moment, was revelatory.

Reflections on Work in the United Kingdom and Serbia

Participatory community music work, when it is approached as a collaborative and immersive venture, has the power to engage and empower people, young and old, who would otherwise remain marginalized within society. This approach contrasts strongly with conventional music education.

There is no such thing as a neutral education process. Education either functions as an instrument which is used to facilitate the integration of generations into the logic of the present system and bring about conformity to it, or it becomes the "practice of freedom," the means by which men and women deal critically with reality and discover how to participate in the transformation of their world. (Shaull, 1970, p. 11)

Process is an important part of understanding and approaching community music (Pestano & Lissimore, 2007). It is essential that process reflects—throughout all stages of the work—the values of creativity, inclusion, self-expression, and diversity. Both the journey and the destination matter. Community arts work is catalytic, providing energy and uplifting the spirit. It can offer a stimulus for the renewal of people's artistic creativity, freeing them to respond imaginatively to their circumstances. Community music techniques that emphasize the awakening of individual ideas, an awareness of personal agency, and finding the expressive voice in all its forms, have strong components for achieving success.

One crucial challenge that arises for a coordinator of community music projects is finding the right people to deliver a project in a given setting. While technical or specific skills are a consideration, it is as important that the practitioners have some understanding of the communities with whom they are working and of the life experiences that the people in those communities have had. Having experienced oppression or challenges in different forms may allow a person to become a particularly inspirational role model, providing empathy and a deeper contribution to a project.

The training and development of people with non-formal music backgrounds who want to enter this work presents a challenge for higher education institutions. In developing community music-related training courses at all levels, the question arises of how access can be extended, how potential candidates should be assessed, and how students' interpersonal skills in creating respectful relationships in the community can be developed. In order for community music principles to continue to thrive, university lecturers and trainers must maintain a commitment to inclusion and diversity in music-making experiences and outcomes.

All of the work described here involves reaching out to the marginalized. In the United Kingdom, our work with adults and young people is with marginalized individuals and groups, often in institutions or localities that are themselves marginalized from society, whether geographically or in relation to mainstream service provision. In Serbia, the projects took place within a newly constructed country that was marginalized in relation to Europe: in post-conflict time Serbia was not allowed to join the European Economic Community (EEC). We worked with groups marginalized because of their disabilities and with those for whom their ethnicity represented a marginalization within Serbian society. This was greatest for the Roma population, who were excluded even by their neighboring marginalized minority ethnic groups.

It is interesting to reflect that community musicians are themselves marginalized within UK society. Universities struggle with the term *community music*, often preferring *applied music*. Mainstream music services and funders pay rates that leave workers struggling to construct viable careers or earn a living wage. Perhaps this is an inevitable consequence of aligning with those who lack power in society. Individual choices by practitioners and commissioning organizations matter if community music is to retain the qualities that help it engage and inspire people. The way an organization negotiates, the way one relates to competitors, the way one treats other freelance workers whose services are commissioned—all are as significant as individual interactions with music-making participants.

CONCLUSION

This chapter has focused on programs serving individuals and groups that are excluded from society and the usual opportunities to pursue musical interests that might be available to most. In reaching out to provide inclusion, these programs offer socially interactive musical activities that foster self-fulfillment, develop skills for lifelong enjoyment of music and diversion from crime, and promote social reintegration. These programs provide one template for the establishment and growth of programs for marginalized communities across the globe.

ACKNOWLEDGMENTS

The DIME project was supported, in part, by the Open Foundation, the USF Collaborative for Children, Families and Communities, the USF Institute on Black Life and the USF College of Performing Arts. The work in Vojvodina, former Yugoslavia, was funded by the inaugural ISME Gibson award for community-based music projects. The work in London was funded by the Positive about Young People (PAYP) funds from the London Borough of Croydon.

BIBLIOGRAPHY

Csikszentmihalyi, M. (1990). *Flow: The psychology of optimal experience.* New York: Harper & Row.

Elliott, D. J. (1995). *Music matters: A new philosophy of music education.* New York: Oxford University Press.

Gardner, H. (1983). *Frames of mind: The theory of multiple intelligences.* New York: Basic Books, Inc.

Herrera, C., Sipe, C., McClanahan, W. S., Arbreton, A. J. A., & Pepper, S. A. (2000). *Mentoring school-age children: Relationship development in community-based and school-based programs.* Washington, DC: National Mentoring Partnership and the US Department of Education.

Jekielek, S. M., Moore, K. A., Hair, E. C., & Scarupa, H. J. (2002). *Mentoring: A promising strategy for youth development.* Washington, DC: Child Trends. Retrieved from www.childtrends.org/PDF/MentoringBrief2002.pdf

McCord, J., Widom, C. S., & Crowell, N. A. (Eds). (2001). *Juvenile crime, juvenile justice: Commission on behavioral and social sciences and education.* Washington, DC: National Academy Press.

Mullen, P. (2002). *We don't teach, we explore: Aspects of community music delivery.* Retrieved from www.worldmusiccentre.com/uploads/cma/mullenteachexplore.pdf

Muntingh, L. (1998). *A longitudinal study of diversion.* Cape Town: NICRO.

O'Neill, S. A., & McPherson, G. E. (2002). Motivation. In R. Parncutt & G. McPherson (Eds.), *The science and psychology of music performance; Creative strategies for teaching and learning* (pp. 31–46). New York: Oxford University Press.

Pestano, C., & Lissimore, T. (2007). Get your act together. In H. Coll & J. Finney (Eds.), *Ways into music: Making every child's music matter.* Reston, VA: National Association of Music Educators.

Roper v. Simmons, 541 US 1040 (2005).

Scott, E. S., & Steinberg, L. D. (2008). *Rethinking juvenile justice.* Cambridge: Harvard University Press.

Shaull, R. (1970). Foreword. In P. Freire, *Pedagogy of the oppressed.* Harmondsworth: Penguin.

Skelton, A. (2008). Restorative justice in child justice systems in Africa. In J. Sloth-Nielsen (Ed.), *Children's rights in Africa: A legal perspective* (pp. 129–145). Aldershot: Ashgate Publishing Limited.

Sloth-Nielsen, J. (2001). *The influence of international law on juvenile justice reform in South Africa* (Unpublished master's thesis). University of the Western Cape, Cape Town, South Africa.

Sloth-Nielsen, J. (2003). The business of child justice. In J. Burchell & E. Erasmus (Eds.), *Criminal justice in a new society.* Cape Town: Juta & Co., Ltd.

Slobin, M. (1993). *Subcultural sounds: Micromusics of the West.* Hanover, NH: Wesleyan University Press.

Small, C. (1998). *Musicking: The meanings of performing and listening.* Middletown, CT: Wesleyan University Press.

South African Law Commission. (2002). *Report on Juvenile Justice.*

South African Law Commission. (2003, October). *Draft of the Child Justice Bill.*

Steyn, F. (2003). A preliminary evaluation of the Open Society Foundation funded diversity programmes. (Unpublished report. Open Society Foundation).

Veblen K., & Olsson, B. (2002). Community music: Toward an international overview. In R. Colwell & C. Richardson (Eds.), *The new handbook of research on music teaching and learning* (pp. 703–756). New York: Oxford University Press.

Chapter Thirteen

Personal Growth through Music: Oakdale Prison's Community Choir and Community Music for Homeless Populations in New York City

Mary L. Cohen and Marissa Silverman

This chapter explores the following community music projects: (1) the initial eighteen months of the Oakdale Community Choir and (2) community music activities involving homeless persons in New York City: Music Kitchen, a homeless shelter outreach project and a music therapy treatment program at Bellevue Hospital. Mary L. Cohen discusses her work with the Oakdale Prison community choir and Marissa Silverman explores musical interventions of both community outreach and music therapy in New York City.

In addition to examining these community music sites in situ, we discuss the skills, dispositions, and values—musical, emotional, social, and personal—that these "homeless" persons develop in and through their participation in such programs. We reflect on how these respective programs provide a means for participants to develop social skills.

DIFFERENT CONTEXTS: SIMILAR PURPOSES

The programs examined in this chapter serve similar purposes. All programs use music to address problems of social alienation. The choral singing and music intervention programs cultivate a sense of social identity as well as self-worth for participants. The contexts are different in that the prison is a legally enforced separation from society, while the homeless shelters offer protection to individuals who are without a home base of belonging. In our descriptions of these community music practices, we highlight traditions, participants' perspectives, and illustrations of social bonds that accrue through participation.

OAKDALE COMMUNITY CHOIR

The underpinning philosophy of the Oakdale Community Choir (OCC) is an African concept, *Ubuntu*, meaning "a person is a person through other people" (Fisher,

2006/2007). One learns and grows from the experiences in the choir because of the interactions with others, musically and socially, and through the writing component. Related to this grounding concept, the choir embraces a restorative justice model (Zehr, 2002).

Restorative justice is rooted in a commonsense understanding of wrongdoing: "Crime is a violation of people and of interpersonal relationships. Violations create obligations. The central obligation is to put right the wrongs" (Zehr, 2002, p. 19). Restorative practice is an emerging field of study intended to restore and build community. The Oakdale Community Choir is an example of restorative practice.

The choir's goals are to provide choral singing experiences for (a) general population male offenders who are not restricted to their units at the Iowa Medical and Classification Center (IMCC) and (b) female and male community volunteers who have an interest in learning more about the prison system and being actively involved in prison education. As the educational mission of the choir and a related prison partnership program continues to evolve, the choir intends for the broader goals of community involvement to expand and further the overall hope of improving the US justice system.

Since beginning this choir in February 2009, Mary Cohen has been in the process of developing a coalition of prison partnership programs. These programs include any courses, programs, or projects created to benefit both partners. People involved from the University of Iowa or from the community partner with IMCC or other correctional facilities enter the project with the intention of learning from one another. The mission for these programs is to empower participants to embrace the joys of hard work for a meaningful purpose, build companionship rooted in sharing one's self and responding to others, gain confidence that each one can contribute to a greater good, and learn to honor oneself individually and as a community.

Getting into Prison

About five years before starting the OCC, while employed full-time as an elementary music specialist, Cohen attended an East Hill Singers prison choir concert (see www .artsinprison.org). Cohen had friends who sang in this choir as community volunteers and became curious about this unique program. This men's choir, composed of minimum-security offenders and male community volunteers, had a rich, warm sound and performed in public venues. The prisoners recited narrations before the selections, and prisoner-created visual art pieces and creative writing filled the gathering space outside of the performance space. Cohen was impressed with the idea of community members joining prisoners to bring a choral performance to the public and became curious about the outcomes of such an innovative program.

In 2003, Cohen began a full-time PhD program in music education at the University of Kansas (KU) and further researched prison choirs. She found very few published data-based research studies. Most of the prison choirs in US correctional facilities were inmate-conducted or religious-based and sang during prison worship services. With the support of the music education and music therapy department at KU, Cohen spent time in the Lansing Correctional Facility researching the East Hill Singers, assisting and directing a small male prison choir, and thinking about the role of choral singing in prison contexts. She constructed a theory of choral singing pedagogy in prison contexts based on Christopher Small's (1998) concept of musicking (Cohen, 2007).

After moving to Iowa City to begin her position as assistant music education professor at the University of Iowa, Cohen continued researching prison choirs and met with Warden Lowell Brandt at the IMCC, who supported her plans to put her theory into practice by starting a choir in the facility. The planning stage of approximately one year involved visiting a music therapy session at the prison, talking with prison staff, designing a research project in conjunction with the start of the choir, coordinating a graduate seminar to occur alongside the choir, choosing literature to perform, seeking funding to purchase choral scores, and recruiting community singers to join the prisoners.

In December 2008, just eight weeks before the first rehearsal with the prison choir, Warden Brandt died unexpectedly. Although the prison administration was struggling with the change in leadership, they continued to support the start of the choir. On February 3, 2009, the choir had its first rehearsal. The choir rehearses for ninety minutes on Tuesday evenings in the prison's testing room. Cohen brings between fifteen and thirty outside singers with her into the facility for rehearsal. The prisoners (she call them "inside singers") set up the room prior to rehearsal. They start and end each practice and performance with two different "anchoring" songs.

To help the full choir develop a social as well as a musical identity, Cohen ritualized certain social functions in rehearsals to anchor shared social experiences, memories, and associations for inside and outside singers alike. The most obvious of these are the meeting and leave-taking song rituals that begin and end each rehearsal session. Lyrically, both the opening and closing songs concentrate on the virtue of beauty. The first announces a recognition of beauty in one's own life: "Beauty before me, beauty behind me, beauty above, and below, and all around." The second bestows a wish for beauty in the lives of others: "May you walk in beauty in a sacred way, may you walk in beauty each and every day." While it is impossible for Cohen to say how these rituals resonate with all the choir members, they do appear to facilitate social-identity formation within the choir. One of the inside singers, for example, shared these ideas about the choir's closing song:

> To me, it seems as though we are all bidding one another farewell, or au revoir (till we meet again), after having come together for a time of sharing something very special. Even though I may not have the opportunity each week to have a meaningful conversation with everyone that was present for rehearsal, I can still send them a message from my heart as I sing with them and look into their eyes, giving them a little part of me to take with them for their journey back out into the real world.

Providing time for small talk among choir members is another way in which rehearsals help build a social identity that brings inside and outside singers together. The few minutes the members have to interact at the beginning and end of rehearsals are treasured by both groups of singers. For example, one inside singer wrote that sometimes even one word spoken to him from an outside singer is meaningful to him. Inside singers have described outside singers as "family—when one is absent, they [sic] are missed."

An outside singer reflected on one of the prisoners being released: "When I learned that one of the inside members would be leaving us, I felt a sense of loss I hadn't anticipated."

In April 2009 the choir dedicated their first performance, themed "Peace and Place," to the memory of Warden Brandt. When Cohen asked the choir members to reflect on the theme of peace and place, one prisoner remarked that when he was first incarcerated he did not think he could ever find a sense of peace in prison. After three weeks in choir, he wrote:

> Every voice I hear reminds me of what is possible. Togetherness, teamwork, acceptance, and the list can go on. Those voices carry with me as the volunteers leave on their good-byes and I return to prison. While we sing I'm not in prison. I'm in peace. I'm in a choir of gifted musicians who share my passions and joys. The choir helps me along my path to find my place in peace.

Two Disparate Groups Join as One

The Oakdale Community Choir, like most choirs, creates a new community, but theirs, by its very nature, is different because it joins two groups of people who are otherwise prevented from meeting. A group of prisoners join singers from outside the prison. As the director, Cohen is aware of three groups: the prisoners, the community singers, and the combined full group. The prisoners and community singers do not rehearse independently, but the community singers socialize at a choir member's home after each season's final concert. Cohen works carefully to develop camaraderie among the groups. To help the community singers get to know one another, she asked them to write a short biography that she shares only with the other community members, because some of this information is personal and rules prevent sharing such information with prisoners. Through this writing exercise, two of the community singers realized they had known each other as youths in the same Lutheran church and had not seen each other in over forty-five years.

During the first eighteen months of the choir, the only social bonds Cohen has been able to facilitate among the prisoner singers occur during weekly practices and concerts. However, the writing component (explained in detail later) has given the men an opportunity to interact in a way they would not within their regular prison routines. Some have mentioned they now have new friends among fellow prisoners. After the summer 2009 choir season, the prison administration asked that volunteers not rehearse with the prisoners in the summer because the correctional officers could not coordinate the community singers entering the prison weekly while coordinating the many outdoor activities available to prisoners. For this reason, during the summer of 2010, Cohen taught a songwriting class to the prisoners to provide opportunities for the men to develop and strengthen social bonds with one another through musical expression.

With respect to the whole choir, Cohen worked to build their community through interactions at rehearsals such as singing together, changing formation within sections, mixing members into new places in the choir, having members lead musical activities, and supporting one another through applause as they progressed with learning parts and singing solos. Structured feedback sessions before and after concerts provide opportunities for the members to talk. However, because of restrictions on topics of conversation, there is, as noted by one of the community members, a "certain lack of authenticity" in the relationships between community singers and prisoners.

A description of what happens immediately before rehearsal for the prisoners and community singers illustrates the contrasting contexts of their lives. From the perspective of the prisoners:

> It was Tuesday, and some of us had finished dinner quickly, leaving some of the food untouched. There was over an hour left before the rest of the choir would arrive, but in prison it is best to get things done early, making time to deal with problems as they arise. Four men split duties with little comment, falling easily into practiced roles learned from setting up the testing room for church services. The testing room needed to be opened by staff. One man looked to that. The piano and chairs needed to be brought out from storage behind security, which means getting staff to open elevators. Others worked at that. By the time the piano and chairs were rolled down the hall, the testing room was open, and men were moving tables to the side. As always, there was discussion as to the best placement of the tables, chairs, and piano. None of it really matters, but it is part of the ritual, and ritual is everything in prison. (prisoner choir member)

From the perspective of the community singers:

> Volunteers begin arriving around 5:15[1] in the reception area. We sign in, show our IDs to the guy in the front office, get our hands stamped, and wait for the stragglers to show up before we start through the multiple sets of doors that finally lead us to the testing room. While we wait, volunteers chat about the weather, what kind of work we do, and our experiences with this choir. There is an air of anticipation for us as well, and we are eager to begin the journey to the testing room where we will find you [prisoner members] already gathered and the room prepared for us. (community singer)

The contrasting contexts of their lives are evidenced by differences between inside and outside singers' family relationships. Some inside singers are alienated from their families and therefore receive no social support (in the form of letters and visits) from family members on the outside. Several inside singers have remarked that negativism is extensive in prison; one expressed his sense of how such differences distinguish inside singers from the rest of the choir: "I now measure my years in parole-denial letters. New Year's Day and birthdays mean less to me as years pass. It's this difference in mindsets that separates me from the volunteers. It's probably the one main thing we can't understand between us."

Such real and perceived differences challenge Cohen to devise ways to bridge the divide and make connections between the groups.

Writing Component[2]

The writing component initially began as a means to focus singers' attention on the choir between rehearsals. Cohen quickly realized this component could also help bridge the divide between inside and outside singers. She began designing prompts encouraging singers to identify themselves as individuals, as musicians, and as members of the choir, and experimented with ways to facilitate exchanges of writing among choir members as well as between herself and the choir. Some of these writings eventually become song introductions for performances to audiences of prisoners, prison staff, and community guests. Some writing prompts, therefore, encourage singers to articulate the personal meanings they find in the lyrics in the concert selections.

In addition to shared writing, communal reading is another activity inside and outside singers may elect as a means to build the social identity of the choir. Cohen has paired the writing prompts with three books, one focusing on writing itself (*On Writing* by Stephen King), one focusing on prison (*We're All Doing Time* by Bo Lozoff), and one focusing on musicianship (*Musicking* by Christopher Small). Like the writing activities, reading activities are optional for both inside and outside singers, and Cohen tries to design questions to accommodate those singers who want to participate in the writing but not the reading activities. Participants bring their writing to rehearsal, exchange via a drop-off basket, and respond to one another's writing. The following week they place their responses in a basket for Cohen to read.

About half of the members participate in the reading or writing activities, or both aspects of the choir, although all of them periodically receive the choir newsletters, composed of excerpts from the writings of choir members who have indicated a wish to share with the full group. As of spring 2010, one of the outside singers, a rhetoric professor at the University of Iowa, has compiled and distributed six newsletters containing themed collections of excerpts from choir members' writing. This component of the choir offers members yet another avenue for interaction with one another, encouraging members to think critically about connections between their experiences in the choir and their lives as a whole and between their own life experiences and those of others.

The choir members' weekly writings also helped Cohen assess their understanding (or lack thereof) of musical aspects of the practice. In the fall of 2009, after reading members' reports that they were struggling with activities such as reading musical notation, finding pitches, or understanding terminology, Cohen began adding "Musical Tidbits" to the writing prompt menu to introduce various elements of musicianship.

Most recently, written social exchanges among choir members have included sharing of musical biographies. In the spring 2010 semester, Cohen received permission from prison officials to collect and distribute the musical biographies of members. She currently includes two of these brief biographies, one from an inside singer and one from an outside singer, on each weekly writing menu. These brief musical summaries extend members' capacities to learn about each other in a safe, participant-generated way.

Benefits of Choral Singing in the Oakdale Community Choir

Cohen collected data on members' perceptions of benefits derived from their participation in the choir. Inside singers' responses indicated that community volunteers' willingness to come into the prison and their eagerness to sing with prisoners enhanced their self-esteem. Some explained that the participation of the outside singers makes them feel valued: "It's nice to know there are people in the outside world who really care about us. It's nice to know we can be in a group and be accepted as a real person." More than one outside singer has described the relief of not having cell phones with them, so they can fully devote themselves to the rehearsal, and that the inside singers are more grateful than they deserve. One remarked: "To the prisoners, I say 'Thank you! Thank you for accepting this motley crew of men and women as fellow travelers on the road of life.'"

The focus on teamwork and collaboration through writing, singing, and talking with one another seems to help some of the prisoners make connections outside of themselves and to be more aware of others and their environment. Some of the offenders remarked that because of their time in the choir, they have become more other-centered rather than self-centered. This point may be significant in light of research that indicates that crime against another person or against property is more likely committed by someone with high narcissism and high antisocial personalities (Baumeister, Smart, & Boden, 1996; Visser, Bay, Cook, & Myburgh, 2010).

Many of the benefits the prisoners wrote about relate to personal benefits they have received:

- "I have a much better attitude and feeling about myself inwardly since joining the choir."
- I feel "less stressed, healthier, and happier with this choir in my life."
- I am able to "connect with a better side of myself."
- "Singing in the choir also has proven to me that if I put my mind into something I didn't think I could succeed in and take the chance, it can open the door to many possible opportunities."

These personal benefits are an important part of their growth and development; however, Cohen wonders about deeper levels of the impact their participation has on their thinking. Are they more focused on individual benefits than the process of the group? If so, is that self-focus feeding their narcissistic personalities?

One of the inside singers wrote about these issues:

The biggest downside to the choir, as far as I'm concerned, is that I see men who are in prison basically because of behaviors dictated by overinflated egos continue to feed their self-centeredness. I see this because it is something that I have to combat in myself. How do you balance efforts to lift up self-esteem against the possibility of enabling a person to stay stuck in a narcissistic delusional world where the wants and needs of others are always subservient or non-existent? Encouraging someone to step up and perform may be forcing them out of a shell of shyness or self-pity. It may also, in his mind, validate his belief that he is better than those around him. It's a swampy mess that I think needs to be in the back of our minds.

Obviously, the prisoner singers have committed crimes resulting in their current incarceration. Now as they join with community singers, they are working to create something beautiful together with members of the broader community they have harmed. A community singer described one aspect of this process: "The contribution of one pitch to a well-tuned chord is a metaphor for belonging."

The medium of choral art allows the individuals to come together to create a product more beautiful than any of them could do individually. This need for teamwork in order to create a cohesive sound is similar in some ways to the work the offenders must do upon their release from prison: they need to be able to function cooperatively with others in their personal relationships and professional acquaintances. This point resonates with the ideas of beauty in the choir's opening and closing rituals.

Some outside singers have described the choir as being "outside of [their] comfort zone" and reported some anxiety about entering a prison. But they also have reported a sense of responsibility to remain involved and a sense of reward for meeting that responsibility. One wrote, "They [prisoners] need the functional community relationships that we maintain with them, and supplying that need is a profound experience." Some of the writing from inside singers indicates they had little to no previous interactions with people who care about them. One wrote, "Never have I met people that I wanted to be like because of the way they talked to me."

This same inside singer described the community singers as a "breath of fresh air." The prisoners enjoy the interaction with volunteers because it breaks up their usual prison routine. According to a one inside singer, the prisoners behave better during choir rehearsals than in everyday regular prison life. He remarked they do not use profanity, pass gas, tell dirty jokes, or belch when they are rehearsing with the outside singers. He also remarked that on Tuesday nights, rehearsals prompt him to shave and look presentable for choir practice.

Connections among Prisoners, Family Members, and the Community

Cohen's intent is that the choir helps build connections among prisoners, their family relationships, and community members. Each choir season, they perform two concerts, the first concert for prisoners and a few outside guests, and the second concert for inside singers' family members and other outside guests. Each prisoner can have a maximum of two guests. The audience guest lists coordinated for these concerts have ranged between thirty-five and sixty-five guests. Because the prison administration does not want the prisoner singers to go through a strip search after the concert, they do not allow any physical interaction, such as shaking hands, between outside guests and prisoners. Beginning with the December 2009 concerts, the second concert was moved from a Tuesday night to a Wednesday night, so prisoners' family members who have a long drive to the prison can spend the night in the area and return to the prison the next evening for Thursday visiting hours.

Concerts were audio recorded and CDs sent to prisoners' families in an effort to help prisoners bridge the gap between themselves and their families. Prisoners have mentioned that these CDs and the choir as an activity they take part in give them specific topics to discuss with their families. Cohen has received a few thank-you notes from family members who seem to genuinely appreciate the fact that their relative is participating in the choir.

Outside singers also receive benefits from the choir. One of the goals for bringing community members into the prison to sing with the inmates is to educate the broader community about criminal justice issues. Cohen has integrated three different university classes with the choir thus far (two graduate music seminars and one undergraduate human rights topics class) and has offered a panel on restorative justice at the university. Some of the outside singers have gone on to participate in other prison education programs such as the Inside Out Prison Exchange Program at Temple University, an institute for teachers who want to integrate inmates and students in their classes, and the Alternatives to Violence Program, a three-day intensive anger-management training.

COMMUNITY MUSIC AS INTERVENTION
FOR HOMELESSNESS IN NEW YORK CITY

Homelessness in New York City has been consistently on the rise. Legally, the city must provide adequate housing for homeless citizens. In New York City, homeless shelters are organized in three categories: shelters for families, for women, and for men. Besides shelters, other proactive methods have been successful in alleviating issues surrounding homelessness. In this section of the chapter, Marissa Silverman discusses two therapeutic interventions in New York City's homeless shelters.

The mission statement of the New York City Department of Homeless Services (DHS) is:

> DHS prevents homelessness wherever possible and provides short-term emergency shelter and re-housing support whenever needed. These goals are best achieved through partnerships with those we serve, public agencies and the business and nonprofit communities. (www.nyc.gov/html/dhs/html/about/agencyintro.shtml)

As of June 2011, the number of adult and youth homeless persons on a given day in New York City's shelters is approximately 36,492 (statistics are tabulated daily and can be found at www.nyc.gov/html/dhs/html/homeless/famserv.shtml).

The physical and emotional environments of the shelters lead one to ask: How can men, women, and children living in shelters obtain the necessary legal, therapeutic, medical, and social assistance, and the inner strength to make the life-altering changes needed to improve their lives? Can music help?

Silverman will discuss two such programs: the Music Kitchen and 30th Street Men's Shelter. The Music Kitchen is a non-profit organization that presents performances of live classical, jazz, and world musics in homeless shelters. It brings highly regarded, professional musicians (e.g., Emmanuel Ax, Albrecht Mayer, Mark O'Connor) to perform chamber music for residents of New York City shelters. The 30th Street Men's Shelter at New York City's Bellevue Hospital has two different divisions: a general intake shelter and a clinic serving men who suffer from psychiatric illnesses and substance abuse/dependency issues. Music therapy is one program offered to the men who live in the clinic. The music interventions provide ways to serve as a medium for healing.

Music as Healing

Ian Cross (2003) writes that music predates human history:

> The earliest unambiguously musical artifact identified to date is a bone pipe dated to around 36,000 BP found near Württemberg in southern Germany, which was uncovered in a context that associates it with modern *Homo sapiens.* The pipe predates almost all known visual art, and in any case a capacity for musicality (most likely vocal) would predate the construction of a sophisticated musical artifact such as a pipe, probably by a considerable period. (p. 21)

While scholars are still unsure about the evolutionary role of music, using music as a tool for healing is an ancient practice. In the Old Testament, Joshua uses the long blast of trumpets not only to break open the city of Jericho, but to symbolize healing of cultural ills, and David dispelled the evil spirits of King Saul by playing the harp. The ancient Chinese used music as a cosmological prescription for human conduct (Benson, 1998; Sutton, 2000) and Vedic chants were a source for healing (Sumathy & Sairam, 2005). In classical traditions, music and medicine have been closely intertwined. Apollo was god of both medicine and music, and Hippocrates, the father of modern medicine, took his patients to the temple to hear therapeutic music. According to Pythagoras, the daily "use" of music would contribute greatly to one's health. Similarly, scholars have documented how mothers sing to their infants to relieve stress and sometimes pain (Milligan, Atkinson, Trehub, Benoit, & Poulton, 2003).

The following passage from the American Music Therapy Association provides a context for explaining the purpose of music therapy as an intervention in trauma, depression, and substance abuse:

> Music therapists commonly serve persons with mental health and functional wellness issues in a variety of settings including public and private psychiatric hospitals or schools, mental health centers, private practice, community-based programs, correctional and forensic facilities, and substance abuse treatment programs . . . Music therapists use music to enhance social or interpersonal, affective, cognitive, and behavioral functioning. (www.musictherapy.org/factsheets/bib_mentalhealth.pdf)

Music therapy's mission, generally speaking, is to meet the physical, psychological, neurological, emotional, behavioral, social, and environmental needs of patients and/or clients. Indeed, one of the basic advantages of music as a means of therapy is that it is often effective in supplementing medical interventions, or "penetrating" where medicine cannot. As Doron K. Antrim (1944) explains, medicine "prescribes for the physical man" and music seeks to "restore balance to the person as a whole" (p. 409). Music therapy functions within the domain of community music in multiple ways.

According to Gary Ansdell (2002), music therapy and community music originate from a common belief in music making, and it is through music making that we can have a clearer idea of the nature of each one's goals. He notes the following similarities:

- *Who* is worked with, and *how many* people are worked with
- *Where* the work happens, and what resources are available
- *Why* they work with people (agenda, aims, theoretical assumptions)
- *What* continuity and depth of work is possible
- *What* status is given, what reward received
- *How* far successful practice has led to building a discipline and a professional structure to further the work and its body of knowledge (2002, p. 7)

Jessica Atkinson (2000) concurs: "If community music is the making of music with people to meet their needs, it would not be unreasonable to suggest that music therapy falls within this category" (quoted in Ansdell, 2002, p. 22). Indeed, community musicians and music therapy practitioners often integrate various forms of knowledge, including performing, composing, improvising, arranging, and music listening; psychology; fund-raising, grant writing; diplomacy; and cultural studies. Moreover, music therapy and community music share similar goals: enhancing people's self-growth, self-esteem, self-knowledge, friendship, and a sense of community. Through musical development and musical performance, practitioners, clients, and music makers are connected to each other through various means of musical participation.

The Music Kitchen

Traditionally, community music scholars have focused on music making as one definitive aspect of community music. However, taken more broadly, there is emerging scholarship (e.g., Higgins and Phelan) that suggests that community music is any musical "intervention" that exists for, and whose aims are, the betterment (social, emotional, cultural, physical, spiritual) of a group of people. Silverman suggests that community music listening activities also qualify as interventions that can improve people's social, emotional, cultural, physical, and spiritual well-being. Therefore, community music is any musical intervention that exists in line with the above-mentioned aims. Consider the Music Kitchen.

Founded in 2005, the Music Kitchen (whose motto is "Food for the soul") has applied its premise that music can serve homeless citizens by providing what founder Kelly Hall-Tompkins calls "a spiritual, uplifting help" at a time when some may need sustenance most. According to Hall-Tompkins, homeless populations are not only "musically underserved, but nonserved" (Lee, 2009, p. 22).

Over the past six years, NYC homeless persons have been treated to concerts at the men's shelter at Holy Trinity Lutheran Church and the Antonio G. Olivieri Drop-in Center for homeless women (both in Manhattan). Hall-Tompkins has also organized and performed Music Kitchen concerts at the Holy Apostle Soup Kitchen, the largest soup kitchen in New York City, serving 1,200 meals everyday (www.holyapostles soupkitchen.org). Because this venue is a soup kitchen, the musicians play while the hungry come and go during the performances. As Hall-Tompkins says: "At any one time, I'm estimating that there are about 700–800 people who pass through listening to our concerts. It is terrific that we can share music with so many people . . ." (personal communication, 2010).

After each concert, Hall-Tompkins asks shelter residents to write down their thoughts on index cards.[3] One person wrote:

It put me in a real mellow cool mood. I enjoyed your songs so much. The theme was terrific bought [sic] me to a place where I could reach my inner child. You made an impact on me greatly.

Another wrote: "I loved the singing. It was inspirational. And the singing keeps my hope and faith alive." Another wrote: "Please come back when you have the time." Yet another wrote:

EVER SiNCE MY PARENTS passed, I can't gEt my life together. BASKETball AND MUSIC has helped ME, but I still don't KNOW where MY life is going. THANK YOU!

Yet another said:

Thank you for your gift of music today as we endure some extremely difficult times. You both were a breath of fresh air where hard times exist. A temporary relief!! Thank you for your expression of care and concern. God bless.

The Music Kitchen intervention not only aids the homeless shelter population it serves, but also the musicians serving that population. As Brett Deubner, violist, said: "When we go there and play from our hearts, there's a therapeutic back-and-forth for both the listener and performer. Both are being fed" (Lee, 2009). Albrecht Mayer, principal oboist for the Berlin Philharmonic, said: "Music feeds our soul and I'd wish that there would be many more places like Music Kitchen where musicians can offer their art to people in need of comfort and encouragement and, in return, get a unique feeling of what it means to share the sensation of music. The intense interaction of giving and receiving has been a very special experience for me and has moved me deeply" (www.musickitchennyc.org).

While the Music Kitchen is not a traditional community music program insofar as the music making is delivered to the audience, there have been a few instances where homeless citizens have participated. At one particular Music Kitchen concert, a program was performed by the Bach Vesper vocal soloists (singers who specialize in Renaissance and Baroque cantatas, motets, etc.). At this concert, Hall-Tompkins asked the audience if anyone had questions for the singers. The first question was "Can I sing, too?" (personal communication, 2010). As Hall-Tompkins states:

I often think to myself when people ask this: is this going to work? Here was period (Renaissance/Baroque motets) music being sung, in German. So, I thought: no way. This is not going to work. But I was wrong. And it really made me think that it doesn't really matter what music it is, or what people's prior experience has been, people gravitate towards all music. This young man, in his early 20s, did not have any prior "formal" experience with making music, and he certainly did not have any experience speaking German or reading music fluently, but he just looked over the director's shoulder and did his best on one song, and sat down when finished. And he felt really good about himself.

And satisfied. It was truly amazing that he felt so much a part of the concert experience that he had the desire to be even more connected to the music in this way.

Surprisingly, the same thing happened two [days] later. I presented a concert in a homeless youth center in Brooklyn. For that concert, we were all playing instruments. One of the young homeless women wanted to play, but not what we were playing. She just wanted to get her hands back on a string instrument, again, because she was clearly regretful that circumstances in her life had taken her away from being in a stable home and taking music lessons. She was just beside herself when the violist let her play her viola. (personal communication, 2010)

Hall-Tompkins finds that music listening has a lasting, therapeutic component. The mission of the Music Kitchen is as follows:

To bring top emerging and established professional musicians together in order to share the inspirational, therapeutic, and uplifting power of music with New York City's disenfranchised homeless shelter population. I believe a shelter exists to provide not only physical but emotional and spiritual support to those who, for whatever reason, have lost the foundation of their homes and communities. I believe that music reaches the core of our being and can play a vital role in nourishing hope, love and strength, particularly when performed at an extremely high artistic level and in a *friendly, relaxed setting*. (www.musickitchennyc.org/index.htm)

The 30th Street Men's Shelter at New York City's Bellevue Hospital

Noah Shapiro has been the activity therapies supervisor at the 30th Street Men's Shelter at New York City's Bellevue Hospital since the program's inception in 1987. This music therapy program is only one type of therapeutic intervention that Bellevue offers to homeless men suffering from psychiatric illnesses. The program was originally conceived as a multi-disciplinary approach. Therefore, in addition to music therapy, the men participate in drama therapy, recreational activities, current events groups, and dance therapy. According to Shapiro (2005), the purpose of the program is to re-socialize the men and "to find them more stable, permanent housing" (p. 31). Shapiro continues:

These men are suffering from isolation because of their illness, their homelessness, and in many cases, because they are in a foreign country. At the present time, half of the program's population of 30 men was not born in the United States. Music with these men is a unique conduit for communication. (p. 31)

Many in the shelter are newly immigrated to New York City. Although different kinds of therapeutic strategies are available to the men at Bellevue Hospital, Shapiro notes that some men do not benefit from strategies that use spoken language as a means of communication. Shapiro (2005) states: "As a music therapist, I find myself in the role of 'integration-facilitator,' helping to integrate the clients unto the music therapy group and into the community they are living in. At the same time I try to honor the individual cultures from which they came" (p. 31). Hence, Shapiro prefers to engage the men in multicultural musical styles as this seems to be the best way to enhance a sense of community and respect for diversity among the men.

In Shapiro's therapy sessions, the men listen to, perform, and improvise a variety of musical styles and genres. Shapiro states: "In this community, people from various countries and cultures are trying to live together in some kind of 'harmony'" (p. 32). As Harriett Powell (2005) says:

> Small group music therapy in this kind of setting facilitates meaningful communication and connection between people with different languages and cultural backgrounds, with different physical and mental difficulties—all can be enabled and empowered by being listened to and heard in musical terms (Proctor, 2002, pp. 101–102), and connected in making music with others. (p. 174)

Stige (2002) concurs: "Music therapists need to be able to relate to a plurality of musics in order to meet the individual needs of clients coming from different backgrounds with different histories of music use" (p. 93).

While there are thirty men in the Bellevue Shelter group, those participating in the music therapy sessions vary. The men are not forced to go to music therapy; rather, they choose to attend because they enjoy the musical/communal interactions. As the men walk into the session, a variety of musical instruments is placed in the center of the room and they are free to choose any instrument they prefer on that given day. As they sit in a circle and wait for the session to begin, they individually improvise upon their chosen instruments, reacquainting themselves with musical materials. "Musical improvisation puts people in a unique kind of contact with each other, one which does not rely on . . . verbal language or social status" (Wood, Verney, & Atkinson, 2004, p. 60).

As the men sat down, they introduced themselves to me by explaining what we would engage in together. As stated by one patient: "We sing, we play instruments. We get to know each other better through our singing and our music making." According to Luck et al. (2008), "There is always musical and non-verbal communication present in the improvisational situation through which the therapist tries to communicate with the client" (p. 26). Sessions at the 30th Street Men's Shelter began with each patient "introducing" himself musically. This meant musically expressing himself on a self-chosen instrument through improvisation. This activity allowed the men to get re-acquainted with each other as individuals.

Karl, a male with violent tendencies and a form of mental retardation,[4] asked a graduate music therapy student from New York University if she could explain the music she had made when it was her turn to "introduce" herself. The intern replied: "That's my music. That's how I feel." The group continued to talk about the many meanings of music, and spontaneously discussed philosophical questions such as: What is music? Does music have meaning? What is the difference between music and noise? Can anyone make music?

Mark, a physically "closed" man with a defiant demeanor became tired of talking. Mark, who has a history of severe depression and a prison record, said: "There's too much talking. Not enough music." Noah then directed the group back to music making, and asked Mark whom he wanted to improvise with. Mark chose the intern (according to Shapiro, he always chooses her) and myself. He also chose our instruments for us and began our improvisations. Robert, another patient, remarked on the fact that this was the first time in music therapy that anyone chose three similar instruments to play with—Mark wanted us all to play mallet percussion. Robert found this interesting and the sounds soothing. Mark stated that he enjoyed playing together.

Upon first seeing him, I was taken aback by my initial perception of Mark's hardened appearance. As he sat down next me in the circle, Mark introduced himself: "My name is 'Iron-Tech,' or you can call me 'Spider-Man.'" Despite this, there was something very caring about his musical and social interactions. As Mark smiled to us during our improvisations, I slowly began to see a different side of him. I interpreted his musical improvisations as extremely well-mannered; he looked to the intern and myself as he began to shape fluid musical lines. Shapiro remarked privately that Mark was very controlling in his improvisations. He chose the instruments, he decided whom he wanted to play with, and he picked the duration of the music-making activity. Though there was a sense of freedom of expression, it was very controlled. Shapiro elaborated: "He's in a men's homeless shelter, he's been in prison, and he's mentally ill. Why can't he have something he can control?" For Mark, music therapy is very beneficial. It is working for him, and inside him. And this is unlike the rest of his chaotic world.

A trio of men improvised next. Following the trio, the remaining quintet played together. Shapiro and Leon (a depressive who is prone to self-injury) were not only playing similar African drums, they were mirroring, matching, and reflecting each other's improvised beat patterns; over this ostinato, Robert played an Irish harp, Karl played a bass mallet instrument, and Reiss (a depressive and suicidal client) played the marimba. The group seemed most impressed that five people were able to work together to make music. Karl noted insightfully: "Musical communication is challenging. The eye contact and body language is what kept us together to make beautiful music."

Wood, Verney, and Atkinson (2005) note that in improvisational music therapy sessions, barriers come down and social roles change. These authors quote Rudd (1998) who notes that in such moments, patients or clients experience *communitas,* and this state is particularly common during improvisation:

> Improvisations in music therapy seek to build a community ("communitas") through a temporary leveling-out of all social roles. During improvisation, all traditional expectations regarding the role of the therapist do not apply. (Rudd, 1998, pp. 131–132)

As is clear from the above, active musical engagements—performing, improvising, listening—motivated these men to act and feel positively about themselves, each other, and their guests. In short, music-as-action transformed the ordinary, mundane circumstances of the hospital-shelter situation, and these men's tentative "hospital lives," to an embodied experience of personal and group affirmation and joy. As the men proceeded to their next group activity, we said our farewells. Shapiro observed that the session was transformative in yet another way: the introduction of a guest/musical-participant also motivated the men to "move" their personas in socially positive directions. As we all sat in a circle, we were all equal, all civilians, all members of a community working together, where everyone was musical.

CONCLUSION

A common purpose in these community music examples is the promotion of opportunities for social exchange, experience, and transformations among people who
are living without a traditional home life. Through group music making and music
listening, these disenfranchised citizens find relief from social alienation. The process
provides opportunities for enhanced self-worth and beauty through musical sounds
and human transactions.

In the Oakdale Community Choir, the grounding philosophy *Ubuntu* maintains that
a person is a person through other people. The common bond of choral singing gives
the two disparate groups one unifying purpose. In the New York City shelters, the
various constituents come together for the communal experience of music listening
and music making. These people have experienced large degrees of isolation related to
their illnesses and/or their homelessness. However, by joining a musical community,
they come together as individuals belonging to a musical collective.

The community music contexts explained in this chapter provide the participants
with many means of developing social skills. Social barriers are broken down as the
participants contribute together toward musical goals greater than any individual
could achieve alone. Through a deep awareness of the role each individual plays in the
larger ensemble, members develop a sense of group responsibility and accountability.
As one Oakdale Community Choir prisoner stated, "I find that working as a group can
be a lot of fun if I just try."

Viewed for the Aristotelian perspective of happiness, or "living well and doing
well," flourishing human societies require that individuals interact positively, productively, and ethically. This chapter's community music practices demonstrate how
people dealing with separation from families and isolation can cope with such stresses
positively, productively, and ethically. Group music making and listening appears
to help these participants develop a more positive self-concept and improved social
interaction abilities. More research is warranted to examine and understand how these
experiences impact participants' lives.

NOTES

1. The arrival time has moved to 5 PM with rehearsals lasting from 5:15 to 6:45 PM.

2. Cohen is co-authoring a paper about this unique aspect of the choir with a choir member
who teaches a writing class at the prison and another instructor of this writing class at the
prison. The paper is called "Voice as Intersection between Music and Language: The Writing
Component of the Oakdale Prison Community Choir."

3. For these and other examples of the notes, see http://documents.nytimes.com/the-music
-kitchen#p=1.

4. All names are pseudonyms to protect for anonymity. In addition, all descriptions of the
illnesses were explained by Shapiro and the NYU music therapy intern.

BIBLIOGRAPHY

Ansdell, G. (2002). Community music therapy and the winds of change. *Voices: A World Forum for Music Therapy.* Retrieved from www.voices.no/mainissues/Voices2(2)ansdell.html

Antrim, D. K. (1944). Music therapy. *The Musical Quarterly 30*(4), 409–420.

Baumesiter, R. F., Smart, L., & Boden, J. M. (1996). Relation of threatened egotism to violence and aggression: The dark side of high self-esteem. *Psychological Review, 103,* 5–33.

Benson, J. (1998). Mind and body: Qigong for pianists. *Piano & Keyboard, 194* (48), 51–52.

Cohen, M. L. (2007). *Christopher Small's concept of musicking: Toward a theory of choral singing pedagogy in prison contexts* (Unpublished doctoral dissertation). University of Kansas.

Cross, I. (2003). Music and biocultural evolution. In M. Clayton, T. Herbert, & R. Middleton (Eds.), *The cultural study of music* (pp. 19–30). New York: Routledge.

Fisher, S. (2006/2007). Why we need choral music—Ubuntu. *The Voice of Chorus America, 40.*

Higgins, L. (2006). The community in community music: Hospitality-friendship. In D. Coffman & L. Higgens (Eds.) *Creating partnerships, making links, and promoting change* (pp. 1–20). Singapore: Commission for Community Music Activity Seminar.

Lee, L. (2009). Food for the soul. *Strings.* March, 22–23.

Luck et al. (2008). Modelling the relationship between emotional responses to, and musical content of, music therapy improvisations. *Psychology of Music 36*(1), 25–45.

Milligan, K., Atkinson, L., Trehub, S., Benoit, D., & Poulton, L. (2003). Maternal attachment and the communication of emotion through song. *Infant Behavior & Development, 26,* 1–13.

Phelan, H. (2008). Practice, ritual, and community music: Doing as identity. *International Journal of Community Music 1*(2), 143–158.

Powell, H. (2005). A dream wedding: From community music to music therapy with a community. In M. Pavlicevic & G. Ansdell (Eds.), *Community music therapy* (pp. 167–185). London: Jessica Kingsley Publishers.

Rudd, E. (1998). *Music therapy: Improvisation, communication, and culture.* Gilsum, NH: Barcelona Publishers.

Shapiro, N. (2005). Sounds in the world: Multicultural influences in music therapy in clinical practice and training. *Music Therapy Perspectives, 23,* 30–35.

Small, L. (1998). *Musicking: The meanings of performing and listening.* Middletown, CT: Wesleyan University Press.

Stige, B. (2002). *Culture-centered music therapy.* Gilsum, NH: Barcelona Publishers.

Sumathy, S., & Sairam, T. V. (2005). Music therapy traditions in India. *Voices: A world forum for music therapy.* Retrieved from www.voices.no/country/monthindia_march2005.html

Sutton, D. S. (2000). From credulity to scorn: Confucians confront the spirit mediums in late imperial China. *Late Imperial China, 21* (2): 1–39.

Visser, B. A., Bay, D., Cook, G. L., & Myburgh, J. (2010). Psychopathic and antisocial, but not emotionally intelligent. *Personality and Individual Differences, 28,* 644–648.

Wakin, D. J. (2009, December 18). For the homeless, music that fills a void. *The New York Times.* Retrieved from www.nytimes.com/2009/12/19/arts/music/19soup.html?_r=1&sq=music%20kitchen&st=cse&adxnnl=1&scp=1&adxnnlx=1276355212-nRpSIO-Q2LQkkGaROOinNcg

Wood, S., Verney, R., & Atkinson, J. (2004). From therapy to community: Making music in neurological rehabilitation. In M. Pavlicevic & G. Ansdell (Eds.) *Community music therapy* (pp. 48–62). London: Jessica Kingsley.

Zehr, H. (2002). *The little book of restorative justice.* Intercourse, PA: Good Books.

Chapter Fourteen

Reaching out to Participants Who Are Challenged

Don DeVito and Arthur Gill

Community music programs provide activities that enhance music participation, aesthetic awareness, and self-expression for populations in need. This chapter examines programs from the United States, West Africa, and Pakistan. In addition, we look at current international initiatives and partnership links, specifically at programs for individuals who are challenged, in the Asian Pacific, the Middle East, the United Kingdom, and North America.

PROGRAM NARRATIVE: THE SIDNEY LANIER COMMUNITY MUSIC PROGRAM

The Sidney Lanier Community Music Program (CMP) in Gainesville, Florida, combines music education and community-based instruction for students and adults with moderate to profound disabilities, in some cases in assisted-living facilities and their families. Participants face challenges associated with cerebral palsy, autism, Prader-Willi syndrome, Down syndrome, Williams syndrome, and other developmental disabilities. Performances throughout the Alachua County community in north central Florida exhibit the ability of students with special needs to be functional musicians and active members of society transcending their challenges to participate in the ensemble.

CMP partners with local public schools and colleges for resources and technological leadership to provide services, which include: (a) community-based music instruction; (b) drum circles; (c) dance programs; and (d) a virtual classroom component. Local community musicians from a variety of ethnic backgrounds and a range of musical expertise lead the ensembles, which meet monthly with a different guest musician leading each activity. CMP participants are provided with unique opportunities to enhance their knowledge of world cultures and have experienced traditional European Classical, Australian didgeridoo, and Brazilian *pifano* (a three-hole fipple flute) performances; Kenyan singing; Guinean drum circles; and dances from Peru and the Ivory Coast.

The Sidney Lanier community-based instructional trips (CBIs) allow CMP participants to attend these music experiences in a variety of locations, providing members
with opportunities to interact with people in the community, which would otherwise
be unavailable to them. These trips serve as an extension to general music education
by utilizing local artisans as the educators and the community as the classroom. CBIs
have included listening to folk music at historic farms, performing for senior centers,
and interacting with members of the University of Florida percussion and dance ensemble *Agbedidi Africa,* where the members learned to perform structured and improvisational rhythms and dances in the context of an African drum circle.

A recent project combined the Sidney Lanier School Music Ensemble with Dr. Steven Bingham and the Santa Fe College Jazz Band, performing a percussion arrangement of Benny Goodman's arrangement of "Sing, Sing, Sing." For a year, the Sidney
Lanier Percussion Ensemble, the Santa Fe College Jazz Band, and CMP members participated in small group and full ensemble music activities, rehearsals, performances,
and picnics, culminating in an evening performance on the campus of Santa Fe College. As a result of the interactions fostered by CBIs, Carl, a student with Williams
syndrome, enrolled in a guitar class offered at Santa Fe College. Without experiences
like these, visiting a college, utilizing its resources, or interacting with other students
in a college environment would have been highly problematic for students.

Community dance programs incorporating a variety of themes (harvest dances,
Mardi Gras, and Hollywood) provide opportunities for Sidney Lanier students to interact in social engagements with students from other schools. Participants dance in
choreographed and improvised patterns to a variety of music (e.g., jazz, rap, hip-hop,
disco, and cajun), generating improved self-confidence through creative self-expression and enhancing cultural appreciation through social interaction.

Functional Musicianship

The common musical denominator in this ensemble is a steady beat. Whether accompanied with hand-over-hand assistance by a parent, self-generated through dance
movements, instrumental performance on a djembe, or verbally, a steady beat provides
a baseline for participation. CMPs that include students with special needs, along with
their family and friends, provide an inclusive music environment with participants of
differing levels of abilities. Within this context, a variety of methods of participation
take place. While music therapy provides many one-on-one and small group clinical
benefits to clients' speech, language, and physical challenges, the primary purpose of
the Sidney Lanier CMP is to create and enhance functional musicianship.

Methods of Participation

Participants are able to select the method of participation that best fits their abilities
and comfort levels.

Instrumental performance is generally based on one of three degrees of complexity, from maintaining a steady pulse to repeating a given single measure rhythm to

improvising rhythms based on the music being performed. During singing activities, students learn to adjust their vocal performance, based on the syllables and words they can pronounce, to the style of the song. For students who are unable to participate by using one of these methods, assisted performance and recognition of affective behavioral communication may also be useful alternatives.

Hand-over-hand assistance allows participants with profound challenges to accompany their peers. However, for many students with more profound challenges, an alternative approach is the observation of self-generated behavioral responses. These behaviors are often communicative of musical affect directly related to the performance. Student participants who are confined to wheelchairs, are non-verbal, or have significant cognitive impairments may rock their bodies back and forth to the beat of the music. These affective behaviors can be recognized as forms of dance as the participants engage in the performance.

Some participants with autism spectrum disorders who, before they participated in CMP, had stereotypical repetitive hand gestures, have learned to coordinate these manual patterns with the rhythm and style of the music. While this is not a traditional method of performance, it is nevertheless these students' method of participation. By observing the behaviors communicated by a participant during the music performance and profiling which behaviors directly relate to responses indicating affect, the communicative intent of behavioral patterns is often self-evident or made clear after repeated observation. Family members observe behavioral indicators of affect in non-music activities and can identify them during music performance.

When indicating positive musical affect, Eric (a secondary school student with autism) will stand, rock his body back and forth with his feet extending outward, smile, and focus his visual attention on the performer nearest to him. This behavior will cease almost immediately upon the cessation of the music. Daniel (a student with profound mental and physical challenges) will sway his head in time with the music and clench his hand in a repetitive pattern with the steady beat of the music. His bodily expression often draws attention to him as a performer himself. This method of functional musicianship becomes evident to the audience, and he is a participating member of the ensemble.

Self-Expression and a Sense of Community

Community music ensembles in the United States often take the form of choral, band, and, to a lesser degree, orchestral programs. While these programs may be available to most members of the community, they seldom suit the needs of people with disabilities. It is often difficult for parents of students with special needs to provide opportunities for music and creative self-expression. While sports activities such as Special Olympics or therapeutic riding are available in many communities in the United States and abroad, they do not address the arts.

Since the emphasis of CMP is on functional musicianship, performance creates an opportunity for self-expression within a community consisting of family and peer participants and is a model for enhancing traditional methods of music performance for students with disabilities.

Parental Response

Several parents have indicated their positive opinion of the integration of their children into the mainstream population through community music experiences. Loretta Bondsdale, the parent of a child with autism, states: "With the drum circle there is no way she can mess up. It's just so hard to find recreational and cultural things for disabled kids. She just fits right in and I'm very thankful for it" (personal communication, 2005). Gloria Butler, a teacher at the Sidney Lanier School, has two sons with autism. She has attended the Sidney Lanier CMP performances and has noticed the positive impact this program has had on her own children and students. "[The community music program] has brought out a lot of the hidden talents of our kids. It's a joy to just see the students come up and participate in drumming and be involved with kids from other schools and see the talents they've had hidden all this time" (personal communication, 2005).

Effie McClellan, a parent of a high school student with Down syndrome, has attended several Sidney Lanier CMP activities. She has noticed the interest in music performance indicated by her child. "I remember when she first got into it, she came and said, 'Granny, I have that beat.' I said, 'I know you did.' It was really nice" (personal communication, 2005).

Another Sidney Lanier CMP participant who has demonstrated a significant aptitude for the percussive arts is Lyndon White. This high school student has profound hearing loss, cerebral palsy, and a reliance on non-verbal communication. His former general education teacher Brenda Littlejohn has noticed his positive responses when given opportunities for music performance in both his music education class at Sidney Lanier and the community music program:

> Lyndon is a child who is profoundly deaf. You can tell he mimics all the actions of the drummers he sees on TV. It's just so incredible a child with the severity of the hearing loss he has can express himself so remarkably with the drums. It's everybody being free to be themselves, and I think that's the most positive thing about it. Everyone is free to do just what they want to do with the drum that way. There are so few opportunities in life where we have the opportunity to do that. It's just such a wonderful thing to watch. (personal communication, 2005)

Lyndon is the lead drummer in the school's drumline and the winner of the Council for Exceptional Children's national Yes I Can Award, given nationally to children who overcome significant physical and cognitive challenges in order to excel in life.

Leadership through Technology

Sidney Lanier parents and students have participated in music lessons that incorporate online music instruction adapted to accommodate the needs of each child and provide an ethnically diverse curriculum through video conferencing from undergraduate and graduate music majors at Universidad de Londrina in Brazil (Dr. Magali Kleber), Syracuse University (Dr. Emma Rodríguez Suárez), Weber State University (Dr. David Akombo), and the University of North Texas (Dr. Debbie Rohwer). This online community of educators has taken a leadership role in the field of community music with the goals of

- bridging the distance between institutions by networking universities, public schools, and community musicians through using a variety of technology;
- enhancing the variety and quality of instruction of graduate and undergraduate music majors in the field of community music and special education;
- enhancing the quality and variety of instruction provided by public school music educators for their students with special needs by including instructors associated with community music; and
- promoting cultural interaction and demonstrating the community music activity's vision of complementing, interfacing with, and extending formal music education structures. In addition to training music educators, these professors have direct experience in developing and enhancing community music programs.

GROUP LAIENGEE, A MUSIC APPROACH FOR CHILDREN WITH DISABILITIES IN CONAKRY, GUINEA

In addition to networking and the sharing of musical experiences, a supplementary goal of the Sidney Lanier CMP is outreach and development. Group Laiengee is a performing troupe in Conakry, Guinea (West Africa) composed of children with significant disabilities. The troupe was founded by Lansana Camara, who comes from a long line of griot family musicians dedicated to the crafting of instruments and the performance of traditional songs for ceremonies, social occasions, and stage performances. Camara is currently visiting the United States as a freelance musician for the purpose of providing workshops and generating resources for the ensemble in Conakry and was a guest musician at one of Sidney Lanier's evening drum circles. A cooperative music project between Sidney Lanier and Group Laiengee was begun.

The theory behind Group Laiengee's approach is that all human beings have an innate responsiveness to music similar to that of the infant and the sound of its mother. This natural instinct remains intact despite physical, cognitive, or emotional disabilities. Musicality is a basic human characteristic and a binding element in the socialization of a community. The children of Group Laiengee perform traditional songs on handmade instruments, including the *kora* (African harp), *balofone*, and *djembe*.

"Travail Patient" (patient work) is a traditional griot song that epitomizes the Group Laiengee approach. This title reflects the work of the musicians who raise previously homeless children of the ensemble to overcome their challenges. Camara tells of a child who came to the ensemble without the use of his legs and of the daily, continuous care a child with this type of disability requires. Years later, the young man rejected assistance and used the strength of his arms to move (wheelchairs are rare). It is this kind of "patient work" and music education that makes Group Laiengee so important in Conakry.

The Sidney Lanier School and Group Laiengee project includes:

- organizing music performances and workshops for schools in Florida and Guinea by Mr. Camara and members of the ensemble; and
- distributing information about the program to help establish artist-in-residency programs for the musician-educators of Group Laiengee.

Proceeds from performances, workshops, and instruments help to provide a home, food, clothing, and other essential needs for the child musicians in the ensemble. Future goals to ensure the self-sufficiency of the group include purchasing a van to transport the children to performances in Conakry and leasing of a building to act as a school and music store.

Networking Community Music Programs and Practitioners

Current initiatives taking place through the International Society for Music Education (ISME) include an emphasis on collaboration and interaction between community music programs and practitioners. Research developed through this program has been presented at the ISME's commission for Community Music Activity (CMA) since 2006: Leading Beyond the walls: *CMA Interdisciplinary Cooperation through the Virtual Classroom for Students with Disabilities Project* (DeVito, Kleber, Rodríguez Suárez, & Akombo, 2009) and *Harmony through DIScovering ABILITIES: An Interdisciplinary Music Approach for Students with Disabilities with the Sidney Lanier Center, ISME CMA, and NACCM* (2010).

Collaborative CMA Projects: DIScovering ABILITIES and Carnegie Hall

Collaborative projects with the ISME's CMA have been a growing trend and a desired theme for the past several years. Last year, the formation of a DIScovering ABILITIES performance in Carnegie Hall came to fruition thanks to CMA members working together to generate the resources for an inclusive event that demonstrated the abilities of international underserved populations. This evening of music was a demonstration of shared experiences based on these research projects conducted by both university music professors with community music experience from around the world and the Sidney Lanier School Music Ensemble. Each student who participated in this event has either autism, cerebral palsy, Down syndrome, or another developmental disability. The general public, music majors, and public/private schools in New York were invited to observe and interact in this uplifting and inclusive music workshop. David Elliott (New York University) provided rehearsal facilities during the week of the performance.

Syracuse University music education majors, under the direction of Emma Rodríguez Suárez, performed a music selection taught to Sidney Lanier musicians through the published study *Leading Beyond the Walls: CMA Interdisciplinary Cooperation through the Virtual Classroom for Children with Disabilities Project* (DeVito et al., 2009). The paper was published in the proceedings of the 2009 International Society for Music Education Conference in Italy.

The Santa Fe College Jazz Band, under the direction of Steven Bingham and whose members are active participants in the community music program at Sidney Lanier, performed six arrangements of Benny Goodman songs, including "Sing, Sing, Sing." Prior to the performance, two students from the Lanier community music program were added to the ensemble on percussion. Students were switched on percussion for each song so every student had an opportunity to be integrated into the ensemble. Rehearsals took place in the CMP at Lanier and on the cafeteria stage leading up to the trip to Carnegie Hall. Santa Fe professors Brian Holder and Chris Sharp took part in an improvisational performance that incorporated Lyndon White, a Sidney Lanier percussionist with profound hearing loss and cerebral palsy and who is unable to speak, performing on a drum set. A jazz combo of the Santa Fe ensemble adapted their performance to the rhythms created by Lyndon.

Phil Mullen, 2010–2012 board member of the International Society for Music Education, Julie Tiernan, and Thomas Johnston, all of Limerick University in Ireland, were among the community music practitioners who taught traditional Irish music to the students prior to the performance. Tiernan included two of her students who were representatives of the Irish Traveller community in Carlow and the Nomad Project at the University of Limerick.

Lansana Camara, director of Group Laiengee and visiting musician with the Sidney Lanier program, led the students in the traditional West African songs originally taught to the students at the Sidney Lanier School. Andrew Krikun, professor of Bergen Community College, led the college's popular music ensemble highlighted by Jimmy Vonderlinden, a Bergen College alumnus who is blind with special physical needs. His performance included "Hey Jude" and a spirited duet of Sam and Dave's "Hold On, I'm Coming" with Lina Cloutier, a musician in the Sidney Lanier ensemble. Lina was born in Haiti with hydrocephalus and was placed in an area of the hospital for infants who cannot be helped. Rescued by a missionary, she was adopted in the United States where she had life-saving surgery over a decade before her Carnegie Hall debut. According to Lina's father, Raymond Cloutier:

> What the children experience brings great joy to them; especially in a world that does not always see their value through the disabilities . . . Who would have thought it possible that a group of disparate music educators from all over the world could help teach the students via the internet throughout a school year and then unite for the first time the day before giving a moving concert in New York City? (personal communication, 2010)

The next portion of the performance included traditional Brazilian songs "Marche de Pifano" and "Bande de Pifano." Original music from the *Leading Beyond the Walls* study (DeVito et al., 2009) paired students from Sidney Lanier with Magali Kleber of the Universidad de Londrina in Brazil. Regarding the original *Virtual Classroom* study (DeVito et al., 2010), Kleber wrote:

> This experience showed a large possibility to share musical knowledge and pedagogy for both the teachers and students. In addition, the experience provides the possibility to discuss, from a socio-economic-cultural perspective, the importance of cultural diversity as a symbolic richness in the process of cross-cultural identity. Even in low-tech conditions,

because the University of Londrina does not have a videoconference room, the workshop with students of both institutions was a grateful and gainful musical moment. This report shows [that] important shared experiences of this complexity can be a guide for reflection leading to concrete actions in the music education field and public policies that aim at promoting social change. The Virtual Classroom for Students with Disabilities Project provided the participants with a discussion for integration of the pedagogical process related to citizens' values, articulated with several dimensions of humanity.

David Akombo, researcher in the field of music and medicine at Weber State University in Utah, performed the music of Kenya, including his arrangement of the traditional folk song "Jambo Bwana" with a combined Syracuse University and Sidney Lanier ensemble, and moderated a brief discussion on techniques in the field of music and medicine.

Breaking Down Barriers through Community Music

Increasing ISME CMA Representation and Engagement from Low to Medium HDI Countries[1]

Through Don DeVito's position as chair of the International Society for Music Education (ISME) commission for Community Music Activity (CMA) for 2010–2012, the CMA commission initiated a two-year project to increase the representation of community musicians from low to medium HDI countries in ISME and ISME CMA. Through the ISME CMA Seminar in Hangzhou, China, and the ISME Conference in Beijing, China, two programs were initially selected for this pilot project. The first is the Special Education Center for children with visual and physical impairments in Gujrat, Pakistan, under the direction of Arthur Gill; the second is the Hui Long Center for people with special needs in Beijing, under the direction of Cassie Liu.

The initial goal is to link these music programs with community music practitioners and arts programs from around the world. Initial contact was made with Gill at the ISME world conference in Beijing, China, in August 2010. After the conference, music interaction continued through online performances and discussions between Gill's Special Education Center in Pakistan and the Sidney Lanier Center in Florida. Through this CMA initiative, innovative and adaptive lessons and experiences for the programs were developed. A series of wonderful music experiences, information, resources, and social capital have been shared between the programs in the United States and Pakistan in the first year. These resources may be accessed through the links instead after Mr. Gill's introduction.

Letter of Introduction: Arthur Gill   My name is Arthur Gill and I teach music to visually and physically handicapped children and lead my choir in my church. I am a graduate in Arts and passed the IELTS (International English Language Testing System) from the British council. My school is the Special Education Center of VHC (Visually Handicapped Children), Gujrat City 50700, Pakistan. Gujrat is a small city of Pakistan which is three hours' drive by car from Islamabad, the capital of Pakistan.

I have been working with these children since 2002. We have about eighty students, girls and boys, ages five to fifteen. Our specific needs for these students are a building, water, electricity, books, uniforms, teaching aids, furniture, etc. We have a rented building and can't afford it. My Music students have no proper musical instruments for learning, but they have good talent. Most of my students belong to poor families that have incomes less than $100 US per month.

There is no infrastructure for music education here in Pakistan. I have learned some South Asian classical music from my church and from my teacher. I have applied for university training in music education in England and Australia but have been refused a visa because of insufficient finances. There is a miserable condition in Pakistan; my city is also affected by flooding. I would appreciate all avenues of engagement from the ISME community to come forward to help the people who belong to third-world countries. It is my humble request to you that help my music students to get proper music education, teaching, and learning. I will be very thankful to you for my whole life.

With thanks,

Arthur Gill, Music Teacher

Special Education Center, Gujrat City, Pakistan

(personal communication, 2010)

Student and Parent Responses to the Program in Pakistan Gill's students and their parents extol the benefits of his program. Member Anam Shabir states, "Music class is my favorite, and I feel life when I learn music." Saqlain Mushtaq comments, "When I sing and play piano, I forget about my disability; music gives me courage and hope" (personal communication, 2011). Mrs. Tasneem, a parent of one of the students in the program, believes the program for music education has given new life to her child (personal communication, 2011). This is a common theme among the parents associated with Gill's choir. In fact, several parents have requested that Gill extend the program to other communities in Pakistan. Thanks to a grant from SEMPRE (the Society for Education, Music, and Psychological Research) and ISME president Graham Welch, this dream is becoming a reality.

Picture and Video Links of Interactive Online Experiences The links below include video clips of Gujrat, Pakistan's Special Education Center and some of the shared experiences with the Sidney Lanier Center, USA.

Video:

Sidney Lanier Center website: www.oncoursesystems.com/school/webpage.aspx?id=24619&xpage=891572

www.youtube.com/watch?v=Pb2UZgNDwcg

www.youtube.com/watch?v=-i01VPHWCpY

www.youtube.com/watch?v=IHu5_x8gYdI

www.youtube.com/watch?v=yGL7SNZ4sYk

Photos:

www.oncoursesystems.com/school/webpage.aspx?id=24619&xpage=888956

www.oncoursesystems.com/school/webpage.aspx?id=24619&xpage=889114

Needs:

The needs of the program in Pakistan include a more permanent structure where the children can meet, additional technology and equipment to enhance the music program and the quality of the center's interaction with the outside world, books, and additional food and medical supplies. Besides fulfilling these needs, the overall goals of the project are:

1. Developing social capital through community-based support. This includes linking technology, such as Skype software, for educational opportunities, shared cultural experiences, and presentations at professional organizations that enhance the interaction and education of all project participants.
2. Training and assisting with grant writing (National Endowment for the Arts, COS funding systems, and university networking, for example). By the end of the project, the staff at the Special Education Center should be fluent in the process of locating and submitting grant proposals to enhance their program and participation with ISME and ISME CMA.
3. Connecting populations underserved in the arts in low to medium HDI countries through a variety of fund-raising techniques.
4. Continuing to enhance social capital, grant writing, and fund-raising development during the second year to make the programs in Pakistan and China self-sufficient and increasing music and special education interaction between the centers and the general public. This includes generating sufficient funds to allow Gill and some of his students participation in future ISME and ISME CMA events.
5. Increasing representation and interaction in ISME and ISME CMA by members who can provide related services to programs in low to medium HDI countries. Enhancing the contacts, materials, and experiences shared at ISME and ISME CMA will create resourceful engagement opportunities in the fields of music education and community music. This pilot project was designed to be replicated every two years with new participants in order to regularly add to the representation of music educators and programs from low to medium HDI countries.

The CMA website lists complete details of new collaborative initiatives:

1. *The Middle Eastern Initiative,* created by Dochy Lichtensztajn, pedagogical director of the Community Program at the Levinsky School of Music in Tel Aviv, Israel, will call for papers from Middle Eastern community musicians to enhance participation and opportunities for cooperation at the 2012 ISME CMA Seminar in Corfu, Greece.
2. *The Asia Pacific Community Music Network* (APCMN) was formed at the ISME Conference in Beijing in 2010 and is closely affiliated with the ISME Community Music Activities Commission. The network serves as a vehicle for activating relationships, developing cross-cultural partnerships for community music activity, and disseminating research about community music in the Asia-Pacific region. The network is not restrictive in terms of geography but, rather, includes anyone with ties to or an interest in the region. The network's website (http://apcmn.edublogs.org) provides general information about APCMN as well as membership details.

3. *The North American Coalition for Community Music* fosters collaborative engagement between more than sixteen university and community arts programs representing Canada, the United States, and Mexico. Kari Veblen and Don Coffman, professor of music education at the University of Iowa and 2008–2010 ISME CMA chair, have taken leadership positions in this developing coalition.

Progress in the CMA Initiative in Pakistan: University of London (SEMPRE) and DIScovering ABILITIES Online (Queensland University, Australia)

University of London (SEMPRE)   ISME President Graham Welch supports the CMA initiative through SEMPRE, the Society for Education, Music, and Psychological Research in the arts. He arranged for a £3600 (British) grant for the Special Education Center for the purchase of music and technology to enhance the quality of instruction and Internet connectivity. Since Gill does not have the opportunity for university training in music or in special education in Pakistan, Welch also arranged for Gill and DeVito to visit special education schools and community music programs in England through the University of London, which provides access to and instruction in high-quality programs. Maria Harneed, one of Gill's students, commented: "After getting music instruments and other equipment, we are really getting music knowledge properly. Thanks to SEMPRE" (personal communication, 2011).

Queensland University, Australia   Steve Dillon of Australia's Queensland University agreed to partner with Gill in his Sweet Freedom project, which provides international distribution of the choir's musical performances with all of the proceeds going to the center. The "Save to DISC" link (http://savetodisc.net) leads to a resource that documents innovations in sound communities throughout the world. The use of Jam2Jam technology to create interactive online music performances should increase the Pakistan program's access to many more musical artists worldwide.

NASDSE and CEC Conferences

Mr. Gill has repeatedly interacted in the field of community music and special education by networking with the students at the Sidney Lanier Center (Florida). The students at Sidney Lanier were honored as presenters at the 2010 National Association of State Directors of Special Education (NASDSE) seminar in Nashville, Tennessee, where DeVito was the closing speaker. Their presentation included Gill's description of his program and the Sidney Lanier pilot project, via Skype. On October 23, 2010, Mr. Gill taught music to special education teachers at the Florida Council for Exceptional Children Conference in Clearwater, Florida, again utilizing Skype. His center recently celebrated White Cane Safety Day, an international day of recognition of people with visual impairments, with guest speakers and a reception in Gujrat, which was provided by members of ISME CMA.

ISME CMA Low to Medium HDI Project

The Pakistan Special Education Center serves a variety of children with visual and physical special needs. Engagement has currently been between the Center and schools; however, the Center's goal is to garner support for this project from local communities, universities, and individuals and organizations internationally. This three-stage model (social capital, grant-writing training, and fund-raising development) could be replicated to serve other international arts programs that assist underserved populations in a variety of low to medium HDI countries. Engagement with the Hui Long Center in Beijing, China, under the direction of Cassie Liu, is also progressing. A grant has been written to obtain the technology so that these two centers can communicate and engage via Skype. The same goals and procedures for assisting and interacting with the Special Education Center in Pakistan will be used to benefit this important program in China. Future updates on this CMA initiative can be found in articles on the ISME Community Music Activity website and the ISME newsletters.

CONCLUSION

In countries where children and adults with disabilities do not receive public school education, as well as in societies where inclusive education is legally mandated, community music programs are beneficial. Parents of children with special needs may not be aware that there are other families facing similar challenges within their communities. An established community music program, or CMP, provides opportunities for networking and mutual assistance for families and practitioners through a variety of technologies. Demonstrating the musical abilities of children provides a united front for, at a minimum, gaining recognition and acceptance.

Community music programs can be adapted to bring people together through the arts and motivate and assist all individuals to transcend their challenges through creative self-expression. Programs of this nature can be modified to suit the particular communities in which they are established. While drum circles are popular in Gainesville, Florida, the community where the Sidney Lanier CMP is located, programs in other regions can and should include performance ensembles relevant to local musical traditions. Specific benefits of this style of CMP include:

1. supplementing music education experiences, in addition to those that may be offered through their public school systems, for children and adults with special needs;
2. establishing and reinforcing bonds between parents of children with special needs through frequent meetings in a positive social and arts setting;
3. informing communities of the abilities of children and adults with special needs through music performance; and
4. providing opportunities for community-based music education, such as visits to museums, integrated performances with other public school music programs, and training from artisans located within the community.

NOTE

1. HDI refers to Human Development Index, a composite indices of statistical information comparing conditions internationally. Compiled by the United Nations, the HDI is used to understand many components of wealth, sustainability, and equity.

BIBLIOGRAPHY

DeVito, D., Kleber, M., Rodríguez Suárez, E., & Akombo, D. (2009). Leading beyond the walls: CMA interdisciplinary cooperation through the virtual classroom for students with disabilities project. *CMA XI: Projects, perspectives and conversations: Proceedings from International Society for Music Education (ISME) 2008 seminar of the commission for community music activity* (pp. 193–201).
DeVito, D., Suárez, E., Akombo, D., Bingham S., Kleber, M., & Kriken, A. (2010). Harmony through DIScovering ABILITIES: An interdisciplinary music approach for students with disabilities with the Sidney Lanier Center, ISME CMA, and NACCM. *CMA XII: Harmony and futures of the world (ISME) 2010 seminar of the commission for community music activity* (pp. 92–97).

Chapter Fifteen

Diverse Communities, Inclusive Practice

Magali Kleber, Dochy Lichtensztajn, and Claudia Gluschankof

In educational research, great emphasis has been placed on "located knowledge," the belief that that each body of knowledge is connected to the specific experience from which it emerges. Findings show that collectivity and interaction underlie music practices as a sociocultural network. The transformation of individuals and social groups depends on the networks that connect individuals in a community and the networks that connect these individuals to other social groups: the social capital of the community. This chapter focuses on the role of social capital in music-focused social networks and in individual and community development in diverse socio-economic conditions.

Magali Kleber from Brazil describes how social capital, social networks, and music education positively affect many lives and discusses the issues associated with social capital and social inclusion/exclusion in the context of the Villa Lobinhos Project, a non-governmental organization, or NGO, in Rio de Janeiro, Brazil. Dochy Lichtensztajn draws upon nearly fifteen years of initiating and participating in community programs in music education that focus on live concerts. She examines the success of the Kadma program, Live Music Encounters, in the north of Israel, where Jewish and Palestinian elementary school students, although divided by cultural and national splits, unite by listening to symphonic concerts. Claudia Gluschankof discusses a joint music education initiative by Jewish and Arab-Palestinian neighbors who wanted to live together in peace, equality, and mutual respect.

SOCIAL MUSICAL NETWORKS AND SOCIAL CAPITAL: THE ROLE OF MUSIC EDUCATION IN A BRAZILIAN NGO

The goal of Projeto Villa Lobinhos, a non-governmental organization (NGO) in Rio de Janeiro, Brazil, is to promote the inclusion of children and young people from underserved communities. NGOs in Brazil have developed in new sociocultural configurations, paralleling the work of universities. Using social capital and building social networks have been shown to be meaningful structural elements in the success of music learning and teaching activities for at-risk children and youths from underserved communities. Music education in other contexts can benefit from knowledge gleaned from these emergent environments (Kleber, 2003). Musical practices demarcate cultural and aesthetic frontiers and are a means of socio-political mobilization. In spaces where content is flexible and underlain by the emergent demand of the communities being served, sociocultural actions are being constantly redefined to meet the demands of clients' lives. Where there is a locus of knowledge production in the non-profit sector, emergent fields trace new paths for professionals and their activities.

THEORETICAL FRAMEWORK

Music Pedagogical Process as Social Fact

Some theoretical frameworks consider musical practices as the result of human experience in a multiplicity of interrelated contexts. First, music is a social practice, which generates a cultural system that incorporates itself into the sociocultural structure of groups and individuals (Blacking, 1995; Shepherd & Wicke, 1997; Small, 1995). Second, the pedagogical process inherent in music is seen as a "total social fact" (Mauss, 2003), which emphasizes the systemic, structural, and complex character of this process in NGOs. Finally, as proposed by Kraemer (2000) and Souza (1996), music pedagogy is a process of music appropriation and transmission that appertains to relationships between people and music.

Any discussion of the dimensions and functions of pedagogical musical knowledge should be based on the understanding that these are aspects of the one phenomenon/object that cannot be separated. Thus, an analysis that incorporates the interconnection of different dimensions and the meaning of "music pedagogical process as total social fact" (Kleber, 2006) is not only related to the musical learning and teaching process, but should also be seen as a connected multidimensional field (as shown in Figure 15.1). This epistemological view of the field of music education seeks to define the boundaries and intersections of this area, considering specific knowledge that converges with other fields of knowledge. This perspective reveals four categories of context:

1. institutional—the bureaucratic, judicial, disciplinary, and morphological (the manner of working and the organization of working within a physical space) dimensions;
2. historical—a dimension focusing on the historical processes of an NGO and its constitution, taken from histories, reports, interviews, and talks with the research participants;
3. sociocultural—a dimension which includes symbolic values, inter-institutional relations, conflict, and negotiation; and
4. the music learning and teaching process—a dimension focusing on the how, where, why, and what music was being taught and learned.

Social networks and social capital depend on cultural, political, and social factors. A field of knowledge production must be thought of systematically; the multiple contexts used in the analysis cannot exist in isolation.

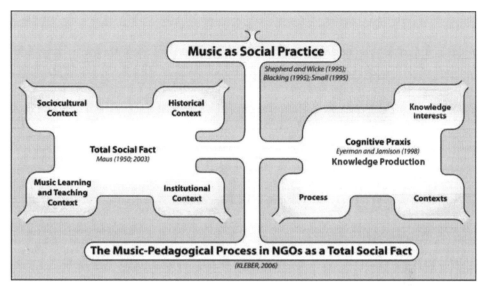

Figure 15.1. Linking concepts and theories in model of music pedagogical process as total social fact.
Source: Kleber (2006).

Social Capital and the Social Network

Social capital is related to the social connections that are the theoretical bases of business, political science, public health, and sociology. Bourdieu (1983/1986) presents three different forms of capital: economic capital, cultural capital, and social capital. He defines social capital as

> the aggregate of the actual and potential resources which are linked to possession of a durable network of more or less institutionalized relationships of mutual acquaintance and recognition—in other words, to membership of a group—which provides each of the members with the backing of the collectivity owned capital. (pp. 248–249)

Social capital may be thought of as the content of social relationships in networks (Gyarmati & Kyte, 2004, p. 3) that underlies the interactions that create social bonds. Social capital has two aspects: individual and collective. It exists for the individual from the moment that that person can use given resources. It exists as a collective entity because social capital is an integral part of the relationships of a given group or social network and exists only with them. Therefore, social capital has a double nature: it's a collective resource that can be used individually. In addition, it can be accumulated, deepening the bond and increasing the cohesion of a group. Social capital depends on individual effort because every network of relationships is the product of individual or collective, conscious or unconscious, investment strategies that are aimed at establishing or reproducing social relationships that are directly usable (Bourdieu, 1983/1986, p. 249).

This study identifies and examines the structures and contents of music social networks, examining the forms of social capital that are embodied in these social networks and paying particular attention to the meaning of music in participants' lives and the consequences of taking part in a music social project. If one is to understand the forms of social capital and the effect of social relationships found within a network, one must understand that network's content and structure. In other words, how is social capital used in a social network to support and empower participants' lives?

Participants and Context: The NGO Projeto Villa Lobinhos and the NGO Reciclarte

Villa Lobinhos Project/Projeto Vila Lobinhos (VLP/PVL) has established a network of sociability with several other social projects and institutions, presenting shows in theaters, schools, slums, and companies. The exchange of learning and teaching among the participants is emphasized by VLP's coordinator, Rodrigo Belchior:

> I think they arrive there with some previous knowledge, and it is cool to accept their proposals, and, then, to introduce ours. What is our proposal? Theirs. They exchange ideas. One learns with each other, and the teacher is there to polish . . . (personal communication, December 6, 2004)

The music learning and teaching context encompasses the classroom as well as concerts featuring *choro* ("The New Orleans Jazz of Brazil," Souza, 2011), MPB (Música Popular Brasileira), and other groups with eclectic repertories that have been developed both individually and collectively. Turíbio Santos' pedagogical conception of the project reinforces this idea: "The proposal and conception of the project was only one: we would teach children and learn with them. The school, for me, begins when you realize who will take part in it . . ." (personal communication, June 30, 2004).

The field study involved six participants who would graduate in 2004 and thirteen participants, all between sixteen and nineteen years of age and all but one male, from two institutionalized groups (seven from the *choro* group and six from the MPB group). Most of the students live with their families in three regions of Rio de Janeiro: "Dona Marta" and "Rocinha" communities in Baixada Fluminense and "Favela (Slum) Grota do Surucucu" in Niterói City. The stories of two of these young people, Marquinhos Silva and Walther Caldas, are exemplary.

Marquinhos Silva, a sixteen-year-old, said that before he began the music-learning process in the slum where he lives, he was not very interested in music. "There wasn't any music I liked, I didn't like anything; I was used to hearing funk, at high volume, because of my neighbors and that was music for me." After participating in the project, Silva recognized that his universe had broadened: "I was learning what music was; I saw that music was not only funk; it was MPB, rock (or pop), several things, popular, 'samba,' several things . . . music is a different world . . . different from that of my neighbors."

Marquinhos lost his mother when he was three years old and grew up at crèches in the slums. He explains how the community social network contributed to the construction of his musical aesthetic.

> Since I was a child, my mother and I walked on the streets asking for food. I was growing, and she died when I was three. I didn't have anything for me, it was empty. When I knew music, I was becoming full, I could see that with music it was totally different from the

way I lived before; the feeling of music makes you . . . feel the music! I don't know how
to say that, I only know that my life changed, a lot, a lot, a lot, a lot . . . .

Music is a potential element of social identity construction and a path away from
marginalization, violence, and criminality. For Marquinhos, taking part in the social
projects in his community and meeting other young musicians and music educators
like Rodrigo helped to change his life.

> I could leave this world because I had Rodrigo and the help of the project in our com-
> munity, there in "Morro Dona Marta," where he taught music to poor guys like me. I
> had all the characteristics to become a criminal, to be a trafficker. Rodrigo, as my first
> teacher of music, encouraged me. He noticed I was good at music, deciding my future.
> Now, I am who I am because of him. I loved music because it was the only thing, beyond
> that bad dream (becoming a criminal) that I had before, when I was eight. This project
> was a different thing, a new thing that I didn't know. I really didn't know anything about
> this wonderful thing! Rodrigo began to believe in me, giving me value as a person with
> dignity! I am here today because of him.

Walther Caldas, a seventeen-year-old violinist, aligns his participation in VLP with
his family history and with another NGO, Reciclarte (at Favela Grota do Surucucu,
in Niterói, near Rio de Janeiro). Walther's brother, Felipe (also a violinist), was in
his first year at VLP when they were interviewed, and his twin, Wagner, finished the
music course in violin at VLP in 2003. They are celebrities in the slums because they
were the first to study a musical instrument, and this is almost inaccessible for that
cultural environment. At the beginning, Walther did not like studying the violin:

> It was terrible; we didn't play anything, tried and faced the prejudice—because we were the
> only guys who played from the slum, among more than a thousand boys. But after we began
> playing well, we started to leave the slum to perform, to know places, new people; then the
> community was accepting, and they saw it was a good thing! (personal communication)

Walther's life at Favela Grota do Surucucu was empowered by alternatives and opportunities through the NGO:

> There is a mathematical calculation. Two thousand, nine hundred and ninety guys are in-
> volved in trafficking. They were our friends and many of them [have] already died. Eight
> study and two play violin, and this was what happened. Many people became traffickers
> because they had the same opportunity, but it didn't work. And suddenly, even us, if we
> didn't have the opportunity to study music, as I said before, we didn't have any expecta-
> tion of life, we have to thank our father because he called our attention and everything
> is going well.

This experience of music and the project carried out at Grota is reflected in the young
men's behavior in the community and promotes other values. As Walther states

> That is, now [in] the community, we are the heroes of the slum, we are the heroes, be-
> cause I think we are, suddenly, avoiding that they follow the wrong way and, as they are
> involved in music, they don't have anything to lose. Today, we can say that half of the
> community is doing something. Many children, many children, many people walking up

with violin cases, people I didn't know. Wherever you look, you can see violin cases, many people attending classes.

These young men became strong advocates of connecting with other networks. Walther continues:

> We began to play in other projects too and to take part in several projects. Through the "Cordas da Grota" orchestra we found this [VLP], from which we found other NGOs that offered musical practices; one was leading to the other. The work at the slum, "Favela da Grota" by "Cordas" orchestra, and the pleasure of playing musical instruments and music that were strange to them has changed the dynamic of that place.

Actions and activities that were initially seen as prejudicial to the violinists from the slum, because the violin was considered a strange instrument there, began to be seen as positive, motivating other students to learn how to play orchestral instruments. The positive visibility of the music was a determining factor that attracted the community's attention to a repertoire that was far from their experience. Taking part in a string orchestra made the students feel included: "Because we play this classic repertoire and we are not here just to hear and applaud the others. This makes a big difference" (Walther de Oliveira).

The relationship and music pedagogy result in a positive association between the two NGOs because the students of string, brass, and woodwind instruments are provided with a performance-oriented education that enables them to reach a high technical and interpretative level. The movement between the two cities provides the opportunity for both projects to develop and present socio-educational music proposals in schools and other public and private institutions, making them well-known for the quality of their music pedagogical work.

Discussion

Belonging to an acknowledged social group contributes positively to the construction of individual and collective identity, and the statements of the two students reveal that, while neither had money to pay for instruments or private music classes, both joined social projects (through NGOs and social networks). Through musicking and music education, the students received opportunities to feel included and empowered.

Just as shared values and aims define the identity of a network, the principles of a more practical nature characterize the processes of its components. In the case of VLP, the individuals' and social groups' musical practice is the foundation of activities promoting networks of personal and musical relationships. These are spontaneous networks that arise from human interaction mediated by musical practice and the activities that support the project.

Collectivity and interaction underlie any practices in a sociocultural network. Notions of belonging, visibility, and human dignity exemplify the participant experience of these NGOs, but musical practice is the focal point that aligns all other collective activities. In both NGOs (VLP and Reciclarte), proposals are focused on musical pedagogy, musical practices and interactions are emphasized in daily activities, and individual and group identities are formed and become meaningful in the students' lives through their participation.

The interviews show that personal transformation is ameliorated by the interaction between existing networks, individuals of a community, and members of other social groups utilizing the social capital of a community. Like in any other capital (human or financial), investment in social capital has a great rate of return.

The musical practices of NGOs are positive factors that can change individuals and groups. The multi-contextual perspectives of NGOs reflect the complexity that is present in the music pedagogical process and offer the possibility of learning different aspects of social interaction. In a network such as the one constructed in VLP, the members are very close to each other, and sharing information is facilitated by the close links between trusting participants. The kinship experienced within a network is itself a source of social capital for its members.

The implications for music education are reflected in an acknowledgment that the production of pedagogical musical knowledge should consider multiple contexts of social reality and dissolve hierarchical categories of cultural values. In order to accomplish this goal, one must reflect on the dominance of traditional artistic and pedagogical categories, questioning and re-forming the evaluation and judgment of musical practice. Moreover, it is important to re-examine the relationship between academic knowledge and knowledge of popular culture, as some in the field of music education have proposed.

Finally, NGOs have been shown to be meaningful alternatives in the development of socio-educational music works and can provide important social capital where musical social networks play an essential role. They offer great mobility and, at the same time, guarantee an institutional stability. This research is aimed at contributing to knowledge about the role of music education in politically aware social movements and projects in NGOs which seek transformation and social justice by minimizing poverty and eliminating inequality and social exclusion by using social capital to advance human dignity.

THE MULTICULTURAL COMMUNITY PROGRAM
LIVE MUSIC ENCOUNTERS IN THE SCHOOL OF MUSIC
EDUCATION, LEVINSKY COLLEGE OF EDUCATION

This community program, which is composed of four projects, is based on three major goals of music education and music listening:

1. to cultivate a creative dimension of music listening as a way of thinking, in and with sound, through a common experience;
2. to expose the young audience to a wide repertoire of symphonic and chamber music with the goal of enhancing listening and appreciation skills; and
3. to develop an integrated vision of leadership, good teaching, and facilitation practice for graduate students from the Levinsky School of Music.

Education

To this end, the Live Music Encounters (LME) program is made up of three components:

1. in-class activities (in which young students learn with their music teachers the works that are played at live concerts),
2. in-school or kindergarten chamber ensemble performances (which are held prior to the concluding concerts and focus on the works performed at the final concerts, which are moderated by graduates of the Levinsky School of Music Education (LSME), and which allow the pupils to get to know the performers in a more intimate setting),
3. concluding live concerts (which are the culmination of the in-school classes and ensemble performances held at the community auditorium).

First Project: Musica Viva—Intergenerational Live Music Encounters in the Community (Since 1998)

High school music students and kindergarten children are partnered in this project. The older students serve as role models for the younger students by initiating a series of vocal and instrumental chamber encounters and mini-concerts for kindergarteners in the neighborhoods where they live and learn. This project was inspired by the literacy method in Freire's *Pedagogy of the Oppressed* (1970), which advocates dialogue and guided reflection between educators and learners.

Second Project: KeyNote: Outreach Program between Children in Schools, the Israel Philharmonic Orchestra's Program, and the Levinsky School of Music Education (Since 2000)

KeyNote is the Israel Philharmonic Orchestra's (IPO) program for music education and community outreach, established in 2000. Over 15,000 children of all ages take part each year in a diverse collection of activities centered on the symphonic repertoire, in cooperation with the music educators at their schools.

From elementary school (where the program activities are led by supervisors from the Ministry of Music Education), to high school, through Colleges of Education, the Orchestra reaches out to the young audience with intimate sessions in the classroom and specially designed school concerts at community halls. The KeyNote program promotes tolerance and mutual respect, serves all of Israel's citizens (Jewish, Christian, and Muslim), and regularly reaches out to communities that previously had no exposure to the Orchestra.

Third Project: The Academic Course: The Live Concert—Community Initiatives in Music Education (Since 2001)

For the first time in Israel, a course on communal initiatives centered around the live concert was introduced at the tertiary level.

Fourth Project: The Kadma Program for Elementary Schools in Haifa and Surroundings (Since 2003)

The Kadma program, Live Music Encounters, in the north of Israel takes place in elementary schools that are divided by cultural and national splits. The program seeks to select appropriate repertoire for concerts and shares traditions most appropriate for the different cultures in Israel. The project was based on the belief that the live concert permits an examination of a framework of musical constructs from cultures in conflict and highlights the ways in which music learning occurs.

Haifa is the largest city in northern Israel, the third largest city in the country, and yields a mixed population of more than 264,900 Jews and Arab-Palestinians. The Arab-Palestinian population was once predominantly Christian, while some of the Jewish population were Russian immigrants.

Religious and secular conflict between Jewish and Arab-Palestinian students, as well as with immigrant children of foreign workers, was the stimulus which led the Levinsky School of Music Education's Live Music Encounters project leaders to initiate the Kadma program for didactic concerts, using music as a cultural bridge to co-existence understanding, and education." The Live Music Encounters multi-year program emerged to create a new or renewed historical portrait of the people it serves, to allow LSME to learn and hear about "many voices," and to move toward "a collective identity between non-equals" (a melting pot), initiating a process of equality in a multicultural society.

The Kadma program was based on a social capital rationale. Two types of social capital are particularly important here: bonding and bridging. Bonding social capital exists in social networks with common attributes among members; bridging social capital exists in social networks with members of different demographic categories (Frank, 2003). The project was initiated by a broad consortium of institutions: the Levinsky School of Music Education, the Haifa New Symphonic Orchestra, the Ramsis Sakis Arab-Palestinian Ensemble, the music education district inspectorate, and the municipal authorities of Haifa.

Dilemmas Concerning the Selection of Repertoire in the Kadma Program

May 15th, 1948, has different meanings for Israeli Jews and Israeli Arab-Palestinians. For Jewish Israeli citizens, it is the festive day of the establishment of the State of Israel. For Arab-Palestinian Israeli citizens, this day commemorates a catastrophe and marks the date their lands were confiscated by the new State of Israel. Most of the Arab-Palestinians who remained in Israel continued to live in their communities, but some of them became refugees and were forced to move to other Arab communities either within the State of Israel, in the West Bank–occupied territories, or in the neighboring Arab countries.

In July 2007, in an unprecedented move, the former Minister of Education Yuli Tamir (a past leader of the Peace Now Movement) announced that the Ministry had approved a school text, describing the establishment of the State of Israel in 1948 as *Nachba* ("catastrophe"), for use in Israeli Arab-Palestinian schools. The Education

Ministry defended its decision, arguing that the Arab-Palestinian citizens' narrative deserved recognition in the State of Israel.

> The Arab public deserves to be allowed to express its feelings. It will generate debate in the schools and will only contribute to Israeli children's learning about the need to live with one another. It's a mistaken pedagogic approach to teach Arab students that everyone took to the streets in joy when the State of Israel was established. You have to give expression to the feelings of the other side as well, so it will be able to become connected to the Jewish narrative and to historical facts—including those that mention that the Arabs did not agree to a partition of the land. (*Haaretz Daily Newspaper*, 2007)

Kadma was originally designed for Jewish and Arab-Palestinian primary schools in the multicultural town of Haifa. Nevertheless, rancor between the majority and minority groups, the different learning and teaching traditions of the participants, and the short-term intervention programs have recently spawned controversy, encapsulated in two contretemps:

1. the appropriate balance between Middle Eastern/Arab works and Western symphonic repertoire that have been taught in the 2006–2008 academic years, and
2. the chosen repertoire for the 2007–2008 season of the didactic concerts, including the 60th Anniversary of the State of Israel Celebration (May 15, 1948) which is commemorated by the Arab-Palestinian population of Israel as *Al-Nachba*, the Day of Disaster.

Long disputes and polemic arguments led to a compromise among the program's leaders, the music education inspectorate, and the orchestra's administration in regard to the repertoire's selection:

- The 60th anniversary celebration of the establishment of the State of Israel, on the one hand, and the commemoration of Al-Nachba on the other, would not be expressed or manifested in the Kadma concert programs;
- The types of repertoire to be taught and performed would include two main foci:
  - Symphonic and chamber works concentrating on the genre of dance music in a cultural-geographic context ("Music Tiptoe"). The program presented a wide repertoire, from Western classical music (e.g., Bach, Mozart, Tchaikovsky, Prokofiev) to dances and songs that emerged from the oral and written traditions of Palestinian, Druze, Bedouin, and Israeli-Jewish communities.
  - Symphonic and chamber pieces under the topic "Fiesta Española—El Andaluz" for fourth and fifth graders who had studied works whose influence was expressed, both at the historic-geographic and stylistic-cultural level, in southern Spain (El Andaluz) by Isaac Albeniz and Manuel de Falla, on one hand, and Adam Beq Elsanturi, on the other.

The Kadma Report

Based on the report from 2007–2008, which involved semi-structured interviews, testimonies, and open discussions with the young students, school staff, music educators, and school principals (from both Jewish and Arab-Palestinian schools), response from program participants indicate that the Kadma program is a potentially powerful tool for multicultural bridging (Shteiman & Vinograd-J'an, 2008):

> I feel that the program takes our pupils to new dimensions in the educational process. It is different: new codes of listening, observing and learning, with difficulty (because of the novelty of the concerts dynamics and because of the long-term time of some works) and with enjoyment, when they recognize the performing works and the programmatic contents. At this point they can participate in expressing corporal realization, body percussion, and singing. (music teacher from an Arab-Palestinian school)

> The workshops and stages organize my year from the onset of my studies . . . I looked forward to the first meeting between Jewish and Arab teachers that took place in the 2006–2007 academic year . . . I inquired as to the reception that the classic Western repertoire received from their students, and they shared their problems with me. (music teacher in a Jewish school)

> It's good that Arab musicians perform together with Symphonic Orchestra musicians in concert. I want there to be more joint musical activities between Jewish and Arab children. I would be happy if there were to be joint musical activities between Jewish and Arab children in my school. (principal from a Jewish school)

> It's good that Jewish and Arab pupils listen to a concert together. The chamber encounter's [encounters] in-school link, among all projects' stages, is perceived as the most successful one by both music educators and principal, not only as a preparation stage towards the symphonic concert but also as an event that encompasses and embraces the program's goals and secret charm. At the intimate chamber encounters at the school, there are new understandings/insights of Western classic music. (Arab-Palestinian music teacher)

The Continuity of the Kadma Program—Assumptions and Conclusions

The success of the program and its continuity is an acknowledgment that advocacy for live music and music education and for the inclusiveness of each member—the young listeners, the general staff teachers, the music educators, the administration staff, parents, supervisors, and therapist workers—strengthens diversity, increasing cross-border flow on a magnitude that has never before been experienced. Principals and music educators who participated in the program express agreement and identification with the programs' objectives and a willingness to strengthen the multicultural closeness.

The diversity of traditions in teaching and learning, the shared and divergent features of responses to selected patterns of music representing different cultures, and the dissention that characterized the political space became crucial topics of discussion among the Kadma program leaders. The Kadma program is, in itself, a mechanism for a new beginning where East can meet West in an artistic learning environment. It comes as no surprise that, in a multicultural, war-torn society such as Israel, every music educator, designer, promoter, and implementer of music education programs is challenged to act responsibly and communicate and interact from a perspective of truth and a deep recognition of multicultural experiences, joys, and pains.

BRIDGE OVER THE WADI: MUSIC EXPERIENCES, DILEMMAS, AND INSIGHTS IN A BILINGUAL PRESCHOOL

One of my [Claudia Giuschanhof] main concerns during late childhood and teens was my dual identity. What was I? A Jew first and then an Argentinian? Or the reverse? Or equally both? Or sometimes only one or the other? In the 1970s, there was no one to tell me that being bi-cultural was normal. Being raised in a liberal, Jewish home in Buenos Aires at that time meant developing a political conscience, sensitive to the needs of the oppressed and minorities.

This social consciousness led me to teach music, as a volunteer, in the Pre-K and kindergarten classes in a Muslim town, Kfar Kara. The Bridge over the Wadi was an integrated, bilingual (Hebrew-Arabic) school that was established as a joint initiative of Jewish and Arab-Palestinian neighbors from the Wadi Ara region who sought to live together in peace, equality, and mutual respect. This is the only school in Israel where Jewish children attend a school in an Arab town; in other words, the majority ventures into the minority's territory.

The kindergarten class, as all the other school classes, is taught by two teachers: a Palestinian and a Jew. Each of them speak to the children mainly in their own first language, Arabic and Hebrew, respectively. Both Muslim and Jewish religious holidays are celebrated and learned about in a curriculum that emphasizes humanistic values.

The singing repertoire taught in the class presents a challenge. On the one hand, the early childhood Hebrew singing repertoire holds a modern, Western perspective of the child (Minks, 2002) and is an expression of the new Hebrew culture (Gluschankof, 2008; Lichtensztajn, 2010). This repertoire is large, heterogeneous in musical and textual quality, and includes developmentally appropriate material (i.e., narrow range, syllabic narrow intervals, clear tonality, text related to the child's world, short sentences) (Gluschankof, 2007). On the other hand, the early childhood singing repertoire in Palestinian Arabic culture is small (Khallaf, 2003), probably because traditional Middle Eastern musical education did not, until recently, encourage writing and composing for children (especially for very young children) (Mdallel, 2004). Due to Arabic diglossia, repertoire from other Arab-speaking countries written in the spoken language is not relevant to Palestinian children (Maamouri, 1998).

This situation presents two pedagogical dilemmas:

1. Should the children be exposed to good repertoire (developmentally appropriate to Western singing standards with content relevant to young children, at least by contemporary Western standards) that has the potential of further empowering the dominant Israeli culture?
2. Should parental permission for this teaching methodology be obtained? Constructivist, student-centered, process-based teaching is seldom found in Palestinian classrooms. The co-teachers are aware of the differences between the two teaching styles that are present in these Pre-K and kindergarten classrooms, but are supportive of the Western model.

Data gathered through ongoing ethnographic research shows that the children—both Jewish and Palestinian—took ownership of Hebrew singing games, using them as artifacts for their self-initiated free play. While the Jewish children hardly ever sing Palestinian songs in their play, the Palestinian students sing Hebrew songs, replacing Hebrew words with Palestinian words depending upon the context. Palestinian songs are seldom used in this type of play. Palestinian girls are more engaged than Palestinian boys. Parents voluntarily reported that their children engaged in this type of singing play at home and asked to learn the singing repertoire. These findings may indicate that (a) developmentally appropriate singing repertoire is not only appropriate for Hebrew-speaking children but also for Palestinian children raised in a dominant Western culture and (b) parents who send children to this type of educational setting accept and value a repertoire and teaching styles that encourage children's own agency.

This kindergarten is not only integrated and bilingual, but a place where a modern culture (the established Hebrew culture) and a traditional culture (the developing, modern Palestinian culture) meet and negotiate. Spaces like this may serve as a hothouse for the seeds of a just peace.

ACKNOWLEDGMENTS

Magali Kleber is grateful to all participants of NGO Projeto Villa Lobinhos, especially the people who shared their lives, values, and music with her. This work could not have been possible without their generous contributions.

BIBLIOGRAPHY

Besnard, P. (1980). *L'animation socioculturelle.* Paris: Editions Sociales de France (Spanish Version).

Blacking, J. (1995). Music, culture and experience. In J. Blacking (Ed.), *Music, culture and experience: Selected papers of John Blacking.* Chicago: University of Chicago Press.

Bourdieu, P. (1983/1986). The forms of capital. In J. Richardson (Ed.), *Handbook of theory and research for the sociology of education* (pp. 241–258). Westport, CT: Greenwood Press.

Brand, M. (2000). Music teachers' role in preparing students for live symphonic experiences. *Research Studies in Music Education, 15,* 24–30.

Bridge over the Wadi. (n.d.). Retrieved from www.handinhandk12.0rg/index.cfm?content .display&pageID=73

Cohen, D. (2007). Music in different cultures: Shared and divergent features. *Music in Time* (pp. 1–29).

Elliott, D. J. (1994). Music, education, and music values. Paper presented at the 21st World Conference of the International Society for Music Education on Musical Connections: Traditions and Changes, Tampa, Florida.

Eyerman, R., & Jamison, A. (1998). *Music and social movements: Mobilizing traditions in the twentieth century.* Cambridge: Cambridge University Press.

Ferez, K., & Adair, D. (2005). *Social capital, communities, and recent rationales for the performing arts.* Griffith University, Australia. Retrieved from www.engagingcommunities2005.0rg/ abstracts/Ferres-Kay

Finnas, L. (2001). Presenting music live, audio-visually or aurally—Does it affect listeners' experiences differently? *British Journal of Music Education 18* (1), 55–78.

Frank, J. (2003). Making social capital work for social policy. *Horizons: Policy Research Initiative, 6* (3). Retrieved from www.engagingcommunities2005.0rg/abstracts/Ferres-Kay

Freire, P. (1969a). *La educación como práctica de la libertad.* Madrid.

Freire, P. (1969b). *Pedagogy of the oppressed.* New York: Herder & Herder.

Ginzburg, C. (1991). Checking the evidence: The judge and the historian. *Critical Inquiry, 18* (1), 79–92.

Gluschankof, C. I. (2008). Music everywhere: Overt and covert, official and unofficial early childhood music education policies and practices in Israel. *Arts Education Policy Review, 109* (37–44).

Gluschankof, C. I. (2007, June 26–28). Research and practice in early childhood music education: Do they run parallel and have no chance to meet? The case of preschool singing repertoire. In *Proceedings of European network for music educators and researchers of young children* (pp. 27–31). Nicosia, Cyprus: University of Cyprus.

Gruppetta, M. (2010). *Autophenomenography? Alternative uses of autobiographically based research.* University of Western Sydney. Retrieved from www.aare.edu.au/04pap/gru04228.pdf

Gyarmati, D., & Kyte, D. (2004). Social capital, network formation and the community employment innovation project. *Policy Research Initiative, 6* (3). Retrieved from http://policyresearch .gc.ca/ page.asp?pagenm=v6n3_art_05

Haaretz Daily Newspaper, Israel (2007, July 22). Print Edition.

Khallaf, R. (2003). *Where is the music?* Retrieved from http://weekly.ahram.org.eg/2003/626/ fe1.htm

Kleber, M. O. (2003). *O terceiro setor e projetos sociais em música. Revista do Terceiro Setor, Rio de Janeiro, 9 Maio 2003.* Retrieved from. http://arruda.rits.org.br/notitia1/servlet/newstorm .notitia.apresentacao.ServletDeSecao?codig oDaSecao=11&dataDoJornal= 1052517652000

Kleber, M. O. (2006). *Music education practice in non-governmental organizations: Two case studies in Brazilian urban context.* Retrieved from http://sabix.ufrgs.br /ALEPH/ 8MYX2II JR5C1TE2PV59MKPIPKPC4 QPUVLDKQB7S72JNA44DDM3–09504/file/start-0

Kraemer, R. (2000). *Dimensões e funções do conhecimento pedagógico-musical. trad.* Porto Alegre: Em Pauta, 11(16/17), 50–75.

Lichtensztajn, D. (2010). The Israeli song in the Jewish community in Palestine (1880–1948) and its projection on music education narratives. In D. Coffman (Ed.), *CMA XII: Harmonizing the diversity that is community music activity* (pp. 53–56). Hangzhou, China: International Society for Music Education.

Lichtensztajn, D. (2008). Live music encounters: An integrate vision of leadership, good teaching and facilitation practice. In *Proceedings from the 2008 ISME Seminar of the commission for Community Music Activity: Projects, perspectives, and conversations* (pp. 202–216).

Lichtensztajn, D. (2007). The "live" concert: A transient episode or a continuous educational event in a multi-culturally divided society? In *Proceedings from the 2006 ISME Seminar of the Commission for Community Music Activity: Creating partnerships, making links, and promoting change* (pp. 120–131).

Lichtensztajn, D. (2000). Exploring connections between music education and multicultural communities in Israel. Paper presented at ISME CMA Seminar and Conference, Toronto and Edmonton.

Maamouri, M. (1998). *Language education and human development: Arabic diglossia and its impact on the quality of education in the Arab region.* Retrieved from http://eric.ed.gov/ ERICWebPortal/search/detailmini.jsp?_nfpb=true&_&ERICExtSearch_SearchValue_0= ED456669&ERICExtSearch_SearchType_0=no&accno=ED456669

Mauss, M. (2003). *Sociologia e antropologia.* (Paulo Neves, Trans.) São Paulo: Cosac & Naify.

Mdallel, S. (2004). The sociology of children's literature in the Arab world. *The looking glass: New perspectives on children's literature.* Retrieved from www.lib.latrobe.edu.au/ojs/index .php/tlg/article/view/177/176

Minks, A. (2002). From children's song to expressive practices: Old and new directions in the ethnomusicological study of children. *Ethnomusicology, 46* (3), 379–408.

Ortega y Gasset, J. (1935, 1962). *History as a system and other essays toward a philosophy of history.* New York: W. W. Norton & Company.

Peterson, E. (2002). *The creative dimension of the music listening experience.* (Unpublished doctoral dissertation). Northwestern University, Illinois.

Shehan, P. (1986). Music instruction for the live performance. *Council for Research in Music Education Bulletin, 88*, 51–57.

Shepherd, J., & Wicke, P. (1997). *Music and cultural theory.* Malden: Polity Press.

Shteiman,Y., & Vinograd-J'an., T. (2008). *Kadma program. Multicultural live music encounters. Annual Report.* Tel Aviv, Israel: Levinsky School of Education.

Small, C. (1995). *Musicking: A ritual in social space.* Retrieved from www.musikids.org/musicking.html

Souza, J. (1996). Contribuições teóricas e metodológicas da sociologia para pesquisa em educação musical. *Encontro Anual da Associação Brasileira de Educação Musical,* 5, Londrina. Anais . . . Londrina: ABEM.

Strauss, S., & Shilony, T. (1994). Teachers models of children's minds learning. In L. A. Hirschfeld & S. A. Gelman (Eds.), *Mapping the mind: Domain specificity in cognition and culture* (pp. 445–460). Cambridge: Cambridge University Press.

What is Choro Music? (2011). *Saint Paul Sunday. American National Public Radio.* Retrieved from http://saintpaulsunday.publicradio.org/features/0109_choro/

Part IV

PERFORMING ENSEMBLES: ARTISTRY, ADVOCACY, AND SOCIAL JUSTICE

Chapter Sixteen

Community Choirs: Expressions of Identity through Vocal Performance

Susan Avery, Casey Hayes, and Cindy Bell

As the first decade of the twenty-first century concludes, choral singing at the community level remains a vibrant and energetic activity for many adults. A 2009 study by Chorus America re-affirms what community and music educators have already known: participation in choral singing is the most common musical activity practiced by American adults (Chorus America, 2009). This survey confirms and strengthens earlier national studies by Chorus America (2003) and the National Endowment for the Arts (1998). Over thirty-two million Americans (or approximately one in six adults between the ages of eighteen and sixty-four) sing weekly in community-based choirs, with some of these singers participating in more than one choir. These numbers are remarkable.

The nature of educational outreach in its own right deserves special attention. Why is there such a strong communal need to place one's belief structure out in front of the general public to be scrutinized, accepted, or rejected? Is it just as simple as the need to feel that one belongs to a greater community than oneself? If that were the case, wouldn't it be enough just to "belong" and not to "reach out" to a community that may or may not accept your belief structure? Many choral organizations have utilized primitive tools of educational outreach simply to preserve their past heritage. German choral organizations such as Liederkranz or Mannerchor have for centuries existed to preserve German heritage, either musical or cultural. Particularly in this country, the Mannerchor have consistently been the face of the German people in America. To this day, many American cities have some form of Germanic musical organization whose primary mission is to preserve the past (German-American National Congress).

However, America is in the midst of a grand cultural and social transformation. According to the 2010 US Census, by 2020 Hispanic-Americans will outnumber white Americans. The ubiquitous main street of suburban America has largely disappeared as chain stores and Internet purchasing have replaced shopping in town. Mainline church denominations face shrinking membership as evangelical branches and megachurches draw Sunday morning worshippers (Iannaccone, Olson, & Stark, 1995). How does this changing social environment affect our community choral groups?

America of 2010 is a vastly different from America of 1950. Indeed, the many community choirs and choral societies founded in the patriotic surge of the post-World

War II years are now populated primarily with older singers (Bell, 2004). Still, the numbers reported above indicate a healthy singing environment. This chapter explores the current community choir scene as it presents three contemporary perspectives on choral singing and identity. A larger perspective and then a case study provide a special lens through which to view the contemporary choral singer. By weaving a multifaceted tapestry of community choral singing, the authors show how choir members join together to create and express their respective identities through singing.

The first section, by Susan Avery, provides an update on the traditional community choir: the long-standing, widespread choral group with a geographical home base that is largely sustained by working or retired adults. The second section, by Casey Hayes, highlights the growth and success of the GLBT (gay, lesbian, bisexual, transgender) choral movement, a phenomenon attributable to the emergence of the gay community in America over the past thirty years (Hayes, 2009).

PORTRAITS OF COMMUNITY CHORUSES

Community choruses have as many diverse forms as the people they serve. The singers who form each ensemble define the group's personality and, ultimately, their choral sound. These ensembles function in ways that allow each member to enjoy and learn from the experience and further commit to lifelong participation in the choral arts. The various constituents create an amalgam of possibilities, each considered by the director and/or a governing body. The components of a community chorus' personality can be viewed as parts of a machine: some are relatively simple and others are complex. Through exploring hundreds of websites of community choruses in the United States, portraits of the participating singers, the artistic leadership, the organization, and the representation of the chorus as a living, musical entity came into focus.

Portrait of the Singers

Singers who compose community choruses come from all walks of life and represent a true portrait of their communities. Many websites proudly declare the breadth of their members' vocations (lawyers, secretaries, engineers, financial analysts, nurses, etc.). A majority of choruses set minimum age requirements of sixteen, but a few have no age limit listed. Certainly there is no upper age limit; however, some websites articulate the need for members to be able to learn and memorize music. Several choruses are truly multigenerational and take pride that there are families involved who represent three current generations.

Most community choruses are mixed (SATB—soprano, alto, tenor, bass) choirs, although there are women-only and men-only ensembles as defined by their chorus organization (e.g., gay ensembles or choruses that specialize in SSA [soprano I, soprano II, and alto] music). A few choruses state that "all are encouraged to join, especially tenors and basses."

The level of singing and musical expertise varies widely; many choruses encourage singers from the most basic through the most highly experienced levels of ability to join. Choruses are welcoming of new members who have no previous choral experience, those who haven't sung since high school, and even those who cannot read music. Some community choruses utilize section leaders who, in part, assist novices to feel more confident.

Several websites indicate that their community chorus joins with other singing ensembles, usually from local (often community) colleges. In many cases, the director of the local community chorus conducts the college choir, facilitating an easy arrangement. One such partnership encourages not just area residents and college students but also community college employees to be part of the chorus. Another partnership requires all chorus members to register for one course credit from the community college.

Portrait of the Artistic Leadership

The conductor and accompanist of each community chorus are integral parts of the chorus performing personality. A biography (sometimes brief, sometimes extended) of the conductor may be posted on the website, accompanied by a professional photo. Some websites feature photos of the chorus in performance or in a posed shot.

The amount of experience and training among community chorus conductors varies greatly. These maestros range from current or retired college professors, high school choral conductors, and teachers with voice studios in the area to musicians who do not have college degrees in music but who are lifelong participants in choral singing and proffer their talents as church choir or community chorus directors. The accompanists (if any), like the conductors, have varying amounts of training and experience.

One differentiating aspect that is revealed on choir websites is the fact that some directors are paid. Some websites indicate that chorus members' dues go in part to paying the director, but no website disclosed the amount of pay a conductor receives.

Chorus members' dues may help to pay the accompanist. Choruses who utilize orchestral, chamber ensemble, or guest artist accompaniments or interpreters often declare that the subsidy for these instrumental collaborators derives from local business donations or corporate sponsorship.

Portrait of the Organization

The organization of a community chorus frequently includes a governing board of directors. The conductor may be a member of the board and is often listed as "artistic director," while other board members are identified as officers and members-at-large. Several websites list specific member positions that focus on philanthropic endeavors, public relations, or librarian or fund-raising duties.

Many of the choruses provide a mission statement. While some are fairly formal, most are informal and articulate a general sense of existing for the "joy of singing" and having fun. Some of the statements specify information such as being organized around the study and performance of choral literature appropriate for a large, symphonic choir or not affiliated with any religious or private groups. In some fashion, all of these community choruses' websites indicated the importance of providing music both to their immediate geographic communities as well as the global musical community.

Several choruses were sponsored by local civic organizations (for example, a city's community service department or parks and recreational department). Many of the websites indicated the chorus had not-for-profit status and encouraged monetary donations through that venue. One chorus highlighted a wish list of needs, such as office equipment and music folders, sought through donations. Some community choruses are affiliated with theater groups, providing members opportunities to perform in choral activities and musicals. Many larger community chorus organizations have children's choirs that perform in concerts with the adult chorus or in other venues (for example, when a children's chorus is required in a local opera production).

Community choirs may sponsor scholarships for local high school graduates who intend to pursue music in college. The money is obtained from concert admissions, donations specifically for the scholarship, or membership dues. More affluent choruses occasionally commission choral works and perform them as world premieres. Well-established community choruses look to their future and identify goals that include touring, creating endowment funds, creating outreach programs, paying section leaders, and hiring professional management.

An important part of a chorus structure is its volunteers. Specific jobs (ushers duties, refreshments, public relations work, photography, grant writing, envelope stuffing, etc.) are listed on many websites, and members or friends of members are encouraged to fill the positions. A few choruses mandate serving on a committee or working on projects as a requirement for membership in the chorus. Through all of these organizational requirements, it is evident that a community chorus is just a smaller community that is intent on serving the musical or social needs of a larger community.

Portrait of the Chorus as a Living and Musical Entity

A healthy community chorus is a dynamic and multifaceted entity. Its energy flows among all of its members and their music making. The earliest date for a chorus noted in this website search was 1948; while many began in the late 1970s and 1980s, many others have been established since 2000. No two choruses are exactly alike. And while there are decisions that are made by the conductor (and the board of directors) that inform the chorus and its musical personality, all stress community.

Most choruses provide a formal or informal mission statement on their websites. Other articulated information gives insight into the philosophy of the ensemble. One chorus specifically chooses repertoire "of compassionate music that unites people in good causes and helps singers and audience feel involved in society" (Teaneck Community Chorus) and declares its commitment to songs from many cultures by looking at the deep feelings behind the songs.

Joining a Community Chorus

Entrance into a community chorus occurs through either demonstrating interest or an audition process. Those choruses that have open invitations to any and all singers define membership as attendance at the first rehearsal (a few specify that membership becomes closed after the third rehearsal). When no auditions are required, choirs offer somewhat vague requirements such as having the ability to match pitch, a good ear for music, a good sense of rhythm, and the ability to memorize words and music or to carry a tune. One chorus suggests that interested members who cannot match pitch work with the director for six months to see if improvement occurs.

Required auditions may be indicated on the chorus' website. Choruses that have auditions sometimes have applications that are then reviewed by the conductor and an admissions committee; acceptance is based on the needs of the existing group.

While many of the choruses adopt a membership rule that has no ceiling number, several choruses limit the number of singers and have a waiting list for those who are interested in joining at a future date. Other entrance statements emphasize that members have a desire to sing, display musical ability, and commit to a set period of time. There are community choirs that accept interested members who do not read music. But no matter what the entrance procedures are, the chorus' websites are filled with statements declaring a welcoming and accepting atmosphere, an enthusiasm for working hard and improving musical ability, and the importance of making friends and having fun in a social setting.

Membership Guidelines

Many websites articulate membership rules or guidelines for all singers. Member handbooks in portable document format (PDF) are available on websites (some under password-protected formats) while other sites describe their regulations in a short paragraph or in bulleted form. The guidelines refer mostly to attendance and punctuality, expected volunteer participation, preparation, willingness to provide selected concert attire, and paying of dues and fees. Almost all of the community choruses have a dues requirement. Some are nominal ($20 or $30) and some more costly ($100 for a year's participation or $60 per concert); a few choruses provide a seniors' discount or a reduced fee for couples participating. The need for dues is explained as necessary for the purchase of music, services of a director and accompanist or instrumentalists, and scholarships. One chorus provides the opportunity to earn dues by securing advertising or sponsorships. Additional fees are sometimes charged for concert attire maintenance, purchase of music (which then belongs to the singer), costumes, or refreshments.

The money issues facing community choirs are daunting. Besides the dues and fees collected from each member, donations are often sought from local businesses or corporations. Sponsorship of a piece of music by members or non-members is offered as a means of helping to defray the ensemble's costs by purchasing the appropriate number of copies and donating them to the chorus in honor or memory of a loved one or important occasion.

Another fee structure that is mentioned in websites is that of admission costs to concerts. The typical ticket prices are between $10 and $12 with some price reductions for senior citizens. A few choruses indicate that concerts are "free to students through corporate sponsorship." One chorus proudly declares that they have never charged admission for concerts; many websites do not mention concert admission costs at all.

Literature

The entire spectrum of choral music is represented by these community choruses. While some websites do not indicate which specific pieces are being or have been performed, others list entire concert programs from the inception of the ensemble. There are choruses whose performance repertoire is focused on large symphonic works with orchestral accompaniment (Beethoven's *Ninth Symphony,* Bach's *Magnificat,* or Mendelssohn's *Elijah*); others simply indicate that they perform masterworks of previous centuries to more contemporary works. Other traditional choral literature mentioned include Brahms' *Liebeslieder Waltzes,* Vivaldi's *Gloria,* Orff's *Carmina Burana,* Rutter's *Requiem,* and Britten's *A Ceremony of Carols.*

A more common statement on the websites indicates that the chorus performs many styles, including Broadway, spirituals, pop, and holiday. In general descriptive paragraphs, specific titles are mentioned so interested members may know the songs ("River in Judea," "Hallelujah Chorus") or categories, such as jazz, folk songs, Beatles tunes, or Jewish songs, that the chorus performs. There are ensembles who focus their literature choices; one chorus may specialize in the performance of spirituals and works of African-American composers, and another chorus may focus on the music of female composers.

A strategy that encourages musician independence and allows ownership in the chorus emerges when a conductor presents performance opportunities to small groups led by interested members of the chorus. These small groups choose the music (that is appropriate to the concert programming), rehearse at times and sites other than the main chorus rehearsal, and make artistic decisions either by consensus or under the guidance of the director.

Theme concerts are a popular means of choosing literature. Many choruses offer seasonal fare in December and a more eclectic program in spring. "Salute to Armed Forces," "Music of the Americas," "Movie Music," "Sounds of the '60s," "A Tribute to Mr. (Richard) Rogers" (in which his widow participated), and "Broadway Themes" are themes that are mentioned in the chorus websites. Several community choruses began by performing Handel's *Messiah*, after which the ensemble decided to continue as a formalized chorus.

Learning Music

Many choruses declare that interested members need not have music reading ability in order to join. To maximize group rehearsal time, conductors provide rehearsal materials for the members to practice in the privacy of their homes. Whether the singer is given a CD that has his or her part recorded or an MP3 embedded on the website, it is expected that the singer will come to rehearsal having learned the music. Most websites that provide the rehearsal material on the site itself have that area password-protected while some simply make it available for anyone to hear. These materials usually take the form of the singer's part played by an electronic keyboard or the part with accompaniment (with the part emphasized). No information is given on the websites as to the source of these materials. Commercial sources can provide this service, or the director, an accompanist, or ambitious tech-savvy members can create the material with the assistance of technology and software such as GarageBand, Finale, or Sibelius. In addition, to ensure a comfort level of each singer's part, sectional rehearsals are sometimes scheduled along with the weekly ensemble rehearsal.

Rehearsal and Performance Times and Venues

There is no state in which community choruses do not exist. They are found in urban areas as well as rural, drawing members from extensive geographic areas. An important issue, both financially and logistically, that must be decided early in the creation of a chorus is where to rehearse and ultimately perform.

Community choruses are creative and secure a variety of sites, which are used as rehearsal halls and performance venues. Choruses rehearse in church social halls, school chorus rooms, community centers, retirement community centers, Centers for Council on Aging, and college rehearsal halls. While the chorus' websites gave little information as to the cost of rehearsal sites, it can be assumed that some sites will charge a set fee or accept member pass-the-hat-type donations to help cover the cost of utilities.

Performance venues can be imaginative and are often community based. Many websites declare that their choruses perform in local churches or school auditoriums for traditional concerts. It is heartening to note that many choruses perform at community functions such as the lighting of the town Christmas tree, singing the national anthem at local sports arenas, celebrating the arrival of dignitaries, and performing at the opening of community facilities and at awards ceremonies. Many choruses give performances at retirement and nursing homes. In addition, the listed concert performances indicate these choruses occasionally perform with local school choruses or bands. Several choruses proudly indicate that they have toured or hope to tour to foreign countries such as Italy, Spain, France, Germany, Austria, and China.

The traditional community choir allows people of all levels of musical expertise, with the single commonality of wanting to sing, to join with like-minded souls in a creative community. Today, in every part of the United States, an unprecedented number of singers, directors, and the organizations they have joined ensure that community choruses continue to be living musical entities.

THE GLBT CHORAL MOVEMENT

"Values: We [GALA (Gay and Lesbian Association) Choruses] believe

- in the power of music to change lives.
- that there is unity in diversity, that the diversity of our associates strengthens us all, and that all people are welcome to the stage.
- that we can sing together with respect and understanding, and in so doing, we offer community, hope, inspiration, and healing.
- that every time a member chorus of GALA Choruses sings, the chorus commits a political act.

- that GALA Choruses can assist in strengthening and inspiring our member choruses.
- that striving for musical excellence strengthens the GLBT choral movement."
  (GALA Choruses)

Three Decades of Growth

The struggle for equality within the gay, lesbian, bisexual, and transgender (GLBT) community, as played out in the public arena, is a relatively new phenomenon. The identification of a collective group of individuals distinguishing themselves as either gay or lesbian emerged within American culture during the middle of the twentieth century, largely after World War II, and was largely limited to urban areas. As Americans adjusted to a changing post-war society on the eve of a national civil rights movement, the GLBT movement found its roots: a movement designed to bring together individuals who longed for social rights and the freedom to love. One vehicle that has emerged within the GLBT community as a catalyst for societal change is that of the community chorus.

The community choral movement has been a popular form of musical expression within American society for hundreds of years. However, the formation of choral organizations labeling themselves as either "gay," "lesbian," "GLBT," or "transgender" is a new articulation within the musical realm. Not until the late 1970s did members of the GLBT community recognize the potential that the choral movement offered to alter the lens through which mainstream America viewed their emerging society. GLBT choruses sprouted up in a few large urban areas where, historically, large numbers of gay men and lesbian women congregated during the first half of the twentieth century. The first cities to cultivate these choirs were San Francisco (Gay Men's Chorus), Philadelphia (Anna Crusis Women's Chorus), and New York City (Gay Men's Chorus).

These choruses were founded for a variety of reasons. A GLBT chorus provided a surrogate family for gay men and lesbian women, who were often turned away from their biological families. Choruses became a central force within the social life of GLBT individuals, creating a feeling of acceptance and belonging that many of their heterosexual counterparts would also find within their community chorus of choice. Drawing upon past inspirations, such as the Fisk Jubilee Singers and the Mormon Tabernacle Choir, GLBT choruses quickly acknowledged the power of music to reshape common misconceptions of their community by mainstream American society. GLBT choruses focused upon the non-threatening nature of music to reach out to non-GLBT communities in order to educate people about key issues of GLBT justice, civil rights, and tolerance.

As the GLBT choral movement spread across the continent, it was necessary to develop a national agency for choirs who aligned themselves with issues of gender identity. In 1981, Gay and Lesbian Association of Choruses (GALA Choruses) was formed in Washington, DC, to aid in the growth of gay and lesbian choruses within their respective communities (Hayes, 2005). Today, GALA Choruses lists 261 member choruses and over 10,000 individual members. Additionally, the Seattle Men's Chorus, with over three hundred members, is considered to be the largest community chorus in North America (coincidentally, the New York City Gay Men's Chorus, with 286 members, ranks second [Sparks, 2005, p. 8]).

San Francisco, 1979

From its inception in 1981, GALA Choruses has worked tirelessly to unify the collective voice of an element of society that was fragmented as a result of the assassination of a national icon of gay rights, San Francisco City Supervisor Harvey Milk.

Although Harvey Milk began his political career in a very modest, unassuming way—being urged to run for a seat on the San Francisco City Council by his friends and neighbors from the densely populated and heavily gay Castro section of the city—he quickly became a fierce advocate in the war for equal rights (Shilts, 1982, pp. 109–110). Milk was elected a city supervisor and, as the new face of GLBT people, spearheaded an aggressive campaign to unify the political voice of the GLBT community. Encouraged by the support of San Francisco's GLBT-sympathetic mayor George Moscone, the GLBT community viewed themselves as an accepted and valued part of the San Francisco community as a whole. San Francisco became known as the nation's most accepting city of GLBT people. Milk wrote legislation calling for the end of anti-gay discrimination within the city. This legislation was ardently fought for and quickly passed, making San Francisco the first city in the country to legally recognize its GLBT community (www.time.com/time/magazine/article/0,9171,991276–1,00 .html). This powerful social movement, however, suffered an enormous loss in late fall of 1978 when Harvey Milk and Mayor Moscone were shot and killed on the very steps of the city hall they so ardently fought to open to all of San Francisco's citizens.

The seed of GLBT choral movement germinated on the steps of the San Francisco City Hall because it was here, in the early spring of 1979, that Edward Weaver congregated with fellow members of the San Francisco gay community to protest the shooting death of Milk (Vivyan, 2004, p. 6). Weaver, an avid musician who loved to sing, gathered with friends who spontaneously broke into verses of "We Shall Overcome" in reaction to the hate crime against one of their own. That impromptu gathering marked the beginning of the San Francisco Gay Men's Chorus, an organization in which Edward Weaver played a vital role. Weaver worked diligently with other members of the San Francisco Gay Men's Chorus organization to solidify the structural foundation of this new musical community during the critical first months of its development (Vivyan, 2004, p. 6).

When Weaver relocated to New York City in the summer of 1979, he brought with him both the desire and the organizational knowledge to create a similar organization on the east coast. During that summer, with the aid of Edward Dryer, the manager of the National Gay Task Force in New York City, flyers were posted throughout Greenwich Village and other predominantly gay areas of the city announcing the formation of the New York City Gay Men's Chorus. Under the musical direction of Jonathan Fey, the new organization's first rehearsal was Monday, September 17, 1979 (Vivyan, 2004, p. 7). The eighty men who showed up for that inaugural rehearsal at the Washington Square United Methodist Church could not have imagined the impact that their fledgling organization would have upon New York City and the world. Thirty-two years later, the New York City Gay Men's Chorus continues to change the lives of individuals within and outside the GLBT community.

Building Bridges through Song: Outreach

From the outset, GLBT choruses worked to raise the awareness of GLBT issues throughout the United States and the world. Edward Weaver, and all of the other men who came together in song on that September evening, intended to create an organization that would change lives through song. In order to accomplish this, from their inauguration, these choruses engaged in educational outreach. By utilizing the basic tools of educational outreach, the San Francisco Gay Men's Chorus and the New York City Gay Men's Chorus simply teach tolerance, acceptance, and breaking down the many barriers that prevent the non-GLBT community from understanding issues that relate to the greater GLBT community.

There is also burgeoning interest in the utilization of community musical organizations to not only preserve the past but to influence the future of society. The Mormon Tabernacle Choir, for example, is recognized as the face of the Mormon faith to the world. Although many Americans initially viewed Mormonism with tremendous skepticism and trepidation, these fears were largely calmed by the widespread fame of the Mormon Tabernacle Choir. During the 1960s and 1970s, the Mormon Tabernacle Choir was the face of not only of the Mormon religion, but, to a strong degree, of Christmas itself, as its outreach programs utilized the very holiday that meant peace and joy to teach tolerance of their own unique form of Christianity. Rarely was there a Christmas special on television that did not showcase the vocal excellence of this community chorus.

Utilizing a choir to influence thought and perception is not new. Gospel choirs have had a major influence upon American society, both musically and culturally, in the understanding and tolerance of African-Americans. Whereas most mainstream white Americans would never have visited an African-American church in the 1960s, they would listen to a gospel choir sing in the town square and, effectively, be exposed to the choir's own form of educational outreach. In short, the utilization of musical ensembles in educational outreach is not new.

In addition, GLBT choruses have a history of commissioning unique musical works which address issues relating to the understanding and tolerance of the GLBT community. Choirs utilized the finest composers to commission works specifically for the chorus. These works were not simply gay-specific musical products but works meant to transcend the boundaries of gender-specific issues, as each commission has its own special story to tell. The New York City Gay Men's Chorus has commissioned no fewer than sixty-five major musical works in its three-decade history, as well as giving the New York premiere of an additional 110 works. Furthermore, the roster of composers whose services were engaged by the chorus reads like a Who's Who of the American musical scene: Leonard Bernstein, Samuel Adler, William Bolcom, David Conte, Joseph Jennings, Daniel Pinkham, and Conrad Susa, to name a few.

Although some of these new works deal with GLBT-specific issues, the majority of the commissioned pieces were composed to perpetuate the choral music idiom. Most works were written, primarily, to achieve beauty of sound, and a sizeable canon of literature exists that deals with specific GLBT-related issues, to put words to the melodies. Whether it is in using the words of gay poet Walt Whitman or the creation of an original text by gay composer John Corigliano, the canon of commissioned works appeals to the audience on many levels and brings a much more familiar face to homosexuality for those outside of the GLBT community.

Crossroads of Identification

Today, the GLBT chorus finds itself at a crossroads of identification. The gay rights movement, as well as positive gay and lesbian subject matter on television and in the media, has changed the landscape for gays and lesbians. Most Americans have contact with someone who identifies as either gay, lesbian, bisexual, or transgender, whether directly (someone at work) or indirectly (on the TV show "Will and Grace"). The focus on societal education has paid off, and all of the years of singing to build bridges through song are reaping benefits.

As a community, GLBT members are on the threshold of finally gaining the basic civil rights that all Americans deserve and most Americans have. This is partly due to the role of GLBT community choruses, which have tirelessly been singing for the past thirty years to help change the way a larger American community views them and their non-singing counterparts. GLBT choruses took a lesson from the Mormon and African-American playbooks: singing breaks down barriers in the most non-threatening of ways. As GLBT choruses begin redefining their roles within the community, shifting from communal education to musical excellence, some groups may feel that they have lost their purpose. Perhaps it is time for GLBT choruses to join the ranks of other community choruses who sing for the love of music and work toward the commonality of membership that fosters a greater sense of family within their respective communities. Regardless, the necessity for GLBT choruses to effect change continues, but the fact remains that the finest impression any musical organization can make is in its ability to create great music.

As with all community choruses, the love of music is at its core, as it should be. It is that music that will continue to aid the GLBT community, as well as all minority communities, in building bridges through song.

BIBLIOGRAPHY

Bell, C. L. (2004). Update on community choirs and singing in the United States. *International Journal of Research in Choral Singing, 2* (1), 39–52. Retrieved from http://www.choralresearch.org

Chorus America. (2003). Retrieved from http://www.chorusamerica.org/impact03.cfm

Chorus America. (2009). *How children, adults, and communities benefit from choruses: The chorus impact study.* Retrieved from www.chorusamerica.org/about_choralsinging.cfm

GALA Choruses. (2011). Retrieved from www.galachoruses.org/about/mission_vision.html

German-American National Congress. (n.d.). *German singing societies.* Retrieved from http://www.delawaresaengerbund.org/GermanAmericanHistory/PDF/GermanSingingSocieties.pdf

Hayes, C. J. (2009). *Building bridges through song: A qualitative study of educational outreach by the New York City Ambassador Chorus* (Unpublished doctoral dissertation). New York University.

Hayes, C. J. (2005). Community music and the GLBT chorus. *International Journal of Community Music, 1* (1), 63–67.

Iannaccone, L., Olson, D., & Stark, R. (1995). Religious resources and church growth. *Social Forces, 74* (2), 705–731.

National Endowment for the Arts. (1998). Retrieved from www.nea.gov/about/98Annual/First.html

NYC Gay Men's Chorus. Retrieved from www.nycgmc.org/

Shilts, R. (1982). *The mayor of Castro Street: Life and times of Harvey Milk.* New York: St. Martin's Press.

Sparks, J. D. (2005). Gay and lesbian choruses—then and now. *Voice* (Summer), 28–31.

Teaneck Community Chorus. (2011). Retrieved from www.facebook.com/pages/Teaneck-Community-Chorus/105307001058?v=info

US Census. (2010). Retrieved from http://2010.census.gov/2010census/

Vivyan, J. (2004). *New York City Gay Men's Chorus 25th anniversary journal.* NY: New York.

Chapter Seventeen

Instrumental Ensembles: Community Case Studies from Brazil and the United States

Don Coffman and Joel Barbosa

Instrumental music education has received wide acclaim as an enjoyable and beneficial activity. Research studies have documented the numerous possible benefits of a music education, citing musical development as well as social benefits, among others. This chapter will highlight the experiences of instrumental musicians in two settings (older adults in concert bands and musicians in Brazilian concert bands) in order to add context to the understanding of how music education is produced, received, and perceived by a variety of constituents.

NEW HORIZONS FOR OLDER ADULT MUSICIANS (DON COFFMAN)

> *I think I should have no other mortal wants, if I could always have plenty of music.*
> *It seems to infuse strength into my limbs, and ideas into my brain. Life seems to go*
> *on without effort when I am filled with music.*
>
> —George Eliot

The Iowa City New Horizons Band (ICNHB) is part of the New Horizons International Music Association (NHIMA), an affiliation of more than 160 bands, choirs, and orchestras across the United States, Canada, and Ireland that share a newsletter, Internet website (www.newhorizonsmusic.org), and national institutes or "camps." The first New Horizons band began in Rochester, New York, in 1991 under the leadership of Roy Ernst, professor of music at the Eastman School of Music (Ernst & Emmons, 1992). Each NHIMA group is autonomous and usually works with a local music merchant who offers support such as rehearsal space, administrative oversight, or discounts on purchases.

New Horizons groups differ from other amateur community performing groups because we do not simply rehearse music for a performance. We are dedicated to teaching participants how to play better. For many players, the band is an opportunity to improve the skills they acquired years ago in school. For some players, this program fulfills their desires for making music that they have dreamed of for decades. For others, this program is an invitation to an experience that they thought was not possible.

Most groups rehearse once or twice a week in music stores, schools, or churches and are led by retired high school or college ensemble directors or by college professors. The ICNHB relies on a teaching staff of six to eight assistant instructors who are University of Iowa undergraduate and graduate music education students. Since the program's inception in 1995, more than one hundred music students have gained practical experiences in real-life, supportive, low-stress teaching situations prior to obtaining their degrees. Even though the leaders and the university students are the official teachers in the program, we learn a great deal from our elders, the students. Most of the instructors come to the program without much teaching experience and with some understandable nervousness. The older adults often mentor the student instructors, gently making suggestions. Sometimes they simply tell the instructors what they are having trouble playing or understanding. Sometimes they ask for a clearer conducting pattern from the instructors. On rare occasions, they have private conversations with me to let me know about an instructor who seems disorganized or unsure.

On Tuesday and Thursday mornings, teachers and students congregate at the Iowa City/Johnson County Senior Center for forty-five minutes of small group instruction or chamber ensemble coaching, followed by a sixty-minute band rehearsal. The Center is a multi-floor, former post office, with ornate woodwork and a sweeping staircase, built in the early 1900s, which has been renovated to house a modern ceramics room, an exercise room, an assembly room/cafeteria, a computer lab, a television production studio, a library, and a consignment shop. On New Horizons mornings, music emanates from rooms on all three levels of the building. During coaching sessions, student instructors also teach playing the instrument. The players ask student instructors for more opportunities to practice technical skills (e.g., scales and arpeggios). We are thrilled that this chamber program has spawned other self-directed groups of musicians who rehearse weekly on their own, and we believe that the concert band's technique, tone, and intonation have improved because of the instruction that occurs in these smaller groups. The small groups focus on preparing for chamber concerts that occur every December and May.

The program has expanded from one band to many ensembles, and the concert band, the centerpiece of the program, has nearly tripled in size, from twenty-six players in 1995 to seventy-seven at present. Some groups were formed and named through members' initiatives: the Polka Dots, Second Wind (a woodwind quintet), Post Horns, Jazzy Flutes & Friends, and the Old Post Office Brass quintet. In 1998, Silver Swing, which plays Big Band swing music from the 1930s and 1940s, was added, and this group has been led by a series of student instructors. As the concert band matured in musicianship, there was a need for a new entry-level band, so in 2004, I added a Monday evening band for novice players, the Linn Street Band. Because this band meets after the typical workday, adults who have not yet retired from work can participate. Some members of the Linn Street Band have since moved up to the more advanced Tuesday/Thursday morning band.

We rehearse year-round, pausing for four weeks over the winter holidays and during August. Nominal member fees and donations sustain the program expenses for student instructor stipends, music, and equipment. The concert band performs about six concerts annually, usually at the Senior Center, but the array of performance venues for all the small groups is extensive and includes pedestrian malls, shopping centers, parks, churches, schools, and area adult care centers. We have traveled a couple dozen times to other Iowa towns. Our most prestigious appearances have been for two state conventions of music teachers and the Iowa Governor's Conference on Aging. The number of performances by the small groups exceeds ninety performances annually.

Some of the concerts have been intergenerational, with New Horizons' band members sharing the stage with young players from elementary school, middle school, high school, and university bands. Each band performs alone, and then the groups merge for mass band performances, allowing players of varying ages to musically and socially "rub shoulders." I design seating arrangements that scatter the New Horizons players in sections of the school bands. Then we briefly rehearse and allow time for players to converse within the sections.

It takes a sense of humor to put oneself in situations where there is a risk of making audible mistakes. Everyone does his or her best, so I coach them by teasing them gently about playing problems. When the band first started, I resisted singling out players for performance errors as much as possible. I tried to call attention to problems by only identifying group problems (e.g., tubas or woodwinds or melody line). No one likes to have his or her mistakes identified publicly, so if the band has some rhythmic struggles, I might say something like, "We are improvising some new rhythms today." When individuals make early entrances due to not counting rests properly, I have remarked, "You all have the right sense of what to play, you're just not agreeing on when it occurs." My goal is to address the problem indirectly while, at the same time, affirming the value of the players. I want them to feel that the band rehearsal is a safe environment and that there is no reason to fear making errors. I do my best to honor the trust they have placed in me.

Our goal is to balance playing our best with not taking ourselves too seriously. Without the ability to laugh at themselves, this group would not have progressed to its current state of excellence. If someone plays at the wrong place or misses a pitch or rhythm, there is never any embarrassing awkwardness—someone is bound to come up with a gentle, witty remark about it. For instance, one player wryly remarked during one rehearsal, "At our age, every day is sight-reading!"—a witty reminder that sometimes memory falters.

The best way to describe the New Horizons experience is through the players' words and stories. Their comments reveal the beneficial aspects of group music-making:

> I had continued to sing in church choirs, so never left "making music" behind entirely. However, I had forgotten the very real pleasure that comes from being part of an ensemble where the total is greater than the sum of the parts. There is great satisfaction, to say nothing of the fun involved, in making music with a group. Even when it doesn't go well; it's fun to play—and in those occasions when it's better than we thought possible, it becomes a spiritual adventure. There is a physical and emotional high that comes from being a part of the band that I don't find in anything else that I do.

I think making music does more for me spiritually and emotionally than anything else. What makes it fun is that it is challenging, and even if I am not great, I can get better than I am now. Piano and voice have hit their peak for me, and it's all downhill. But with a new instrument I can progress. With music, the whole is great[er] than the sum of its parts. I do not enjoy being a soloist, and I play (and sing) much better in a group. I can't make myself practice for myself (piano), but I work hard to bolster my section in the band. And every now and then this band of blue hairs and aches and pains, people who forget their shortcomings and concentrate on their parts, this band makes glorious music, and I'm proud to be a small part of it.

I often receive emails from band members after concerts, but this message from a member after a concert has been particularly meaningful to me:

I do not know whether I played well or not, but I do know that I made an impression on one young man. He thought I played well, and that was a giant compliment to me. A mother, son, and daughter were waiting for me in the lobby at Clapp Hall. The young man, around twelve, with his program in hand, approached me and asked if I was the Beverly Mueller listed in the program. I told him I was, and he asked to shake my hand. His mother also shook my hand and said her son loved the sax. I asked him if he played, and he said he was playing the euphonium but wanted to play the sax as he really loved it. The realism of playing in the New Horizons band really hit home. We are actually making an impression on the younger generation. I thank each and every one of you for the opportunity of playing with you all.

The band functions like an extended family. Band participants have coffee or lunch together, rehearse at members' homes, and go to concerts together in the community. Some single women have paired up for vacations. Two marriages have resulted from friendships formed in the band. Comments from band members show that the socializing is a mixture of making new friends and often renewing old friendships:

The band has been the main influence in finding my way into the community. Band activities give me a natural way to get to know men—something not easy for a widow new in the community.

I consider all of the band members to be very good acquaintances. And given an out-of-band situation, each would come to another's aid. Given the age we all are, it is less likely that a goodly number would become close "chums" because we all have too many other personal, health, housing, and financial concerns. Yet there is a togetherness as we come together in band and sectional practices . . . Maybe it is because we are more dependent on each other's presence at each gig for our success. We compliment each other a lot and do cause each to put in extra effort because we want our group to do well. The NHB [New Horizons band] and its many subgroups is the catalyst for a group of people to do many activities together, [people] who otherwise would probably have few, if any, associations with each other.

While their health is generally good, it is not unusual for members (or their spouses) to suffer sudden setbacks (e.g., heart attacks, strokes, broken bones, cardiac bypass surgery) or long-term ailments (e.g., Alzheimer's, Parkinson's, cancer). Many times, ailing members make remarkable recoveries that allow them to return to the band. The importance of the band in forming a genuine community is evident during these tough times. When one person copes with illness, the other members help with visits, meals, and transportation. In cases of bereavement, members provide what comfort they can. According to one member,

> The NHB has become my main group. I love the men in the clarinet group—they are concerned about me and for each other, like when someone doesn't make it to rehearsal. One member even came to the visitation when my husband passed away, and I had just met her! That's the kind of loyalty the band has for each other.

New Horizons Research

In 2007, I conducted a research study that surveyed 1,652 older adults participating in New Horizons bands and orchestras in the United States and Canada in order to confirm that the benefits I had observed in my program were being experienced in other bands and orchestras. One of the survey questions asks:

> Do you believe that playing an instrument in a New Horizons group has affected your health, either favorably or unfavorably?

A majority of the survey participants answered this question ($n = 1,156$ [70 percent], yielding 1,626 statements), and they indicated that NHIMA participation had affected their health in some way. Comments were almost uniformly positive (98 percent, or 1,593 statements). Negative outcomes (thirty-two statements) were almost all associated with (a) some discomfort in playing or carrying instruments or (b) some stress from not being able to perform as well as they wished. Responses were coded into four areas:

- *Emotional Well-Being*
  ($n = 1,203$ statements, 74 percent of 1,626 statements). This category had two subcategories: happiness and sense of purpose.
- *Physical Well-Being*
  ($n = 390$ statements, 24 percent). Many comments ($n = 260$ statements, 16 percent) indicated that playing a wind instrument had improved the respondents' lungs, breathing, or cardiovascular system. Others respondents (5 percent) believed that NHIMA participation had improved their physical condition (e.g., posture, dexterity, muscle tone, flexibility, coordination). Some respondents (1 percent) noted that playing the instruments and carrying the instruments was good exercise, while others (3 percent) reported that the desire to participate in a NHIMA group had motivated them to adopt more healthy lifestyles (lose weight, watch nutrition, seek exercise). A handful of individuals believed that playing a musical instrument had kept them from illnesses, like a cold, or had helped them recover from illnesses and surgery more effectively.
- *Mental Stimulation*
  ($n = 341$ statements, 21 percent). Some asserted that playing an instrument had kept them mentally sharp (mental challenge, concentration, alertness, focus, improved

brain power, improved memory, exercise the imagination, improved hand-eye co-ordination).
* *Socialization*

  (*n* = 325 statements, 20 percent). For many respondents (18 percent), NHIMA groups provided a sense of belonging or camaraderie, new friends, and an opportunity to improve social skills. Some cited the support they received during difficult times such as the death of a spouse or family member.

Music educators generally assert that music is a lifelong activity, yet our efforts are heavily focused on youth. Opportunities for adults to make music and learn about music are limited in comparison. In the United States, there has been a long-standing gulf between music education (school music) and music in the community ("real music"). These older adult bands and orchestras are excellent examples of what can be done to bridge the gap between school music and community music. I find their love of music making inspirational and the members' words stirring:

> The most astounding aspect of my involvement in band, chorus, and orchestra is the extreme enhancement of my joy in listening to music. The education of my ears and that part of my brain adds immensely to the intellectual, emotional, and kinesthetic pleasure of listening . . . deepens and expands it and, therefore, my life. Where else are people crazy enough to haul a bass drum, timpani, and a xylophone across rough terrain to play music, with the wind ruffling the pages and overturning music stands, and call in[it] FUN? It's satisfying at this age to be part of an educational experience that demonstrates that performance really improves with practice. One may not get "good," but one gets better! An atmosphere which encourages all learners is a very good place for a retired person.

> Returning to band and playing clarinet once again after years away from it felt like a wave had washed over me and I'd woken up to discover life.

> It's a relief to find like-minded souls. Musical amateurs seem to have many common political, social, recreational views. In addition, they have similar family backgrounds to mine. Music was the leitmotif in my family life—all kinds, not any one type. I see and hear about it in other band members . . . Making music has been the fourth meal of my day ever since the neighbor who dressed me at birth became my piano teacher. Singing in the family and especially together in the car was a given. Words and rhythms were put to music like other families work puzzles together. Music means memories. Music brings joy.

THE WIND BANDS FROM BRAZIL:
ACTIVITIES, PRACTICES, AND TRADITIONS (JOEL BARBOSA)

The civil wind bands from Brazil are non-profit organizations which began in the second half of the nineteenth century. Military bands gained social prestige in the first half of the century when Portugal's king Dom João VI and his court fled to Brazil in 1808 to escape from Napoleon. The first civic bands came into existence at the end of the nineteenth century and played at religious and social feasts. According to Binder

(2006), the influence of the military bands has contributed to the military characteristics of the civil bands' instrumentation, repertoire, uniforms, and hierarchy.

The bands are an indispensable part of city life in Brazil. The bands contribute to the official agenda of the cities through social, religious, civic, and cultural events. The bands also play a significant role in their participants' lives and in the musical life of the country. Brazilian civic bands are teachers of community music practices, participants in community music activities, and keepers of community music traditions.

History and Research on Brazilian Bands

Civil bands have been a growing national phenomenon over the last century. The governments of some of the states of the Federative Republic of Brazil provide support to the bands through a variety of projects. The Ministry of Culture, through FUNARTE (the National Foundation for Art), maintains a program called Projeto Banda, which accepts only civil bands. Pereira (1999) states that there were 742 bands registered in this program in 1975, 1,027 in 1984, and 1,302 in 1999. The official catalog of registered bands on the Projeto Banda website lists 2,086 bands in every state and in 1,768 of Brazil's 5,562 cities as of 2009. They are distributed throughout the five regions of the country with 36 percent in the southeast, 33 percent in the northeast, 15 percent in the south, 9 percent in the central-west, and 7 percent in the north (Amazon region). If military, municipal, religious, conservatory, and school bands were counted, these numbers would be even higher. In *Perfil dos Municípios Brasileiros 2006—Cultura*, the Brazilian Institute for Geography and Statistics (IBGE) documented that 44 percent of the cities had bands in 2001, growing to 53 percent in 2006, an increase of 22 percent (IBGE, 2009), and according to Granja (1984) and Bendedito (2005), the number of youth in the bands is growing as well. The bands obtain their financial resources from playing for the municipal governments and for Catholic churches. In addition, they may qualify as tax deductible projects financed by private companies or benefit from contributing partnerships.

History documents the bands' important place in the city's agenda. Granja (1984, p. 42) explains how the performances of the bands fell within the sphere of *communitas,* occurring "at the moments in which the collectivity share experiences of pleasure and equality, when all the men feel in brotherhood, disappearing . . . the hierarchic differences of the quotidian life." Granja (1984) documents where and when the bands participated—at public performances in municipal plazas, in parades, and at circuses, auctions, and balls.

Figueiredo (1996) discusses how the institution of the band suffered interference from outside and how this influenced the members of the band. Prejudice against the band, for instance, was related to two factors. Slave bands were active relatively recently—until the end of the nineteenth century. More contemporary bands were composed mainly of people from the interior and from the poor suburbs of big cities. This same prejudice was not shown toward symphonic bands because the bands' musicians were considered to be peers of the musicians in symphonic orchestras, and both of these groups performed at prestigious venues. In terms of social relations within the bands, Salles (1985, p. 11) states that "in the popular communities, the band . . . is a democratic association which [aspires] to bring back the associative spirit and to level the social classes." As the bands played in the parades and in the plazas of a city, they became a part of that area's heritage and traditions.

Figueiredo (1996) investigated five bands in Barra do Piraí, Rio de Janeiro. Four of them had been in existence for more than seventy years and the other for more than a century. The men who created this musical culture created the bands and worked to ensure their survival as institutions in order to protect themselves, concluded Figueiredo; the bands became social, educational, and cultural phenomena as well as cultural artifacts.

The civil bands are groups composed of wind (B flat clarinets, alto and tenor saxophones), brass (trumpets, E flat saxhorns, slide or valve trombones, euphoniums, B flat and E flat tubas or sousaphones), and percussion instruments (snare drums, bass drums, and idiophones).

During its history, the bands contributed with the creation of new music genres such as the *maxixe*, the *dobrado*, and the *frevo* (Granja, 1984). These genres had their origins in the civil wind band milieu and became very popular throughout Brazil. The *maxixe* was a musical genre and dance that began at the end of the nineteenth century and continued into the twentieth century. The *dobrado* is a Brazilian march genre for band, played mainly at civic and military events, that began in the second half of the nineteenth century. The *frevo* has been one of the most exciting carnival musics (Granja,1984); its uniforms helped to give every member of a band equal standing. It hid the anonymous participant, incorporating one into a collective individuality—the band—that was respected by the public and defined the role a member played in the ritual. Granja (1984) studied two bands from the city of Nova Friburgo, in the State of Rio de Janeiro, the Sociedade Musical Beneficente Euterpe Friburguense, founded in 1863, and the Sociedade Musical Beneficente Campesina Friburguense, founded in 1870. As in many cities that have two bands, the later band was begun after a rift split the original band; in this case, the disagreement was due to local politics.

Figueiredo (1996, pp. 56–58) writes that "tradition, [the] past, conservativeness, uniform[s], and discipline build up the group's identity." She explains that the preoccupation of maintaining hierarchical behavior through old genre repertoire, uniforms, and formal activities serves to preserve a band's tradition. The past is present in these bands' board meetings. At the end of each meeting, the board members pause for a minute of silence in remembrance of deceased members. The past is also acknowledged at the All Souls' Day holiday, when the band plays for the departed at the cemetery.

Granja (1984, pp. 57–58) writes of "the respect to the veterans, the hierarchic relation, the transmission of knowledge from generation to generation, the participation of people linked by parental ties reproduces . . . the characteristics of a family structure." She points to the bands' gallery, where portraits, banners, flags, trophies, symbols, and books of minutes conserve the bands' traditions and history in order to preserve the clan.

Granja (1984, pp. 71–72) adds that "these groups establish a constant competition among themselves . . ." According to Da Matta (1980, p. 45), ". . . in a hierarchic structured society as the Brazilian, when escapes from the dominant scheme (of hierarchy) take place, the groups enter in competition." This may be seen in the intensity of the contests held throughout the country.

The bands are headed by a president, followed by the conductor (the "bandmaster" in the Brazilian band tradition). The latter "occupies the main role among the musicians . . . he is an example of authority" (Figueiredo, 1996, p. 55). The assistant conductor (or "countermaster," as it is called in this tradition) substitutes for the bandmaster as necessary. The students are at the bottom of the pyramid. In a parade, the band's traditions are evident in the hierarchical behavior of the musicians, in the uniforms they wear, and in the repertoire they play.

The bandmasters are usually retired military band musicians with years of experience. But musicians who have graduated from schools of music have also become band directors. Besides teaching and conducting rehearsals and performances, the bandmasters also act as arrangers and composers. There is no course to prepare bandmasters in the Brazilian schools of music, but there are short courses at music festivals.

Bendedito (2005) studied the band Teodoro de Faria from São João Del Rey, Minas Gerais State, which was founded in 1902. Besides participating in traditional civil wind band performances, this band has played at official receptions, soccer championships, presentations of plays, and outdoor church festivals. Salles (1985) examines the history of the bands of Para State, in the Amazon region, and mentions the bands' presentations at lunches, dinners, tours in pleasure boats, feast days, baptisms, baby funerals, feast eves, and shows at the doors of theaters. Not all of these kinds of events require the bands' presence nowadays, but bands continue to play at most of them.

The community music tradition of the bands contributes to the socialization of their student musicians with musical practices augmenting social practices. Holanda (2002) writes about the Banda Juvenil Dona Luíza Távora from Fortaleza, the capital city of the northeastern State of Ceará. This band belongs to the Centro Educacional da Juventude Padre Joao Piamarta, an educational institution affiliated with an Italian religious organization, and works with youths ages nine to eighteen who attend the institution, focusing on music and citizenship.

The youths' education begins with an explanation of the "game's" rules, "a group of regulations that aim to control and to start them in a better way in the disciplinary experience" (Holanda, 2002, p. 48) for the new students. These regulations concern attendance, involvement, mutual respect, hygiene habits, and good behavior in the classroom. The language used by both teachers and students is simple, sincere, and direct, without subterfuge.

Holanda believes that the success of this musical and social training is due to the combination of collective participation, the personal and academic achievements of the students, the challenges and rewards of the musical and social training, the rigid discipline, the family approach, and the band's repertoire.

In the case of the Banda Juvenil Dona Luíza Távora, the musical work had a social impact as much as the citizenship work did. Many of the band members have become professional musicians. Some ex-members have worked as instrumentalists and band directors in Brazil and Italy, and others have become arrangers, composers, music teachers, and music producers (Holanda, 2002). Bendedito (2005, p. 75) writes that the bands are "centers of integration and education on social and music values." Moreira

(2007), in a study of two bands from Sergipe State, also reveals the importance of the bands in terms of socialization, human development, and social responsibility.

The case of the Banda Juvenil Dona Luíza Távora is not rare. Researchers acknowledge that the bands contribute to the formation of professional musicians. Civil bands have made a significant contribution to Brazilian professional ensembles (military bands, symphonic bands, symphonic orchestras, and ensembles of urban pop music). The majority of military instrumentalists receive their first musical training in the civil bands. After entering a military band, some musicians continue playing in civil bands, and others come back to them in retirement as bandmasters or musicians.

Salles (1985) affirms that "the band is then the people's conservatory . . . it has been a cellar of the symphonic orchestra musicians in Brazil" (p. 11). Indeed, the bands are the only schools of music in many cities. The number and quality of the band members who have become professional musicians has contributed significantly to Brazil's musical ensembles. Granja (1984) identifies fifty-four musicians who had started in the bands as members of the two professional orchestras of Rio de Janeiro. The bands have made great contributions to the nation's music and to the musicians themselves.

Pedagogy of Brazilian Bands

Figueiredo (1996) declares that the pedagogical function of the bands is a natural extension of the group experience and not an isolated, externally imposed process. Struggling, working, and fighting to grow on the part of the students mixes with the band's history (p. 81). The learning and teaching processes for wind and percussion instruments are similar in bands across the country. The bandmaster usually teaches all of the instruments, but in some cases, the countermaster or an instrumentalist serves as the teacher. The pedagogical approaches concentrate on music reading, instrumental technique, and ensemble practice, divided into three phases (Barbosa, 1994).

In the first phase of training, the student receives instruction in music reading by reading the rhythm and speaking the name of the notes without singing the pitches. The most commonly used materials are exercises in a published method book or written by the teacher. With few exceptions, the elementary music theory classes of this phase are group lessons while the music reading instruction is done individually.

In the second phase, the student begins instruction in his or her instrument through individual lessons. The selection of the instrument depends more on the needs of the ensemble and the availability of the instrument rather than on the student's choice. Instrumental training starts by learning to produce the instrument's tones, including the instrument's diatonic scale. Once the tones and scales have been mastered, practice consists of transferring vocal music reading abilities to the instrument. Students may learn to play the same music on the instrument that they used as reading material in the first phase. Some teachers use method books to develop finger dexterity. These materials are usually Italian or French instrumental books from the nineteenth century or Brazilian books from the first half of the twentieth century. This phase concludes with the student learning the band's repertoire.

The third phase consists of the students practicing the band's repertoire with the band. Some bands have student bands to prepare students to enter the main band. The band director determines when a student is ready to become a regular member of the band and receive his or her uniform.

Studies document the pedagogical difficulties and deficiencies with the Brazilian band instructional sequence. The first phase of the learning processes has the highest drop-out rate of the course. This may be due to the fact that there is no musical or instrumental practice in this phase. Figueiredo (1996) noted that "the classes are expositive . . . [and] follow formal process of teaching . . . There is no practice of improvisation, teaching through imitation, or even freedom to create" (p. 83). She adds that the music reading classes are disassociated from the instrumental instruction, concluding that the band's pedagogy has postures of controlling, obligation, and repression. The band schools have a very high drop-out rate, around 75 percent (Barbosa, 1994; Figueiredo, 1996).

Benedito (2005) adds that "the destitution of physical structure, specialized teachers, and pedagogic material plaster this music practice" (p. 81). Pereira (1999) interviewed fifty students between the ages of ten and eighteen from ten bands from the São Paulo State, one from Minas Gerais and one from Rio de Janeiro, to observe that technique is prioritized to the detriment of the music and that the instruments are of low quality and poorly maintained. Finally, Granja (1984) cites a bandmaster who declares that the music quality of the bands is not good because of the poor condition of the instruments, the lack of good teachers, and the paucity of competent conductors.

The pedagogical approach is not the only factor that contributes to a student's motivation and success. The combination of a band's activities, traditions, social relationships, and prestige affects a student's progress. According to Holanda (2002), "the quality of the repertoire stimulates the instrument's practice . . . the interpretation, and the human promotion . . . the youth . . . feel the need of continuing practice to overcome bigger challenges" (p. 109). A band's prestige and performance in parades and at religious feasts (*communitas*) helps to recruit young people to learn instruments in its schools. Even though the bands have failed to retain the majority of their students, they have managed to prepare a sufficient number of musicians to have kept them active for more than a century despite crises and transformations.

Bands as Community Music Tradition

The literature demonstrates that the civil wind bands are Brazilian institutions that have been a constitutive part not only of their local communities, but of the music of the nation. The similarity of their practices in the areas of music performance, music education, and social integration characterize them as patrimonies, giving them unique identities with their own concepts, values, beliefs, and knowledge. The bands not only constitute a community activity but, moreover, a phenomenon. Because of that, the bands have become an essential part of their communities and of their nation. In this sense, the Brazilian bands form a community music tradition, the unique body of community music practices (especially music education and public performance) the bands have carried on, within and outside of their contexts, during their history. Each community music practice includes its own community music activities, units employed to accomplish specific tasks.

CONCLUSION

While each of the ensembles described in this chapter has a distinct story to tell, they all send one coherent message: music can be a powerful mechanism for the betterment of individuals and society. The writings in this chapter tell but a small portion of the global context of how music is produced, received, and perceived in community settings. The moral of each story is the importance of investigating and understanding the complex world of music in communities.

BIBLIOGRAPHY

Barbosa, J. L. (1994). *An adaptation of American band instruction methods to Brazilian music education, using Brazilian melodies* (Unpublished doctoral dissertation). University of Washington.

Benedito, C. J. R. (2005). *Banda de música teodoro de faria: Perfil de uma banda civil Brasileira através de uma abordagem histórica, social e musical de seu papel na comunidade* (Unpublished thesis, Univeritaria Sao Paulo, Brazil).

Binder, F. P. (2006). *Bandas militares no Brasil: Difusão e organização entre 1808–1889* (Unpublished thesis, Univeritaria Sao Paulo, Brazil).

Da Matta, R. (1980). *Carnavais, malandros e heróis: Para uma sociologia do dilema Brasileiro* (2nd ed.). Rio de Janeiro: Zahar.

Eliot, G. (1914). *The mill on the floss.* Boston: Ginn and Company.

Ernst, R. E., & Emmons, S. (1992). New horizons for senior adults. *Music Educators Journal, 79* (4), 30–34.

Figueiredo, L. M. G. C. (1996). *Bandas de música—Fenômeno cultural e educacional no contexto da microrregião de barra do piraí* (Unpublished thesis, Univesidade Federal, Rio de Janeiro, Brazil).

Granja, M. F. D. (1984). *A banda: Som e Magia* (Unpublished thesis, Consevatorio Brasilierio de Musica, Rio de Janeiro, Brazil).

Holanda, F. J. C. (2002). *A Banda Juvenil Dona Luíza Távora como fonte formadora de músicos e de cidadãos Na Cidade de Fortaleza-Ceará.* Nossa Senhora da Conceição, UFBA-UECE.

IBGE. (2009). Retrieved from www.ibge.gov.br/home/presidencia/noticias/noticia_visualiza. php?id_

Moreira, M. S. (2007). *Aspectos históricos, sociais, e pedagógicos nas filarmônicas do divino e Nossa Senhora Da Conceição, do estado de sergipe.* Nossa Senhora da Conceição, UFBA. noticia=980. Retrieved on July 10, 2009.

Pereira, J. A. (1999). *A Banda de Música: Retratos Sonoros Brasileiros* (Unpublished thesis, Sao Paulo State University, Brazil).

Salles, V. (1985). *Sociedades de Euterpe.* Brasília: Edição do autor.

Chapter Eighteen

Expressing Faith through Vocal Performance

Hussein Janmohamed, Cindy Bell, and Mehnaz Thawer

"For heights and depths no words can reach, music is the soul's own speech" is an unattributed adage that describes the power of music as it invigorates the individual and collective spirit. For generation upon generation, humans engage in music—in this case, singing—to offer praises to the "Great One" in times of bountiful harvest and blessing, or to sustain downtrodden people in their darkest hours of life's journey.

In 1000 BCE, David sang to the Lord a song of thanksgiving, as recorded in the Book of Second Samuel. Three millenniums later in 2010, Hanif, a Canadian Ismaili Muslim, professes: "To me, music is a form of devotion in itself" (Shariff, personal communication, 2009). No culture is without music and singing, and no culture is without a philosophical discussion as to the existence of the supernatural. Theism, deism, pantheism, mysticism: such a brief snippet from the long record of man's attempt to pinpoint the mysteries of the soul. But despite the numerous differences in belief systems, one thread holds constant for all these communities: the use of music to express one's faith and feed the soul.

In this chapter, the authors consider how religious communities use music to propel their faith and to essentially expand their foundations. In particular, we examine the role singing plays in the individual and corporate worship experience. Hussein Janmohamed and Mehnaz Thawer detail the captivating story of how a community youth choir is transforming the lives of Ismaili Muslims in Canada. Cindy Bell discusses how in the United States the Sunday morning church choir has spilled into the community via choir festivals and community gatherings. Both of these stories offer intriguing depictions of how music provides the fundamental underpinnings of the spiritual experience.

BISMILLAHIR RAHMANIR RAHIM
HUSSEIN JANMOHAMED: THE BACK STORY

Born in Nairobi, Kenya, an Ismaili Muslim[1] of South Asian origin, Hussein Jan-mohamed immigrated with his family to Canada as a child. As new immigrants, his family dealt with issues of integrating into a new society and educating young children who would learn about their cultural histories and faith in Canada, possibly never coming into personal contact with their countries or languages of origin. For Janmohamed, it was the efforts of his family, the foundations they laid and the opportunities they provided, that allowed him to understand faith, explore identity, and express himself in a language he would understand and that he could communicate with others. Music became an integral part of that language and a naturally unifying force for Janmohamed.

It was making music with others, ensemble music, which particularly resonated with Janmohamed. Group singing reflected a spirit of community, confidence, and ministry. The feeling of reciting unison devotional poems at *jama'atkhana*[2] aligned with similar feelings evoked through singing choral harmony in jazz and chamber choirs at school. This alignment spoke to him about an esotericism, a deep connection to the spirit and with others beyond which words could convey. Group singing and music making affirmed for Janmohamed the values of caring for others, joining with others to create beauty, working together, generosity of spirit, compassion, inclusion, pluralism, and connecting to the divine. Jose Abreu (2009), founder of *El Sistema,* a children's choir and orchestra in Venezuela, eloquently describes how ensemble music making is an example of a school for social life:

> . . . because to sing and to play together means to intimately coexist toward perfection and excellence, following a strict discipline of organization and coordination in order to seek the harmonic interdependence of voices and instruments . . . a spirit of solidarity and fraternity among them, [to] develop their self-esteem and foster the ethical and aesthetical values related to the music in all its senses.

For Janmohamed, music became a metaphor for life itself, a life that resonated and reflected the shared values of his faith, of his cultural heritage, and of Canada itself. Music made it possible to feel comfortably Muslim and Canadian at the same time.

The Journey

Janmohamed's ongoing personal search for identity informed his passion for bringing people together and enabling a sense of belonging through music. His love for music and building community eventually came together through the formation of the Vancouver Ismaili Muslim Youth Choir (VIMYC).[3]

As the conductor, Janmohamed's first task was to work with the Ismaili community to establish a vision for the choir and an artistic direction that would meet both musical and community goals. The vision was initially set: to create a safe space for youth who shared a passion for singing and choral music, to become a world-class choir, and to aim for excellence in a cappella choral music through folk and popular songs that resonated with the youth and community experience. However, world events and negative media perspectives on Islam soon compelled Janmohamed and some members of the choir to think beyond the choir's initial goals. The call for increased dialogue with others and putting forward a positive view of Islam became apparent. The choir would make the ongoing search for identity and its expression in a plural Canada an integral part of the vision and process.

The Artistic Direction—Repertoire

> Whatever its vernacular forms, the language of art, more so when it is spiritually inspired, can be a positive barrier-transcending medium of discourse, manifesting the depths of the human spirit.
>
> —Aga Khan (2003)

The artistic programming and repertoire became the primary focus to meet the goals of the choir. A major challenge (and strength), however, was the fact that Islam would not be a monolithic faith and that Ismailis, an ethnically diverse community, lived in more than twenty-five countries around the world. Which music would the choir sing? How would the choir bring focus to the repertoire? Fortunately, although their traditions, languages, and art forms varied from country to country, Ismaili ethical and spiritual life would be deeply rooted in the esoteric use of the intellect to provide the conduit for spiritual search, under the guidance of the Imam. It was through this element of using the intellect, engaging reason, ethics, and aesthetics, that the choir underwent a process of inquiry and research. The artistic direction included several criteria to select and program repertoire.

- First, to determine music that was familiar to the group—music that reflected not only the students' contemporary/popular experience but also the Ismaili community's diverse cultural heritages; the music would contain recognizable melodies, rhythms, languages, intentions, and/or narratives
- Second, to research music that was unfamiliar to the group—music from around the world that demonstrated linguistic and stylistic diversity, spiritual inspiration, and shared values, regardless of religious or cultural affiliation
- Third, to program music for which scores of arrangements and compositions already existed

The choir's programs often juxtaposed familiar with unfamiliar, traditional with contemporary, and spiritual with the material. Whatever it was, in some way the repertoire was relevant to the group, to the faith community, and to the larger context of a diverse and plural Canada. A naturally intercultural repertoire emerged, creating a spirit of inclusion, acceptance, dialogue, and exchange.

Despite the joy the choir found in singing music such as Duruflé's "Ubi Caritas," Celine Dion's "My Heart Will Go On," choral arrangements of "Lor Lai Bache Ma" (from Afghanistan) or "Malaika" (from Kenya), something was missing. The choir still did not perform or present devotional music specifically rooted in the Ismaili religious traditions. The reason was twofold: First, much of the Ismaili devotional poetry and chants (*ginan, qasida,* and *zikr*) were ceremonial in nature and not easily accessible for public presentation. Second, congregational recitations were traditionally sung in unison. Very little, if any, choral arrangements or compositions of this devotional music existed. To perform any of this repertoire, the choir would need to research, discuss with, and obtain guidance or permission from community elders and leaders. The choir would also need to commission arrangements or compose choral renditions themselves.

As the choir began to expand beyond interpreting and performing the music of others, it was an altogether profound experience to walk into rehearsal and hear "Halleluiah" mixed with "Allahu Akbar," or traditional chants in three-part harmony as a member in the back of the room added a beat box to the already full choral sound. Improvisation allowed for experimentation and sowed the seeds for future intercultural compositions and arrangements. Choristers combined traditional Ismaili chants with songs of other faiths and cultures and added elements from popular genres of music such as spoken word, rap, poetry, and vocal percussion. In the safety of the rehearsal room, singers discovered different combinations of sounds, finding ways to respect and understand commonalities, embrace differences, make connections, and create unique expressions of identity. When improvisations became unwieldy, the students themselves intervened, asking each other questions and negotiating creative license with informed, responsible expression. Whether conscious or not, the choir's commitment to their ethical and historic traditions guided them every step of the way.

For the choir, these organic moments of creativity, problem solving, and inquiry strengthened relational bonds and added layers of depth, inspiration, and profound spiritual and ethical engagement in the traditions. When the choir found itself in almost any informal space, it was an unspoken invitation for harmony to burst from within the circle, whether in the courtyards of the Ismaili Centers, on the public transit system on the way to a concert, or in the waiting lounge at the airport. Singing became a catalyst for dialogue about faith, identity, personal stories, histories, music, and life. Hanif, a longtime musician and Canadian Ismaili Muslim Youth Choir (CIMYC) alumnus, remarks:

> Before becoming involved in Ismaili choirs, I was a musician and an Ismaili Muslim—neither world played a part in the development and growth of the other, and both remained separate. Now the idea of the two being unrelated seems ludicrous. To me, music is a form of devotion in itself, and when performed with a spiritual undertone, the result is surreal. I have certainly become much more cognizant of my faith, and performing with my fellow Ismailis has triggered a series of feelings within me, which have driven me to independently learn more about the practices and ethics of my faith. [I] am able to take part in the making of music, in a way that's so different from anything I know, and give back to my spiritual community. (Shariff, personal communication, 2009)

The Narratives

How the choir programmed the repertoire was as significant as the repertoire itself. The choir wove narratives linking the repertoire and framing their choices within an overarching artistic vision. Ongoing mentorship from elders and scholars well-versed in Ismaili and Muslim history, theology, civilization, and contemporary thought helped the choir to critically review the repertoire and weave the music into narratives relevant and vital to the ethical and spiritual underpinnings of the community. The artistic program often sparked dialogue in rehearsals about relevance, meaning, and association, informing the narratives and contributing to an even stronger sense of identity and connection to the music.

The rehearsal became a laboratory and vehicle for search and learning where the choir made meaning and shaped unique expressions of identity. The ongoing quest for choral beauty and relevance fostered critical inquiry, creativity, understanding, compassion, and intellectual engagement. The musical juxtapositions (the familiar with the unfamiliar, the Muslim with the Christian, the African with the Afghan, folk songs with devotional songs) enabled the choir members to understand themselves and informed their understanding of others within a multicultural Canada. Nafeesa, a longtime VIMYC member and CIMYC alumnus, notes:

> In Ismaili choir we fostered an environment where young people could explore their creativity, culture, and spirituality and not worry about being judged harshly. We forged ahead and melded religious fare with harmony, improvisation, jazz, and even beat-boxing. The choir for me became a symbol of where my community is currently and where it is going. We are at a crossroads where young people want to take the reins and create their own understanding of their identity, but we still have one foot firmly planted in the world of our parents who came from outside Canada. Whether it was through a traditional choral piece, a Swahili folk song, or devotional poem in four-part harmony, the choir taught me how we can use music to express the conflicting "hats" we wear. (Karim, personal communication, 2009)

Singing choral music together touched a sacred core, illumined a way of life, and connected the choir members to each other and the world around them. The inherent social values, spiritual connections, and unified pursuit of beauty and inquiry resonated with the teachings of the faith and compelled the choristers to learn more. Musical journeys and life journeys were not separate from their faith; for the choir members, their material and spiritual lives informed each other. As it was for Janmohamed, it was indeed possible for the choir as well to be Canadian and Muslim at the same time, affirming the co-existence of their multicultural identities.

Growing Up Choral

Choir members' families were also "growing up choral." Siblings, some at the same time and some years apart, joined the choir. Parents and families became a part of the social fabric of the choral community. Parents and grandparents ensured that students got to choir rehearsals, attended concerts, volunteered in various capacities, and contributed to the formation of the students' spiritual, social, and musical identities. It became common to hear parents and grandparents sharing personal reflections after a concert, reminiscing, telling stories, and dialoguing about topics as wide-ranging as what a song meant to the importance of music as a door to communication. Mehnaz Thawer, co-author, longtime VIMYC member, administrator, and CIMYC alumnus recalls:

> My mom would talk about our practice sessions at home. My mom grew up in a very different cultural context, and yet, she would go so far as to give words of musical advice: "Honey, that was a little off, I think!" Over the many years I've been in choir, the musical experiences have augmented and deepened our relationships and these experiences have stayed with us. (Thawer, personal communication, 2008)

Although choral music (in the Western sense of the word) was not historically part of the social, cultural, or religious fabric of the Ismaili community, it was a formative part of the lives of many parents and grandparents who participated in church-based musical activities during their time at Catholic boarding schools in Europe, Africa, and elsewhere. Singing hymns, playing the piano, or attending Christmas mass was, for some, their only access to a spiritual heritage while away at school. Hearing the Ismaili choir singing choral music, particularly hymns or Christian spiritual music, reinforced for these members of the community a sense of belonging and reconciled any sense of separation between their Muslim and Canadian/Western identities.

Community Investment

The community's investment went much deeper than simply a supporting role. Community leaders began to understand and see the value of choral music and its benefits. In an effort to "go national," the community leadership initiated the Canadian Ismaili Muslim Youth Choir—first as a pilot project in 2005, and again in 2007 to commemorate the Golden Jubilee of His Highness the Aga Khan. The national choir was an auditioned chamber choir of sixteen youths from across the country, modeled after groups like the provincial and national youth choirs of Canada. The CIMYC performed for Ismaili community audiences and high-profile events during several weekend retreats in various cities across Canada and recorded a CD in 2008. The choir members brought with them very different histories and musical backgrounds. Some singers had only had the experience of singing devotional poetry while others had taken private voice lessons, sung in musicals, and sung in choirs on a regular basis. Because of the range of experience, the choir worked through many challenges to find a place of ease and common ground on which to begin its work. The jaw-dropping moments when individual singers sang for each other what they knew best fortified the choristers' resolve and taught the members of the choir to respect each other and work with unique differences to achieve excellence in choral music. Diverse audiences pushed the singers to work harder and find new ways to make meaning and bring relevance. Like the VIMYC, the national choir became a pathway for creative expression, formation of identity, and building strong and lasting friendships.

Audience Response

While the choir was proud to perform for external audiences, they were equally proud to perform for Ismaili community audiences. Audiences of up to eight hundred people (families, children, parents, and grandparents) would attend local concerts, sitting wherever they could find space, whether on a chair, against a wall, or on the carpeted floors of social halls and community centers. At concerts in Edmonton and Montreal, the audience members were even seated at the base of the conductor's podium.

The choral concert took on a new identity where the audience and choir were one. There was no separation. The line between performer and audience, the distinction between formal and informal, was blurred. What at first was quite disconcerting for the choir was quickly embraced. The choir were no longer entertainers. They were a source of knowledge, sharing their music with family. The choir felt empowered and supported. They belonged. Nafeesa reports:

> Regardless of how our music touches someone, I'm amazed at the power we have to connect with people. It's a testament to how music is the ultimate bridge builder and how the human voice is truly the universal instrument. (Karim, personal communication, 2009)

The choir became a source of pride for the community. Audiences responded and made connections that in turn uplifted and empowered the choristers to be and give the best that they could. Janmohamed recalls a conversation with an audience member who reported how each layer of harmony on the devotional chants led her one step closer to reaching the divine. After a summer outdoor concert, another audience member felt that her "outside world matched her inside world." In a green room in a local social hall before a concert, a volunteer greeted the choir with open arms exclaiming, "Our choir is here! Welcome!" She only knew two of the choir members, yet she greeted the whole choir as her own. After a concert in Edmonton, one community member remarked: "The choir is like a flower blossoming. All the different voices come together to make something beautiful, just like our Ismaili volunteers work together in unity." Members of the choir began to feel the impact that choral music had on themselves, their audiences, and their community.

The choral experience became a metaphor and a catalyst for insight and understanding. What started out as a singing initiative evolved into the choir members' own search for identity and gradually became a vehicle of search and identity for many community members as well. In this close-knit community, the conductor's story became the choir's story, the choir's story became the community's story, and the community's story in turn became the choir's.

Something More

For audiences and choristers alike, the Ismaili choir was certainly something more than a reason to be entertained. It was about a journey and a process for young people to contribute to the dynamic social and spiritual fabric of the community. It was about building trust and safe space for youth searching for a sense of belonging and identity. It was about empowering and enabling individual strengths to come together for the betterment of the whole. It was about beauty and relationships. It was about who the singers had become through inquiry, making mistakes together, improvising in stairwells, interpreting the music of others, collaborating, and singing together. It was about a journey that touched the hearts and minds of not only the choir members but of their families and their audiences. Finally, it was about young people confidently expressing who they are in a plural Canada, putting forward a positive view of Islam, shaping stories, and building for the future.

As the poet Mevlana Rumi (Barks & Moyne, 1995, p. 36) exclaimed, "There are hundreds of ways to kneel and kiss the ground." For the Ismaili choir, choral singing became one of the ways to revere the divine. Singing became a gateway to something intangible and ineffable. It became an essential part of the choir members' identities. It was who they were, who they had become, and who they imagined themselves to be.

Transformation

Working with the Vancouver and Canadian Ismaili Muslim Youth Choir has been transformational for both the choir members and the musical director, Janmohamed. Community music can definitely focus on achieving a magical choral sound and vocal excellence, yet effective community music making pushes its participants beyond technical and aesthetic pursuits. Community music is about knowledge transfer. It is an exchange, not a top-down approach. Community music is about establishing a safe space to critically inquire, to make meaning, to search for identity, to engage community, and to create together. Community music allows us to feel, think, and dream together. Community music offers a pathway to seek understanding of God's creation, of beauty, of oneself, of others, and of the world around us.

Moving Forward

Working within one faith community illuminates one way of engaging in choral music. However, can these lessons be applied in or across diverse cultural contexts? Can these lessons be applied in public settings where participants are not from the same faith community or do not share spiritually inspired value systems? What would that look like, and how would it play out? How would the practitioner adapt the process to make it work? It is definitely an exciting road ahead. May we continue to engage and teach to our passion to bring positive community music experiences to all people worldwide.

COMMUNITY CHOIRS IN FAITH-BASED SETTINGS

In the United States, the Sunday morning church choir is a longtime mainstay of the Christian worship setting. Even today, with the emergence of praise bands and song leaders as alternatives to traditional music, many churches still offer a worship service whose singing is led by a choir. And in many instances, the American church choir has spilled out of its pews and into musical venues in the local community. Unfortunately, it is difficult to identify these faith-based community choirs, as they often function under the radar.

Professional choral organizations (American Chroal Directors Association; Chorus America) and most choir directors view community choirs and faith-based choirs (i.e., the church choir) as two distinct entities: (1) the typical adult community choir, having no religious affiliation, but more of a geographical connection, and (2) the church choir, a group of singers attached to a specific church (building, if you will) who perform weekly for purposes of worship. Therefore, community choirs in faith-based settings defy easy categorization and, consequently, identification.

A recent study by Chorus America (2009) claims that there are twelve thousand professional and community choirs in the United States, and 216,000 choirs found in the various religious denominations. Other research shows there is much overlapping of these communities: 67 percent of chorus members surveyed say they regularly attend a church, synagogue, or mosque (Chorus America, 2009), and 24 percent of community singers surveyed also sing in faith-based choruses (Bell, 2004).

What, who, and where are these community choirs with faith-based affiliations? How do these organizations come together, and what are their performance goals? How do these choirs represent or cut across the denominational spectrum? This section will present three particular settings where choral singers join together in organized choirs that have faith-based underpinnings.

Ecumenical Church Choir Festivals

Probably the most common example of a community choir gathering with a faith-based membership is the church choir festival, an assembly of members of various church choirs who come together to perform a specific concert or worship service of sacred choral music. This may be a one-time event or, in some cases, an annual occasion. These choir festivals are difficult to document as they tend to be localized (drawing from specific geographical areas) or restrictive of their participants (featuring choirs from only the Presbyterian or Methodist denominations).

With an ecumenical church choir festival, a smaller community can produce a large choral performance by combining singers from many area church choirs. Much of the responsibility for such a festival rests on a creative and energetic organizer who must plan all of the programming logistics. Several directors may share the responsibilities of leading rehearsals, conducting the performance, and providing the performance site. The challenges are numerous: finding a sanctuary with a chancel area or choir loft big enough to hold several dozen singers, having enough copies of music for everyone, printing programs, coordinating schedules, and so forth. But such an event, while heavy in minutiae, provides an opportunity for choirs to sing choral literature that the average small church choir could not present on its own. Whether it is an annual Messiah performance (rehearsed ahead of time), or a Messiah "Sing" (i.e., bring your own score, with no rehearsal) or a festival of worship anthems, these choir festivals bring together unique communities of believers who willingly share their faith.

An outstanding example of such an ecumenical gathering is the Choral Festival Weekend at the Northport (New York) First Presbyterian Church. For ten years, the Music and Ministry Committee, led by organist Deborah Jenks, has sponsored a weekend festival that offers area church choirs and individual singers the opportunity to sing under the direction of an accomplished choral conductor. To participate in the October weekend, participants must learn the repertoire ahead of time, and they may attend "preview" rehearsals before the weekend, but no audition is required. Up to fifty volunteer singers have packed the small choir loft for the unique opportunity to sing under well-known conductors like Anton Armstrong, Marguerite Brooks, Timothy Sharp, Constantina Tsolainou, and Simon Carrington (who conducted in 2010).

Sometimes these small choir festivals take on a life of their own, as in the case of the annual Ocean Grove (New Jersey) Annual Choir Festival, now in its fifty-fifth year. What began in 1955 as a small gathering of area church choirs has evolved into an annual event with a festival choir of one thousand voices. Singers come together on a summer Sunday afternoon, rehearse pre-selected popular church anthems, and perform them that evening during the regular church service. Contributing to the success of the Ocean Grove Annual Choir Festival is an ideal facility for supporting and sustaining a festival choir: a 6,700 seat open-air auditorium and 10,000-rank pipe organ, normally used for camp meeting services. Some years, singers from 250 different church choirs participate (Ocean Grove Annual Choir Festival, 2009).

Faith-Based Community Choirs Beyond Sunday Morning

Faith-based community choirs—a collection of singers that draw their membership from different churches and rehearse and perform above and beyond the regular weekly Sunday church choir—are found primarily in urban areas. Again, the leadership of such an organization must be an energetic choral director wishing to extend a musical ministry beyond Sunday morning.

An excellent example of this is the Community Christian Choir, Inc., in New Jersey, an interfaith group of auditioned singers that began in 1995. The singers now represent more than forty-seven churches of various Christian denominations throughout central and southern New Jersey and Bucks County, Pennsylvania. This non-profit, ecumenical choir performs benefit concerts and has raised and donated over $135,000 to many local charities. The adult choir also has an outreach program where they sing and minister to the inmates at the Federal Correctional Institution at Fort Dix, New Jersey.

So successful is the Community Christian Choir (CCC) that there are now several singing divisions for adults as well as children. Adult and children's choirs are composed of singers of a variety of skill levels, and the children's choir has divisions for kindergarten and up. Since 2004, the CCC has been focusing its collective energies on building a Christian Center for the Arts. Although their primary goal is buying land and building a permanent facility, many arts activities are already in place, including summer theater camps and piano, strings, drama, art, and technology programs. Their website (www.ccchoir.com) includes a link to a fifteen-minute video on the history and mission of the choir and an extensive interview with founder and director Pat Weitz.

Another example of a faith-based community choir is the National Christian Choir (NCC) in the greater Washington, DC, area. NCC has a performance history of more than twenty-five years, and more than 150 singers from over one hundred different churches rehearse weekly for their ten to twelve annual concerts. Performance tours to popular venues (the National Cathedral, Crystal Cathedral in California, and various religious conventions) keep the choir busy. The choir records annually and sponsors a weekly inspirational radio broadcast, "Psalm 95," which is heard on more than three hundred Christian radio stations across America and Canada. The NCC is a non-profit corporation governed by a board of directors and financed primarily through the supporters' gifts. Founded in 1984 and directed by C. Harry Causey, the choir's vision is "to be widely recognized as a national and international model of excellence for Christian choirs and worshipers, providing materials and events to equip and inspire others to better serve our Lord." The NCC website (www.nationalchristianchoir.org) provides details about performances, tours, recordings, and the radio program.

Community Choirs for Religious Events

Special religious events—church assemblies, evangelical revivals, and denominational conventions—utilize choirs to support and enhance the immediate worship experience. For such occasions, a choir is usually composed of volunteer singers from the immediate area in the tradition of Protestant camp-meeting choirs. Even today, two of the oldest active camp-meeting sites in Chautauqua (New York) and Ocean Grove (New Jersey) have summer-only choirs, composed of residents and vacationers who enjoy religious music. One or two rehearsals per week prepare the choir for Sunday services.

Perhaps the best-known example of special religious meetings is the long-running "Crusades" with evangelical preacher Billy Graham. An advance team arrives in town, ahead of the Crusade, to find volunteers for the numerous jobs. A choir director recruits and rehearses volunteer singers to perform as a united chorus for the Crusade, which can run for several days. Of course, any singer in the choir is guaranteed a fairly good seat in the house and a close view of Mr. Graham as he preaches. At the conclusion of the Crusade, the choir is disbanded, the stage is struck, and Graham's personnel move onto another town.

Graham's last New York City evangelistic Crusade was held in June 2005 and demonstrated a vigorous attempt by organizers to create an urban religious community, provide staff for the crusade, and pool necessary resources (Newman, 2005b). The Graham organization attempted to contact every Protestant church (over twelve thousand) within fifty miles of New York City, and 1,400 congregations, representing eighty denominations, agreed to participate. Assembled from these churches was an amazing 1,200-voice Billy Graham 2005 Crusade Choir.

Cliff Barrows, Graham's longtime music director, explained the choir's membership formula as "first come, first served." In the brief practice just before the opening service, volunteer singers quickly rehearsed the music, ranging from Graham's signature song "How Great Thou Art" to contemporary praise music. Assembled on a makeshift stage in front of a crowd of seventy thousand people, the mass choir led the music for three days of programs, while the message was simultaneously translated into thirteen languages.

Similar special community-based religious choirs were needed for the many ecumenical services and masses led by Pope Benedict XVI during his April 2008 visit to New York City (Catholic News Service, 2009). Most memorable among these services were the mass at St. Patrick's Cathedral for priests, deacons, and members of religious orders (St. Patrick's Cathedral, 2009) and the public mass at Yankee Stadium for fifty-five thousand celebrants. Service music ranged from traditional Gregorian chants and Renaissance polyphonic motets to the music of well-known composers such as Mozart, Bach, and Brahms. In keeping with the increasing Spanish-speaking population in the archdioceses, the services incorporated bilingual hymnody. Several composers contributed with new works or arrangements of existing works for orchestra. At Yankee Stadium, a fifty-eight-piece orchestra and select two-hundred-member chorus from the diocese led the music from behind home plate.

While choirs in faith-based settings are not usually thought of as community choirs, they fulfill all of the requisites of the definition of a community choir. The members come from all walks of life and represent their communities; the singers create unique choral personalities and sounds which are grounded in faith and which are socially and culturally diverse. Choristers enjoy and learn from their experience and demonstrate their commitment to their faith through their participation in the choral arts.

In summary, music continues to play a significant role for communities of faith. Whether Buddhist or Jewish or practitioners of other belief systems found throughout the world, music is the common denominator for spiritual expression and a corporate worship experience. This writing only presents two specific examples— Ismaili Muslim and Christian; other communities are encouraged to share their stories of success with us.

ACKNOWLEDGMENTS

Hussein Janmohamed gratefully acknowledges his family, community, and alumni of both Vancouver and Canadian Ismaili Muslim Youth Choirs.

NOTES

1. The Shia Ismaili Muslims, generally known as the Ismailis, are a community of ethnically and culturally diverse peoples living in more than twenty-five countries around the world, united in their allegiance to His Highness Prince Karim Aga Khan (known to the Ismailis as Mawlana Hazar Imam) as the forty-ninth hereditary Imam (Spiritual Leader) and direct descendant of Prophet Muhammad (peace be upon him and his family) (Islamic Publications Limited, 2009).

2. A *jama'atkhana* is a gathering place for Muslims to worship and join in fellowship. Although this congregational space is most frequently a mosque, other spaces may be used.

3. The Vancouver Ismaili Muslim Youth Choir was founded in 1998. However, the first Ismaili Choir in Canada was established in Toronto in 1982.

BIBLIOGRAPHY

Abreu, J. (2009). Transforming kids through music. *TED.* Retrieved from www.ted.com

Aga Khan, H. H. (2003). Opening address. *The Qur'an and its creative expressions* (pp. xix–xxi). London: Oxford University Press in association with The Institute of Ismaili Studies.

Barks, C., & Moyne, J. (1995). *The essential Rumi.* San Francisco: HarperCollins.

Bell, C. L. (2004). Update on community choirs and singing in the United States. *International Journal of Research in Choral Singing, 2* (1), 39–52. Retrieved from www.choralresearch.org

Canadian Ismaili Muslim Youth Choir. Retrieved from www.theismaili.org/cms/620/Golden-Jubilee-marks-the-formation-of-the-Canadian-Jamats-national-youth-choir

Catholic News Service. (2009). Retrieved from www.catholicnews.com/data/stories/cns/0801745.htm

Chorus America. (2009). *How children, adults, and communities benefit from choruses: The chorus impact study.* Retrieved from www.chorusamerica.org/about_choralsinging.cfm

Community Christian Choir. (2009). Retrieved from www.ccchoir.org

Islamic Publications Limited. (2009). *The Ismaili community.* Retrieved from www.theismaili.org/cms/16/The-Ismaili-Community

National Christian Choir. (2009). Retrieved from www.nationalchristianchoir.org

Newman, A. (2005a, June 19). 1,200 voices with faith in a formula for success. *The New York Times*. Retrieved from www.nytimes.com/2005/06/19/nyregion/19choir .html?ref=billygraham

Newman, A. (2005b, June 23). Mounting a Billy Graham crusade takes prayers, mailings and many, many chairs. *The New York Times*. Retrieved from www.nytimes.com/2005/06/23/ nyregion/23crusade.html?ref=billygraham

Northport (New York) Choral Festival Weekend. Retrieved from www.fpcnorthport.org

Ocean Grove Annual Choir Festival. (2009). Retrieved from www.ogcma.org/pages/choirfestival

St. Patrick's Cathedral, New York. (2009). Retrieved from www.saintpatrickscathedral.org/ papal_visit.html

Chapter Nineteen

Community Music and Sustainability Worldwide: Ecosystems of Engaged Music Making

Huib Schippers and Richard Letts

Community music activities distinguish themselves from most other music practices in Western cultures by their manner and level of engagement and participation. While it is easy to get the impression, on the basis of a literature overview, that community music making was "invented" in the 1970s (Higgins, 2006), in fact, the very strength of the phenomenon—its deep roots in community—is, and has been, characteristic of many musics across the world for many centuries. This chapter explores this diversity and relates it to issues of sustainability, an understanding of the ecosystems of community music worldwide.

Writing from Australia, it is difficult to ignore the longevity of the musical traditions of the Aboriginal people (more than forty thousand years old) and the strong role their songs still play in forging and supporting community links and linking community to their country, history, and law (e.g., Marett, 2005). In Africa, the very concept of *Ubuntu* (which Desmond Tutu defined in 2008 as "the fact that you can't exist as a human being in isolation; it speaks about our interconnectedness") illustrates the importance of community, which resonates in every aspect of music making. This approach is widely shared below the Sahara. "One monkey, no show," they call it in West Africa (Schippers, 2010).

At the same time, brass music traditions in European villages and towns share very similar characteristics: all generations in a village find joy and take pride as they engage in joint music making. Playing music together becomes a distinctive feature of that community, contributing to both an individually and collectively constructed sense of identity. Much the same can be said for the community choirs and community orchestras, which tend to flourish in more urban areas. The key to sustainability rests with the profound connections among those involved in the various components of music making. This does not only apply to community music in Western countries but across the world. In addition to the practices common in Europe, Australia, and Africa, a myriad of traditions throughout North America, Latin America, and Asia have developed on these principles.

Although many traditional practices remain fertile, forces of globalization have eroded some of this ground, especially over the past fifty years, and this is perhaps illustrated most readily by the plight of many forms of traditional music. While community music is, of course, not confined to the practice of traditional music, an overview of the state of the latter for the International Music Council (Letts, 2006) reveals a large number of issues related to social dynamics and community. This study voices great concern for the vitality of traditional musics, many of which are in danger of extinction.

The reason for this eradication, in most cases, is change in the community context from which these musics grew. The "Rice Pounding Song" is not sung anymore because machines have taken over the task. As villagers migrate to the cities, village music has been replaced by city music or international music. Traditional music slides toward oblivion; in many situations, only a very few elders still carry the knowledge.

> Some of these [minority styles of music] might become extinguished or disappear forever, unless government and citizens protect and promote them properly (at mass media level) by distributing them nationally (through recordings, thematic festivals typical of one style or the other, cultural weeks abroad, documentaries, publications, and print). Up to now this musical diversity has survived against all the odds. However, how much longer will it be able to survive in the face of globalization? (Hassan Mégri, quoted in Letts, 2006, p. 129)

Sometimes, governments do act to preserve musical traditions. While they may record and archive these legacies, one can argue that programs that attempt to bring them back into the regular life of the community are of greater urgency. The question is whether they will remain unchanged as museum pieces or will be allowed to change to adapt to new contexts. This represents a fundamentally different approach.

The Chinese government is one of many to inaugurate a formal program for the survival of traditional musics. In 1979, the Chinese Ministry of Culture initiated a program of rescuing the ethnic cultural heritage (called "The Great Wall of Chinese Culture") aimed at "inheriting while keeping [cultural heritage] alive" (quoted in Letts, 2006, p. 122). "The significance of this program lies in the 'keeping alive' and 'inheriting,' which are distinct from the usually called 'rescue,' which is static (only aimed at preserving them in the form of characters, audio and video)" (Zhang Xian, quoted in Letts, 2006, p. 123).

An educational group, the Pumi People's Traditional Culture Learning Group, is an example of the "keeping alive" or cherishing cultural heritages. The group "organizes the young people in the village to learn the traditional culture and performing skills with the senior artists. It is expected that the ethnic culture now facing extinction can be carried forward in this way" (Letts, 2006, p. 123). However, Chen Zhe expresses concerns about the wider viability of such an approach; he argues that the situation remains critical:

> The fundamental causes are the change and disappearance of the forms of production and the lifestyle that the Chinese people have depended on over thousands of years. Large-scale collective labor has disappeared, hence the extinction of the folk songs that were associated with those productive modes, e.g., work songs (boat trackers' work, transplanting rice seedlings, ramming), sacrifice ceremony music (sacrifice ceremony), etc. The deaths of

the old people who were engaged in these labors have caused the disappearance of most of the music, too. Pessimistically speaking, I think it still remains questionable whether we can keep the traditions and cultures (including those listed by UNESCO [United Nations Educational, Scientific and Cultural Organization]) alive in China through the programs that have already been carried out or just put them into the museums. (Letts, 2006, p. 123)

Vietnam, as a case in point, is fascinating and multifaceted and reveals issues faced by many cultures worldwide. Since the commencement of the feudal dynasties (938–1884), the Vietnamese have had to contend with invasions and fight for their independence. Letts (2006) writes:

> Over the 15th to 18th centuries, the areas that minorities inherited were given their autonomy and blood relationships were established by marriage to the Vietnamese royalty. Thanks to that policy, the minorities were entirely free to preserve and develop their own ethnic cultures . . . That is why the diversity of cultural generally and of traditional music of each Vietnamese ethnic group particularly, could develop and exist until our times. (p. 124)

After turbulent periods with French and American wars, Vietnam is now headed by Communist Party leadership,[1] which has actively supported continuation of the traditional ethnic cultures. And as in China, a major long-term program, spanning fifty years, has collected traditional musics in archives that currently contain over twenty-five thousand musical works. The community basis for much of this music, however, is rapidly waning. Leading traditional music scholar To Ngoc Than comments:

> The biggest part of traditional music is the folk music. This music was created and existed closely with the everyday life of the people, 95% of whom are farmers living in rural, self-sufficient communities. Now [that] the economy in the country is moving toward industrializing and modernizing, the life of these people fundamentally changes. Many social-cultural activities occupied a very important role in the former society; now they have lost the social bases for which they were created and existed. They are no longer unseparated from the everyday life of the people. (quoted in Letts, 2006, pp. 124–125)

To Ngoc Than mentions the rise of Western-style pop music as an additional threat to community music, but the government-driven "so-called improvement, modernization and theatricalization which in fact is a process of Europeanization using traditional culture and music" (quoted in Letts, 2006, pp. 124–125) also places traditional community music practices in an exigent environment.

An informant from East Africa notes the role of the colonists in undermining local cultures and imposing alien concepts on various aspects of cultural and political life. He writes about Kenya, Uganda, and Tanzania and refers specifically to the situation of local musics, making the point that many African countries are constructs of convenience of former colonizers who agglomerated peoples of different languages and cultures into an artificial national structure. Given this history, the idea of national traditions is a difficult one. The colonial authorities and missionaries suppressed local cultures and imposed a Western education system that influenced the thinking of the indigenous people. In music, this has resulted, for instance, in composers working in hybrid genres, not necessarily to universal approval. Despite this, local musics survive often in the interest of their own communities (Letts, 2006, p. 127). The circumstances of a general loss of local traditions are similar to those in Vietnam. The notion of a national music has also been imposed by governments on their own people, the most dramatic example being that of the Union of Soviet Socialist Republics (USSR) in Eurasia between 1922 and 1991.

Reports from Latin America show the same issues with regard to traditional musics. Argentina reports that "local practices are not supported or weakened, they are ignored" (Letts, 2006, p. 130). In ancient times, the Aymara culture occupied common territory in what are now Perú, Chile, and Bolivia. In October 2005, at Tiwanaku's sacred hill, these countries celebrated a first re-encounter of Aymara culture, revaluing native dance and music (Letts, 2006, p. 111). The Mexican National Council for Culture and Arts (CONACULTA) has developed several programs that effectively support traditional genres. One of these programs promotes the creation of music with traditional characteristics. Another one offers grants for composers of national genres. There are workshops to develop performance, traditional techniques, and the construction of instruments (Letts, 2006, p. 130).[2]

Traditional musics arose from contexts of time and place when travel and communications were very limited. Each, therefore, served a small population, and differences between practices, even within a small geographical area, could be very marked. As communications widened, local differences could fade. In the current era, "wide" seems to equal "global." The influences of new technologies, urbanization, and globalization have undercut the basis for sustaining that rich diversity. This is both inevitable, to some extent, as part of a system of discarding and renewal, and regrettable where communities are not given the time and resources to adapt to change. While there are examples of efforts to replant musical traditions into new social contexts, if the connection between a traditional music and its community is broken, from the point of view of the community music philosophy, what is most important is that there are other musical forms in which community members are participants and not merely consumers. There is ample evidence of that.

NINE DOMAINS

One of the most extensive studies of community music to date juxtaposes six community music settings across Australia (Bartleet, Dunbar-Hall, Letts, & Schippers, 2009). Rather than define community music, we identified nine domains of community music to help understand this phenomenon in its myriad forms, as shown in Table 19.1.

Strikingly, almost all of these domains not only constitute characteristics of community music making, but also point to factors crucial to sustainability. It is worth briefly reflecting on each of the domains and considering how they relate to sustainability.

Infrastructure

Community music activities tend to be highly flexible in their demands and use of infrastructure, rehearsal spaces, instruments, and other equipment. While many

Table 19.1. Nine Domains of Community Music in Australia

	1) Infrastructure	2) Organization	3) Visibility/PR
Structures & practicalities	• Buildings • Performance spaces • Equipment • Regulations (e.g., council by-laws) • Funding • Earned income • Legal issues (e.g., copyright, insurance, incorporation)	• Method of organization • Inspired leadership structures & roles • Division & delegation of tasks (e.g., artistic, administrative) • Mentoring of new leaders • Membership issues • Forward planning • Links to peak & related bodies	• Public visibility of CM activities • Community centers as identifiable places of activity • Attention to promotion • Audience development • Membership development • Networking/building influence/ building loyalty • Exposure in local press/media • Awards/prizes and champions • Issues of prestige for participants
	4) Relationship to place	**5) Social engagement**	**6) Support/networking**
People & personnel	• Connections to location (e.g., urban, regional, rural, & remote) • Sense of belonging (e.g., connections to cultural identity) • Cultural heritage (e.g., Indigenous, immigrant communities) • Creating pride of place	• Commitment to inclusiveness (and sensitivity to issues of exclusiveness) • Creating a sense of well-being • Links to cultural & personal place • Shared musical interest in genre • Engaging the marginalized 'at-risk' or 'lost to music' at-large • Providing opportunities • Empowerment • Links to local concerns • Relationship to audience	• Links to the local community • Links to other community groups • Links to local council • Links to local businesses • Links to local service providers (e.g., police, fire, health) • Connections to national peak bodies
	7) Dynamic music making	**8) Engaging pedagogy/facilitation**	**9) Links to school**
Practice & pedagogy	• Inclusive, engaged, inspiring • Active involvement by all • Understanding how people engage • Need for training (differences between teaching adults and children) · • Short- vs. long-term orientation • Responsive to ambitions & potential of participants • Flexible relationship between audiences & performers • Purpose driven (e.g., performance goals) • Balance between process & product	• Sensitivity to differences in learning styles, abilities, age, & culture • Nurturing a sense of identity (within individuals & groups) • Commitment to inclusive pedagogies (ranging from formal, to non-formal to informal) • Sensitivity to cultural diversity • Recognizing the need to balance process & product • Embracing multiple references to quality (e.g., musical & social outcomes) • Attention to 'training the trainers'	• Identification of mutual interests • Locating CM activities in schools • Sharing of equipment & facilities • Financial/non-financial rewards for collaborations • Marrying aspects of formal & informal learning • Realizing CM as part of the curriculum • Exchange of pedagogical approaches • Support & commitment from school leadership • Awareness of regulations

Bartleet, Dunbar-Hall, Letts, & Schippers, 2009.

forms of heritage music (such as Western opera) are dependent on large amounts of support, community music is not as dependent on resources outside the community. What is striking in exploring community music practices across the world is the resourcefulness of the people involved, ranging from the village *gamelans* in Bali to the large *samba batucada* groups preparing for Carnival in Rio. Operating without any governmental support in most cases, communities find ways of realizing their musical ambitions. In some countries, however, this spirit of innovation is increasingly threatened by laws and regulations, particularly taxes, sound restrictions, and liability insurance.

Organization

There is an ambiguous relationship between organization and community music activities. One striking characteristic of almost all community music activities is the presence of very strong and inspired leadership. Seemingly, the "community music movement" in the West has reacted to the over-organization of formal musical practices. Letts (1997) describes community music as comprising "programs that, unconstrained by any educational bureaucracy, have found solutions that fit the needs of particular communities" (p. 27). Higgins (2006) takes this further and describes community music as "an active resistance towards institutionalized structures." These are interesting reflections in the face of musical ecosystems. The underlying thought appears to be that formal organization and institutionalization threaten to undermine the sustainability of a musical practice and create distance between the practice and the community.

Visibility/Public Relations

Across the world, community musicians are celebrated in their local press. Many community organizations have built excellent relationships with newspapers and news stations. Still, many great community music projects fly under the radar simply because there are no reporting structures to make them visible. As a result, there is little awareness that almost all community music projects represent fabulous value in terms of return on investment (or "bang for the buck"). This sometimes works against the interest and sustainability of community music activities but, at the same time, represents a great advantage and strength in the musical ecosystem at-large.

Relationship to Place

This chapter began with a reference to the profound and long-standing connection between song and place (or country, as Indigenous people usually call it) among Aboriginal Australians. This has yielded a remarkable longevity to some of their traditions. But similarly, we see community music being used to garner a sense of pride in even the most desolate of contemporary concrete jungles. The often-cited work of Pete Moser in Morecambe-on-Sea, "More Music in Morecambe," is a striking narrative of how a town can come to songwrite, compose, and sing about old stoves and even garbage cans in the alley behind the house and create a vigorous and enduring organization devoted to "building confidence and spirit in individuals and communities through the arts, especially music" (More Music).

Social Engagement and Support and Networking

Engagement lies at the heart of community music. Inclusiveness, interconnectedness, and relevance to contemporary issues are all keys to any vibrant and sustainable practice although, paradoxically, they also imply constant change as circumstances and issues alter.

Support and networking are closely related to social engagement. They involve anchoring music practices in an organizational environment. While professional orchestras and opera companies focus on wealthy bankers and foundations, many community music facilitators have developed great skills to increase their sustainability by creating close connections to local churches, small businesses, hospitals, or even the police.

Dynamic Music Making

The participatory nature of community music dictates musical idioms that are accessible to all and flexible in being able to adapt to the needs of specific circumstances and occasions. This creates both stability and change.

Engaging Pedagogies

While formal music education still largely depends on one-way didactic teaching, community music most often emphasizes group learning and giving everyone a voice in the final musical product to secure continuing involvement of participants with different levels of skill and ambition.

Links to Schools

While the rigid education structures of traditional schools and the fluid practices of community music practitioners may seem worlds apart, close collaboration can strengthen both. Despite obvious aspects such as sharing spaces and combining events, the interchange between musical material and pedagogical approaches holds the promise of more sustainable practices for both school and community music groups.

UNDER THE RADAR

These characteristics are vividly illustrated in eight examples of community music from Down Under. Aware of an enormous variety of community activity responding to unique, unconnected, and unreported local circumstances, the Music Council of Australia established the annual Music in Communities Awards to publicize and honor exemplary programs. Some of the winners have been the usual suspects, doing great work: bands, orchestras, and choirs. Others were not on the radar, and in some cases, jostle preconceptions about the nature of community music.

- The Gunalda Hotel Music Club is located in a pub in a small regional town. It operates on three simple principles: anyone can get up and have a go; people learn from each other; and performance needs a live audience. It fosters local talent, providing a safe place where beginners and amateur musicians get support and mentorship from professional musicians who drop in to the club for jams.
- The Mungindi Music Festival was established in a very small, isolated town. It draws audiences and participants from the entire surrounding area (even from the city) and has transformed the town's regard for itself, its place in the region, and the musical opportunities offered.
- The Women in Harmony choir, formed in 2005 after several racist incidents had rocked the local community, enables women from all cultural backgrounds to celebrate diversity by learning music in each other's languages and, at the same time, sending a powerful message about tolerance and togetherness on its own doorstep.
- The Willunga Academy of Rock provides tuition, mentoring, resources, and facilities for budding young musicians in the regional town of Willunga, South Australia. It has become an integral part of its community, helping otherwise socially isolated young people connect with others through music and performance.
- Drum Atweme is a percussion project begun as a means of encouraging school attendance by Indigenous children. Rhythms are woven around the songs and stories of the Indigenous participants' culture. The program has transformed the lives of countless Alice Springs camp-based children.
- Madjitil Moorna is an all-inclusive community choir led by Indigenous musicians; they sing contemporary and traditional Aboriginal and Torres Strait Islander music. Performances at schools and at significant cultural events enable the choir to take the music beyond the traditional community and to share its message of reconciliation and healing.
- The Sweet Freedom project creates opportunities for asylum seekers to speak for themselves through music.
- Ambient Orchestras has forty members with disabilities who come together regularly to put their own stamp on the concept of "orchestra." Instruments are modified, rhythms are loose, and an environment is created that is totally at the service of each musician's capabilities.

It is tempting to liken the diversity represented by these examples, and the hundreds of practices not mentioned here, to biodiversity. While the many different incarnations of community music may defy definition, drawing this parallel may strengthen their position in the musical ecosystem, making them tenacious enough to resist unwanted change. If all government grants and subsidies for the performing arts were suspended tomorrow (the equivalent of a meteorite for dinosaurs), almost all conservatories, schools of music, and concert halls would close their doors. One can be certain, however, that community music would still flourish in its diverse incarnations.

UNPACKING SUSTAINABILITY

Recent research into the sustainability of music traditions points strongly in the direction of the importance of community. The international research collaboration *Sustainable*

Futures for Music Cultures: Toward an Ecosystem of Musical Diversity (Schippers, 2008) identifies five key domains that strongly influence the survival of musical practices, most of which resonate strongly with the nine domains of community music:

Systems of Learning Music

This domain assesses balances between informal and formal training, notation-based and aural learning, holistic and analytical approaches, and emphasis on tangible and abstract aspects of musicking. It explores contemporary developments in learning and teaching (from master-disciple relationships to systems based on technology/the Internet), and how non-musical activities, philosophies, and approaches intersect with learning and teaching. These issues play key roles in musicking, from community initiatives to the highest level of institutionalized professional training.

Musicians and Communities

This domain examines the roles and positions of musicians and the bases of traditions within a community. It looks at the mundane realities in the existence of creative musicians, including the role of technology, media, and travel, and issues of remuneration through performances, teaching, portfolio careers, community support, tenured employment, freelancing, and non-musical activities. Cross-cultural influences and the role of the diaspora are also examined, as well as the interaction between musicians within the community.

Contexts and Constructs

This domain assesses the social and cultural contexts of musical traditions. It examines the realities of and the attitudes toward recontextualization, cross-cultural influences, authenticity, and context, and explicit and implicit approaches to cultural diversity resulting from travel, migration, or media, as well as obstacles such as poverty, prejudice, racism, stigma, restrictive religious attitudes, and issues of appropriation. It also looks at the underlying values and attitudes (constructs) that steer musical directions. These include musical tastes, aesthetics, cosmologies, socially and individually constructed identities, and gender issues, as well as (perceived) prestige, which is often underestimated as a factor in musical survival.

Infrastructure and Regulations

This domain primarily relates to the hardware of music: places to perform, compose, practice, and learn, all of which are essential for music to survive, as well as virtual spaces for creation, collaboration, learning, and dissemination. Other aspects included in this domain are the availability and/or manufacturing of instruments and other tangible resources. It also examines the extent to which regulations are conducive or obstructive to a blossoming musical heritage, including grants, artists' rights, copyright laws, sound restrictions, laws limiting artistic expression, and adverse circumstances, such as obstacles that can arise from totalitarian regimes, persecution, civil unrest, war, or the displacement of music or people.

Media and the Music Industry

This domain addresses the large-scale dissemination and commercial aspects of music. Most musicians and musical styles depend, in one way or another, on the music industry for their survival. Over the past one hundred years, the distribution of music has increasingly involved recordings, radio, television, and the Internet (e.g., podcasts, YouTube, MySpace). At the same time, many acoustic and live forms of delivery have changed under the influence of internal and external factors, leading to a wealth of new performance formats. This domain examines the ever-changing modes of distributing, publicizing, and supporting music, including the role of audiences (including consumers of recorded product), patrons, sponsors, funding bodies, and governments who buy or buy into artistic product.

Using this framework, *Sustainable Futures* explores nine highly divergent traditions to identify triggers for sustainability: Indigenous Australian music, Balinese *gamelan*, Mexican mariachi, music from the Amami Islands (Japan), North Indian classical music, Vietnamese *ca trù*, ewe percussion from Ghana, Korean *samul'nori*, and Western opera. All of these have a strong historical and/or present basis in community. In fact, it is obvious that, in this framework, the importance of community is not limited to the second domain but stretches out across the five other domains. Systems of learning music are very often community-based, as are the contexts, values, and attitudes that steer musical activity. Even infrastructure, regulations, and the music industry are often driven, or at least strongly influenced, by communities.

This allows us to conclude that, across the world, community is a key driver for engaged and sustainable music practices with great flexibility and responsiveness to ever-changing circumstances. At the same time, community music practices are more vulnerable to social change than highly commercial or government-funded music styles or genres and need to be valued and nurtured to ensure optimal benefit for the societies in which they can thrive.

NOTES

1. The Communist Party in China has a similar policy of maintaining traditional ethnic cultures.
2. See www.conaculta.com.mx/convocatorias/ for more information.

BIBLIOGRAPHY

Bartleet, B., Dunbar-Hall, P., Letts, R., & Schippers, H. (2009). *Sound Links: Community music in Australia.* Brisbane: Queensland Conservatorium Research Centre.
Green, L. (2001). *How popular musicians learn: A way ahead for music education.* Burlington, VT: Ashgate.
Higgins, L. D. (2006). *Boundary-walkers: Contexts and concepts of community music* (Unpublished doctoral thesis). University of Limerick, Limerick.

Letts, R. (1997). Music: Universal language between all nations? *International Journal of Music Education 29*, 22–31.

Letts, R. (2006). *The protection and promotion of musical diversity*. Paris: International Music Council. Retrieved from www.unesco.org/imc

Marett, A. (2005). *Songs, dreamings, and ghosts: The Wangga of North Australia*. Middletown: Wesleyan University Press.

More Music. (2010–2011). Retrieved from www.moremusic.org.uk

Schippers, H. (1997). *One monkey, no show—Culturele diversiteit in de Nederlandse muziekeducatie*. Utrecht: LOKV, Netherlands Institute for Arts Education.

Schippers, H. (2008). *Sustainable futures for music cultures: Towards an ecology of musical diversity*. Brisbane: Queensland Conservatorium Research Centre.

Schippers, H. (2010). *Facing the music: Shaping music education from a global perspective*. New York: Oxford University Press.

Small, C. (1998). *Musicking: The meanings of performing and listening*. Hanover, NH: University Press of New England.

Veblen, K., & Olsson, B. (2002). Community music: Toward an international overview. In R. Colwell & C. Richardson (Eds.), *The new handbook of research on music teaching and learning* (pp. 730–753). New York: Oxford University Press.

Chapter Twenty

Resources in Community Music

Janice L. Waldron, Steven Moser, and Kari K. Veblen

BOOKS

Cahill, A. (1998). *Community Music Handbook: A Practical Guide to Developing Music Projects and Organisations.* Strawberry Hills, NSW: Currency Press.

    Australian-based practical guide to generating and working with instrumental and vocal ensembles and community music schools.

Higgins, L. (2012). *Community Music: In Practice and Theory.* London: Oxford University Press.

    Drawing upon extensive practical experiences, this resource looks at active music making outside of formal contexts. Working with historical, ethnographic, and theoretical research, Higgins provides a rich resource for those who practice, advocate, teach, or study community music, music education, music therapy, ethnomusicology, and community cultural development.

Higgins, L., & Campbell, P. (2010). *Free to Be Musical: Group Improvisation in Music.* Lanham, MD: MENC/Rowman & Littlefield Education.

    Comprehensive and adaptable, this book offers a wealth of strategies for group musical improvisation. Suggested activities will help community musicians, educators, and therapists create expressive musical experiences with multiple participants.

Moser, P., & McKay, G. (2005). *Community Music: A Handbook.* Dorset, UK: Russell House.

    Based in UK contexts, this book provides inspiring exercises, ideas, and stories for use by communithy music (CM) workers and others.

Schipper, H. (2009). *Facing the Music: Shaping Music Education from a Global Perspective.* NY: Oxford University Press.

    Advocating a contemporary, positive, and realistic approach to cultural diversity in music education and transmission, this book is a rich resource for reflection and practice for all those involved in teaching and learning music, from policy maker to classroom teacher.

JOURNAL

The International Journal of Community Music. UK: Intellect Press. ISSN: 17526299 Online ISSN: 17526302. www.intellectbooks.co.uk/journals/view-Journal,id=149

    The *International Journal of Community Music* publishes research articles, practical discussions, timely reviews, readers' notes, and special issues concerning all aspects of community music. The editorial board is composed of leading international scholars and practitioners spanning diverse disciplines that reflect the scope of community music practice and theory.

PROJECT REPORTS

Hesser, B., & Heinemen, H. (Eds.) (2010). *Music as a Natural Resource: Solutions for Social and Ecomomic Issues: Compendium.*
   The International Council for Caring Communities (ICCC) is a not-for-profit organization that has Special Consultative status with the United Nations' Economic and Social Council (ECOSOC).

McKay, G., & Higham, B. (2011). *Connected Communities: Community Music: History and Current Practice, Its Constructions of "Community," Digital Turns and Future Soundings.* http://salford.academia.edu/georgemckay/Papers/1117860/Community_Music_History_and_ Current_Practice_its_Constructions_of_Community_Digital_Turns_and_Future_Soundings
   This is a UK-based critical examination of research into aspects of community music.

OUTREACH, EDUCATION, AND RESEARCH

The Internet's ability to bridge distance makes it a natural tool for networking and exploring resources. For community music, some helpful resources are easily accessed online. Locating these resources can be helpful in broadening the perspective of the practitioner, researcher, and community music advocate.

International

Music as a Natural Resource Initiative. (n.d.). www.musicasanaturalresource.org
   An Internet reference site of global initiatives and ongoing projects promoting music for the "sustainable community, mental and physical health, trauma survivors, learning, and peace building."

Music Without Borders. (1999—). www.musicianswithoutborders.org
   International network organization dedicated to the development of projects and events that promote healing and reconciliation through music practice and performance specific to cross-cultural exchange and development of individual and community identities.

Voices: A World Forum for Music Therapy. (n.d.). www.voices.no
   An "international journal and online community" promoting research and practice of music therapy in all delivery modes, including community music therapy.

Africa

Field Band Foundation: Developing Life Skills in Youth Through Music for Eradicating Poverty and Promoting Development. (2000—). http://www.fieldband.org.za
   South African foundation "developing life skills in youth through the medium of music and dance" using the show band or drum and bugle corps model.

The Firemaker Project. (2003—). www.zakheni.org.za/the-firemaker-project.html
   A training program for the use of music, art, and drama for clinical psychologists dealing with children affected by political conflict.

Ntonga Music School: Playing for Change. (2007—). www.playingforchange.com
  South African school focused on social learning programs, described as a "multimedia movement created to inspire, connect, and bring peace to the world through music."

Australia and New Zealand

Music Council of Australia. (1978—). www.mca.org.au
  A nationally funded music organization promoting music in all aspects of life and community throughout Australia.
Music in Communities Network. (n.d.). http://musicincommunities.org.au
  Australia's first network linking CM workers and programs, provides resources.
Sweet Freedom Inc. (n.d.). http://sweetfreedom.org.au
  A record label promoting social justice and engagement through creative projects and the development and sharing of resources and effective community engagement through scholarly research.

Central America

Departamento de Arte y Cultura. (n.d.). www.musicacedrosup.org.mx
  Collaborative community music school between the Centro Escolar Cedros and American University in Mexico.

Europe, Britain, and Ireland

Choral Allegro ONCE Valencia. (1982—). http://sites.google.com/site/coralallegrooncevalencia
  Community music organization for the blind and visually impaired in Valencia, Spain, highlighting participant success through performances throughout Europe.
Centro Didattico Musicale, Bambino al Centro, City of Rome, Italy. (1999—). www.centro didatticomusicale.it
  A community music initiative funded by the City of Rome, Italy, focusing on family relationships through music learning and engagement.
Community Music Wales (Cerdd Gymunedol Cymru). (n.d.). www.communitymusicwales .co.uk/
  An all-access community music charity in Wales providing resources and training to encourage all aspects of lifelong music engagement.
Music Bus, Children's Music Theater Blog. (n.d.). http://musicbussrebrenica.blogspot.com
  BlogSpot highlighting the Children's Musical Theater Activities in Srebrenica, Bosnia, and affiliated with Music Without Borders international organization for healing and reconciliation through music.
Music Education Network (meNet). (2006–2009). http://menet.mdw.ac.at/menetsite/english/index.html
  A European Commission-sponsored program for the "collection, compilation and dissemination of knowledge about music education in schools and the training of music teachers in Europe."
Music Village. (2006—). http://site.music-village.gr
  A collaborative music project in Agios Lavrendios, Greece, organized to promote "prescheduled and spontaneous performances" and the exchange of ideas and projects among artists of diverse nationalities.

Resonaari Figurenotes Special Music Centre. (1995—). www.resonaari.fi

A Finnish research center focused on the Figurenotes© teaching methods serving music educators, therapist, teachers, and community-based programs.

School for Social Entrepreneurs (SSE). (1997—). www.sse.org.uk/person.php?personid=197

Focused on social change, an educational outreach organization providing opportunities for the development of creative and entrepreneurial abilities in the United Kingdom.

University of Limerick, World Academy of Music and Dance: *The Nomad Project.* (n.d.). www.ul.ie/~iwmc/nomad/index.html

A community engagement and outreach program promoting the ongoing legacy of Traveller music culture within the Irish society.

World Music Centre. (n.d.). www.worldmusiccentre.com

Based in Rotterdam, the Netherlands, this networking website promotes cultural diversity in music education, links European partner programs, and houses papers from a CM seminar in 2002.

Middle East, India, and Asia-Pacific

UNESCO-NIE Centre for Arts Research in Education (CARE). (n.d.). www.unesco-care.nie .edu.sg/

A clearinghouse of research on the instrumental benefits of arts in education in Singapore and the Asia-Pacific rim.

Levinsky School of Music Education: Live Music Encounters. (n.d.). http://sites.levinsky.ac.il/ livemusic

Community music program for schools addressing social inclusion and the development of mutual respect among the Jewish and Arab-Palestinian population in Israel.

Music Bus Goes Middle East. (n.d.). www.musicbusgoespalestine.blogspot.com

A BlogSpot highlighting training programs for young adults working with children in Palestine and affiliated with the Music Without Borders international organization for healing and reconciliation through music.

North America

Cal Community Music. (n.d.). www.ocf.berkeley.edu/~ccm/resources.html

A University of California at Berkeley-sponsored community service outreach program targeting neighborhood retirement centers and convalescent hospitals.

Chamber Music Network. (1947—). www.acmp.net

A non-profit organization promoting informal music making "by people of all ages and nationalities, from beginners to professionals."

College Music Society's Committee on Community Engagement. www.acmesrig.org

Community Arts Resources (CARS). (1990—). www.communityartsla.com/about

A community arts resource firm focused on the "collaboration, connectivity, exploration and celebration" of the arts in community events.

Community Band and Orchestra Home Pages. (1995—). http://boerger.org/c-m/commother .shtml

A website listing more than 1,200 community band and orchestra hyperlinks.

Guitars in the Classroom™. (n.d.). www.guitarsintheclassroom.org

A non-profit 501(c)(3) promoting the use of guitars, singing, and songwriting across the curriculum for teachers as a means to reinforce and enrich subject area content.

Michigan State University Community Music School. (1993—). www.cms.msu.edu

A university outreach program targeting community and therapy clients with opportunities for the study, appreciation, and therapeutic use of music.

MUSE: Musicians United for Superior Education. (1990––). http://musekids.org

A Buffalo, New York-based organization committed to connecting professional artists with area children to foster "cultural vitality" in the community.

National Association for Music Education, Adult and Community Music Education Special Research Interest Group (SRIG) (1998). www.acmesrig.org

This group promotes research, sponsors colloquia, and posts useful information concerning adult and community music education.

National Guild for Community Arts Education. (1937––). www.nationalguild.org

A national service organization supporting access to "arts learning opportunities" for all ages and consisting of a membership network that includes "schools of the arts, arts and cultural centers, preparatory programs, and arts education divisions of performing arts companies, museums, parks and recreation departments and others."

North American Coalition for Community Music. (2008––). http://naccm.info

This think tank offers online resources for teachers and others establishing community or outreach programs.

Sidney Lanier Music Program. (n.d.). www.oncoursesystems.com/school/webpage.aspx?id=24619&xpage=642411

A cooperative music project associated with programs in Guinea, Pakistan, and China. (Sidney Lanier is a public school in Gainesville, Florida, for students with disabilities.)

Temple University, Boyer College of Music and Dance: The Arts and Quality of Life Research Center. (n.d.). www.temple.edu/boyer/ResearchCenter/index.html

A university-sponsored research center whose goals include community music outreach programs such as their Hear Our Voices: Songwriting with At-Risk Youth.

Tufts Community Music Program. (2007––). http://as.tufts.edu/music/musiccenter/program/index.htm

A community music outreach program offering Saturday music classes for children and teenagers, weekday evening classes and ensembles for adults, guest workshops with community musicians, a concert series, and family and children's concerts.

South America

Guitarrissima. (n.d.). www.guitarrissima.com.br

Community school for the study of guitar, located in southern Brazil.

Orchestra Villa_Lobos. (2003––). www.myspace.com/orquestradeflautasvillalobos

Community orchestra promoting social inclusion and cultural awareness for children and youth of Porto Alegre, Brazil.

University of Buenos Aires Extension Programs and Projects. (n.d.). www.uba.ar/ingles/about/extensionprograms.php

An outreach program in Buenos Aires whose objective is to improve the quality of life for its regional citizens through interdisciplinary programs, including music.

ORGANIZATIONS

International

International Society for Music Education. (1953––). www.isme.org

An international, interdisciplinary organization of music educators engaged in the understanding and promotion of lifelong music learning by virtue of their commitment to culture, education, conservation, cultural preservation, and evidence-based policy and practice. Visit the ISME Community Music Activity Commission page for resources and events.

New Horizons International Music Association. (1990—). www.newhorizonsmusic.org
   An all-inclusive music organization providing entry points for music-making opportunities to the inexperienced and out-of-practice adults.
Sound and Music Alliance. (2009—). http://soundandmusicalliance.blogspot.com
   An interdisciplinary membership organization of therapists, clinicians, educators, musicians, researchers, sound and music practitioners, Indigenous teachers, program developers,
   and product manufacturers promoting the intentional and transformative power of sound and
   music throughout the full spectrum of life cycles.
Sweet Adelines International. (n.d.). www.sweetadelineintl.org
   "A worldwide organization of women singers committed to advancing the musical art
   form of barbershop harmony through education and performances," characterizing itself as
   a non-profit music education association.
World Federation of Music Therapy (WFMT). (1985—). www.wfmt.info/WFMT/Home.html
   An international organization promoting music therapy as an art and science through edu-
   cational programs, clinical practice, and research.

Europe, Great Britain, and Ireland

European Music Therapy Confederation (EMTC). (2003—). www.musictherapyworld.de
   A online journal archive for music therapy, hosted in Germany.
Sound Sense. (n.d.). www.soundsense.orgs
   A membership organization that provides professional development opportunities, net-
   working, issues awareness, and advocacy and lobbying efforts in support of organizations
   and individuals who make music in their communities.

Middle East, India, and Asia-Pacific

My Peace Music Institute. (2006—). www.mypeacemusic.net
   An independent, not-for-profit organization dedicated to providing disadvantaged and
   musically interested children with opportunities for basic and music education.
SVARAM, Musical Instruments and Research. (n.d.). www.svaram.org
   An instrument manufacturer dedicated to creating musical instruments that are relevant
   and accessible to anyone on the Indian subcontinent.

North America

Music National Service. (n.d.). www.musicnationalservice.org
   A national non-profit organization that supports music as a strategy for public good
   through direct programs, public advocacy, and leadership development.
ServiceArtist.Net. (n.d.). www.serviceartist.net.
   A membership driven network of artist devoted to "improving lives and strengthening
   communities" through creativity and service.
Songs of Love. (1996—). www.songsoflove.org
   A national non-profit 501(c)(3) organization that creates free, personalized, original songs
   for children and young adults experiencing medical, physical, or emotional challenges, based
   in New York.

About the Contributors

David O. Akombo (Kenya; USA) is Assistant Professor of Music Education at Jackson State University in Jackson, Mississippi. A music educator, musician, ethnomusicologist, and music therapist who works with communities both in Kenya and North America, Akombo has presented workshops and lectures, created CD/DVDs, and authored books and articles. His research interests include music education, ethnomusicology, choral and instrumental arranging, multicultural music education, African music, community music, teaching and learning theory, music and technology, the psychology of music, and music and the biomedical sciences. Dr. Akombo is the founder of the Interdisciplinary Society for Quantitative Research in Music and Medicine.

Chris Alfano (Canada) is a musician and educator who works with adolescents and senior music learners in public school settings and with jazz ensembles in community and university outreach programs. He performs on clarinet, saxophone, and flute in classical and jazz idioms. Arranger, soloist, and director, Dr. Alfano earned his dissertation from University of McGill in 2008 with his ground-breaking study "Seniors' Participation in an Intergenerational Music Learning Program." He conducts, lectures, and performs throughout North America.

Susan Avery (USA), Associate Professor of Music Education at Ithaca College, is a specialist in vocal ensembles. Her published research focuses on adult rehearsal preferences. In addition to serving on national music education committees, she currently conducts the Seneca Singers, an adult community choir, and Voices, the faculty-staff choir at Ithaca College. Dr. Avery's choral ensembles consistently receive high awards at festivals and her students participate in all levels of local, state, and national ensembles. A conductor, a clinician, and an adjudicator, Dr. Avery works with choirs, including honors choirs, at local, state, and national levels.

Joel Barbosa (Brazil) is active as a lecturer, presenter, conductor, and performer, creating, coordinating, and working on projects in social orientation in music education. As Professor Titular at the Universidade Federal da Bahia, Brazil, he works as clarinet professor and coordinates social projects. His research is published nationally and internationally and focuses on clarinet performance and music education in community bands and in NGOs (non-governmental organizations). He wrote the first Brazilian band method. A former president of the Brazilian Clarinet Association, Dr. Barbosa has served on the ISME Community Music Activities Commission.

Brydie-Leigh Bartleet (Australia) is Senior Lecturer in Research and Music Literature at the Queensland Conservatorium, Griffith University, and commissioner for ISME's Community Music Activities Commission. As a community music facilitator, she conducts ensembles in Australia, Thailand, Singapore, and Taiwan. She has published widely on the contemporary realities of music making such as community music, women's music, cross-cultural music projects, conducting, and music autoethnography. Her books include *Music Autoethnographies: Making Autoethnography Sing/Making Music Personal* with C. Ellis; *Navigating Music and Sound Education* with J. Ballantyne; and *Musical Islands: Exploring Connections between Music, Place and Research* with E. Mackinlay and K. Barney.

Cindy Bell (USA) is Associate Professor of Music Education and director of the 140-voice University Choir at the Hofstra University (Hempstead, New York) music department. A specialist in music teacher training, choral music education, and community choirs, Dr. Bell researches, publishes, and presents clinics nationally and worldwide, often performing as a guest conductor for festival choirs. She also directs the Mariners Chorus at the US Merchant Marine Academy, Kings Point, NY. Her research in community music and adult singing is presented and published internationally.

Carol Beynon (Canada) serves as Vice Provost of Graduate and Post-Doctoral Studies and Associate Professor of Education at the University of Western Ontario, London, Ontario. She is the founding and co-artistic director of the award-winning Amabile Boys & Men's Choirs. Her research focuses on gender issues in music education, particularly as they pertain to representations of masculinities in relation to singing, teacher development and identity, school music education and policy development, and arts education. Her publications include *Critical Perspectives in Canadian Music Education* (2012) with K. Veblen and *Learning to Teach: Concepts and Cases for Novice Teachers and Teacher Educators* (2001) with A. N. Geddis and B. A. Onslow.

Chelcy Bowles (USA) is Professor of Music and Director of Continuing Education in Music at University of Wisconsin–Madison, where she directs professional development programs for music teachers and performers, the community adult music education program, and the Madison Early Music Festival. She is a professional harpist, co-founder of NAfME's Adult and Community Music Education Special Research Interest Group, and a member of the North American Coalition for Community Music. Dr. Bowles is an influential author and music education researcher with a particular interest in the adult music learner.

Shelley Brunt (Australia) is a Lecturer in Music Industry and Media at RMIT University (Royal Melbourne Institute of Technology) in Melbourne, Australia. With a varied performance background, ranging from classical cello and choral singing to contemporary electronica and experimental pop, her research concerns ethnomusicological approaches to popular music, focusing on community and identity. Recent publications can be found in *Home, Land and Sea: Situating Music in Aotearoa New Zealand* (2011) and *Many Voices: Music and National Identity in Aotearoa/New Zealand* (2010).

Jeffrey E. Bush (USA; Canada) is Director of the School of Music at James Madison University. Active as a presenter, researcher, and musician, Dr. Bush's interests include adult music making, music curriculum, and middle/high school general music. His professional service includes numerous positions with NAfME, including Western Division President and National Executive Committee member, president of the Adult and Community Music Education Special Research Group, and executive member of the Society for Music Education. He has also served as a member of the editorial review boards of national and international music education journals.

Sylvia Chong (Singapore) is Associate Professor and Associate Dean with the Visual and Performing Arts Academic Group, National Institute of Education (NIE), Singapore. She is also the Associate Dean for Programs Planning and Development, which is responsible for initial teacher preparation programs at NIE. Her main interests are elementary education and mass media and how both support local music curricula. Her research projects include an interdisciplinary project on music and language acquisition. Dr. Chong served on the ISME Music in Cultural, Educational and Mass Media Policies and Community Music Activities Commissions and as a board member for the Asia Pacific Symposium on Music Education Research (APSMER).

Don Coffman (USA) is Professor and Chair of Music Education and Music Therapy at the University of Miami's Frost School of Music. An active researcher in lifelong music learning, Dr. Coffman is the former chair of NAfME's Adult and Community Special Research Interest Group and a board member for ISME's Community Music Activities Commission. His passion is making music with "chronologically gifted" people in wind bands.

Mary L. Cohen (USA) is Area Head of the Music Education Department at the University of Iowa, where she teaches a variety of undergraduate and graduate courses. She combines her research into choral singing and well-being and teaching in her work with the Oakdale Community Choir, composed of male prisoners and female and male community members. Her research investigates the roles of music, writing, and songwriting activities in incarcerated people's lives. Published internationally with journal and book chapters, she edited the 2010 issue of the *International Journal of Community Music* focusing on criminal justice and music.

Will Dabback (USA) is Associate Professor of Music Education at James Madison University in Virginia, where he teaches courses in conducting as well as instrumental methods and pedagogy. Conductor, clinician, and adjudicator for middle and high school students, he formed the Harrisonburg New Horizons Band in conjunction with the James Madison University Lifelong Learning Institute. He publishes research on the relationships between sociological interactions, learning and identity, musical improvisation, teacher preparation, and instrumental pedagogy.

Kathryn Deane (UK) is Director of Sound Sense, the UK association for community musicians. On behalf of Sound Sense, she carries out advocacy work as author, advisor, and project instigator. For decades, Ms. Deane has served as researcher, editor, and author, penning the influential Music Manifesto report *Making Every Child's Music Matters* among other writings, and is in constant demand as lecturer on community music.

Don DeVito (USA) is the music director of the Sidney Lanier School in Gainesville, Florida, USA, which serves students with intellectual disabilities. He spearheads numerous projects linking music education and community music practitioners from diverse regions and countries with people with special needs. Dr. DeVito is the 2010–2012 chair of the International Society for Music Education Community Music Activity (CMA) Commission, is a founding member of the North American Coalition for Community Music (NACCM), and is on the research committee of the Florida Music Educators Association and the review board for *Research Perspectives in Music Education.*

David J. Elliott (Canada; USA) is Professor of Music Education at New York University. Author of *Music Matters: A New Philosophy of Music Education* (1995) and *Praxial Music Education: Reflections and Dialogues* (2005), Dr. Elliott lectures and presents worldwide. He is currently Chief Editor of *Action, Criticism, and Theory for Music Education* and serves on several other editorial boards. As an award-winning composer and arranger, Dr. Elliott has published many choral and instrumental works. His primary interests are music education philosophy, curriculum, creativity, composition, and community music.

Donna Emmanuel (USA) is Associate Professor of Music Education and coordinator of the PhD program in music education at the University of North Texas. Her areas of expertise include immersion field experiences, intercultural competence training, urban/inner city training, and elementary general music, as well as group piano instruction, student teacher supervision, interdisciplinary curricula, qualitative research, and the musics of Mexico, Africa, and Southeast Asia. Dr. Emmanuel is the Academic Sponsor for the Mariachi Águilas.

Arthur Gill (Pakistan) is Director of F. G. Special Education Centre for Visually and Physically Handicapped Children in Gujrat, Pakistan. The Society for Education, Music and Psychology Research (SEMPRE), under the auspices of Dr. Graham Welch, funded the purchase of equipment and supplies for Mr. Gill's program and made it possible for him to travel to England to observe the special education and music programs at the University of London and surrounding community in 2011. Gill's work is recognized internationally, and he has visited China, the United Kingdom, and North America. Mr. Gill is keyboardist and vocalist in Seven Tunes Musical Band, and his music may be sampled on YouTube.

Claudia Gluschankof (Israel; Argentina) is Head of Music and Movement Studies at the Early Childhood Department at the School of Music, Levinsky College of Education, Tel-Aviv, Israel. She holds a PhD from the Hebrew University of Jerusalem and an MA from the University of London, along with Orff and Kodály certificates. Her research interests focus on the musical expressions of young children, particularly on the self-initiated play of young children in various cultural contexts, especially among Hebrew and Arab speakers. Dr. Gluschankof has presented her research at many international conferences and peer-reviewed journals. She serves on the ISME Early Childhood Music Education Commission.

Casey Hayes (USA) is Assistant Professor of Music at Franklin College (FC), in Franklin, Indiana, where he conducts the FC Singers, Women's Chorus, and Men's Chorus. He also serves as Artistic Director for the Cincinnati Men's Chorus. Dr. Hayes received his PhD in music education from the Steinhardt School of Education, New York University, with a pioneering dissertation on educational outreach within gay/lesbian/bisexual/transgender (GLBT) choruses. Known for his research and for his fervent advocacy, Dr. Hayes is in world-wide demand as a clinician and speaker on issues facing GLBT community choruses.

Lee Higgins (UK; USA) is Associate Professor of Music Education at the Boston University School of Music. As a community musician, he has worked in education and health settings, in prison and with probation service, with youth, and in orchestra outreach. His professional practice embraces a gamut of music genres, most notably samba drumming, improvisation, pop/rock, and music technology. A prolific author, Dr. Higgins' forthcoming book is *Community Music: In Practice and Theory* (2012). He is the senior editor of the *International Journal of Community Music* and a past chair of the ISME Commission on Community Music Activity.

Hussein Janmohamed (Canada) is a choral conductor, composer, and community music educator living in Vancouver. He has performed with some of Canada's finest choirs, including Chor Leoni Men's Choir, Laudate Singers, and the National Youth Choir of Canada. Hussein is recognized as a leader in choral music for community building, cultural development, and inspirational leadership. Co-founder of the Vancouver and Canadian Ismaili Muslim Youth Choirs, he has conducted choirs for Canadian audiences and in the presence of His Highness the Aga Khan and Governor General Adrienne Clarkson. Janmohamed's compositions and arrangements integrate spiritual expressions of Islamic, Christian, Jewish, and other faiths for healing and community.

Sidsel Karlsen (Norway; Finland) is Professor of Music Education at Hedmark University College in Hamar, Norway, and Adjunct Professor at the Sibelius Academy in Helsinki, Finland. With experience as a freelance classical singer, a community musician, and a festival administrator, Dr. Karlsen currently teaches general music education theory and has published articles in Scandinavian and international journals. For the period of 2009–2011, she conducted research, funded by the Academy of Finland, on multicultural music education in the Nordic countries. Her main research interests include exploring music-related learning in informal contexts as well as music education in multicultural societies.

Magali Kleber (Brazil) is Professor at Londrina State University (UEL). An active and internationally known researcher in music education and ethnomusicology as well as a concert pianist, Dr. Kleber has initiated and written about a number of projects in Brazil at the grassroots level. A current project—Associacao Menoinos do Morumba in São Paulo, Brazil—offers Afro-Brazilian music to two thousand adolescents who would not otherwise have access to music-making opportunities. Currently the president of the Brazilian Association in Music Education, Dr. Kleber is also on the ISME Community Music Activity Commission.

Andrew Krikun (USA) is Assistant Professor of Music at Bergen Community College in New Jersey and a doctoral candidate in music education at New York University where his research focuses on popular music pedagogy in the community college curriculum. Active in the field of community music, Krikun is a founding member of the North American Coalition for Community Music (NACCM) and music curator for Riverspace Arts, a non-profit performing arts center. He presents and publishes in popular music, lifelong learning, and historical research areas while maintaining an active career as a performer, composer, and recording artist.

Nathan Kruse (USA) is Assistant Professor of Music Education and Coordinator of the Master's Program in Music Education at the University of North Texas. A specialist in instrumental music education, Dr. Kruse teaches methods courses and supervises student teachers at the undergraduate level, teaches the sociology of music at the graduate level, and assists the Denton New Horizons Senior Band. Active as a conductor, clinician, and performer, his research interests include adult music education, ethnographic traditions of community music, and school-university partnerships. In addition to presenting at national and international conferences, he is published in national and international refereed journals.

Richard Letts (Australia) is founder and Executive Director of the Music Council of Australia. He has served as director of the East Bay Center for the Performing Arts in San Francisco and director of the University of Minnesota's MacPhail Center for the Arts. From 2005 to 2009, he was president of the International Music Council. Dr. Letts is a journal editor and author of books, hundreds of articles, and research reports, including *The Protection and Promotion of Musical Diversity* for UNESCO

(United Nations Educational, Scientific and Cultural Organization). His current interests include policy formation and advocacy in a broad range of music issues, including music education at all levels. He is a member of the Order of Australia.

Chi Cheung Leung (Hong Kong) is Senior Lecturer at the Hong Kong Institute of Education. Leung researches curriculum development, cultural and education policy, extracurricular activities, music composition and its pedagogy, issues concerning the teaching of traditional music and Chinese music, and technology in education. Leung's musical compositions have been performed in the United States, Hong Kong, and Singapore. He serves as coordinator and column editor of the Comparative Music Education feature initiated by the MayDay Group and Chairperson of the Commission on Music in Cultural, Educational, and Mass Media Policies of the International Society for Music Education.

Dochi Lichtensztajn (Argentina; Israel) is a musicologist (PhD in Musicology, Tel Aviv University), a music educator (Levinsky College of Education, Tel Aviv), and founder and musical director of the Vocal and Instrumental Ensemble Shiruli, for young concert audiences. She works as the pedagogical director of the Levinsky School of Music Education Community Program "Live Music Encounters" (in partnership and collaboration with the Israel Philharmonic Orchestra, for primary and secondary schools); the Kadma program (New Haifa Symphonic Orchestra), for a Jewish and Arab-Palestinian primary school; the Musica Viva program for students; and the Divertimento Series for adult audiences. Dr. Lichtensztajn serves on the ISME Community Music Activities Commission.

Stephen J. Messenger (USA) is a public school teacher who teaches a diverse student body at the secondary level (his training includes special education and the teaching of reading and English as a second language) and a visiting instructor in english composition at St. Mary's College of Maryland, the public honors college of the University of Maryland system, where he teaches English composition focused on the students' musical lives. Dr. Messenger plays guitar, mandolin, octave mandolin, and bass guitar and is active in a variety of online musical communities. His research interests include popular culture, poetry and imagistic prose, blues and American roots music, Mexican folk art, and British motorcycles.

Steven Moser (USA) is Dean of the College of Arts and Letters and Professor of Music at the University of Southern Mississippi. Having served as senior associate dean in the College of Arts and Letters, Professor Moser is a 2007 fellow of Harvard's Graduate School of Education Management Development Program and has served in various leadership roles at the University of Southern Mississippi since 2002. Active as a consultant, clinician/conductor, and adjudicator for marching and concert events throughout the United States, Dr. Moser specializes in instrumental conducting, music administration, and adult and community music education.

Phil Mullen (Ireland; UK) is a UK-based community musician and trainer. He has facilitated music making for three decades with diverse populations ranging from vulnerable youth, including those with mental-health issues and special educational needs, to homeless people, people in prisons, and a range of ages from seniors to students in primary and secondary school settings. He has long-standing working relationships with Goldsmiths College, London University, Limerick University, London Philharmonic Orchestra, Music Leader, and Sing Up, the UK national singing program from primary-age children. A former chair of ISME's Community Music Activity Commission and ISME board member, Phil continues his work on an international scale.

David Myers (USA) is Professor and Director of the School of Music at the University of Minnesota, an internationally regarded music educator, and a proponent of innovation in higher music education. He founded the Center for Educational Partnerships and its groundbreaking Sound Learning partnership with Georgia State University, the Atlanta Symphony Orchestra, community musicians, and inner-city schools. He consults, serves on national panels, presents, and publishes widely. Dr. Myer's primary interests are teacher education, lifespan music learning, and collaborative music education programs. A longtime advocate of arts education programs involving higher education, cultural institutions, and schools, he is actively involved in forging new paradigms in this field.

Elizabeth Oehrle (South Africa; USA) is Professor Emeritus at the University of Natal, Durban, South Africa, whose work centers on creativity, equality, and expression through music. She directs Ukusa, a community music project for historically disadvantaged people (funded through the Swedish group the Swedish International Development Association, or SIDA). Dr. Oehrle organized the first multiracial conference for all music educators at tertiary institutions (in South Africa) in 1985 and has initiated numerous projects for intercultural education in Southern Africa including a national network (NETIEM) and the journal *The Talking Drum*. She served as chair for the ISME Community Music Activities Commission, continues to hold other prominent offices, and publishes widely.

Heidi Partti (Finland; UK) is a musician, educator, and researcher working both at Sibelius Academy, Finland, and at Griffith University in Australia. She completed her doctorate at Sibelius Academy in 2012 with her thesis "Learning from cosmopolitan digital musicians: Identity, musicianship, and changing values in (in)formal music communities."

Catherine Pestano (UK) is Chair of Sound Sense, the UK National Development Agency for community music. Her work focuses on community development, corporate, youth, early years and schools/pupil referral units (PRU) music, and the training of community musicians. She is studying for a PhD at Winchester, investigating how music can benefit socially excluded youth/adults. Her organization, the Croyden Intercultural Singing Project (CRISP), was recipient of the inaugural ISME Gibson award for Community-based Music Education Projects in 2007. Having trained with Frankie Armstrong, Phil Mullen, and Chris Philpott, Catherine works across all age groups and is passionate about music's potential to inspire.

Debbie Rohwer (USA) serves as Chair of the Division of Music Education at the University of North Texas. A specialist in instrumental music education, Dr. Rohwer teaches methods courses and supervises student teachers at the undergraduate level and teaches research and statistics courses and psychology of music courses at the graduate level. In 1997, Dr. Rohwer founded the Denton New Horizons Senior Citizen Beginning Band. She currently serves as conductor, administrator, and arranger for the thirty-piece band. Dr. Rohwer has concentrated her research on skill-learning of musicians at a variety of experience levels. She has been published in numerous research journals and serves on state and international research review boards.

Huib Schippers (Netherlands; Australia) is Director of the Queensland Conservatorium Research Centre and Associate Professor of Music Studies and Research at Griffith University, Brisbane, Australia. Having trained as a sitar player for over twenty years, his research interests include world music, cultural diversity in music education, arts policy, and musical ecosystems. He is the author of numerous articles across these areas, including a recent book on learning and teaching music in culturally diverse environments: *Facing the Music: Shaping Music Education from a Global Perspective* (2010).

Mari Shiobara (Japan) is Professor of Music Education at Kunitachi College of Music and currently on the ISME Community Music Activities Commission. Educated in both Japan and the United Kingdom, she received a doctoral degree from the University of London, Institute of Education, and a Dalcroze licentiate from the London Dalcroze Society. Involved in community music activities as a practitioner as well as researcher, she also engages in music therapy work. Dr. Shiobara has written chapters for handbooks for both primary and secondary music teachers as well as numerous publications on community music activities, music transmission, cultural music identity, and comparative studies of music education.

Marissa Silverman (USA) is Assistant Professor and Coordinator of Undergraduate Music Education at the John J. Cali School of Music of Montclair State University in Montclair, New Jersey, and an active professional flutist in New York City. Previously she taught secondary school band, general music, and English literature in New York City. A Fulbright Scholar, her research interests include urban music education, music and social justice, interdisciplinary education, community music, secondary general music, curriculum development, and topics in the philosophy of music and music education. In addition to articles in peer-reviewed journals, Dr. Silverman has published book chapters in *The Oxford Handbook of Music Education Philosophy*; *Music, Health and Wellbeing*; and *The Oxford Handbook of Music Education*.

Rineke Smilde (Netherlands) has been Professor of Lifelong Learning in Music & the Arts at the Prince Claus Conservatoire in Groningen and the Royal Conservatoire in The Hague since 2004. She leads an international research group that examines questions about what engaging with new audiences means for the different roles of musicians and artists. Her particular research interests focus on learning styles of musicians and the role of biographical learning in the context of lifelong and life-wide learning. She has served as vice president of the European Association of Conservatories (AEC) and as a board member of the European Association of Music in Schools.

Einar Solbu (Norway) serves on the executive committee of the International Music Council (IMC). Former Chief Executive Officer of Rikskonsertene—the Norwegian Concert Institute—he has an academic background in church music and worked for a number of years in the State Academy of Music in Oslo. Einar Solbu's contributions to music research are reflected in his internationally published books and articles on music education and communication. He has been involved in a number of organizations for music and music education, chaired the Norwegian opera and the Lindeman Foundation, was the initiator and first chair of the ISME commission for Community Music Activity, and served as president of ISME from 1998 to 2000.

Anja Tait (Australia) is Library Program Advisor at Northern Territory Library who blends music therapy, education, research and community arts in her work to develop intergenerational literacy programs in multiple contexts. She is a music therapist and senior research fellow at ArtStories at Charles Darwin University, and works extensively in youth music as conductor/artistic director with the Tasmanian, Melbourne, and Western Australia youth orchestra councils. An improviser, composer, and broadcasting musician, her research interests include sustainable models of professional learning and mentoring relevant to those in isolated, transient, or volatile school communities and the links between arts participation, educational success, and social and emotional well-being for young children and their families.

Mehnaz Thawer (Canada) is a writer and communications professional based in Vancouver, British Columbia. She grew up surrounded by music and had the pleasure of being part of the Vancouver Ismaili Muslim Youth Choir and performing with a variety of musicians locally and nationally. Mehnaz's work can be found in the *Ismaili Canada Magazine*, *Moxy Magazine*, and *National Geographic*. She writes regularly on her blog, titled Speak Softly and Carry a Red Pen, which was recently nominated for the 2012 Canadian Weblog Awards.

Catherine Threlfall (Australia) is a music therapist and educator. She works in the educational system in the Northern Territory and Victoria as an advocate, catalyst for community development, and mentor for teachers, enabling innovative practice for shared art-making in school communities for well-being and learning. An active member of the Music Council of Australia and member of the American Music Therapy Association (AMTA) National Council, she is a visiting lecturer at Charles Darwin University, Royal Melbourne Institute of Technology (RMIT), and the University of Melbourne.

Kari K. Veblen (Canada; USA) is Assistant Dean of Research and Associate Professor of Music Education at the Don Wright Faculty of Music at the University of Western Ontario, Canada. A musician and educator, Dr. Veblen studies international trends in community music and writes on the intersections of music, education, the arts, and society. As well, she pursues a twenty-five year fascination with transmission of traditional Irish/Celtic/diasporic musics. An international representative to the NAfME Adult and Community Special Research Interest Group, she has served on many professional boards, including the ISME board. She is associate editor of the *International Journal of Community Music*.

Janice L. Waldron (Canada; USA) is Associate Professor of Music Education at the University of Windsor, where she teaches instrumental music and world music education. A band director since 1980 at middle schools and high schools in Texas and Ontario, Dr. Waldron's research interests include informal music learning practices, community music, Celtic-Canadian and Irish traditional music, virtual music learning, and adult music education, and her findings are published and presented internationally. In 2011, Dr. Waldron was awarded a research grant from the Canada Social Science and Humanities Research Council (SSHRC) to pursue research on music learning and teaching in convergent on- and offline communities of practice.

Elias Weldegebriel (Eritrea) is Director of Asmara Music School, well-known for his advocacy and expertise in Eritrean music and culture. Mr. Weldegebriel oversees music instruction ranging from theory and history to technology to performance of all kinds. Moreover, he sets the standards for this government school, which has its roots in the Eritrean liberation struggles from Ethiopian colonization. Asmara Music School is the first of its kind in Eritrea to consciously train musicians who will preserve indigenous musics as well as generate creative new forms.

Heidi Westerlund (Finland) is Professor of Music Education at the Sibelius Academy in Finland, where she teaches postgraduate research methods, history of music education, and philosophy of music education. Widely published in the field of philosophy and pedagogy of music education, she examines the meaningfulness of music education from the learner's perspective. Concepts such as musical interaction, transaction, musical experience, context, situation, and event are central in her work. She reviews for international journals and has served as past co-chair of International Society for Philosophy of Music Education and editor of the *Finnish Journal of Music Education*.

Sheila Woodward (South Africa; USA) is Chair of Music Education at the University of Southern California, Thornton School of Music. Dr. Woodward's research focus is music and well-being from before birth to adulthood, with studies on the fetus and neonate, the premature infant, the young child, the at-risk youth, the juvenile offender, and the adult musician. She has created important collaborations between musicians and youths in her native South Africa and communities in North America. She has served on numerous professional boards in South Africa, the United States, and throughout the world, including the ISME Commission on Early Childhood and the ISME board.

Christine Yau (China; UK) studied piano at the Central Conservatory of Music and Shanghai Conservatory of Music in China and continues work as an accompanist, piano teacher, and manager for music community centers in China, Australia, and the United Kingdom. Currently a doctoral student at University of Cambridge, UK, her research interests include instrumental community music in China and a cultural perspective on the instrumental teacher-student relationship in music conservatories.